CHARTIST PORTRAITS

CHARTIST
PORTRAITS

BY

G. D. H. COLE

WITH AN INTRODUCTION BY
ASA BRIGGS

MACMILLAN & CO LTD
NEW YORK · ST MARTIN'S PRESS
1965

Asa Briggs's Introduction
Copyright © Macmillan & Co Ltd 1965

First Edition 1941
Reissued 1965

MACMILLAN AND COMPANY LIMITED
St Martin's Street London WC 2
also Bombay Calcutta Madras Melbourne

THE MACMILLAN COMPANY OF CANADA LIMITED
70 Bond Street Toronto 2

ST MARTIN'S PRESS INC
175 Fifth Avenue New York 10 NY

PRINTED IN GREAT BRITAIN

CONTENTS

INTRODUCTION

CHARTIST PORTRAITS is one of the most readable and interesting of G. D. H. Cole's many books on labour history. It has more in common, indeed, with his biography of William Cobbett than with his more descriptive and analytical works. Written mainly on the basis of secondary sources, it presents a sequence of pen sketches of a number of outstanding Chartist personalities. Each personality is meant to be ' representative ', and the book as a whole sets out to provide ' something like a general picture of the rise and fall of the movement and of the widely differing elements that made it up '.

Unlike some labour historians, Cole did not underestimate the personal element in labour history. He gets into some difficulties with his search for the ' representative ', but he reaches many useful conclusions about the effect of particular personalities on the development of Chartism. He notes, for example, how O'Connor was able, paradoxically, to heighten the appeal of Chartism just because his personal faults included ' a total incomprehension of the new forces with which Chartism was called upon to deal '. He also writes perceptively of Lovett's last years: ' he had lost faith not in his doctrinaire principles, but in the men through whom alone they could be made actual '.

Whatever the social complexities of Chartism — and they were many — the strength and weakness of individual human beings must always be taken into the reckoning by historians of the movement. So, too, must the variety of individual human beings. The Six Points of the Charter, first set out in slogan form in 1838, attracted men of different ages and occupations, from different parts of the country, and with different educational and religious backgrounds. They were also men of different temperaments. Some were sanguine; others gloomy. Some were prudent; others rash. And there were as many nuances as contrasts. The same individual Chartist — O'Brien, for example — might think and behave in different ways at different times, for the movement itself provided an education in political action. There were ' lessons ' to learn or to avoid.

Two kinds of biography are relevant to an understanding of the rôle of individuals in the development of Chartism — first, the life stories of outstanding individuals, the ' leaders ' of the movement either locally or nationally; second, the life stories of less prominent Chartists, the men who stood firm during all the vicissitudes of the agitation. Cole found it difficult to collect details even about some of the leaders: their lives were shrouded in mystery. About the ' militants ' or the fluctuating rank-and-file he could find out still less. More recent research, based on the pursuit of primary materials and the careful scrutiny of newspapers, has enabled us to supplement his account and in some places to modify it. A. R. Schoyen, for example, in his brilliant portrait of George Julian Harney, *The Chartist Challenge* (1958), has explored many aspects of Chartism which find little place in Cole's pages, while enough has been written about Thomas Attwood to modify many of the points Cole makes about him, not least his relationship with ' toryism ', which Cole does not take sufficiently seriously. About the rank-and-file, the contributors to *Chartist Studies* (1959), approaching central problems of the sociology of Chartism from local sources, have uncovered a level of the agitation which Cole did not reach.

In every centre of Chartist action there seem to have been at least four groups of Chartists — a hard core of reformers, whose association with Chartism was one phase, sometimes a formative phase, in careers devoted to political protest movements of one kind and another, including ' republicanism ', Owenism, trade-unionism, the struggle for the unstamped press, or the fight for increased working-class power in 1831 and 1832; a group of new recruits to working-class politics, often consisting of young men for whom Chartism provided a political apprenticeship; a body of ' loyal supporters ', men who were eager not only to sign petitions and to attend meetings but to participate in the social activities which offered ' fellowship ' — the procession, the rally, the institute, the Chartist church or the education class; and a fluctuating rank-and-file, capable of being stirred to enthusiastic activity, but just as capable of remaining silent and apathetic.

Within each of these four groups, the divisions already mentioned can often be traced — that, for example, between
those people who believed in an ' ideology ' and those who
were driven simply by hunger or discontent, or that between
those people who preferred the noise and bustle of mass
demonstrations to the calm of adult education classes. We
know very little, however, about ' apathy '; we do not even
know whether it is the right word to use.

Cole suggested in *Chartist Portraits*—and it was a most
important suggestion which has provided a point of departure
for more recent historical research—that there were significant differences not only between people but between
localities. Alongside the profiles of individuals it was
necessary to consider the profiles of villages, towns, cities
and regions. He begins, therefore, not with psychology but
with geography, with a country which was imperfectly
unified either economically or politically. Lovett can be
explained in terms of London, but the next two portraits,
those of Joseph Rayner Stephens and Richard Oastler, are
concerned with the North of England, where a new industrial working class had already been brought into being.
As late as 1839 Bronterre O'Brien, the leading Chartist
' ideologist ', was writing that ' the men of the North would
soon be marching to London, there to constitute a Parliament of their own. But the South, East and West have still
to be organised '. This was an overstatement, as is shown
in the work of Henry Vincent, ' the Demosthenes of the
West ', whom Cole did not choose as one of his subjects.
Yet there was a special dynamism about the North of England,
only one element of which has been vividly described in
Cecil Driver's *Tory Radical: The Life of Richard Oastler*
(1946).

There is more to Cole's suggestion than this. London, the
North of England, Birmingham and the West, to take four
areas alone, were so different in social and economic structure and political traditions that Chartism meant different
things in each of them. It could appeal to depressed workers
in stagnating industries and to organised workers in areas of
economic growth. The relatively sophisticated London
artisan, with a tradition of independence, did not think in
the same terms as a Dorsetshire labourer. Nor did a Lan-

cashire cotton spinner think in the same terms as a Leicester framework knitter. When those differences are taken into account, the significance of Chartism in national history must be re-examined. Older historians emphasised the internal conflicts within the Chartist movement, often making moral rather than sociological judgments about them. More recent historians underline the fact that Chartism to an unprecedented extent united people in different parts of the country in a common movement of mass protest. It drew on snowballs of local grievances until it became a national avalanche. London artisans took up the grievances of Dorsetshire labourers; the National Petition was written in Birmingham, but read everywhere. 'Missionaries' were active in almost all parts of the country in the decade which followed 1836.

By choosing to deal with Feargus O'Connor towards the end of his book rather than at the beginning, Cole showed that he recognised the importance of O'Connor in pulling together all the diverse elements in the movement. His work on Cobbett must have seemed relevant in this context. O'Connor more than any other leader was responsible for the shift in Chartism from a series of local movements, each with its own momentum, to a national movement, although, as his Chartist opponents often pointed out, he cared little for the common stock of ideas which might have provided the basis of a more effective unity. Not worrying too much about principles, willing at times to underplay the Six Points, captivated by panaceas of his own, exploiting popular Messianism, O'Connor seized, often brilliantly, on the hopes and fears of a torn generation, a generation accustomed to violent talk and craving for dramatic leadership. It was also an overworked generation, pitched, as the Leeds socialist, John Francis Bray, put it, between periods of 'inordinate idleness and incessant toil', an uneducated generation easily stirred by bold symbols and romantic language.

O'Connor encouraged the proliferation of grievances rather than canalised them; he followed as much as he led. Yet he could defeat Attwood in Birmingham, overshadow Stephens in Lancashire, supplant Oastler in Yorkshire, and hold his own against local figures who emerged later, like Thomas Cooper in Leicester. 'Feargus is irresistible',

Reynolds Miscellany proclaimed judiciously as late as 1848.
' He has great declamatory powers, but he is wholly destitute
of original ability. He declaims admirably; but he would
not do for debate. He has vast energy . . . and energy always
tells well in a speaker, especially a popular speaker.'

Donald Read and Eric Glasgow in their book *Feargus
O'Connor* (1961) touch on some of these themes without
exhausting them. They do not fully exhaust, for example,
the ' land question ' which is particularly important in the
social context of the 1840s. They also quote Francis Place's
scathing denunciation of O'Connor, which is so comprehensive that it demonstrates in itself the danger of relying too
much on Place's voluminous papers, as Mark Hovell did in his
The Chartist Movement, for an understanding of early labour
history. Read and Glasgow's conclusions about O'Connor
should be set alongside those of Cole — just as John Saville's
conclusions about Ernest Jones in *Ernest Jones: Chartist*
(1952) should be set alongside the brief conclusions in Cole's
final chapter. With Jones many of the assumptions of
socialism were written into Chartism, as the extracts quoted
by Saville reveal. Just as the sponsors of the *Poor Man's
Guardian*, an invaluable historical source, had discovered
during the early 1830s a connecting link between Owenite
views of economics and radical programmes of political action,
so Jones during the late 1840s and 1850s discovered a connecting link between Chartist politics and socialist programme
building. The failure of Jones is as interesting to the historians
as the failure of O'Connor, and it is impossible to attribute
it too mechanistically to the onset of ' good times ' in the
1850s. Schoyen's last four chapters are particularly illum-
inating and perceptive in this connection — ' From Green
Flag to Red ', ' Defeat ', ' Retreat ' and ' Looking Backward '.

Throughout the whole of the Chartist agitation the
Chartists had to clear their minds about difficult tactical
questions. What, above all else, was to be political relationship, if any, between their movement, as a movement of
working-class protest, and middle-class radicalism ? Such
questions came to a head with the growth of the Anti-Corn
Law League and with Joseph Sturge's Complete Suffrage
Union venture, to which Cole devotes one chapter. Behind
the emergence of these new political organisations there were

powerful new social forces. Both Chartism and the Anti-Corn Law League were expressions of militant class consciousness, the one working-class, the other essentially middle-class. Each form of class consciousness strengthened the articulation of the other. It was fear of working-class solidarity as well as hatred of the landlords which buttressed middle-class consciousness. It was irritation and frustration with the well-organised Anti-Corn Law League, itself a child of the depression, which was set up *after* the Chartist movement had established itself and was regarded by Chartists at best as a deviation, at worst as a conspiracy, which provoked the Chartists to their most violent class declarations. 'The movement is, in fact,' the *Annual Register* noted in 1839, 'an insurrection which is expressly directed against the middle classes.' Sturge was quite unable to bridge the gulfs in 1842, even in Birmingham, where Attwood had been far more successful with his currency reform slogans ten years earlier. The strength of class feelings is brought out, indeed, in a casual remark by Sturge's mid-Victorian biographer, H. Richard. After describing the breakdown in 1842 of the negotiations between the Complete Suffrage Union and the Chartists, he adds, 'Mr. Sturge's friends felt thankful that this result left him free to withdraw from much uncongenial fellowship '.

Yet intelligent and shrewd Chartists were compelled to recognise within the logic of social and political relationships in the 1830s and 1840s that a frontal collision between middle and working classes would prevent the Six Points from being realised. If the main place of Chartism in international history is that it was the first large-scale working-class movement, Chartists at the time were often driven to reconsider tactics and strategy both in the light of their own experience and of changing circumstances. Vincent had changed his mind by 1840; he was treated as a renegade. O'Brien, who advanced a fascinating theory of class, on 'Marxist' lines, in the columns of the *Poor Man's Guardian* and the *Midland Representative* long before the Charter was drafted, had come round to the view by 1842 that there was 'a considerable and growing minority of the middle classes ' with whom a 'union' was not only possible but desirable. Harney always hated this line, but O'Connor was prepared to advocate an alliance between working and middle classes in 1848 and 1849, and Jones was taking up a similar position during the late 1850s. 'There can be no doubt,' he wrote in April 1857, 'as to the wisdom of allying with the middle classes and their leaders if they offer such a measure of reform as we can be justified in accepting.'

The analytical study of class relationships and the political issues associated with them is as necessary for the historian of Chartism as an analytical study of the trade cycle and its consequences or of what W. W. Rostow has called a ' social tension ' chart. Only the lead into the subject is concerned with social semantics, with the word ' class ' for example, and what people made of it. The real content of the study is concerned with ways of life and contrasting styles of behaviour. A broader and more imaginative social history is needed to provide the right kind of setting for Cole's biographies. It must be the kind of social history which can deal both with working-class and middle-class ways of life, and which can at the same time provide analysis and coherence. A full narrative history of Chartism, which is greatly needed, will have to be grounded in such study.

Ernest Jones belongs to the twilight years of Chartism, and there is doubtless more to be written on the last phases of the movement and its links with what happened later in the century. There is even more urgent need, however, for a study of the 1820s and 1830s before the words ' Charter ' and ' Chartist ' were coined but when nearly all the materials of the agitation, intellectual and economic, were already there. Edward Thompson's *The Making of the Working Class* (1964) is a long and exciting prelude. The work of Richard Carlile, which greatly interested Cole, needs to be fitted into place. So, too, do the many signs of intellectual ferment in the 1820s. Birmingham has recently been described and analysed in a more thorough fashion than most cities, but the London origins of Chartism still need further research. Many other smaller communities, like Bolton or Stalybridge, deserve to be examined in all their rich detail. The whole position of the Irish in the North of England has become a topic of research, but the research conclusions have not yet been published. Professor David Williams has followed up his admirable life of *John Frost*, which Cole's chapter on Frost skims rather than exploits, with an interesting study of the Rebecca Riots, but the historians of violence have not yet made use of the same methods for the Chartist period as have been employed in monographs on French revolutionary crowds or on the disorders associated with Wilkes. F. C. Mather's useful and scholarly *Public Order in the Age of the Chartists* (1959) is concerned more with the mechanisms of law and order than with the dynamics of disturbance. Detailed studies of ' minor characters ', like Joshua Hobson of Leeds, will provide necessary strands of continuity. He does not figure in *Chartist Portraits*, but his is the kind of portrait which makes us appreciate a whole *genre*. He has links with Carlile and with Oastler, with Owen and with O'Connor. His *Voice of the West Riding* helps us to understand much in the *Northern Star*. Indeed, he was the chief publisher of the *Northern Star* from its inception in 1837 until its removal to London in 1844.

In sum, Cole's *Chartist Portraits* needs to be treated as an introduction to be followed up by other books, some of which have not yet been written. Among the books which have been written, his own collection of documents, edited jointly along with A. W. Filson, *British Working Class Movements, 1789–1875* (1951), is one of the most valuable. *Attempts at General Union* (1953) is also relevant and interesting, and it was under the influence of his advice — ' there is room for a dozen local studies in Chartism ' — that I assembled the miscellaneous essays in *Chartist Studies*, knowing well that far more essays needed to be assembled in the future.

Nonetheless, Cole's last words were never about research. There were certain basic simplicities in the Chartist story which he felt should be communicated to as wide a circle of readers as possible. He would have taken as a fitting starting point for his account lines quoted by Edward Thompson at the end of his *The Making of the Working Class*. They come from the report of the parliamentary committee enquiring into the plight of the handloom weavers in 1835:

Question: Are the working classes better satisfied with the institutions of the country since the change [the Reform Bill of 1832] has taken place ?

Answer: I do not think they are. They viewed the

Reform Bill as a measure calculated to join the middle and upper classes to Government, and leave them in the hands of Government as a sort of machine to work according to the pleasure of Government.

Chartism was born before the name, and no name, however symbolic, could do full justice to it.

ASA BRIGGS

PREFACE

IN this volume I have tried to tell the story of Chartism by means of biographical sketches of some of its leaders. I owe special thanks to Dr. Alfred Plummer, who allowed me to make very full use of his, so far, unpublished biography of Bronterre O'Brien, of whom no other study exists. I have also to thank Mr. Arthur Lehning for help in connection with the study of Julian Harney, and Dr. H. Mars and Miss Rosler for their generous aid in getting the volume ready for the press.

G. D. H. C.

INSTITUTE OF SOCIAL HISTORY
19 BANBURY ROAD, OXFORD
June 1941

Introductory Study

HUNGER and hatred — these were the forces that made Chartism a mass movement of the British working class. Hunger gnawed at the hearts of the people, and seemed to gnaw the more fiercely as, under the spur of the new industrialism, the means of producing wealth increased. The new machines set a pace of output which reduced to dire penury those who were forced to compete with them by the older methods of handicraft. They flung men out of work by thousands, and sent them to struggle wildly for jobs, at any wage the employer would offer and under any conditions of over-work. Hours of labour in the factories were stretched out to almost unbelievable lengths, throwing more workers out of jobs, and making the scramble worse. Even when trade was good, the handloom weavers were near starvation : there were too many of them, but, even so, fresh workers flocked into the dying craft. Even when trade was good, there was no respite from the battle with the machines, which continually displaced more labour and set a hotter competitive place. Even the ' good ' employer was compelled to grind the faces of the poor ; for how else could he survive ? The bad, ruthless employer was in a position to drive him out of business if he did not conform. And ruthless employers were many, and well assured of being justified in what they did. Were they not the masters of implements infinitely more productive than any the world had known ; and did it not stand to reason that the new methods were better than the old, and ought to be used to the full ? If some people suffered, that was but a passing trouble, for if they were left free to develop the powers of production by their enterprise, goods would become cheaper and more plentiful, and society as a whole was bound to be better off. Besides, there were laws that decreed that wages were what they ought to be — laws which the political economists had discovered and written down

I

with unanswerable logic. Free contract was the only rational way of ordering men's economic relationships ; and all the workers who laboured in their mills or mines had contracted freely so to labour — they, or their parents or guardians for them — for the hours and at the wages which competition caused to prevail. If people suffered, this was not the employer's doing, or his fault ; and anything which interfered with the free course of production would be certain to make them suffer more.

The Corn Laws, which made bread dear in the interests of a narrow class of privileged aristocrats — these, said the capitalists, and not any conditions imposed by the industrial employer, were the cause of working-class distress. Repeal the Corn Laws, and the fear of famine would be removed from the people. Work would still be arduous, no doubt ; but the cheapening of production would enable the men of enterprise to flood the markets of the world with their goods, and to bring back in return the cheap corn that would feed the workers. Hard work never hurt anybody : it was good for men, women, and children alike. It kept them out of mischief : leisure only bred bad habits and encouraged vain amusements. Mankind was very sinful, and this world a place of tribulation. The soul mattered : not the body. Give generously to build chapels where the people would be taught to value heaven above riches, and to fear hell. It was the employer's mission to make money, and to spend it to God's glory. If the poor had it, they would only get drunk. They were poor because they were thriftless — not the other way round. Let them profit, if they were fit to profit, by the employer's good example. Did he not work all hours himself, drive himself as remorselessly as his overseers drove the factory children, deny himself luxury in order to pile up capital for the further increase of wealth, and therewith show himself generous in chapel-building and in charity to the deserving poor ? Had he not made himself an employer by his own unremitting efforts, risen from nothing by his own successful enterprise — or at any rate had not his father, which was much the same ? If he was ready to practise abstinence — he who had, unlike the aristocratic landowner, an unquestionable title to his income

— how much more ought the poor to practise the same virtue, instead of demanding wages which the laws of supply and demand made it impossible for him to pay, and running to the Poor Law for relief in times of depression instead of setting aside thriftily a part of their earnings when times were good.

It was a hard generation, with the hardness of men utterly convinced of their own rightness, and of being on the side of economic progress. Nor must it be forgotten that conditions were precarious for the employer as well as for the worker. Competition was fierce. It was not very difficult for a man who could scrape together even a hundred pounds to start in business for himself with a machine or two, renting the use of power. But of those who started, many failed, and were flung back into the working class. Even bigger employers failed in large numbers, when bad times suddenly narrowed markets, or when a bank suspended payment, or a merchant house collapsed. Employer fought with employer, as well as employers together against the overweening claims of the working class. Success in money-making was the best sign of enjoying God's favour : failure and poverty were visitations of the divine displeasure.

In this mood, the new employing class fought against Trade Unionism with the fury of wild beasts. Trade Unionism, with its demands for standard rates of wages and a limitation of the working day, was immoral as well as dangerous. What right could Trade Unions have to claim that bad, or lazy, workmen should be paid at the same rates as good, or to prevent any person from contracting to labour for as many hours as he pleased ? Freedom of contract was a purely individual matter, between the employer and each separate worker whom he engaged. It was a denial of freedom for the workers to combine in an attempt to impose any collective rule. Trade Unions ought to be put down by law ; and if Parliament would not act against them, the employers would have to combine, in the name of freedom, to put such things down with a strong hand. The ' document ', presented to each workman to sign, and requiring him, as a condition of employment, to renounce all connection with Trade Unionism, became a regular weapon in the

3

employers' hands. Most of all did they object to combinations extending beyond a single trade — Trades Unions they were commonly called — both because such Unions were more powerful, and because, by attempting to raise the " general rate of wages ", they were flying most plainly of all in the face of economic law.

The main body of employers objected no less strongly to endeavours to get the conditions of work regulated by law. They saw in the contention that the State could legitimately limit the hours of child labour — because children could not be regarded as free agents — both a dangerous thin end of the wedge (for in many factories how could the grown-ups go on working without the children's help ?) and an irreligious attack on the principle of parental responsibility. It was for the parents to say how long their children should work — not for the State. Moreover, the employer could not afford to do without the " last hour " of the children's labour. If hours were shortened, there would not be enough child labour to go round ; and misguided philanthropy would only result in throwing the children's parents out of work. The bitterest opponents of factory legislation were often found among those who, in matters of politics, professed the most Radical sentiments.

Of course, not all employers shared these views. There were not a few who fought manfully, side by side with the workers and the Tory philanthropists, for the Ten Hours Bill ; and there were some who wanted a compulsory minimum wage in order to put a limit to the competitive driving-down of wages. But these employers were in a small minority, and most of them were established employers of the second or third generation, and not ' self-made men '. They knew that they were secure, if only upstart rivals could be prevented from undercutting them : a recognised rule of the trade, preventing ' unfair competition ', would certainly do them no harm, and might be to their positive advantage. Besides, they had got past the need to be abstinent themselves, or personally to sweat their guts out in their mills and counting-houses unless they chose ; and the less fiercely they drove themselves, the less ready were they to drive their employees to the very limits of human endurance.

Such employers were more numerous in Lancashire than in Yorkshire, because the cotton trade had been the first to pass through the great change to machine production and had begun to settle down under the new technique at a time when the Industrial Revolution was only beginning to hit the woollen and worsted trades with its full force. Well-established firms accustomed to the new methods were numerous in Lancashire in the 'thirties and 'forties ; whereas in Yorkshire the old firms were having a desperate struggle against the new, and cut-throat competition ruled the roost.

From Lancashire and Yorkshire the textile district spread down into the Midlands. There were cotton factories here too ; but the main occupation of the East Midland district was framework knitting, and the stockingers took the place of the spinners and weavers as principal sufferers. There were some large establishments, as at Derby ; but, on the whole, production was still widely scattered, with the merchant employers putting out work to domestic craftsmen who rented their frames on exceedingly onerous terms. In this area, in Nottinghamshire and Leicestershire, had been the centres of the Luddite movement during the Napoleonic Wars ; and ever since then the framework knitters had been fighting a losing battle against falling wage-rates and new methods of production. The textile area also spread west into Wales, round Newtown and Llanidloes especially ; and it extended northwards into Cumberland, where its old centre, Kendal, was still of some importance. Scotland, too, had a considerable cotton-spinning industry, especially round Glasgow and Paisley, and a large body of handloom weavers who were being remorselessly ground down by the new machines ; and there were also considerable manu-factures of linen and of woollen goods.

These textile districts, together with the coalfields, were throughout the storm centres both of the Trade Union struggles of the early 'thirties and of Chartism. Of the coalfields Durham and Northumberland and South Wales were the principal areas of working-class activity ; but there were considerable movements in Lancashire and Yorkshire as well. The collieries, worked sometimes by large com-mercial firms, sometimes by agents employed by the great

5

landowners, and sometimes by small contractors, who rented pits from the landowners and were midway between independent masters and mere sub-contractors, were the centres of some of the bitterest struggles, especially where great ironmasters, as in South Wales, owned the mining villages, the shops, and virtually the whole neighbourhood, as well as the pits, or where, as in some areas in Durham, the pits were parts of great semi-feudal estates in the hands of such peers as Lord Londonderry.

The rest of the country — outside the main textile and mining areas — had in the eighteen-thirties felt much less the impact of the new industrialism. The old, declining textile centres in the South West and in the Eastern Counties were the scenes of sporadic movements ; but they had been so weakened by the competition of the North that there was not very much kick left in them — the more so because they were largely agricultural, and the progress of enclosure and the substitution, after the wars, of pasture for arable had been holding their populations down to a standard of continuous wretchedness which had taken the heart out of them well before Chartism began. At Devizes, Trowbridge, and a few other places in the South West, and also at Norwich, in East Anglia, there were active Chartist movements. But over most of the South of England Chartism never developed into a mass agitation.

Apart from the textile and mining areas, the main centres of Chartist activity were in and around London and Birmingham. But the movements in both these places differed considerably from the hunger-Chartism of the textile operatives and the miners. In London there were in effect always two Chartist movements rather than one. The first of these, which under the leadership of William Lovett actually initiated Chartism and published The People's Charter, developed among a group of skilled artisans, printers, working craftsmen in various trades, most of whom had been connected at an earlier stage both with Owenism and with the National Union of the Working Classes — the principal organ of the London workmen in the Reform struggle of 1830–32. This group, which formed the London Working Men's Association, consisted of relatively prosperous persons, mostly active members of Trade Societies of skilled workers, and some of them in business for themselves as craftsmen-shopkeepers, or as printers or booksellers or coffee-house keepers, or the like. They were educated men — self-educated for the most part — accustomed to decent standards of living, and with no personal contact with the Poor Law, old or new. They were also idealists, strongly under the influence of Owenite or similar doctrines and with an ardent belief in education and in the power of reason. The Industrial Revolution, so far from affecting them adversely, had for the most part left their handicrafts untouched, and indeed benefited them by enlarging the market for their wares among the rapidly growing middle and upper working classes in the towns, and, above all, in London.

But the working class of London was by no means made up exclusively of superior craftsmen. It included also the desperately poor weavers of Spitalfields, and a great host of unskilled, or at any rate underpaid, workers at and about the docks, builders' labourers and navvies, sweated clothing workers, and casuals who had come to London in the hope of finding work. Among these ill-paid grades of labour were many Irish — here, as everywhere, undercutting English standards. These men felt quite differently about politics from the respectable artisans whom alone Lovett and his friends sought to enrol in the L.W.M.A. They were a turbulent mass of starvelings much more closely akin in spirit to the ' fustian-jackets ' of the North ; and their leaders were not Lovett and Henry Hetherington, but men of the ' physical force ' school, such as Feargus O'Connor, before he made his headquarters in the North, and George Julian Harney, who aspired to be the Marat of the coming English Revolution. It was this group that rallied to the London Democratic Association in opposition to Lovett's L.W.M.A., and was responsible for the great crowds which poured out of Southwark and East London upon the City and the West End whenever there was trouble afoot.

Birmingham Chartism, as well as that of London, had two sides. The Birmingham district, though it included some big factories, was still mainly a region of small working masters, half independent and half subject to merchants who contracted to take their wares. Between these small masters and the skilled artisans who worked with them, or for bigger employers, there was no sharp division of class. They could be combined, as they had been in the Reform struggle, under a common leadership ; and this leadership was most likely to come from the ranks of the Radical middle class. In fact, these groups found their common leader in Thomas Attwood, the banker of unorthodox views who had headed the Birmingham Political Union in the earlier agitation, and now reconstituted it and carried it along with him into the Chartist movement.

Attwood was a quite sincere believer in democracy and Universal Suffrage. But the belief which he held most deeply was that a mistaken and monopolistic banking policy lay at the root of the prevailing distress. He held that the issue of currency and credit ought to be based, not on gold, but on productive power. Attwood's financial views were much less nonsensical than his opponents made them out to be, or than they are commonly made to appear even now. Sound or unsound, they made a deep appeal to small masters struggling with adversity in a world of falling prices, and very ready to attribute their difficulties to deflation and the refusal of the banks to grant them financial accommodation. Attwood believed, and told them, that nothing short of the Charter would avail to break the banking monopoly and give them the means of making profits, as they had done during the prosperous years of war. They followed him, and for a time the main body of the Birmingham workers followed him too.

But Birmingham, and, still more, the Black Country near by, had another working class much more impoverished and less educated than the artisans. The nail-makers and other metal workers of the Black Country, and a considerable part of the working population of Birmingham itself, were as near the starvation level as the textile workers of the North, or the lower proletariat of East and South London. Attwood and the group around him — Salt, Douglas, Edmonds, the two Muntzs, and the rest — were determined to appeal only to ' moral force ' in the struggle for the Charter ; but the events in Birmingham itself in

8

1839 showed that not all the local Chartists were of this mind. Altogether, the emergence of ' physical force ' Chartism after Parliament had rejected the National Petition was too much for Attwood and his friends. They dropped out of the movement, leaving the Birmingham Chartists for a time leaderless and at sixes and sevens. Presently Joseph Sturge set to work to reconstitute the ' moral force ' section as the Complete Suffrage Union, without Attwood's currency projects, while the left wing joined forces with O'Connor in the National Charter Association, with which its fortunes were thereafter merged.

This dualism was not confined to Birmingham and London. It appeared in Lancashire as well, where in general Manchester Chartism was moderate in its methods, and the Chartism of the lesser textile centres (where wages and conditions were usually worse) a good deal more violent. It appeared on the North-East Coast, where Newcastle-on-Tyne was more given to moderate courses and to collaboration between the middle and working classes than the coalfield areas. It appeared in Scotland, where Edinburgh was to the right of Glasgow, and there were great contests between the leaders of Christian Chartism, such as Patrick Brewster of Paisley Old Church, and the contingents of starving hand-loom weavers and of cotton spinners (whose Union had been broken by the savage sentences passed on their leaders in the trials of 1837). It appeared in general, as between local Chartist associations dominated by skilled artisans, and associations whose following was made up chiefly of factory workers or miners, or of domestic workers who were being slowly starved out by the competition of the new machines.

In order to understand Chartism it is necessary to go back to the events of the years which immediately preceded the drafting of The People's Charter. During the four years between the passing of the great Reform Act of 1832 and the beginning of Chartism in 1836-7 the working classes had fought and lost two great campaigns ; and at the moment when the Charter was published they were in the thick of a third. They had fought hard for Sadler's Bill — the Ten Hours Bill which they were not to win until 1847. They had flocked, between 1829 and 1834, into Trade Unions —

only to have their Unions crushed by the combined action
of the Whig Government, the Law Courts, and the employers.
And they were, in 1836–7, just beginning the great fight
against the introduction of the New Poor Law into the
industrial areas. Something must be said of each of these
movements if the character of Chartism as a mass agitation
is to be understood, or the reason for its decline appreciated.

The factory reform movement, with the Ten Hours Day
as its principal objective, had two main centres — Lancashire and Yorkshire, the Midlands and Scotland being sub-
sidiary centres. It had a somewhat different character in
the two main areas, dominated respectively by the cotton
and by the woollen and worsted industries. The cotton
industry, the pioneer in adopting the new methods of production and the factory system, had come under regulation
to a slight extent as early as 1802, when the elder Sir Robert
Peel got through Parliament his Act for protecting the Health
and Morals of Apprentices — that is, of the pauper children
who were practically sold into mass slavery by the Poor Law
authorities, by the method of sending them as apprentices
to the cotton factories, there to be worked, fed, housed, and
made in all respects subject to their masters' wills. But
hardly had this Act been passed when the system of pauper
apprenticeship began to die away, as more ' free ' labour
became available from among the children of the growing
body of adult factory workers. Not until 1819 was any
protection given to this ' free ' child labour, under a second
Act sponsored by Peel; and both this Act and amending
measures promoted by John Cam Hobhouse in 1825 and
1831, at the instance of Committees established by the
factory operatives, applied only to cotton factories.

It was in connection with the agitation for Hobhouse's
second Act that the Yorkshire operatives first began, under
the leadership of the land agent Richard Oastler, to play
an active part in the struggle for factory reform. The new
methods of production were at that time sweeping over the
West Riding with a rush; and Michael Thomas Sadler in
Parliament and Oastler outside constituted themselves the
protagonists of the factory children. There was bitter disappointment in Yorkshire when woollen and worsted mills

were left out of Hobhouse's Act and when Hobhouse
expressed the view that it would be useless to press Parliament for further legislation.

But the struggle went on. Sadler, defeated in his contest
at Leeds for a seat in the first reformed Parliament, handed
over the leadership of the movement in the House of Commons to Ashley, later Lord Shaftesbury, who thereafter
acted on behalf of the Short Time Committees in Lancashire
and Yorkshire alike. But the Whig Government would
have nothing to do with the Ten Hours Bill ; and the Bill
introduced on its behalf by Lord Althorp, and duly passed
into law in 1833, was regarded by the operatives as a defeat,
even though it did extend the principle of regulation from
cotton mills to woollen and other textile factories. The
Twelve Hours Day conceded by the Whig measure would
indeed be a substantial improvement on the previous practice of most employers — if only it could be enforced. But
enforcement was bound to be difficult in the absence of
regulation of the hours during which the factories were
allowed to remain open, and the limitation of hours applied
only to persons under eighteen years of age. Children up
to thirteen years of age were indeed to be limited to a day
of eight hours, except in silk mills ; but the operatives, who
wanted a measure which would in practice limit the hours
of adult as well as juvenile labour, found this cold comfort.
Nor did they put any trust in the new travelling Factory
Inspectors, who were appointed for the first time under the
provisions of the Act of 1833.

Through the rest of the 'thirties, and right up to 1847,
when at last the Ten Hours Bill became law, the factory
agitation continued. But from 1833 right up to 1844 the
operatives not merely met with no further successes, but
were repeatedly threatened with adverse modifications of the
law. The textile employers, not content with using every
possible expedient for evading the Act of 1833, brought
continual pressure on the Government to amend it. The
efforts of the new inspectors were systematically thwarted ;
and only to a very small extent was the Act of 1833 actually
enforced.

From 1831 to 1838 Oastler was at the head of the Yorkshire factory movement, and during part of this time he headed the agitation against the New Poor Law as well. But in 1838 he was discharged from his position as land agent and compelled to leave Yorkshire, and in effect to surrender his leadership. His angry and disappointed followers thereupon went over in their thousands to Chartism, taking Feargus O'Connor as their new leader. Similarly in Lancashire the disappointed adherents of the Short Time Committees flocked into the Chartist movement, especially between 1839 and 1842. After the defeats of the great strikes of that year many of them dropped out of Chartism, resumed their place in the Short Time agitation, and had their rewards in the Factory Acts of 1844 and 1847, of which the latter, as we have seen, at last granted in principle the Ten Hours Day.

Between the two main wings of the factory agitation there was a substantial difference. In Yorkshire the factory operatives found their main supporters among the Tories, and were fiercely opposed by the great mass of the Whig and Liberal manufacturers. Sadler and Oastler were both Tories. In Lancashire, on the other hand, the middle-class friends of the operatives were found mainly among Radicals. John Fielden, Joseph Brotherton, and Charles Hindley, the chief supporters of factory reform among the cotton manufacturers, were all Radical M.P.s. This difference was, I think, partly due to the more mature conditions of the cotton industry, which caused some of the well-established manufacturers to favour regulation as a protection against unfair competition ; but it was due also to the greater strength in Yorkshire of Church Toryism and in Lancashire of somewhat Radical brands of Nonconformity. Of course I do not mean that the bulk of Radical manufacturers in Lancashire supported factory reform. On the contrary, most of them were strongly against it, including Cobden and John Bright. But some did — many more than in Yorkshire ; whereas in Lancashire there was, with the exception of Joseph Rayner Stephens (who was a very odd Tory), almost no Tory movement on the side of the factory workers.

The second great movement of which account has to be taken among the forces that went to the making of Chartism is the Trade Union struggle. This reached its height during the years 1833 and 1834 — a period of relatively good trade following the depression which had accompanied the agitation for parliamentary Reform. Most of the published accounts of this struggle, including my own treatment of it in my earlier writings, get the perspective wrong by laying much too much stress on Robert Owen's connection with it, and on the Grand National Consolidated Trades Union which he was largely responsible for bringing into existence in 1833–4. Readers of my later account of the matter (but they are still few) will understand that the G.N.C.T.U. was but one of a number of attempts made between 1830 and 1834 to link the entire working class together in a single grand combination for meeting the persistent lowering of wages and worsening of conditions which accompanied the onrush of the new methods of production. One such attempt was made by John Doherty, the leader of the Lancashire Cotton Spinners, in 1830–31. Another, practically independent of it, was made from Leeds almost at the same time by Simeon Pollard with the workers in the woollen and worsted trades as its nucleus. Elsewhere, for example in the Midland Counties and in Sheffield, there were county or local attempts at General Unions which had little or no connection with either the Manchester or the Leeds central organisation. The half-Owenite Grand National Consolidated Trades Union was no doubt an attempt to join up all these bodies, and the parallel movements in Wales and Scotland, into a single, inclusive Trades Union. But it never succeeded in this ; and the great struggles of 1833–4 were in fact fought out only to a small extent under its auspices. The Yorkshire Trades Union, for example, carried through its struggle for the right to exist practically without any connection with the simultaneous struggles of the G.N.C.T.U.

In effect, what happened was this. About the beginning of 1833 the workers, left voteless by their allies in the successful crusade for parliamentary Reform, and encouraged by the improvement of trade, were joining in very great numbers General Unions based on the previously existing separate societies in the various trades, and were demanding the restoration of the wages lost during the depression and an improvement in their conditions of work. The employers, alarmed at this growth of industrial militancy, banded themselves together in many parts of the country and demanded that the Government should take steps to put down the Trades Unions by re-enacting the Combination Acts, which had been repealed in 1824–5. The Government, however, realising how great a storm any such proposal would arouse, refused the request, but at the same time expressed its abhorrence of the growing combinations, its view that their practices were illegal under the existing law, and its hope that the employers would make, without fresh legislation, every possible effort to put them down. Thus encouraged to direct action, the employers, especially in Yorkshire, but soon in other areas as well, entered into mutual pacts not to continue to employ any workmen who would not sign a ' document ', or at least enter into a pledge, renouncing all connection with Trade Unionism.

The ensuing struggle, bitterest of all in Yorkshire, where it was accompanied by considerable acts of violence, matured at different times and in somewhat different forms in various parts of the country. But it ended, wherever the employers made up their minds to fight it out to a finish, in the complete defeat of the new ' General Trades Unions '. Not only the Grand National Consolidated Trades Union, but also the Yorkshire and other county Unions, and such big industrial combinations as the Builders' Union, were compelled to dissolve, when their powers of resistance had been exhausted. The trial and conviction of the unfortunate Dorchester labourers for administering ' unlawful oaths ' further threatened every member of every Trade Society which used any sort of initiation ceremony — as most of the older craft societies then did. The Trade Unionists were scared as well as defeated ; and a substantial part of their activity was driven for a time underground, out of fear of the combined repression of the employers and of the Government, backed up by the courts of law.[1] Thus to the thwarted

[1] I have given a full account of these struggles in the work " Attempts at General Union ", issued in 1939 in *The International Review of Social History*, published in Amsterdam. But for the war, I should by this time have revised this study, and issued it in England in book form, as

factory reformers were added in the industrial districts the thwarted Trade Unionists, eager to find ways of revenging themselves on the victorious employers, and armed with a new grievance when, in the middle 'thirties, trade began to decline, and a fresh campaign of wage-cutting set in. Side by side with the rise of Chartism in the later 'thirties, Trade Unionism was again raising its head, and in 1838–9 there was a renewed agitation among the manufacturers to have it put down by law. The Trade Unionists, conscious of this danger, were the more disposed to lend their support to movements for Universal Suffrage and other political reforms, in which they saw the hope of a Parliament and a Government more favourable to the rights of combination and to the workers' cause. This close connection between Chartism and a Trade Unionism that was compelled to work largely underground appeared plainly in the great strike movement of 1842. The failure of that movement largely broke the connection, which was never renewed in anything like the same form. For when Trade Union revival came, leading in 1845 to the foundation of the National Association of United Trades for the Protection of Labour, its promoters preferred to hold aloof from the already divided forces of Chartism, and to build up their own movement apart from politics. That was partly why Chartism was never able to regain the mass hold on the workers which it undoubtedly had in 1839, and perhaps even more in 1842.

The third great force making for the development of Chartism into a mass movement was the agitation against the New Poor Law. The Poor Law Amendment Act of 1834, though it was directed primarily against the ' Speenhamland ' system of subsidising wages out of the Poor rates, which had never been applied in most of the industrial districts, did much more than sweep this system away. For the principle of the Act was that outdoor relief should be refused to all able-bodied persons, and that relief should be

it throws a large amount of light on a period of Trade Union history hitherto very inadequately treated by social historians. I still hope to make my study more widely available in this country ; but those who have access to well-equipped libraries can find it, in English, in the files of the above-mentioned *Review*.

given in the new workhouses — the ' Bastilles ' — and even then only under conditions ' less eligible ' than those of the worst-off labourer in ordinary employment. The terms of relief were meant to be as deterrent as possible ; and they involved the segregation of the sexes — the parting of husbands from wives, and of parents from children — and the subjection of the pauper to a discipline based on the idea of his iniquity, proved by his destitute condition. The new system was to be administered, not by the old parish authorities, which were subject to local pressure, but by the new Boards of Guardians, covering wider areas, chosen by a voting method which gave heavy weight to the property owners, and subject to control, in all vital matters of policy, by the Poor Law Commissioners in London — the execrated ' Three Bashaws of Somerset House '.

Against this new system of repression the workers, aided here and there by the old-fashioned Tories, who hated the new-fangled bureaucracy, or by Radical employers, who hated the Whigs, fought a determined guerrilla warfare. The Commissioners, getting to work in 1835, began by enforcing the new system in the agricultural districts of the South, where the Speenhamland system had been in full force. In these areas there was no effective resistance ; for the labourers had shot their bolt in the agricultural revolt of 1830–31, and the savage repression which had followed had left them prostrate and leaderless. Having established their Boards of Guardians and the new methods of relief in the South, the Commissioners proceeded, in 1836 and 1837, to turn their attention to the industrial districts. It happened (but the Commissioners were too certain of the rectitude of the new principles to be deterred by such a conjuncture) that this attempt coincided with the onset of a major industrial depression.

Now, in the industrial areas, the old Poor Law system had not meant that wages were regularly subsidised out of the rates ; but it had meant that, in periods of trade depression, the worker who fell out of employment or could get only two or three days' work a week at most could go to the parish and get outdoor relief to tide him over his temporary difficulty. This relief was not granted everywhere, or without stringent conditions ; but it was widely used as a means of preventing mass starvation in bad times. Under the economic conditions of the later 'thirties, the withdrawal of this kind of relief, with the offer of bare maintenance in the workhouse, accompanied by segregation of the sexes, as the only substitute, meant horrible hardship and indignity for a high proportion of the factory operatives and, still more, of the handloom weavers, stockingers, and other ' domestic ' workers who were, at the best of times, waging a losing battle against the new machines. The economic hardship was severe ; but the personal indignity was even worse. The bitterest resentment was felt at the conditions which the Whig economists were imposing on the working classes in the name of sound economics ; and resentment was made the heavier by the knowledge that the ' Malthusian philosophers ' were set on preventing the poor from breeding. ' Over-population ', according to the orthodox economists, was the primary cause of poverty : it was, above all else, essential to prevent population from outrunning the means of subsistence. Segregation of the sexes in the ' Bastilles ' was one means of preventing ' surplus population ' ; and fantastic stories circulated about the projects of the Poor Law Commissioners for preventing the poor from breeding unwanted mouths. A pamphlet, *The Book of Murder*, by Marcus, proposing the actual infanticide of the children of the poor, was widely believed, though it was plain parody, to be the authentic product of the hated ' Bashaws '. Nothing was too bad to be believed of the Commissioners up in London : the workers saw their only hope in opposing, by every means in their power, the institution of the new bureaucratic system. They tried to prevent the election of the new Boards of Guardians ; and, where they had been elected, they tried to prevent them from carrying out their functions. The institution of the new system was fought, step by step, in the industrial areas. It was fought by the methods of mass resistance — by actual violence, where violence seemed to offer any hope of success. The houses of those who agreed to serve as Guardians were attacked ; and a few Radical employers, such as John Fielden, gave the fullest support to their employees in every step which they took to obstruct the administration of the new system. Moreover even the Guardians, where they were elected, were often reluctant to carry out their duties in accordance with the prescriptions of the Commissioners. They pointed out that the strict enforcement of the new law would speedily fill the workhouses to overflowing, without reducing appreciably the numbers still in quest of relief. They said that they must continue to grant outdoor relief, because the refusal of it would mean riot and mass revolt. The ' Three Bashaws ' fought a battle on two fronts — against obstinate working-class resistance and against the timidities of locally elected persons who agreed with them in principle, but lacked their utter conviction of rectitude and their aloofness from being influenced by the opinion of their neighbours.

In face of everything — undeterred by trade depression, by mass hostility among the workers, or by hesitation among the local administrators of the new law — the Poor Law Commissioners went upon their way, instituting Boards of Guardians and imposing their standard rules for the grant of relief. In the end, they won ; but for years on end, as long as the great depression lasted, the by-product of their unremitting efforts was the hatred of the poor. The ' Three Bashaws of Somerset House ' had more than a little responsibility for turning Chartism into a mass movement of the poor and needy. It is even possible that, but for their efforts, the Charter would hardly be remembered at all.

These three forces, then — the factory reform movement, the ruthless campaign waged by the employers, with Government backing, against the Trade Unions, and the New Poor Law — went to the making of Chartism as a movement powerful enough, for a few years, to threaten revolution, and to command the backing of the main body of the working classes. But for these forces, there would have been nothing to single out The People's Charter from among the many documents and manifestos in which the demands of the Radical Reformers had been set out again and again during the sixty years or so before it was drafted. For the Charter contained nothing new. Each of the Six Points had been a part of the Radical stock-in-trade even before the men who drafted the Charter were born. The times, and not the

precise formulation of the Radical programme by Lovett and
the London Working Men's Association, made The People's
Charter ' a symbol of working-class aspirations, sufferings,
and resentments, and gave to it an almost sacred character :
so that when, in the hour of Chartist defeat in 1842, Joseph
Sturge and his middle-class supporters were ready to accept
the whole of the Charter — except the name — and to go
forward with the Six Points entire under the banner of the
Complete Suffrage Union, even such moderate Chartists as
Lovett would not agree to give up the symbolic name.

They were, however, clinging to a shadow ; for Chartism
never recovered from the defeat of 1842. It had rallied
remarkably after the repressions which followed the abortive
Newport Rising of 1839 ; but the second defeat left it
permanently weakened. It is often said that this was because
thereafter the main body of the movement passed under the
sway of Feargus O'Connor, who led it up a disastrous by-
path with his Land Scheme and made it the instrument of
his own ascendancy rather than of working-class demands. '
But, in truth, the Land Scheme was a symptom rather than
a cause of decay. After 1842 it had become plain to a great
many workmen, as well as to the majority of middle-class
Radicals, that there was no chance for a long time to come
of making the Charter " the law of the land " by peaceful
means, and also that the forces of law and order were too
powerful to be overcome by violence. The rump of the
Chartist leaders accepted the Land Scheme not so much
because they believed in it as because they had to have
something to offer to the people — something closely related
to the people's own wants and aspirations. That the Land
Scheme did make a very powerful appeal is evident from
the money and the devoted service which many desperately
poor workers gave to it during the next few years. Land
hunger was a very strong emotion among large masses of
factory operatives who had been driven out of the countryside by enclosure, new farming methods, and, still more, the
decline of village industries. O'Connor's argument that
wages were low because too many workers were competing
for industrial employment, and that settlement of as many
people as possible as small-holders on their own land was

the best and indeed the only way of raising wages by reducing the competition for jobs, was quite plausible, and would indeed have been true if O'Connor's calculations of the productivity of ' spade husbandry ' had been even nearly correct. That they were wildly incorrect could be seen by Bronterre O'Brien and other rationally minded Chartists who refused to follow O'Connor's lead ; but to the land-hungry factory operative, who was belly-hungry as well and in mortal fear of the new Poor Law ' Bastille ' as the probable home of his old age, the wish to escape was so strong as to make the will to believe in the Land Scheme too insistent to be overcome by rational calculations. Even if O'Connor's estimates were over-optimistic, could the factory operative be worse off than he was, by getting a plot of land he could call his own ? At any rate he would be his own master ; and that meant a very great deal in those days of bitter factory slavery.

But by no means the whole of the working class was of this mind. The skilled artisans were not of it — save a very few. Though they might suffer severely in times of depression, they felt no urge to go back to the land. If they belonged to old handicrafts not yet seriously threatened by machinery, they wanted to become small masters, not smallholders. If they belonged to the new crafts, such as engineering, which were growing rapidly on the basis of machine technique, they wanted to build up Trade Societies powerful enough to limit competition by enforcing apprenticeship, and to exact standard wage-rates and codes of working rules from the employers. They were not perpetually half-starved, like the main body of the less skilled factory operatives. They did not hate the new machines, but saw in them their means of living.

Accordingly, as soon as Chartism went haring off after the Land Scheme, it was bound to forfeit the support of a large section of better-off working class. Moreover, this section was of vital importance from the standpoint of effective leadership. It included the best educated, most capable, and most energetic part of the working class — the very people who were best at organising local Chartist Associations, at conducting propaganda, and at making out

of disorderly mobs of half-starved factory workers a movement having at any rate the rudiments of order and discipline.
I do not mean that all the skilled workers were lost to
Chartism. Many idealists among them remained ; but the
support of the main body was forfeit.

It was among these higher strata of the working class that
Chartism's great rival — the Anti-Corn Law League —
found its principal body of working-class supporters. If
industrialism was to be accepted as the foundation of the
social order, the case for repealing the Corn Laws was over-
whelming. The main body of the Chartist leaders had never
been in favour of retaining them : even O'Connor maintained that they would be unnecessary when the workers
had been settled on the land under proper conditions. The
usual Chartist contention was that it was useless to agitate
for the repeal of the Corn Laws, because the landlord interest
was so powerfully entrenched in Parliament that the laws
were bound to be kept in force until Parliament had been
reformed. Doubtless, the Chartists who argued in this way
usually went on to assert that repeal by itself would do the
workers no good, that the employers wanted it only as a
means of reducing wages, and that, by the laws of political
economy, they would be able to reduce wages as fast as the
cost of bare subsistence fell. But there was a good deal of
polemic about this line of argument. Most of the leading
Chartists did not really believe that free trade in corn would
do nothing to benefit the working class. They believed in
repeal, but held that the way to it lay through the Charter.

Peel's tariff charges of 1842–3 struck a sharp blow at the
doctrine that nothing could be done about the Corn Laws
without parliamentary reform, and strengthened immensely
the Anti-Corn Law League's appeal to those workers who
were already in a mood of disillusionment about Chartist
prospects. The concentration of the O'Connorite Chartists
on the Land Scheme widened the gulf between Chartist-
repealers and Chartists who wanted the Corn Laws kept on
until the new methods of spade husbandry had become
securely established. Chartist-repealers who disliked the
Land Scheme were increasingly disposed to give up working
for the National Charter Association, which now seemed to

have not much to do with the Charter, and to devote their energies to the Anti-Corn Law League instead. There were, however, many anti-O'Connorite Chartists who so hated the capitalists as to be unprepared to work with them in any cause ; and these kicked their heels helplessly, or formed little cliques and groups which were too weak to have any influence on the course of events. There was a temporary rallying of most of these dissidents to the main body in the great ' Year of Revolutions ' — 1848 ; and some of those who had deserted Chartism for the Anti-Corn Law League also came back after 1846, when the Corn Laws had been repealed, and the League's work done. But there was no complete Chartist recovery ; and the movement flew apart again as soon as the affair of Kennington Common had demonstrated both the Government's determination to take a strong line and the Chartist leaders' sense of their own weakness.

After 1848 Chartism was merely a residue. The labours of George Julian Harney and, later, Ernest Jones to keep it alive are interesting to scholars, and especially to Marxists, because it was only at this point that Marx's ideas began to influence the movement. Chartism became increasingly Socialist, and increasingly conscious of itself as a section of a growing international working-class movement. But this did not help it to regain its hold on the main body of the British working class, because Socialism and revolutionary internationalism were not the things in which the British workers were interested, and it was not possible, under the conditions of the 'fifties, for leaders who *were* interested in these things to find means of linking them to positive day-to-day policies capable of enlisting the support of any considerable section of the British working class.

The reasons for this are simple. The main body of workers was coming to be rather less hungry, and a good deal less desperate. What the employers and the political economists had been telling the workers about the results of machinery was beginning to come true. As Great Britain became, on an ever-increasing scale, the world's workshop, and exports rose by leaps and bounds, the scramble for jobs became less intense, and periods of trade depression came to be both less prolonged and much less severe. The displaced hand-loom weavers, stockingers, and other throw-outs of the new industrialism grew old and died off; and a festering sore of misery was removed. Wages — real as well as money wages — rose, albeit not very fast, and probably more for the skilled than for the less skilled kinds of labour. The Boards of Guardians and the Commissioners in London, after the struggles over their establishment had died down, gradually lost some of their zeal for the rigid enforcement of the 'principles of 1834', and even the workhouse became a little less a terror. Employers, getting rapidly richer and less 'abstinent' themselves, shed some of their religious zeal for enforcing abstinence on their employees, and accepted both higher wages and shorter hours as the pressure of competition grew less severe with the enlargement of markets. Joint-stock companies provided new ways of raising capital for industry, and made it less necessary for the employer to set aside every penny he could spare out of profits for the extension of his business. Banking practice ceased to be deflationary as the new gold began to pour in from California and Australia, and as the use of cheques spread and amplified the supply of credit. Talk about the blessings of capitalist enterprise came to be less a mockery in working-class ears; and, for the skilled workers especially, the most urgent tasks seemed to be those of building up their Trade Unions and Cooperative Societies into solid instruments of protection, rather than beating their heads against brick walls.

So Chartism died gradually away; and the new movements for political Reform which began to replace it before the end of the 'fifties were of a less ambitious kind, and had not behind them the mass drive of popular hunger and despair. There were enough hungry people left in Great Britain, heaven knows! But there was no longer mass starvation; and no one was any longer stirring the bottom of the pot of social unrest.

In the following twelve sketches of leading Chartists — or of men whose fortunes were, at one point or another, so closely linked with Chartism as to be inseparable from its story — I have tried to present something like a general picture of the rise and fall of the movement and of the

widely differing elements that made it up. The choice of
' subjects ' was guided by the wish to make my book something more than a series of short biographies of particular
persons ; and, although I had to some extent to be influenced
in my choice by the plenty or scarcity of biographical
material, I was able to find someone about whom enough was
known to make a tolerably plain portrait possible, to serve as
a representative figure for most of the important phases of
the movement, and for most of the main groups that played
a significant part in its history.

There are certain exceptions. I should have liked to find
someone whose portrait would have exemplified the relationship of Chartism to the great Trade Union struggles of
the 'thirties and 'forties. But I could find no representative
figure. John Doherty might have done for Lancashire Trade
Unionism, but he dropped out too soon ; or Simeon Pollard
for Yorkshire, but about him not enough is known ; or
Martin Jude for the miners, but he had not enough connection with Chartism. W. P. Roberts, the ' Miners' Attorney ',
who did play a very active part in Chartism, was also a
possibility ; but I wanted an actual Trade Unionist, and not
a middle-class ally ; and there was no one suitable.

A second gap is that I have included none of the leaders
of Scottish Chartism. Here there were several possibilities
— Abram Duncan, the ubiquitous Dr. John Taylor, or
the Rev. Patrick Brewster of Paisley. But I did not know
enough about any of them ; and I did know that my friend,
Mr. W. H. Marwick of Edinburgh, was collecting material
about them which he proposed to publish. I therefore left
it to him to fill that gap, as I hope he speedily will.

Then there was the question of Temperance Chartism,
at one time a very widespread and social influential movement. I could have used Henry Vincent, the orator from
London who roused South Wales and the West in 1839, as
the subject to illustrate this phase. But there would have
been some overlapping with the story of John Frost ; and
when it came to the final selection, I decided that Vincent
would have to go. Arthur O'Neil, with his gospel of
Christian Chartism, and Dr. Wade, the Chartists' only prominent figure in the Church of England, were also left out

in the end mainly from considerations of space.

Three other ' possibles ' who troubled me not a little were Henry Hetherington, James Watson, and George Jacob Holyoake. But I made up my mind in the end that the story of Hetherington's struggle for the freedom of the press could best be told in connection with the period before the rise of Chartism — the period which begins with the peace of 1815 and ends with the Trade Union defeat of 1834 — and I may perhaps later on attempt another book treating that period in a similar way. By the same line of reasoning, I left out Holyoake, as too much of his story belongs to a period subsequent to that of Chartism. Watson, the indefatigable Radical bookseller, I should have liked to include, but I could not make his life record illustrate any clearly defined phase or aspect of the Chartist movement. So I left him out.

There were of course other names besides these to be considered — Peter Murray McDouall, Peter Bussey, Dr. William Price of South Wales, and a number of others. I seriously considered McDouall as a representative of the ' physical force ' school ; but his story overlapped Cooper's, and in the end I came to the conclusion that I had not enough material. I left out the Irishmen of 1848 — John Mitchel, William Smith O'Brien, and the rest — because I could not have brought them in without bringing in the whole record of Irish Radicalism, including Daniel O'Connell ; and that would have taken me much too far afield. Similarly, I left out the middle-class Parliamentary Radicals, because their relations to Chartism were not close enough, and there was no representative figure to stand for them. Attwood and Fielden, whom I have included, were both M.P.s ; but they appear in this book not as representatives of the ' Radical Party ' in Parliament, but Attwood for his leadership in the Birmingham Political Union, and Fielden for his part in the Poor Law struggle and the campaign for factory reform.

I also hesitated over Charles Kingsley, as a representative of the Christian Socialists. But in the end I felt that this inclusion would mean casting the net too wide. Christian Socialism, though it was active in 1848, belongs essentially to a post-Chartist phase of historical development.

The twelve whom I have included were, inevitably, in the

phases of the movement which I have used them to describe, continually crossing one another's paths. It was therefore impossible to employ the biographical method as a means of telling the story of Chartism without some repetition. But I have tried to repeat myself as little as possible ; and, when I have to tell the same story twice, I try to tell it from an angle different enough to bring out different things. From this standpoint, Feargus O'Connor unavoidably presented the greatest difficulty ; for he was active in the movement so continuously and at so many different points as to overlap everybody else. That is why my sketch of him appears so late in the volume. I have tried to use it for pulling the story together, up to the date of his disappearance m the political scene.

As for the others, Lovett is here because he drafted the Charter and founded the movement, and as the representative of the skilled artisans. Joseph Rayner Stephens is here, though he was never a Chartist in the full sense, because his activities serve best to bring out the essential features of the Anti-Poor Law struggle and the reactions of the factory operatives in and around Manchester. Richard Oastler, the ' Factory King ', was even less a Chartist than Stephens. He was a Tory, and an opponent of Universal Suffrage. He gets in because he led the Yorkshire crusade for factory reform, and Yorkshire Chartism cannot be understood except in relation to that crusade.

Thomas Attwood, the Birmingham banker and currency reformer, stands for the first attempt to unite the middle and working classes under the banner of Universal Suffrage ; and Joseph Sturge, with his Complete Suffrage Union, stands for the revival of this movement after Attwood had withdrawn. John Frost, the ex-Mayor of Newport, is included as the leader of the ill-starred ' Newport Rising ' of 1839, which followed the rejection of the first National Petition ; and Thomas Cooper's life is used to illustrate, among other things, the great strike movement of 1842, after the second Petition had met with the same fate. John Fielden is there both for the Poor Law struggle and for the later phases of the Ten Hours movement.

There remain Bronterre O'Brien, George Julian Harney,

and Ernest Jones. These three, beyond others, gave to Chartism as much as it ever had of a theoretical foundation. O'Brien and Harney both set out, in theorising, from achievements of the great French Revolution, and saw as the mission of the working class the working-out to its logical completion of the slogan Liberty, Equality, Fraternity. O'Brien took Robespierre as his prototype ; Harney took Marat. O'Brien translated Buonarotti's history of Babeuf's *Conspiration des Égaux* ; Harney took to himself the name *Ami du Peuple*, and sported the *bonnet rouge*. But there was more than that to both of them. O'Brien was the foremost advocate of land nationalisation and, extending the principle to all monopolies, of capital as well as land, became a pioneer of collectivism. Harney became the leading exponent of internationalism on a proletarian basis, and was the favourite of Marx and Engels until he took the wrong side, from their point of view, in the contest which rent the Communist League after the defeat of the Revolutions of 1848, and showed too indiscriminate an enthusiasm for continental revolutionaries of every brand and colour. Harney published the first English version of the famous *Communist Manifesto* ; but it was Ernest Jones who, in the 'fifties, became the white-headed boy of British Marxism — only to be discarded in his turn, when, after the eclipse of Chartism, he came round to the idea of class-collaboration in the new Reform movement which led up to the Reform Act of 1867.

Harney, in addition to all this, finds his place in this portrait gallery as the leader of the left wing in London Chartism, and as a prominent member of the ' physical force ' school. O'Brien comes in as the lieutenant of O'Connor, who parted company with him over the Land Scheme. Jones's story is, in its later phases, practically one with that of Chartism in its decline.

Here, then, are my twelve portraits, covering between them most phases and aspects of the great working-class revolt which died away as capitalism emerged from its pangs of growth to the assured stature of adult vigour. It remains only to add a few words about the sources of information.

Two of my ' subjects ', William Lovett and Thomas Cooper, wrote autobiographies, on which my studies have been largely based. Of four others — Stephens, Attwood, Frost, and Sturge — there are published Lives of varying value. The Lives of Stephens (by Holyoake) and of Attwood (by C. M. Wakefield) are both remarkably bad. That of Frost (by David Williams) is excellent ; and there is also a brief sketch of him by Ness Edwards. There are two Lives of Sturge, both fair in their way — one by Henry Richard, the pacifist M.P., who was Sturge's friend, and the other, more recent, by Stephen Hobhouse. Both give more attention to Sturge's pacifist and anti-slavery activities than to the Complete Suffrage movement.

Of Bronterre O'Brien there is an excellent Life, still unfortunately unpublished, by Dr. Alfred Plummer ; and I cannot too cordially thank the author for his generosity in allowing me to make full use of it. I hope it will soon be published, and the extent of my debt to his generosity revealed.

Of three other ' subjects ' there are pamphlet Lives, or rather biographical sketches. These are Richard Oastler (by Arthur Greenwood), Feargus O'Connor (by William Jones), and Ernest Jones (by D. P. Davies — and also a brief anonymous sketch). There is also a rough draft of a Life of Ernest Jones by Ella Twynam (in MS.), of which I have been able to make use. Of Harney and of John Fielden I have been able to find no published or unpublished Lives at all, beyond a brief account of Fielden in *The Dictionary of National Biography*.

There is, however, a good deal of biographical material to be found elsewhere. Oastler's own writings, especially *The Fleet Papers*, are full of autobiographical material. The Lives of Harney and O'Brien can be followed largely in their periodical writings. This also applies, to a smaller extent, to Stephens and to Ernest Jones. *The History of the Chartist Movement*, by R. G. Gammage, who was himself a Chartist, is full of biographical references. So, for Oastler particularly, is Samuel Kydd's *History of the Factory Movement*, which he published under the pen-name of " Alfred ". The trials of leading Chartists, including O'Connor, Frost, Cooper, and Jones, yield up a good deal of biographical information ; and so do the files of the various Chartist journals. Thomas Frost's *Forty Years' Recollections* is a major source for Feargus O'Connor ; and the letters of Marx and Engels (available in English only in a selection) contain many references, especially to Harney and Jones. G. J. Holyoake's writings, *Sixty Years of an Agitator's Life* and *Bygones Worth Remembering*, are also fertile fields ; and there is information in W. J. Linton's *Memories*, in J. A. Langford's *Century of Birmingham Life*, and, for the Poor Law struggle, in the earlier Annual Reports of the Poor Law Commissioners (especially about Fielden). On this, as on all other subjects relating to the working-class and Radical movements of the first half of the nineteenth century, the Francis Place collections in the British Museum are an inexhaustible quarry.

Among modern books I have made full use of the various histories of Chartism — by Mark Hovell, Julius West, Edouard Dolléans, and R. Groves — of the more specialised studies by F. E. Rosenblatt, P. W. Slosson, and G. U. Faulkner, published by Columbia University — of Max Beer's *History of British Socialism*, of J. L. and Barbara Hammond's admirable works, especially *The Age of the Chartists*, and of S. Maccoby's very useful two volumes on *English Radicalism* — particularly the first, which runs from 1832 to 1852. I have used (with caution) T. Rothstein's *From Chartism to Labourism*, valuable for its accounts of internationalist elements in Chartism in the 'forties and 'fifties ; and in this connection I have also profited by A. Mueller Lehning's excellent study of " The International Association ", published in 1939 in *The International Review of Social History*.

Further references will be found in the Bibliography ; but in conclusion I should mention here Engels's *Condition of the Working Classes in Great Britain in 1844* and the great Government reports on *The Sanitary Condition of the Labouring Population* (1842) and on *The Health of Towns* (1841–4) — basic documents for every social student of the period.

It remains only to say how conscious the writing of this book has made me of the vast amount of work that still needs to be done before anyone can hope to produce a really satisfactory history of Chartism. Except here and there, the local newspaper material has hardly been studied at all, and the history of Chartist activity in many parts of the country still remains unrecorded, except in contemporary references, and unknown. There is room for a dozen local studies in Chartism, and for a dozen biographies, on a larger scale than mine, of outstanding Chartist leaders. It is one of the most curious gaps in biographical writing that there is no Life of Feargus O'Connor — surely the most influential figure in nineteenth-century England who has been left lacking such a monument. But then . . . social history is in its infancy : there are no academic endowments for it, and few to care whether it is written or not. Even as I write, doubtless some of its valuable materials are being destroyed by bombs. When the world returns to its senses, perhaps it will care more for these aspects of its past. Meanwhile, I, at any rate, have found writing about the Chartists an excellent by-activity in these times of war.

G. D. H. C.

INSTITUTE OF SOCIAL HISTORY
19 BANBURY ROAD, OXFORD

I

William Lovett

WILLIAM LOVETT was the man who drafted The People's Charter. Others, including Francis Place, who had a hand in nearly every Radical movement for fully half a century, may have contributed suggestions and amendments; but it was undoubtedly Lovett who drew it up. Lovett, again, was the most active and persistent member of the little group of London artisans who, in 1836, founded the London Working Men's Association — the body responsible for launching The People's Charter upon the world. Yet Lovett, though more than any other man he had created the Chartist movement, was right out of it within a few years of its inception and played through all its later phases no leading or effective part. This was not because he had ceased to believe in the Charter : on the contrary, he continued to believe in it fervently up to the very end of his life. But he had ceased to believe in the Chartists, and the main body of the Chartists had come to regard him as an apostate from the democratic cause.

This happened because the Chartist movement developed, from the very beginning, in a way that had not been at all contemplated by its begetters. They, respectable artisans almost to a man, had set out with two main objectives. They had wanted to persuade the working classes to show their fitness for political power by acting for themselves, under working-class leadership and not as mere followers of Radical leaders drawn from the middle class. And at the same time they had wanted to press their demands by peaceful and constitutional means, and had sought with this object the sympathy and support of such middle-class Radical Members of Parliament as could be persuaded to work with them, and to support their claims on the floor of the House of Commons. Their aim had been to guide the middle-class Radicals,

31

instead of submitting to their leadership ; to collaborate with them, without placing the control of the movement in their hands ; to bring to bear upon them a pressure of independent working-class opinion, strong enough to force them into the strait path of democracy. But it was the fate of this little body of skilled and relatively well-paid London craftsmen to set on foot a movement which speedily passed beyond their control, and turned into a vast revolt of the hungry and the intolerably oppressed. They had neither the power nor the instinct needed for the control of such a movement. The Charter was their gospel ; but they had bellies full enough and minds well-stored enough to be able to afford to wait for the fruition of their hopes, and to contemplate the Six Points in a spirit of philosophic detachment which was far beyond the reach of desperate handloom weavers, factory workers faced with the prospect of the detested ' Bastille ' as soon as unemployment befell them, or miners threatened with eviction from home and village if they dared to dispute the authority of the great landlords who were also colliery owners and magistrates and supreme masters over huge tracts of country in the industrial North.

William Lovett, Henry Hetherington, and their fellow creators of the London Working Men's Association wanted the Charter : the main body of the Chartists wanted bread. In the later 'thirties there swept over industrial England a depression deeper and more prolonged than any other in the whole of the century. For seven years on end trade was bad — very bad — with only brief intermissions of partial and illusory revival. Harvests were bad too ; and the price of bread was terribly high. Moreover, to crown the misfortunes of the poor, these were the years during which the New Poor Law, enacted in 1834, was being introduced into the industrial areas : so that the workman who lost his employment could no longer look for maintenance from outdoor relief, even upon the most meagre scale, but was threatened with separation from wife and children and with incarceration in the hated workhouse, the Bastille, under conditions which were deliberately made as unpleasant as possible in order to induce him to seek work outside it — even when manifestly no work was to be had.

The New Poor Law, coinciding in its introduction with the disastrous depression, was responsible for turning Chartism into a hunger revolt. But this was by no means how Lovett and his collaborators had conceived it when they presided over its birth. To them, the demand for the Charter was a continuation of the Radical movement which had been born in the days of John Wilkes and based firmly on the Rights of Man during the years which followed the great French Revolution. They inherited the traditions and the programme of Tom Paine and Major Cartwright, of William Cobbett and of Henry Hunt. They were picking up again the tradition which had been broken by the Whig Reform Act, in which their middle-class allies had banged the door of Parliament in the faces of the workers, after using them to intimidate the upholders of the old aristocratic order. They were trying to do over again what Thomas Hardy and the London Corresponding Society had attempted in the seventeen-nineties — to create a body of intelligent and politically educated workmen who would stand firm for the cause of democracy and, by their very intelligence and manifest fitness for power, persuade all rational men to accept the justice of their claims. They were idealists, thinking men who were well assured of the ultimate rightness of their political creed — and, withal, a little pedantic in their rationality, and ill at ease in the presence of hungry mobs which set more store by bread than by the laws of reason.

Among these men William Lovett was, not leader — for they disliked leadership — but the indispensable organiser. Henry Hetherington, who for years faced fine and imprisonment in defence of the freedom of the press and in protest against the iniquities of the Stamp Tax upon newspapers ; Henry Vincent, the orator of the group, who became a hero among the coal miners of South Wales and the textile workers of South Western England ; John Cleave, who founded the Cobbett Club and put something of Cobbett's bluffness and vigour into his *Police Gazette* : all these men had, much more than Lovett, the power of popular appeal, though none of them could compete in mob-leadership with the stentorian Irishman, Feargus O'Connor, who stole their movement from them and made it his own. But Lovett had,

much more than Hetherington or Cleave or Vincent, or anyone else connected with the Chartist movement, the qualities
of quiet, painstaking assiduity in the day-to-day work of
corresponding, drafting manifestos, seeing whoever needed
seeing, and, in general, ensuring that no one should have any
valid excuse for not doing what he had promised to do.
Lovett, in fact, was the indispensable secretary and director
of the machine. Without him it is improbable that the
Charter would ever have come into being, though the
hunger-revolt in the factory districts would have broken out
in any case, and would have found some other rallying-
point if the Charter had not been there to serve as the
symbol of working-class discontent.

William Lovett was born in 1800 at Newlyn, near
Penzance in Cornwall. His father, who had come from
Yorkshire and had been captain of a small coasting vessel,
was drowned before his birth ; and he was brought up by
his mother, a Cornishwoman and a strict Methodist. His
uncle, a master rope-maker, came to the widow's help, and
at first the family circumstances were fairly good ; but the
uncle died, and thereafter his mother had to support both
him and her own mother by selling fish and doing other odd
jobs. He was sent for brief periods to several schools, and
learned to read and write ; and in due course he was
apprenticed to his uncle's trade of rope-making. Soon after
this his mother married again, and as he did not get on
with his stepfather he set up house with his grandmother,
whom he largely supported out of his exiguous earnings.
Towards the end of his apprenticeship he had difficulty in
getting his wages, and had to go to law with his master in
order to secure payment. He was successful in this ; but
foreseeing further troubles, he induced his master to cancel
the remainder of his indentures, and accepted an offer from
his great-uncle to go to sea on a fishing boat — a career
which he had speedily to abandon on account of persistent
sickness when the weather was rough.

Before this, Lovett had realised that his prospects as a
rope-maker were poor. The trade was decaying, largely on
account of the growing displacement of ropes by chain
cables, but also because the return of peace had reduced

demand. Luckily for him, he was not without alternative resources, for he had great natural aptitude as a wood-worker, and had been able to pick up a good deal of the crafts of carpentry and cabinet-making in his spare time. To this trade he now turned for help in the design which he had formed of seeking his fortune in London. He was able to arrange for his grandmother to find an alternative home ; and by making a number of fancy work-boxes, tea-caddies, and other small objects he got together just enough money to enable him to take the risk of an attempt to estab-lish himself in the Metropolis. He arrived in London in 1821 and, after a vain search for work as a rope-maker, found employment in a carpenter's shop — a non-Society shop, because the Trade Societies would have none of him, on the ground that he had not served a regular apprentice-ship to the trade.

After some buffetings of fortune, Lovett managed to establish his position as a cabinet-maker. Eventually, when he had worked some years at the trade, he was accepted as a member of the closely organised Cabinetmakers' Society, and actually became its president. Meanwhile he had begun to take an interest in working-class politics and in the new economic doctrines which proclaimed the labourer's right to " the whole produce of labour ". He joined a Radical debating society called " The Liberals ", attended courses at the recently founded London Mechanics' Institute, where he heard Thomas Hodgskin's lectures on " Popular Political Economy ", and threw off, in the new atmosphere, the theology, though not the puritanism, of the Methodist environment in which he had been brought up. He also fell in love — with a lady's maid who was a strong Churchwoman, parted from her on grounds of theological incompatibility, and then married her after all — in 1826 — and thereafter found in her a devoted helpmeet in all his vicissitudes.

For seven or eight years after his arrival in London Lovett worked fairly regularly as a cabinet-maker, devoting his leisure to self-improvement and becoming an assiduous reader and student without taking any active part in public affairs. Owenism was then coming to be the gospel of many of the more reflective artisans, and Lovett became a convert to the principles of Owenite Cooperation. He joined the First London Cooperative Trading Association, a body which had opened a shop for the exchange of its members' craft products and for the supply of necessaries at cost price — with the wider ambition of expanding into an agency for the employment of all its members and the supersession of the profit system by the foundation of Cooperative Communities on the principles advocated by the ' Master '. About this time he also met Henry Hunt and other leaders of the advanced Radical movement, and began to launch out a little into public activities, and to form friendships among the leaders of artisan opinion.

At this stage his wife induced him to start in business as a pastrycook, with the intention that she should earn money by minding the shop, while he continued at his trade. But the venture did not answer, and his small savings were speedily lost, and debts incurred besides. Just then his friend, James Watson, later famous as a Radical and free-thinking bookseller and journalist, resigned his post as store-keeper to the First London Cooperative Association, and Lovett, just recovering from a serious illness which had disabled him from working at his trade, was chosen as his successor. Shortly afterwards he added to his responsibilities by becoming honorary secretary to the British Association for the Promotion of Cooperative Knowledge, then the chief agency for Owenite propaganda, which was housed in the same premises as the First London Association.

These offices brought Lovett into contact with many leaders of Trade Union and Owenite opinion in both London and the provinces. But they did not bring him an assured income. The First London Association fell into difficulties, and first reduced his salary and then offered his post to his wife at a still lower rate, while he resumed his work of cabinet-making. These difficulties did not disturb his faith. He continued his unpaid work as secretary of the British Association for the Promotion of Cooperative Knowledge and, in 1829, drew up the first of his many petitions — characteristically, an appeal for the opening of the British Museum on Sundays, in order that working men might have a chance of visiting it, and of putting its Reading Room to effective use.

The following year, 1830, saw Lovett plunged more deeply still into the Radical struggle. Cooperative Associations were multiplying fast, and he had much work to do on behalf of the Association for the Promotion of Cooperative Knowledge. But, in addition to this, he began in this year his long association with the struggle for the liberty of the press. His friend, Henry Hetherington, had decided to defy the stamp duties by publishing a Radical weekly newspaper, *The Poor Man's Guardian*, in defiance of the law, without a stamp ; and this meant that everyone who helped in the editing, printing, or sale of the paper exposed himself to the risk of prosecution for violation of the law. Hetherington had his presses seized more than once, and suffered fine and imprisonment for his stand on behalf of " The Great Unstamped " ; and before long he had many fellow victims who were consigned to gaol for the offence of selling the paper. For their aid, and for the support of their wives and families, Hetherington's friends established a " Victim Fund ", and Lovett became its secretary and the chief dispenser of relief under its auspices. The struggle lasted for four years — until, in 1834, Lord Lyndhurst, the Tory Lord Chancellor, declared, to the general astonishment, that *The Poor Man's Guardian*, though it contained news, was not after all a newspaper within the meaning of the Act, and had therefore been throughout a legal publication, even though scores of unfortunate persons had been sent to prison for the offence of exposing it for sale.

Long before this historic decision was given, Lovett had made himself famous by another highly characteristic defiance of authority. It was customary in those days to hold periodic drawings for men to serve compulsorily in the militia, with the option of providing a substitute or of paying a fine. Early in 1831 Lovett wrote to William Carpenter's *Political Letters* proposing that Radicals should take the opportunity, on being drawn for the militia, to protest against being forced to serve while they were not represented in Parliament. Shortly afterwards, by chance or design, his name was drawn, and he proceeded to act up to his own advice by refusing service. Distraint was thereupon laid on his goods, and most of the furniture which he had been making for his home was taken away, as he refused either to pay the fine or to allow others to pay it on his behalf. This protest, made at the height of the Reform agitation, was remarkably effective. Henry Hunt and Joseph Hume presented to the House of Commons Lovett's petition against the seizure of his goods ; and the authorities, fearful of an epidemic of Radical refusals to serve, promptly abolished the drawings.

This defiance of authority made Lovett a national political figure. About this time he and the group of friends who were later to be collaborators with him in the London Working Men's Association joined the newly founded National Union of the Working Classes, which became the principal mouthpiece of advanced working-class sentiment during the later phases of the Reform struggle. Henry Hunt, who had won a notable by-election at Preston in 1830, was regarded as the leader of this group, which was known as the " Rotundanists ", from its meeting-place, the Rotunda in the Blackfriars Road. Unlike Place and Cobbett, who were in favour from their several points of view of accepting the Whig Reform Bill as an instalment of the Radical demands, the Rotundanists persisted in crying out for Manhood Suffrage, and in denouncing a measure which would only replace the political power of the landlords by that of the propertied classes as a whole. Lovett took an active part in the attempts of the N.U.W.C. to prevent Francis Place and Sir Francis Burdett from enlisting working-class support for their National Political Union, formed to further the Whig Bill ; and it was largely due to the efforts of the N.U.W.C. that the National Political Union was compelled to elect a Council consisting half of working-class members, who were naturally hand-picked by Place with the utmost care to exclude supporters of the Rotundanist policy. As a representative of the N.U.W.C., Lovett had several brushes with Lord Melbourne over the right of public meeting, and became well known as a spokesman of the advanced working-class Radicals of London. But his next serious conflict with authority arose when the Government gave orders for a general fast in the hope of propitiating the Almighty against the spread of the cholera epidemic of 1832. Lovett, who had seen at first hand the pitiable condition of the Spitalfields silk weavers, among whom the cholera was exceptionally prevalent, joined with Hetherington, Watson, and the other leaders of the N.U.W.C. in a symbolic protest. The Rotundanists decided to celebrate the fast day by having together and in public a thoroughly good dinner, and by marching to it in orderly procession through the streets of London. The police broke up the procession, and a few days later Lovett, Watson, and William Benbow, the champion of the Grand National Holiday, were arrested for the crime of organising it. They were brought to trial after some delay ; but a London jury triumphantly acquitted them, as London juries were apt to do in those days.

This affair led, however, to a quarrel between Lovett and his friends on the one side and Benbow and the majority of the N.U.W.C. Council on the other. Lovett held that Benbow had misbehaved, both by leading a successful movement to break through the police cordon on the day of the procession, and thereafter by putting unfair expenses on the N.U.W.C. in connection with the trial. From this point the Lovett group withdrew from active participation in the N.U.W.C. and transferred their main energies to the attempt, under Robert Owen's influence, to build up a Grand National Consolidated Trades Union, in the hope of winning by economic means what the Whig Reform Act had failed to grant. Lovett, as a leading Owenite who had played a prominent part in the Cooperative movement of the preceding years, threw himself with zeal into this new crusade, which received for a time the mass support of the workers who had been disillusioned by the Reform Act. But he continued to believe ardently in Universal Suffrage : and he tried vainly to persuade the Grand National Consolidated Trades Union to include this among its objects.

Between 1832 and 1834 Lovett was dividing his available time between Hetherington's struggle for the unstamped press and Owen's attempt to persuade the Trade Unions to embark upon schemes of Cooperative production, Labour Exchanges for the purchase and sale of Cooperative products, and the enforcement by industrial action of an eight hours day. When, in the celebrated case of the Dorchester labourers, who were transported for the crime of administering unlawful oaths, the Government joined hands with the factory owners in an attempt to destroy the Trade Unions, Lovett's experience as secretary of Hetherington's Victim Committee came in very conveniently ; and he played a leading part in the steps that were taken to organise a mass demonstration and petition on behalf of the prisoners, and to raise money for the maintenance of their wives and families.

The great Union, however, was broken in pieces by the combined force of lockouts and Government repression ; and by the end of 1834 this phase of working-class protest was over. The workers had realised the impossibility of superseding the capitalist system either by the development of Cooperative production or by the organisation of a general strike. The local trade societies flocked out of the Grand National Consolidated Trades Union and the similar " General Unions " which existed in the North of England as fast as they had flocked into them only a few months before. It became necessary to think out a new way of agitating for the satisfaction of the popular claims ; and Lovett and his friends drew the conclusion that what was wanted was a new Reform Bill, embodying Universal or, at least, Manhood Suffrage as its principal provision, and designed to secure the backing of the small group of Radical M.P.s who were prepared to support so drastic a measure, as well as of the main body of Radicals all over the country.

Out of this resolve arose The People's Charter, which was first adumbrated at a joint meeting of a few Radical M.P.s and the leaders of the little group of London artisans who had by that time formed the London Working Men's Association in direct antagonism to the rump of the Rotundanists. For there were now again two opposing views among the working-class Radicals, as there had been during the agitation for the Reform Act. The Rotundanists had been reinforced by their experience of 1832 in their belief that no good could come of collaboration with the middle classes. Had they not then been left in the lurch by their allies in the struggle for Reform ; and had not the Reformed Parliament promptly proved itself the enemy of the people by passing the Poor Law Act of 1834 and transporting the Dorchester labourers ? The left wing among the London workers stood for a policy of no compromise and no alliance with the exploiting classes. Their strength had been shattered by the events which attended the collapse of the Grand National Consolidated Trades Union, even though many of them had stood aloof from it on the ground that a merely economic movement could do no good. But they had continued to growl in the background, hoping that their chance would come again.

As against this view Lovett and his group, now on terms of friendship with their former antagonist, Francis Place, had come round to the view that an attempt must be made to enlist the support of the more Radical middle-class M.P.s in a renewed struggle for political democracy. The Owenite Cooperative Societies had mostly melted away after the Trade Union collapse ; and Lovett, from 1834 to 1836, was losing money by attempting to carry on as a coffee-house and centre of working-class debate premises which he had taken over from one of the derelict Owenite stores. Here it was that he and his friends worked out the plans which led to the formation of the London Working Men's Association ; and this body was founded in June 1836, at the moment when the coffee-house had to be closed for lack of funds, and its proprietor had to go back to his cabinet-making for the means of living.

The L.W.M.A. began as a small body, and without the ambition to enlist large numbers in its ranks. It was to be an educational, fully as much as a political, society ; and mutual improvement stood high among its objects. The members were to prove themselves worthy of the votes which they demanded, and only the respectable and the industrious were invited to apply for membership. Throughout its career the L.W.M.A. never had more than a hundred or two members, almost all of the class of skilled artisans. They met for study rather than for speech-making ; and when they began to issue manifestos to their fellow workers they steadily mingled exhortations to self-improvement with their denunciation of Whig treachery, parliamentary fraudulence, and economic exploitation.

Under Place's influence, the L.W.M.A. was prepared to accept the collaboration of the middle-class Radicals in Parliament. But they were almost as suspicious of these gentry as were the Rotundanists, and very determined not to allow the middle classes to capture the leadership of their movement, or to seduce them into compromise. They would have nothing to do with ' moderate ' proposals for Household Suffrage, or for anything short of the full democratic programme. If some of the middle-class Radicals would go all the way with them, well and good. Let them show their sincerity by their behaviour. But let them not think that they were to do more than present to Parliament demands formulated and insisted upon by representatives of the working class. This was as far towards collaboration as Place could induce them to go. But that indefatigable Radical schemer deemed it far enough to make the attempt worth while.

The first public effort of the L.W.M.A. was a pamphlet drawn up by a committee, and entitled *The Rotten House of Commons*. It was meant to expose the domination of the Reformed Parliament by a combination of vested interests — landowners, capitalists, and the privileged professions ; and it sold widely, for there was little else then being issued on the extreme Radical side. Meanwhile, a second committee was studying the condition of the Spitalfields weavers, and a third was drawing up plans for the creation of societies similar to the L.W.M.A. in all the important towns throughout the country, while the association as a whole was getting ready its programme for the public campaign which it proposed presently to launch. All was to be done lawfully and in order, for from the outset the L.W.M.A. declared its intention of putting its reliance exclusively on peaceful means of reform.

By February 1837 it was ready to begin its campaign. In that month a public meeting held under its auspices at the famous Crown and Anchor Tavern passed a series of resolutions which included all the ' Six Points ' soon to be embodied in The People's Charter — manhood suffrage, vote by ballot, payment of Members of Parliament, annual Parliaments, equal electoral districts, and the abolition of the property qualification for M.P.s. The substance of the Charter was complete before it was formally drafted, and before the middle-class Radicals had been committed to it in any way. They were brought in later — to endorse, and not to amend, what the respectable artisans had proposed on behalf of the people.

The resolutions were enthusiastically adopted, and J. A. Roebuck, M.P. for Bath, and at that time a close collaborator of Francis Place, was invited to present to Parliament the petition in which they were embodied. Roebuck and Place then suggested that other Radical M.P.s should be brought into consultation ; and as the result of a couple of meetings between the leaders of the L.W.M.A. and a few M.P.s, who included Daniel O'Connell, a joint Committee was appointed to draw up a Bill based upon the Six Points.

At this stage the King — William IV — died and Victoria came to the throne. The consequent General Election scattered the M.P.s to their constituencies, and made impossible the early presentation of a Bill to Parliament. Lovett occupied the interval in drawing up a Radical Address to the young Queen ; and the Association proposed to Lord John Russell that a deputation should present this Address in person. Lord John retorted that the deputation would have to appear in court dress, and this caused the project to be given up, to the accompaniment of an Open Letter from Lovett denouncing court flummeries in forthright terms.

Presently Parliament reassembled, and the Committee of six workmen and six M.P.s which had been instructed to draw up the proposed Bill met at last. It instructed Lovett and Roebuck to get on with the job. But Roebuck was too much immersed in the affairs of the Canadian rebels to attend to the Six Points ; and Lovett, wearying of delays, ended by drawing up The People's Charter by himself. He then showed it to Francis Place, who may or may not have amended the drafting, but certainly did not alter the substance. At any rate, in May 1838 The People's Charter was published, in the shape of a detailed Bill for the further Reform of Parliament, accompanied by an Address, also drafted by

Lovett, in which the influence of the vote in promoting popular enlightenment received the principal stress.

From that point events moved swiftly. There was nothing in The People's Charter that had not been in a host of earlier Radical pronouncements. But the name caught on : the Charter speedily became a symbol, and gave its name to a movement immensely wider, and also more tumultuous, than any that had entered into the heads of those who attended at its birth. The reason, as we have seen, was that, by 1837, the New Poor Law Commissioners, the ' Three Bashaws of Somerset House ', were actively engaged in enforcing the Act of 1834 in the industrial areas of the North and Midlands, and that the refusal of outdoor relief in accordance with the principles of the Act coincided with a major depression of trade. The agitation against the New Poor Law had begun from the moment when the Bill was introduced. Cobbett's last articles in his *Political Register* had been devoted to urging the people to mass resistance to its inhuman provisions. But the labourers of the agricultural South and West, upon whom the blow fell first, were too weak to offer effective opposition. Their strength had been crushed in the suppression of the Labourers' Revolt of 1830; and in 1834 the sentence on the Dorchester labourers and the defeat of Owen's Grand National Union had administered the final blows. By 1836 the New Poor Law was in full force in most of the agricultural areas : upon the industrial districts the hammer had not yet fallen, partly because the Commissioners had not yet directed their attention seriously to the North, and partly because, in any case, the main body of the industrial workers turned to the Poor Law only in times of depression — and up to 1836 trade was relatively good. But now, with the coincidence of acute depression and the enforcement of the New Poor Law principles, revolt spread everywhere in the industrial districts. Before the Charter had been heard of, the factory districts were in a ferment. Richard Oastler in Yorkshire and Joseph Rayner Stephens in Lancashire were at the head of a vast hunger movement of protest, furiously denouncing the Whigs as the architects of the people's misery. Political demands played no part in this initial uprising. The cry for the Charter came later, when political missionaries from the South had spread tidings of it and captured the industrial masses with the insistence that there would be no redress of their grievances until they were able to choose their own men to legislate in Parliament on their behalf.

While the North was flaming up into revolt, Lovett in London was busily drafting addresses and laying plans for a Chartist newspaper which William Carpenter was to edit on behalf of the L.W.M.A. He was also doing his utmost to get the artisans in the provinces to follow London's example, by setting up associations of their own on the model of the L.W.M.A. The law against Corresponding Societies, which was still in force, was held to prevent the formation of a national society with local branches ; and accordingly the plan was to have independent local societies, all following the same policy, all committed to the Charter, and all adopting broadly the same methods of organisation. This appeal was astonishingly successful. The L.W.M.A. sent out its own missionaries into the country, as the National Union of the Working Classes had done in the days of the Reform Bill ; and soon there were upwards of a hundred and fifty local associations of various sorts working in loose collaboration with the L.W.M.A.

The organisation of working-class opinion behind the Charter thus seemed to be going on apace. But the collaboration with the middle-class Radicals was less fortunate. 1836–7 were the years of the great strike and trial of the Glasgow cotton spinners, against whom grave charges of violence and intimidation were made. Daniel O'Connell, who had been one of the Radical M.P.s concerned with the drawing-up of the Charter, used the occasion for a frontal attack on Trade Unionism, alleging similar violent practices on the part of the Dublin trades. In February 1838 a Parliamentary Committee was set up to enquire into the Combination Laws, and a new movement for the suppression of the Trade Unions seemed to be imminent. The Trade Societies throughout the country set up special committees for the purpose of rebutting the attack ; and Lovett was chosen for the key position of secretary to the committee set up by the London Trades.

Actually, the Parliamentary Committee led to nothing ; for the Government, having its hands full with the Chartists and finding the Trade Unions mostly too weak on account of the state of trade to give much trouble, took no action. But for a time there was great alarm ; and the effect of O'Connell's attitude was seriously to prejudice the attempted collaboration between the workers and the Radical M.P.s. In particular, Feargus O'Connor seized the occasion to deliver, in his paper *The Northern Star*, a violent attack on the London Working Men's Association, which he accused of having been responsible by its efforts at class-collaboration for encouraging the " Whig Malthusians ", the " Working-class Coadjutors ", to launch the campaign against the Trade Unions. Lovett, as the secretary to the Trades Delegates who were organising the Trade Unions' defence, had of course a perfectly clear answer to the immediate charge. But this did not take the sting out of it ; for a good many of the parliamentary Radicals were in fact strongly hostile to Trade Unionism, and it could not be easy to collaborate with them on the political issue of Reform while they were actually in full cry against the workers' attempts at industrial combination.

In effect, the attack on the Trade Unions brought the collaboration to an end, except for a few Radicals who were prepared to uphold combinations as well as parliamentary Reform. Little more was heard of the help of the Radicals as a group : the Chartists in the country were left to go their own way, and Chartism became almost entirely an extra-parliamentary movement.

The quarrel between Lovett and Feargus O'Connor was of even greater importance than the defection of the Radical M.P.s. At the formation of the London Working Men's Association O'Connor had been among the select few friends of the workers who had been chosen as honorary members. Others so chosen had included Robert Owen, Francis Place, William Johnson Fox of Anti-Corn Law fame, Dr. A. S. Wade, the Radical Vicar of Warwick, and Bronterre O'Brien. But from the first O'Connor had not got on with the leaders of the L.W.M.A. Their slow, educational methods did not appeal to him : trained under Daniel O'Connell in the arts

46

of mass agitation in Ireland, he wanted to build up a vast, menacing popular movement which he could lead — not to waste time in debating subtleties or advocating temperance and respectability as the means to working-class self-improvement. In the early days of the L.W.M.A. O'Connor had tried to build up a counter-movement among the workers on more militant and inclusive lines. But Lovett and Hetherington had been too strong for him on their own ground ; and as soon as the agitation against the Poor Law began to look big in the North, he had moved his headquarters to Leeds, and there, with Bronterre O'Brien's help as editor, set up *The Northern Star*, which speedily outpassed all other Radical journals not only in violence of language but also in the extent of its circulation.

The Northern Star appeared first in November 1837 ; and O'Connor, with its aid to reinforce his own powerful mob-oratory, soon made himself leader of the Northern Chartists, taking over or driving into obscurity the small groups which had been formed there under the inspiration of the L.W.M.A. Soon the challenge was made again in London as well. George Julian Harney, who had been working with O'Connor before his departure for the North, violently criticised Daniel O'Connell for his attacks on the Trade Unions. The L.W.M.A., though it had no sympathy with O'Connell on the point at issue, censured Harney for the manner of his denunciation ; and Harney and his friends thereupon seceded from the L.W.M.A. and formed the rival London Democratic Association, which attempted to build up a mass following on the lines which O'Connor was following in the North.

Meanwhile, the L.W.M.A. was finding fresh friends in the Midlands, where in 1836-7 Thomas Attwood, M.P. for Birmingham, banker and currency reformer as well as Radical, revived the Birmingham Political Union. The old B.P.U. had played an important part in the struggle over the Reform Act ; and its successor now came forward, simultaneously with the L.W.M.A., with a practically identical programme of Radical Reform, except that Attwood and his followers wanted to use Reform as an instrument for securing the abandonment of the gold standard and the establishment of a credit system based instead on the real productive power of the nation. Such a credit policy, they held, would do away with unemployment and banish poverty ; and behind this currency scheme Attwood succeeded in rallying nearly all the Birmingham Radical groups, from the ordinary political Radicals to the Owenites, who had been very strong among the Birmingham workers during the Trade Union uprising of 1833–4. The B.P.U. had began to organise a National Petition of its own quite independently of the L.W.M.A. ; but in 1838 the two groups joined forces. The Birmingham men accepted the Charter, postponing their currency demands until after the reform of Parliament ; and the Chartists took over the Birmingham Petition, which was now to be organised as a united effort of the entire Chartist movement.

The next step was to summon a National Convention of delegates from all over the country, to ratify the Charter itself, and to superintend the presentation of the National Petition to the House of Commons. Feargus O'Connor and his followers in the North could not be excluded from such a movement ; but the London and Birmingham leaders hoped to be strong enough to prevent him from wresting the control of it from their hands. Under the law, the Convention had formally to consist, not of representatives sent by local associations — this would have brought it under the ban of the Act against Corresponding Societies — but of delegates chosen at public meetings, nominally unconnected with the local Chartist bodies. This method gave O'Connor his opportunity. During the latter half of 1838 there was a continual going to and fro of Chartist missionaries sent out from London or Birmingham or Leeds in the hope of bringing over doubtful areas to the support of one or other of the contending factions. The consequence was that, when the Chartist Convention met in London in February 1839, the delegates represented conflicting views. There were currency reformers and advocates of class-collaboration from Birmingham and other places ; followers of the L.W.M.A. from London and from areas such as the West and South of England, where its missionaries had been active ; O'Connorites from Lancashire and Yorkshire ; and, from other parts of the country, delegates whose views were unknown or whose minds were perhaps not made up between the contending factions.

The L.W.M.A. scored its initial success when Lovett was chosen as secretary to the Convention, despite opposition by Bronterre O'Brien and later by O'Connor, who was not able to be present at the opening session.

From the very beginning, the Convention was rent in twain by the controversies between what were known as the ' physical force ' and ' moral force ' schools. Lovett and the L.W.M.A., the Birmingham men, the majority of the Scottish delegates, and some others were upholders of the view that the Chartist agitation must remain strictly within constitutional limits, and that there must be no attempt to gain their ends by force. As against this, the O'Connorites' favourite slogan was " peaceably if we may, forcibly if we must " ; and there was an extreme left which went far beyond O'Connor himself in regarding physical rebellion as the only possible means of winning the Charter. The distinctions were in fact not clear-cut. There were ' moral force ' men who did not object on occasion to the use of threats about what might happen if Parliament rejected the Charter ; and there were ' physical force ' men, probably including O'Connor, who hoped to get their way by the threat of rebellion, without being driven actually to resort to it. There was, moreover, a doubt about the exact point at which ' Moral Force ' ended and ' Physical Force ' began. William Benbow, the untiring advocate of the ' National Holiday ', or General Strike, was there at the Convention ; and it was a question whether a ' National Holiday ' was to be regarded as a peaceable exercise of the constitutional right to abstain from work, or as the first stage in what was bound, if it succeeded at all, to turn into a violent conflict with the authorities.

It would take me far beyond the scope of this study to recite the proceedings at the Chartist Convention of 1839. I am here concerned only with Lovett's part in it. Adhering to the ' moral force ' party, he was nevertheless, as secretary, responsible to the Convention as a whole, and bound to execute its wishes unless he felt strongly enough to be compelled to resign, with the certainty that his resignation would wreck the united movement for the Charter, and probably lead straight to a hopeless hunger rebellion in the industrial districts. Lovett's faith in the Charter and his desire to maintain unity induced him, not to advocate ' physical force ', but to accept responsibility for interpreting ' moral force ' in a very large sense, so as to include at any rate threats that could hardly be regarded as auguries of peaceful intentions, should Parliament refuse to grant the Chartist demands. This, of course, Parliament was absolutely certain to do ; for it could be seen in advance that only a small band of Radicals could be expected to cast their votes in favour even of taking the Charter into consideration, and still fewer in favour of accepting it in full. This being so, the difficulty about threats was that the time would be bound to come when the Chartists would have either to carry them out or to acknowledge defeat. Lovett no doubt saw this, and was full of misgivings ; but what was he to do ? It was his fortune to issue the Charter at a time when its publication unloosed forces much too powerful for the small voice of reason, represented by the L.W.M.A., to be able to control.

For several months matters did not come to a head, because there was, first, delay in getting the National Petition ready for presentation to Parliament, and then further delay, owing to the Government's resignation, before Parliament was ready to debate it. During these months the Convention talked and talked, endeavouring meanwhile to improve its hold on the country by sending delegates to visit weak areas. In face of much talk about possible ' ulterior measures ', some of the most undeviating adherents of the ' moral force ' party dropped away, and the new delegates who replaced them tended to belong rather to the ' physical force ' wing. In May the Petition was at last ready ; and in that month the Convention decided to move temporarily to Birmingham, both in order to be nearer to the main body of its supporters while it prepared to face the outcome of rejection, and in order to be less exposed to arrest than it was while it remained on the Government's doorstep. But its coming to Birmingham caused deep alarm on the part of the Mayor and Corporation, though they mostly ranked as Radicals, or Liberals, of a sort ; and presently, after disturbances had occurred at Chartist gatherings in the Bull Ring, the local magistrates decided to prohibit further meetings in that historic assembly-ground, and imported regular police — ' Peelers ' — from London to aid them in defeating any attempt by the Chartists to defy the ban.

The Chartists did defy the authorities, and there followed a fracas which nearly became a riot. Lovett, outraged by the invasion of the right of public meeting and by the importa- tion of the ' Peelers ', moved in the Convention three strongly worded resolutions of protest, of which the first declared " that a wanton, flagrant and unjust outrage has been made upon the people of Birmingham by a bloodthirsty and uncon- stitutional force from London ". (The new police force founded by Sir Robert Peel was then generally regarded as an instrument of reaction designed to put down popular movements.) The Convention ordered these resolutions to be placarded about the town ; and Lovett, as secretary, appended his signature to the placard.

His arrest, and that of John Collins, the leader of the Birmingham workers, who had taken the copy to the printer, promptly followed ; and the two were gaoled for nine days before they were allowed bail. While they were in gaol the House of Commons rejected the Chartist Petition by 235 votes to 46, and further troubles occurred in the Bull Ring. On the day of their release there was a serious riot, and the military were called in. Though they had nothing to do with this, it was used to prejudice them at their trial.

Lovett's arrest solved what must have been for him a very difficult problem. It kept him out of the later proceedings of the Convention, and released him from the necessity of deciding exactly at what point he, as an advocate of ' Moral Force ', would have to part company with the ' physical force ' Chartists. In May he had been responsible for drawing up the Chartist ' Manifesto of Ulterior Measures ' on which the delegates were to canvass opinion in the country when the Convention adjourned for a time in June in order to seek a further mandate from its constituents. Lovett wrote many years later, in his Autobiography, " I believe that I did an act of folly in being a party to some of its provisions " ; and it is difficult to believe that he ever really liked it. There was, indeed, in the ' Manifesto ' no threat of an unprovoked Chartist rising ; but the Chartists were asked, not only whether they would be prepared to start a run on the banks and to make ' holiday ' for a ' sacred month ', but also whether " they had prepared themselves with the arms of freemen according to their ancient constitutional right, in order to defend " themselves should the forces of reaction levy war upon them when they withheld their labour in the Chartist cause. The ' Manifesto ' was carefully worded so as to advocate the taking-up of arms only as an act of resistance to prior attack. But Lovett can hardly have felt comfortable about its practical conformity with his ' moral force ' principles.

The Chartist Convention, after the rejection of the Petition, had to face the question in earnest. After much debate, a depleted body of delegates — for many of the ' moral force ' men had resigned, or simply gone home — decided by thirteen votes to six to call for the ' Sacred Month ' — the ' National Holiday ' — to begin on August 12. Less than a week later, by twelve votes to six, with seven abstentions, this decision was rescinded, on the motion of Bronterre O'Brien, in view of the evident impracticability of getting a sufficient response. The Trade Unions, well aware that the state of trade was heavily against them, could not be induced to order a strike at the behest of the Chartist Convention ; and most of those who were ready to strike were already out of work, or considerably under-employed. The ' Sacred Month ' was postponed indefinitely ; and after another month or so, spent largely in mutual recrimination, the Convention was dissolved, and the remaining delegates went back to their localities to brood upon their failure, or to plot fruitless insurrection, according to their several bents.

Lovett had no part in these events. On August 6 he was brought to trial at Warwick Assizes on a charge of seditious libel contained in the resolutions published at Birmingham over his name. He conducted his own defence and, together with John Collins, was sentenced to twelve months' imprisonment in Warwick Gaol. He had in fact no chance of an acquittal : the jury was strongly prejudiced against Chartists, and the later scenes of violence in the Bull Ring, in which he had no part, were brought up against him by the Attorney General. In any case, he was not the man to make an appeal for mercy : he stoutly defended what he had done as a legitimate protection of the rights of free speech and public meeting.

In gaol, Lovett's health, which had never been robust, suffered severely. The diet was abominable, and made him ill. He had no fire, even in winter, and he found the sanitary conditions nearly unbearable. He and Collins more than once petitioned the Home Secretary concerning their treatment, and their case was brought before Parliament by Thomas Slingsby Duncombe and other sympathetic M.P.s. Francis Place and the L.W.M.A. also bestirred themselves on their behalf ; but the only concession granted to the two prisoners was the use of pens, ink, and paper — an advantage of which Lovett made use by writing, jointly with Collins, a little book, *Chartism : a New Organisation of the People.*

Release came in July 1840. But Lovett was much too ill to attend the numerous celebrations which had been arranged for him by his fellow Chartists. He went down to his native county, Cornwall, and there slowly nursed himself back to some sort of health. When he was well enough to return to London he opened a bookseller's shop in Tottenham Court Road, but it soon shared the fate of his other ventures in business.

Lovett had intended his book to be published before he came out of prison, and had sent the manuscript to Francis Place for this purpose. But Place, deeming much of it nonsense, did nothing about it ; and it did not appear until some months after his release. When it was published a storm broke promptly over his head, for to the majority of his fellow Chartists, and, above all, to O'Connor and his followers, what Lovett had written seemed to be plain treason to the Chartist cause. The ' new organisation of the people ' which Lovett and Collins now proposed was in effect a scheme for a grand national system of popular education and self-improvement, to be financed by the workers' subscriptions and carried on quite independently of the State. Lovett wanted the workers in every town to club together and build a District Hall, which was to serve as a centre of education, both general and political, for both children and adults. The object in view was still The People's Charter; but the winning of political rights was, in appearance at any rate, postponed to the fitting of the people for their exercise by a long process of mutual self-improvement and rational instruction. Moreover, the middle classes were invited to join hands with the workers in this campaign of national education; and this in itself was evidence enough of treason to assure the O'Connorites of Lovett's apostasy.

The truth was that Lovett, during his imprisonment if not before it, had despaired of the Chartists, though not of the Charter. The threats of physical force and ulterior measures, with no real power behind them, had made him sick of revolutionary slogans and appeals; and, gentle and persuasive by nature and hating force, he had in effect given over politics for education, and despaired of a cause which seemed irresistibly to elevate demagogues into leadership, and to make the Charter the plaything of men whose intellects and characters he despised. Lovett wanted the struggle for the Charter to be as high-souled as he was himself; he could not bear that the cause should be sullied by irrational appeals to violence. In truth, he hated O'Connor and all his works; and by the time he came out of prison, O'Connor and his disciples had entirely displaced the skilled workers of the L.W.M.A. from their position as guides and teachers of the main body of the working class.

There was a massive simplicity about the calculations which Lovett put forward in his little book as a basis for the future activity of the Chartist movement. One million two hundred and eighty-three thousand persons had signed the National Petition. If these persons would but subscribe a penny a week, or even a shilling a quarter, to the cause of national enlightenment, how much could be done! Such a sum would be enough to provide for the creation annually of eighty District Halls and seven hundred and ten circulating libraries, for the employment of four regular missionaries, and for the circulation of twenty thousand tracts a week. How could the human race fail to be elevated by such means — means utterly unlike those which were being advocated by the O'Connorites as the instruments of a renewed Chartist agitation?

Denounced by the main body of the Chartists as a traitor to the cause, Lovett persisted with his educational plans. In 1841 he managed to bring into existence his National Association for Promoting the Political and Social Improvement of the People, with the support of most of his old associates in the L.W.M.A., but in face of the bitter enmity of O'Connor and of the National Charter Association, in which the O'Connorite Chartists were then endeavouring to organise the main body of the Radical working class. Lovett's National Association was well received by the skilled London artisans who had formed the main element in the L.W.M.A., and also — an aggravation of Lovett's offence — by a substantial number of the middle-class Radicals. It succeeded in rescuing Lovett from his unsuccessful venture in bookselling, and in installing him as a director of the first, the one and only, District Hall ever established in accordance with his prescriptions. To all seeming, Lovett had by 1841 dropped clean out of the political agitation for the Charter, and become simply an educationist who believed that the clue to democratic progress was to be sought in the education of the people, and not in popular clamour or mass demonstrations of unrest.

But Lovett had not quite done with politics; for there were others besides himself who, wishful for the Charter, saw no hope of advance towards it under O'Connor's leadership. Already in 1839 there had been a deep division, not only between 'physical force' Chartists and 'moral force' Chartists, but also between Chartists in general and Radical adherents of the Anti-Corn Law League. Working-class misery was crying out to heaven as an evil needing remedy; but how was it to be remedied? Chartists contended that there could be no remedy short of a thorough reform of Parliament, after which the people would take matters into their own hands. Leaguers retorted that parliamentary Reform in itself would butter no parsnips, and that the remedy must be sought in cheaper bread. Many Chartists cried back that the demand for the repeal of the Corn Laws was no more than a device of the Whig factory owners for cheapening the price of labour, and cited the economists as witnesses that, as the price of bread fell, earnings would fall with it in obedience to the inexorable ' iron law of wages '. Many Chartists, hostile to the factory system and resting their hopes on the settlement of the workless workers upon the land, were bitterly opposed to the repeal of the Corn Laws, as a threat to the prosperity of the peasantry which they wished to restore.

To Lovett and to the artisan class, of which he was a typical enlightened representative, this agrarian gospel made no appeal. The town workmen of the skilled crafts were as well aware as their employers that Free Trade would enlarge the prosperity of industry, and lead not merely to higher profits, but also to an improved standard of life. Much as they hated the factory owners, much as they distrusted the Free Trade gospel of the Manchester School of ' liberal ' economists and business men, they too wanted the Corn Laws repealed, and were in this matter on the side of the employing class against the landowning aristocracy. But, though they agreed with the advocates of Corn Law repeal, they were by no means prepared to set aside their own demands for parliamentary Reform in favour of the narrower objectives on which the repealers were seeking to unite the middle and working classes. They believed in the Charter first and foremost, and in Free Trade a long way after it ; whereas the Anti-Corn Law Leaguers put repeal first, even if they were ready to advocate Manhood Suffrage as well, as long as their advocacy did not interfere with their hopes of getting the Corn Laws repealed.

Throughout the years between the publication of The People's Charter in 1838 and the repeal of the Corn Laws in 1846, Chartists and Anti-Corn Law Leaguers were rivals for popular support. In this contest the Leaguers had every advantage that money could buy ; for behind them was the main body of manufacturing employers and traders, who wanted not merely cheap bread as a means to lower wages, as Feargus O'Connor asserted, but also the development of markets for British exports through the encouragement of food imports from the predominantly agricultural countries. Chartism had throughout its agrarian, back-to-the-land

aspect ; but this was a gospel that did not appeal at all
to the skilled artisans, who were simply not interested in
O'Connor's plans for resettling underpaid factory workers
on the land, but were very much interested in securing
cheaper goods for consumption, and in promoting a larger
demand for their own products through a general increase
in the standard of living. The artisans were mostly
' repealers ' ; and, the more agrarian Chartism became, the
less ready were they to support it.

Among the Anti-Corn Law Leaguers also there were
many shades of opinion, from manufacturers who cared only
for the industrial effects of repeal to Radicals who wanted a
wide extension of the franchise in order to bring in the
workers as allies in the continual struggle against the landed
aristocracy — by no means finally defeated in 1832. John
Bright, as well as Joseph Hume, stood for the further demo-
cratisation of parliamentary elections, and wanted the support
of the Chartists for this purpose. But the hostility of such
men as Bright to factory legislation stood powerfully in the
way of any alliance between his group and the Chartists, who,
even when they favoured Free Trade, had no use for *laissez-
faire* doctrines which left the workers at the employers' mercy.

There were, however, Leaguers who, deploring that the
enemies of the privileged aristocracy should fight one
another for popular support instead of joining hands against
the aristocrats, thought it worth while to attempt a reconciliation. Joseph Sturge, the Quaker corn merchant from
Birmingham, became the leader of this group, seconded by
Edward Miall, the editor of *The Nonconformist*, and backed
by the main body of the Anti-Corn Law rank and file.
Sturge and his friends had nothing against the Charter
except its name, which had become after 1839 a synonym for
revolutionary violence in the vocabulary of a large section
of the middle class. They were prepared to swallow the
Charter whole, provided only that they were allowed to call
it something else.

This was the group which, on Sturge's initiative, launched
in 1841 the Complete Suffrage Union on the occasion of
a Conference called by the Anti-Corn Law League. The
delegates who attended this gathering of Sturge's readily

endorsed not only Manhood Suffrage, but also the rest of the Six
Points, and thereupon the C.S.U. made a determined attempt
to secure the support of those Chartists, of the ' moral
force ' party, who were hostile to O'Connor's leadership.
Lovett and his friends were naturally the group among the
Chartists to whom Sturge turned with the greatest hope ;
for Lovett both loathed O'Connor — who was now busy
engineering a second Chartist Petition through the National
Charter Association — and was emphatically a ' moral force'
man, who could be relied on not to scare off middle-class
supporters by threats of violence.

Lovett, for his part, was ready enough to respond to
Sturge's overtures. He had found himself, since the publication of his book, ostracised by O'Connor's followers ; and
he was exceedingly eager to recapture support for a renewed
crusade of the type originally projected by the London
Working Men's Association before O'Connor and the
Northern mass movement had pushed it aside. Accordingly,
Lovett and a goodly muster of Chartist delegates attended
the Conference called in Birmingham in April 1842 for the
purpose of putting the Complete Suffrage movement on an
assured foundation.

At this Conference all the Six Points were adopted by
large majorities ; but there remained the question whether
acceptance of the Six Points involved acceptance of the
Charter itself. Lovett, seconded by O'Brien, moved that it
should, and that the Charter should be endorsed by name ;
but he was at length persuaded to accept a temporising
motion which laid down only that the Charter, together with
other Radical proposals, should be taken into account in
the drafting of the programme of the C.S.U., which was to
be reported to, and finally decided by, a future Conference.
The controversy was thus postponed ; and in the meantime
the C.S.U. went ahead with a Petition of its own, including
all the Chartist demands, but not mentioning the Charter
by name. This was duly presented to the House of Commons
by Sharman Crawford, M.P. for Rochdale, in April 1842,
and was duly defeated, before the rival Petition organised
by O'Connor and the National Charter Association was ready
for presentation.

In May the N.C.A. in turn presented its Petition, through Thomas Slingsby Duncombe, and the House of Commons voted it down as well. There followed the great strikes in the factory areas, which the Chartists contrived to turn into demands for the Charter. But strike action, in the depth of the depression of 1842, was foredoomed to failure. The workers were driven back to work by sheer hunger, and for a second time the Chartists were compelled to face the defeat of their hopes.

During these events, Sturge and his supporters had continued, in face of vehement attacks from the O'Connorites, to organise their Complete Suffrage Union, which was to hold a further conference in Birmingham in December 1842, and was there to determine the vexed question of its programme and its attitude to the Charter. Well aware that the middle-class Leaguers were much too scared of Chartist violence ever to accept the Charter by name, Sturge and his group, without consulting Lovett and in defiance of the decisions of the earlier Conference, drew up for presentation to the delegates a set of proposals which included all the points of the Charter, but avoided any mention of it. O'Connor and his followers, fresh from the defeat of the strike movement, decided to do their best to capture Sturge's Conference, and succeeded in getting themselves elected as delegates to it, in spite of the denunciations which they had hitherto showered on Lovett and those other Chartists who had connected themselves with Sturge's movement. When the Conference met, the O'Connorites were there in force, as well as the adherents of Lovett and O'Brien and the other Chartist groups which had broken away from O'Connor's leadership.

There ensued a curious episode. Lovett, as author of the Charter, and most of his friends, were determined to secure that the Conference should endorse not merely the Six Points, but also the Charter by name. Consequently, Lovett found himself identified with O'Connor, whom he detested, against Sturge, with whom he greatly desired to work. When Lovett moved an amendment to the official resolution, pressing for the acceptance of the Charter as such, O'Connor seconded his motion. When it was carried, Sturge and his supporters withdrew from the Conference, and carried on elsewhere with their attempt to create a Complete Suffrage movement based on middle- as well as working-class support. Lovett and O'Connor were left in joint possession of the field ; but it was out of the question that they, or their several supporters, should work together. They did not attempt to do so. O'Connor was well content to have disrupted the C.S.U. Lovett, deeply disillusioned by what had happened, dropped right out of the Chartist movement, and went back to his attempt to build up his National Association into an agency for the gradual education of the workers for their political tasks.

This fiasco virtually ended Lovett's political activities. He had still his followers among the Chartists ; and in 1843, when O'Connor launched his ill-starred Land Scheme, he was invited to become a candidate for the position of secretary. He refused, in a characteristic letter, to have anything to do with a movement under O'Connor's leadership. Instead, he opened that year a Sunday School in his National Hall. The following year, he took part in the formation of the Democratic Friends of All Nations, a society which did useful work in keeping touch with foreign political exiles in London, and in educating working-class opinion about democratic movements in Europe. But apart from this tenuous association with Chartism, he held aloof from political activities, and devoted himself exclusively to educational work. The excitements of 1848 brought him momentarily back into politics, with an attempt to create a People's League in opposition to O'Connor's National Charter Association, which was then busy with its Third Chartist Petition, and was making renewed threats of ' ulterior measures '. But the People's League was stillborn, and Lovett retired to his National Hall. In 1851 he took over actual teaching in addition to the superintendence, and from that time until his death twenty-six years later teaching occupied most of his time. He was able to collect just enough money to keep his National Hall in existence until, in 1857, he was jockeyed out of it by the publican next door, who wanted the premises for a dance and entertainment hall, and succeeded, by various questionable manœuvres, in compelling him to surrender the remainder of his lease.

Thereafter Lovett taught in other institutions, under various auspices. He also wrote a number of textbooks designed for working-class students, teaching himself a number of scientific subjects for the purpose of imparting their rudiments to others, and compiling manuals better suited than the general run of textbooks for use by adult workers bent on self-improvement. He was thus a pioneer of working-class education of the type attempted in the twentieth century by the Workers' Educational Association. But he met with but a scanty response. For more than twenty years he laboured in the field of workers' education with but little recognition, barely enabled to keep his little movement in being by means of subscriptions flung to him by benevolent middle-class reformers. He had lost faith in politics and in agitation : he simply went on doggedly with his efforts to impart, to however few, the political and general instruction which he deemed to be the necessary concomitant of a claim to a share in political power.

Lovett was in truth, through all these years of middle and old age, a disillusioned man. He had lost faith, not in his doctrinaire principles, but in the men through whom alone they could be made actual. He laboured on, not in hope of the immediate future, but because he had to busy himself somehow about the affairs of his fellow men. His career, as far as it influenced history, was over before he was forty : the rest of his life was merely an epilogue of dogged, disillusioned faith.

Francis Place wrote of Lovett, in the days when he was still an active Chartist, " He is a tall, thin, rather melancholy man, in ill-health, to which he has long been subject ; at times he is somewhat hypochondriacal ; his is a spirit misplaced ". On another occasion Place wrote, " Lovett was a journeyman cabinet-maker, a man of melancholy temperament, soured with the perplexities of the world. He was, however, an honest-hearted man, possessed of great courage, and persevering in his conduct. In his usual demeanour he was mild and kind, and entertained kindly feelings towards everyone who he did not sincerely believe was the intentional enemy of the working people ; but when either by circumstances or his own morbid associations he felt the

F

sense he was apt to indulge in, of the evils and wrongs of mankind, he was vehement in the extreme. He was half an Owenite, half a Hodgskinite, a thorough believer that accumulation of property in the hands of individuals was the cause of all the evils that existed."

William Lovett was in fact a very worthy man— courageous, patient, industrious, rational, and devoted, but entirely without the gifts of leadership. He was the born secretary — but he found no president with whom he could work in harmony. Demagogic arts repelled him — he wanted everything to be done in order, under the direct inspiration of sedate intelligence. He could become angry, at flagrant acts of injustice or oppression. But he had in him no smouldering fire of personal resentment to make him feel the will to smite. He was by instinct a teacher, and not an agitator ; but it was his fate to have his handiwork — the Charter — made into the banner of a great crusade with which he was able deeply to sympathise, but never, because of its irrationality, bred of hunger, to feel himself at one. Lovett failed — his National Association and his National Hall were an anti-climax after he had written The People's Charter. But he would sooner have failed than have done any irrational or ignoble deed. Call him high-minded, or a prig, as you will. He was a very representative figure of the artisan class of his day. Methodism trained him — Owenism set him free to follow the path of reason ; but he remained throughout the respectable artisan, cherishing ideals, but driven by no urgent hunger or thwarted ambition to hate society, or to invoke unreason in the service of the good. Write on his tombstone, " He saved himself — others he could not either save, or leave to destruction, because he was a good man ; but greatness was not in him ".

II

Joseph Rayner Stephens

WHEN a man says openly, at a great public meeting, that, sooner than allow a law duly enacted by Parliament to be enforced, " Newcastle should be one blaze of fire, with only one way to put it out, and that with the blood of all who supported this abominable measure ", it is natural to conclude that the speaker feels strongly on the matter in hand. When he goes on to say that he is " a revolutionist by fire, a revolutionist by blood, to the knife, to the death ", it is natural to regard him as a man of somewhat extreme opinions. When, at another public meeting, he calls upon all his hearers who have firearms to fire them off by way of demonstration, and then on all who intend to procure them to hold up their hands, it is natural to regard him as a man of deeds as well as words, and as likely very soon either to be leading a revolution or to find himself in the hands of the police. Actually Joseph Rayner Stephens, who uttered these sentiments, did soon find himself under arrest. What is surprising is that when he came to trial he got off with a sentence of eighteen months' imprisonment, *plus* a requirement to find sureties for his good behaviour during the following five years. Many men had been transported to Botany Bay, only a few years before, for saying a good deal less than he said, not once or twice, but on many occasions, to great gatherings of workmen all over the country. But, in 1839, the year of the first Chartist Convention, the authorities were going easy with those whose misdeeds were limited to words, however inflammatory. John Frost and his fellow leaders in the Newport affair, having actually taken up arms, were transported to Australia : Stephens and O'Connor and the rest, who had only talked revolution, were let down lightly.

This was, beyond doubt, a matter of deliberate policy.

The Whig Government wanted to crush the Chartists ; but it believed it could crush them most effectively by not being too severe. It wanted to put the Chartists' leaders safely away in gaol, where they would be out of harm's way : it did not want so to exasperate their followers as to provoke a revolution of despair. Even the Whigs knew that the common people in the factory and mining areas had deep and bitter grievances ; but they believed that, if mass revolt could be avoided for the time being, the danger would pass, and the influence of the agitators over the people would begin to fail. The event proved that they were right in this. Armed revolt was localised in 1839, and not attempted thereafter. The great strikes of 1842 did not turn into a Chartist revolution ; and after that calamitous year Chartism, and the popular unrest which had given it strength, noticeably waned. The Whig Government was prudent in its comparative mildness towards the apostles of ' physical force '. It disorganised Chartism by arresting its leaders ; but it stopped short of making martyrs of them, or of depriving their followers of all hope. As the great trade depression of the late 'thirties and early 'forties slowly passed away, the hunger grew less, and there were fewer starvelings ready to take a revolutionary lead. Chartism never again commanded a mass following — not even in the ' Year of Revolutions ', 1848. The day of Stephens and O'Connor was over : they had missed their chance.

The chance was real, while it lasted — of revolutionary uprising, if not of ultimate success. It depended on a certain conjuncture of events, on the coincidence in time of a major depression in industry and trade, a succession of harvest failures and high bread prices, the introduction of the drastic New Poor Law of 1834 into the factory areas, and a mass movement of protest against intolerable factory conditions. The Chartism of 1838 and 1839 was a result of all these influences combined. Into it were swept handloom weavers and factory workers to whom the New Poor Law denied the right of outdoor relief, interested operatives and disinterested sympathisers who could bear no longer with patience the horrible abuses of the factory system, all the victims of high prices and low wages oppressed by the double burden of bad harvests and bad trade. Without all these, the Radical politicians who wanted the Charter would have been but a negligible band of doctrinaires. Hunger and oppression made them formidable ; but the Whigs, wise in their day, did not reinforce the powers of revolt by adding really drastic political oppression to dire economic distress. They carried on with the New Poor Law, which was an essential part of their policy of giving *laissez-faire* capitalism every chance. But they did not persecute : they merely repressed. That was why Joseph Rayner Stephens, who had threatened to slay every man jack of them, was let off with eighteen months' incarceration in Chester Castle.

Stephens was a dissenting minister who had been expelled in 1834 from the Wesleyan Connexion for advocating the separation of Church and State. His father, John Stephens, was of the same calling and persuasion, and high in the Methodist counsels. He was President of the Wesleyan Conference in 1827. One of Joseph's brothers was editor of the *Christian Advocate* ; another was George Stephens, the famous student of early Scandinavian literature and inscriptions. Joseph himself, after receiving his education at Manchester Grammar School and at the Methodist School at Woodhouse Grove, near Leeds, had become in 1825 a Methodist preacher, and had been sent in the following year as a missionary preacher to Sweden. There he had been made domestic chaplain to Lord Bloomfield, the British plenipotentiary, had spread the gospel as far as Lapland in itinerant preaching tours, and had formed a friendship with Montalembert. Returning to England in 1829, he had been ordained as a Methodist minister, and had been stationed in 1830 at Cheltenham, with the care of a number of local chapels scattered about the Cotswold Hills. By 1834 he had shifted his labours to Lancashire, and had there plunged into two movements equally displeasing to his Wesleyan superiors — Church Disestablishment and Factory Reform.

The first of these provided the occasion for Stephens's exclusion from the Wesleyan Connexion ; but it is clear that the second had also something to do with it, for the high authorities of the Wesleyan movement were at that time most determined enemies of every manifestation of Radicalism among the ministers and preachers of the Connexion. Separated from his church, he did not give up preaching, but carried most of his congregation with him to an independent chapel which he set up in Ashton-under-Lyne, in the heart of the South Lancashire cotton-spinning area. This was in the year in which two things of peculiar interest to his congregation occurred. The New Poor Law was passed, and the great Trade Union movement, begun by John Doherty and expanded into a millennial crusade by Robert Owen, was remorselessly crushed. Stephens began his new ministry among men who cherished bitter thoughts of their defeat at the hands of the employers allied with the Government, of the failure of the 1833 Factory Act to relieve their distress, and of the Whig Reform Act of 1832 which had put political power into the hands of their masters.

Stephens began at once to take part in the agitation, led chiefly by Richard Oastler in Yorkshire, for a more effective measure of factory reform. He became a well-known figure on the platforms of the Short Time Committees which were endeavouring to secure legislation providing for a ten hours day. He began to work with Oastler, and to build up his reputation as a highly effective open-air speaker, as well as a preacher, on the side of the factory reformers. Small of stature, he possessed a voice which could be heard by many thousands in the open air ; and he had a remarkable eloquence which, mingling scriptural allusion with impassioned description of factory wrongs, quite carried his audiences away. The more cautious leaders of the factory movement, even if they looked askance at him, could no more do without him than without Oastler, for he was the man whom the Lancashire operatives delighted to hear. His following grew : three chapels were built for him : he preached as he spoke among the factory reformers, as the apostle of the poor. His passionate words gave religion a new, this-worldly meaning to the many who were estranged by the other-worldly pietism of the orthodox Methodists. God, he proclaimed, hated the slavery of the factories : it was God's will that men should rebel against it with all their might.

It seemed to Stephens that his fellow Methodists, as well as the Churchmen, were betraying the cause of religion by their failure to protest against the monstrous abuses of the factory system. He wrote, "We ask whether the ministers of religion in these times of savage and relentless, of stiff-necked and audacious tyranny, have faithfully discharged the duties of their holy office. They have not. Instead of pleading the cause of the poor, they have joined the league against them. They have shared in the murderous assault and are dividing the spoil." [1]

Stephens, on account of his work in the factory agitation, was already a power among the workers in Lancashire when, in 1836-7, the Poor Law Commissioners — the ' Three Bashaws of Somerset House ' — began seriously to attempt to enforce the New Poor Law in the Northern factory districts. They had already applied it in the agricultural South and East, sweeping away the ' Speenhamland ' system which had been in force there since the early years of the French War. Under this system the wages of labourers in work had been regularly subsidised out of the poor rates, and many labourers who could find no ordinary work had been either employed directly by the parishes on road repair or similar tasks, or hired out in gangs to farmers who paid part of the cost of their keep in return for their compulsory labour. This system of relief had resulted in wholesale pauperisation of the rural community in many parts of the country, and had stood effectively in the way of any attempt by the labourers to improve their position. Its abolition, despite the heavy immediate hardships which it involved, was on the whole a thoroughly good thing ; and the primary purpose of the Poor Law Amendment of 1834 had been to get rid of it.

But in the North of England the Speenhamland system had never existed, save sporadically here and there, in anything like the same form as in the South. There had never been in the Northern Counties a class of pauper labourers permanently employed, or hired out, by the parish : nor had subsidies been paid to bring up to subsistence level the earnings of workers in regular employment. Over most of the North the Poor Law had been, for the able-bodied, mainly a source of occasional relief when times were bad and jobs scarce — in effect, mainly a form of unemployment

[1] *People's Magazine*. p. 180.

benefit on which the unemployed or under-employed worker could fall back in periods of depression, and, as such, by no means open to the same objection as the kind of relief paid in the agricultural South.

The Poor Law Act, however, did not make nice distinctions ; and the new Commissioners were inclined to be ruthless in carrying its provisions into effect. Their task, as they conceived it in the spirit of the Act, was to cut off all outdoor relief to able-bodied workers, and to confront those who applied for relief with the ' workhouse test ' — that is, the offer of admission to the workhouse as the only form of relief. The purpose behind this was to make the conditions of poor relief as deterrent as possible, in order to induce the workman to maintain himself by his own labour, on the theory that he could find work if he really tried, and did not attempt to stand out for wages which the employer could not afford to pay. It followed from this policy that the condition of the workers who received relief ought to be made, if possible, " less eligible " than that of the worst-off labourers in ordinary employment, for otherwise the principle of deterrence could not be made to work.

It is easy enough to see now that, in endeavouring to apply these principles to the factory areas, the ' Three Bashaws of Somerset House ' were working on radically false assumptions. It might just possibly be true that, if the Speenhamland system were swept away, the labourers in the agricultural areas would before long all, or nearly all, find employment at wages at any rate no worse than the doles they had been getting out of the rates, and that under the new system each labourer would have some incentive to seek to better his own condition. But it was sheer nonsense to suppose that the unemployed industrial workers could all get work, at any wages, when a slump visited the factory or mining areas, or that there was any sense or justice in deterring them by nearly intolerable conditions from applying at such times for relief. The existence of trade depressions, during which work was simply not obtainable at all by a proportion of the industrial workers, went wholly unrecognised. Workers thrown out of their jobs through no fault of their own were treated as criminals, and left to starve unless they consented to enter the hated workhouses — or ' Bastilles ' as they were widely called among the people.

The violent hatred of the workers for the Commissioners and their ' Bastilles ' was exacerbated by a further fact. The sponsors of the new law, holding ultra-Malthusian views about the tendency of the population to increase faster than the means of subsistence available — Malthus's famous geometrical and arithmetical rates of increase — were determined to do all they could to resist any tendency on the part of the paupers to multiply and replenish the earth. Accordingly, when the pauper and his family were driven by the refusal of outdoor relief to seek entry to the workhouse, rigid separation of the sexes was insisted on. Husbands and wives were parted, children separated from their parents, and deterrence and less eligibility thus happily combined with provision for keeping the birth-rate down. The logical advocates of this plan argued that it was all for the workers' good, because pauperism arose from a redundancy of labour, and a decrease in population would in due course bring about a rise in wages. But the poor themselves saw matters in another light. They felt that they were being treated as criminals for being poor — and they resented bitterly the loss of their old right to claim outdoor relief from the parish when times were bad.

It so happened that the moment when the Poor Law Commissioners set about introducing the new system in the North of England was one of acute depression and widespread unemployment. If the new law had come in at a time of prosperity its terms might have been resented, but there would have been no mass revolt against it, for it would have affected relatively few workers except the handloom weavers, among whom bad times were now continuous, as they fought out their losing struggle against the more productive, power-driven machinery. But, coming when things were bad, and getting worse, the new law inflicted intolerable hardships, and engendered a mood of mass-revolt. Savage indignation swept over the industrial areas : the ' Three Bashaws ' seemed sheer monsters of repressiveness and inhumanity intent on venting their sadistic instincts upon the poor. A passionate spirit of hatred for the Whig oppressors took hold of the suffering people ; they were ready to follow any leader who would give strong enough expression to their desperate sense of injustice.

To Stephens, to Richard Oastler, and to other humanitarians who had been active in the struggle on behalf of the factory children, the Malthusian doctrines of the Poor Law Commissioners seemed wicked to a degree. They did not for a moment admit that there were too many mouths to be fed : they denounced the entire theory of the economists as bunkum and contrary to both Holy Scripture and decent human feeling. They believed that hunger and poverty were due to bad government and evil principles, and not to ' surplus population ' ; and the New Poor Law was, to their minds, the extreme manifestation of commercialism without conscience and without reverence for the divine spirit in man. Preaching in London in May 1839, Stephens gave vehement expressions to his hatred of the New Poor Law and his belief that resistance to it by any means was fully justified. He said : " I have never acknowledged the authority of the New Poor Law, and so help me God I never will. I never paid my rates under it, and so help me God I never will — they may take every chair, every table, and every bed I have — they may pull my house over my head, and send me and my wife and my child wanderers on the heaths and on the hills — they may take all but my wife, my child, and my life, but pay one penny I never will. If they dare attempt to take them, and it becomes necessary to repel force by force, there will be a knife, a pike, or a bullet at hand, and if I am to fall, I will at least sell life for life. I exhort you and all others to do the same. I do not mean to flinch. I recommend nothing which I will not do. I tell you that if they attempt to carry into effect this *damnable law, I mean to fight.* I will lay aside the black coat for the red, and with the Bible in one hand and a sword in the other — a sword of steel, not of argument — I will fight to the death sooner than that law shall be brought into operation on me or on others with my consent or through my silence. . . . Perish trade and manufacture — perish arts, literature, and science — perish palace, throne, and altar — if they can only stand upon the dissolution of the marriage tie — the annihilation of every domestic affection, and the violent and most brutal oppression ever yet practised upon the poor of any country in the world." [1]

Humanity and religion thus worked together to create in Stephens a ferocious hatred of the Whigs and all their works. When he called himself a Tory, as he sometimes did, he meant chiefly that he detested the Whigs with all his heart and soul. In all his political utterances, he was much less the politician than the preacher calling down the vengeance of Heaven upon the ungodly. He would have had God, rather than man, strike down the sinners in the arrogance of their wickedness ; and he felt that the starving workmen, if they were to proceed to extremes against their oppressors, would be but the instruments of the Divine Will. Anything in the way of violence was justified, if only it prevented the victory of the forces of evil — the forces that were driving little children under the lash to labour in factories for fourteen hours a day, that were breaking up the family in the name of sacred Political Economy, and that covered up their sins by pretending to care for the eternal welfare of those whom they condemned to misery in this world. Stephens spoke with the voice of a prophet ; and the people hearkened — for in their wretchedness his passionate hatred, based on human sympathy, sounded the note of hope.

This was the spirit in which Stephens, in 1837, offered himself as a candidate for the borough of Ashton-under-Lyne, against the sitting Whig-Liberal member, Charles Hindley, and a Tory. Hindley was himself a good friend to the factory workers in the struggle on behalf of the factory children ; but he did not go far enough for Stephens, nor was he an opponent of the New Poor Law system. Stephens polled only 19 votes, against 237 for Hindley and 201 for his Tory opponent, James Wood ; and after this defeat he made no further attempt to enter Parliament. Politics, in the parliamentary sense, were not in his line ; he preferred direct action by the people against the transgressors. He said in a sermon preached at Hyde, Cheshire, in February 1839 : " There has already been too much of what is called political reform, the juggling of places from one to another, the

[1] From " A Sermon Preached at Primrose Hill, London, on Sunday, May 12, 1839 ".

passing of the pea from one cup to another cup to amuse and to deceive, and ultimately to destroy the people ; and every step you take is a step nearer to hell. All the laws in England could not make Hyde a bit the better unless the people were a changed people. An Act of Parliament cannot change the hearts of the tyrants Ashton and Howard [local millowners]. These men have made themselves rich by making you poor. . . . Now, all the laws of England could not change the hearts of those wicked men ; and unless their hearts were changed, and your hearts were changed, what could the law do ? There would be a thousand ways of breaking through it. . . . It could do no good. Your minds must be made up. You, husbands ! unless your minds be made up that your wives ought not and shall not work, that rather than kill your wives by allowing them to work, you will allow God to take their lives by gradual starvation. . . . But God Almighty is moving the working classes in the country, and therefore I exhort you to give yourselves to prayer. Pray God to sound the alarum from one end of the land to the other ; and then, in the spirit of self-denial, and self-sacrifice, and devotion, be united as the heart of one man, and as one united and indissoluble phalanx, God leading you by a pillar of fire by night, and by a pillar of cloud by day, wend your way and force your passage through the wilderness into the promised land — the land that flows with milk and honey. It is high time that there was some mighty movement." [1]

Legality, either in making laws or in obeying them, counted for nothing in Stephens's philosophy in comparison with being about the Lord's work. He denied that man could owe any obedience to unrighteous laws : " Are the Spitalfields weavers protected, when not one in a hundred of them, after working twelve hours a day, can earn 12s. a week ? Are the handloom weavers of the North protected, when they cannot, with all their toil, earn more than 7s. a week ? I have known girls eight years of age working at the anvil, making nails from six in the morning until eight or nine at night, and on Friday all night long, and, after all, could not earn more than 1s. 6d. per week. The mother worked

[1] " A Sermon Preached at Hyde, on the 17th of February, 1839."

equal time, and whilst she was at work, one of her children was burned almost to a cinder, and she could only earn 3s. a week, whilst the grandmother could get no more than 1s. 6d. Do these poor creatures owe *allegiance* to the laws ? Are they *protected* ? Do the poor wretches of the factories — the combers, the piecers, the scavengers, dressers, weavers, and spinners — do they owe allegiance to the laws ? Does the agricultural labourer, who can only earn 8s. a week, owe submission to the laws ? The law, in establishing oppression, makes the oppressed its deadly enemy." [1]

It went with this attitude that Stephens, though he became a Chartist and proclaimed his belief in Universal Suffrage, would often go on to say, almost in the same breath, that he had no faith in political reforms. He wanted Universal Suffrage, not because he thought that the people could be saved by votes or by politicians, but because the Charter had become the symbol of the right of the poor to be accounted as men, and not as mere hands to labour for the rich folks' profit. The Charter would not make men happy ; but might not the granting of it, in response to an irresistible movement of the oppressed, jar the whole community into a realisation of sin, and thus bring about that change in the hearts of men without which there could be no real reformation of affairs ? Stephens could shout for the Charter with all the mighty power of his lungs, and yet declare, in all sincerity, that for the forms of government he did not care a rush. He wrote in June 1839 as follows : " Down with the House of Commons — down with the House of Lords — aye, down with the throne, and down with the altar itself — burn the church — down with all rank, all dignity, all title, all power ; unless that dignity, authority, and power will and do secure to the honest industrious efforts of the upright and poor man a comfortable maintenance in exchange for his labour. I don't care about your Charter ; it may be all very right ; it may be all very good ; you have a right to get it, mind you, and I will stand by you in it ; but I don't care about it ; and I don't care about a'republic. You have a right to have it if you choose ;

[1] " A Sermon Preached in Shepherd and Shepherdess Fields, London, on Sunday, May 12, 1839."

and I will stand by you, in defending your right to have it
if you choose. I don't care about a monarchy ; I don't care
about the present, or any other order of things, unless the
Charter, the republic, the monarchy, the present order of
things, or any other order of things that may be brought to
succeed the present, should, first of all, and above all, and
through all, secure to every son of the soil, to every living
being of the human kind . . . a full, a sufficient, and a
comfortable maintenance, according to the will and command-
ment of God. That is what I go for ; that is what I talk
for ; that is what I live for ; and that is what I will die for ;
for I will have it. . . . You have a right, every working
man amongst you has the right to as much for your labour
as will keep you and your families." [1]

The same spirit is expressed in the often-quoted passage
in which he affirmed the essentially economic basis of the
agitation for the Charter : "The question of manhood
suffrage was, after all, a knife-and-fork question. If any man
ask him what he meant by manhood suffrage, he would tell
him : he meant to say that every working man in the land
had a right to have a good coat and hat, a good roof over his
head, a good dinner upon his table, no more work than would
keep him in health, and as much wages as would keep him
in plenty, and the enjoyment of those pleasures of life which
a reasonable man could desire." [2]

The old institutions would serve well enough, would men
but administer them in the spirit of righteousness : at all
events, they were certain to be preferable to the new inhuman
instrument of government that the Whigs were busy making
with their New Poor Law, their centralised bureaucracy
of Malthusian Commissioners, their Parliament of money-
grubbers, and their dishonoured Throne.

This was Stephens's ' Toryism ' — a demagogic Toryism
which was ready enough to call in the old England to destroy
the new. All over the country he went, but principally
throughout the factory and mining districts, using language
of unrestrained violence, inciting the people to revolution

---

[1] *London Democrat*, June 8, 1839.
[2] Speech at Kersal Moor, near Manchester, *Annual Register*, 1838,
p. 311.

against the transgressors, counting no consequences if he could but rouse up in the ruling classes the sense of sin. When he was arrested and brought to trial for his utterances, he defended himself in a speech which many of the Chartists regarded as an act of apostasy. He denied that he was a Chartist, though he had supported the Charter ; he asserted his indifference to merely political programmes and causes ; and he seemed as if he were eating his words in the hope of escaping punishment. But I think there was in this no conscious apostasy. He was, quite genuinely, not a Chartist in the sense in which Lovett was, or even Feargus O'Connor. He really did hold that what mattered was not politics, but sin. He could not see why he should be punished as an inflammatory Radical politician when what he had been about was not politics, but the Lord's work — his duty as a preacher to rebuke evil, and to call down upon it God's vengeance. He felt that he had been misunderstood ; and he came near to repudiating his fellow agitators who stirred up the poor not as God's prophets, but merely as politicians seeking a mundane end. He, too, wanted much that they wanted ; but he wanted it to the glory of God — and that, surely, justified him before his accusers.

His plea, as we have seen, was not wholly without effect ; for the sentence passed upon him in August 1839 was mild in comparison with his offence, judged by purely secular standards. It must have seemed more expedient to muzzle Stephens, if he could be muzzled, than to exact exemplary punishment ; and to a great extent the muzzling was successful. On his release from prison in 1840, he did not resume his activity as a Chartist agitator — he settled down in Ashton-under-Lyne, in a chapel provided for him by his supporters, and gave himself over mainly to his religious duties. True, he also started a journal of his own — *Stephens's Monthly Magazine* — and therein continued to denounce unsparingly the iniquities of the Poor Law and the crimes of factory owners who mercilessly exploited the working people. But he no longer appeared on Chartist platforms in company with men who had no sympathy with his religious approach : nor did his sermons and speeches any longer sound like incitements to immediate, bloody revolution. He had not given up his convictions ; but he stressed more his aloofness from mere politics, and limited his secular activities to continued and energetic collaboration in the struggle for factory reform. His critics said that this was because he had no desire to go to prison again ; and it must be borne in mind that he was bound over in sureties for five years more to keep the peace. But I think the truth is not so much that he had come to be afraid, as that his revolutionism of 1838 and 1839 had been incidental — an outcome of a particular situation, which was never so repeated afterwards as to stir him in quite the same way.

There was, at all events, no change in his essential convictions. In 1846 the period for which he had been bound over ended, and his Lancashire friends made a presentation to him on the occasion of his release from bondage. There was no immediate change in his conduct. He went on with his preaching, much as before, in Ashton-under-Lyne and the neighbouring towns and villages, to congregations mainly of textile workers and colliers, who continued to give him their wholehearted support. *Stephens's Monthly Magazine* had expired speedily, in the year of its birth. In 1848 he started a new paper, *The Ashton Chronicle*, which, two years later, was changed to *The Champion*, and lasted until the end of 1851. These renewed adventures into journalism were the signs not so much of any change of attitude as of a change in the situation. In 1848 political and social excitements were everywhere ; and there was a stirring of Radicalism all over Europe. But *The Ashton Chronicle* and *The Champion* were concerned much less with Radical politics or European revolution than with a narrower cause much nearer home. In 1847 Parliament had at last enacted the Ten Hours Act, for which the factory reformers had been struggling for so long ; and this Act was in danger of being nullified by lawful evasion. The employers were meeting the new law limiting the working day of the factory women and children by working relays — by keeping the factories open for much longer than ten hours, and defying effective inspection by starting workers at different times and even, in some cases, by arranging to employ the same workers at more than one factory, so that the total hours worked were far beyond what the law allowed, but no single employer could be convicted of employing anyone beyond the legal limit.

Stephens, in his new journals, entered wholeheartedly into the struggle of the workers for an effective enforcement of the ten hours day. He joined in the denunciation of Lord Ashley for agreeing to compromise, by accepting a longer working day coupled with a promise of improved enforcement. He backed up vigorously the demand of the Short Time Committees for a " restriction on the motive power " — that is, on the number of hours during which the factories could remain at work, even if they professed to employ no single worker for more than ten hours. He played an active part in the agitation which led up to the amending Factory Acts of 1850 and 1853.

The Champion ceased publication in 1851, by which time the worst abuses under the Factory Act of 1847 had been put right. In the following year Stephens moved his head-quarters from Ashton to Stalybridge, where he rented a chapel in which he continued to preach regularly until 1875. That year his wife died ; and five years later he married for a second time. Throughout, he kept up his connection with the developing Trade Union movement. In the early 'sixties he took a leading part in the agitation to secure relief for the workers who were thrown out of employment by the Cotton Famine during the American Civil War ; and some of his old fire came back into his denunciations of the Poor Law authorities for their failure to bring adequate help to the distressed. In 1863 he was chaplain to the famous Miners' Conference at Leeds, which founded the National Miners' Association under the leadership of Alexander Macdonald, and began the agitation for better mining legislation, which was responsible for the improved safety code laid down in the Coal and Metalliferous Mines Acts of 1872. Four years later he was again serving the Trade Union cause by presiding over a conference of the societies of textile workers in Lancashire called for the purpose of inaugurating a campaign for the eight hours day. After the passing of Forster's Education Act of 1870 he was elected to the new Stalybridge School Board. To the very end he was ready to bestir himself to help any progressive movement among the workers that directly concerned their social and economic good. But he had dropped right out of politics, which he had entered into at all only momentarily, and under the stress of his intense revulsion against the detestable inhumanity of the methods used in applying the New Poor Law of 1834. He died in 1879.

Joseph Rayner Stephens has not fared well at the hands of the historians. They have for the most part dismissed him as a ranting preacher who was so carried away by his own eloquence as again and again to incite the people to acts of violence without counting the cost. There is something in this judgement, but not everything. The Methodists were great ranters, well used to the utmost hyperbole of language in their preachings about the next world. Stephens, trained in this school of religious enthusiasm, committed the crime of transferring his violence of metaphor and adjuration from the affairs of the next world to the affairs of this, and of exemplifying sin in the persons of the tyrannical millowners and Malthusian reformers who were making the lives of his congregations a misery. There was always a risk that this would happen if Methodism were allowed to become a this-worldly gospel. Against this danger the leaders of the Wesleyan Connexion, staunch upholders of the existing order in Church and State, waged ceaseless warfare. But they could not altogether prevent ministers who had to face daily the sight of working-class suffering from becoming advocates of reformation in public affairs, as well as in men's private lives. They did the best they could, by expelling the offenders. Stephens was one of the many Methodist ministers who were driven forth to gather their own congregations among the distressed miners and factory operatives, with a sense of sharing their exclusion from the benefits of the new industrialism and from the religions professed by the well-to-do.

Stephens, the most gifted of these religious pariahs, used the language which he knew for the purpose of expressing his sympathy with the people's wrongs, and of stirring them to action. In doing this, he exposed both them and himself to very serious risks, and it may well be that his eloquence sometimes carried him some distance beyond what he would have said if he had paused to think. But his speeches and pamphlets do not read as if there were in them any element of bluff or hypocrisy. At any rate until his imprisonment had given him ample time for reflection, I feel sure he did mean what he said about the right and duty of resistance to bad laws, and about his readiness generally to go to all lengths sooner than allow factory slavery to continue or the Poor Law Act of 1834 to be enforced. Chartism, when he associated himself with it in the years up to 1839, was much less a political movement than an instinctive uprising of the people against intolerable oppression. It had the quality of a great moral revolt. But by the time he came out of prison in 1840, that phase of Chartism was over. The Chartists had split up into sects and groups following different leaders ; the unity of the oppressed was gone. Chartism had become a political creed ; and political creeds had no attractions for him. I think this, rather than fear for his own skin, explains why he dropped out of the agitation for the Charter, though he continued to work energetically for factory reform and Trade Unionism and other popular causes which were directly related to the living conditions of the people. During the years before 1839 a particular conjuncture had made Stephens, as it made many others, a revolutionary advocate of Physical Force. But that conjuncture did not return.

III

Richard Oastler

'THE Factory King', 'The King of the Factory Children', or, in later years, 'The Old King' — these were the names by which Richard Oastler was known among his contemporaries. He was dubbed 'King' first in derision by his critics ; but he seized on the name, and made it his own. It was appropriate to his position of unquestioned leadership of the Yorkshire operatives in their struggle for the Ten Hours Bill. Oastler at the height of his glory was the 'King' of the factory children, the inspirer of a great crusade against 'Yorkshire Slavery', a personality so large and so keenly alive as to make himself the symbol of the cause which he had espoused with all his restless energy and abounding courage.

Except as a memory, Richard Oastler's kingdom did not endure for long. He began his crusade for the factory children in Yorkshire in 1830, and by 1840 he had been ruined, driven from his native county, and lodged in the Fleet Prison as a debtor. That was by no means the end of him ; but it was the end of his kingdom. Though he edited a weekly journal, *The Fleet Papers*, from his prison, and though he took an active part in the further struggles which led up to the passing of the Ten Hours Act in 1847, though he was still writing and agitating in the eighteen-fifties, and remained 'The Old King' to the end in the minds of many who remembered his past glory, he never returned to his former position of authority. His health had been undermined by the unsparing use which he had made of his great physical vitality during his 'kingship', and by the enervating experience of four years in the Fleet. His contemporaries said that he came out of prison " a changed man ", as earnest as ever in his enthusiasm for the factory cause, but with his old fire gone. When, in 1847, the Ten

Hours Act at last became law, he was ill, and unable to take part in the celebrations of the great event. Oastler has to be judged by what he did between 1830 and 1840, or even between 1830 and 1838, when he was driven from Yorkshire on account of his incitements to the workers to resist the New Poor Law to the bitter end. What came afterwards was only an epilogue — humanly satisfying because to the end it was a record of grateful remembrance by those for whom Oastler had given all he had to give, but of no significance in history.

Richard Oastler's days of greatness were thus nearly over before the Chartist movement was born. He himself was never a Chartist, but, as he was fond of saying, a " Church and State Tory ", whose favourite motto was " The Altar, the Throne, and the Cottage ". He had no use for Universal Suffrage or any other of the ' Six Points ', not merely in the sense that, like Joseph Rayner Stephens, he regarded them as irrelevant to the real issues of poverty and ' English slavery ', but in the sense that he was positively opposed to them. In 1835 he wrote with his usual candour in Hetherington's *Twopenny Dispatch*, " My opinion on Universal Suffrage is, that, if it were the law of the land next week, it would in a very short time produce ' universal confusion ', and would inevitably lead to ' despotism ' ". With Michael Thomas Sadler, his closest colleague in the earlier phases of the struggle for factory reform, he opposed the Whig Reform Bill ; and he never joined, as Stephens did, in any phase of the Chartist agitation as such. Yet he belongs with the Chartists, and finds his place in this gallery of Chartist portraits, because his work as an agitator for factory legislation and against the enforcement of the New Poor Law in the North of England was among the principal forces that went to the making of Northern Chartism. In Yorkshire O'Connor largely inherited what Oastler had made : and when Oastler was gone from among the Yorkshire factory workers, many of them transferred their allegiance from ' The Old King ' to the new. Moreover, Oastler's Toryism, and the close association in Yorkshire between his brand of Toryism and the cause of factory reform, help to explain O'Connor's ' Toryism ' — the ' Toryism ' of which he and his *Northern Star* were often accused. In Yorkshire Whiggism was very closely associated in the workers' minds with opposition to factory reform — much more so than in Lancashire, despite the leading position taken by Bright and Cobden, and despite the reputation of the ' Manchester School '. In Lancashire there were quite a number of important Whig, Liberal, and Radical manufacturers who took the workers' side in the factory struggle : John Fielden, Joseph Brotherton, and Charles Hindley are outstanding names. In Yorkshire there were hardly any. In Yorkshire the Whigs, much more than the Tories, counted as the enemies of the common people.

Richard Oastler was brought up in a thoroughly Tory atmosphere. He was born in 1789, the youngest of the eight sons of Robert Oastler, who had been a linen merchant in Thirsk, but had been made steward of the Yorkshire estates of the Thornhill family. The Thornhills lived on their Norfolk estates, and seldom visited their Yorkshire properties, which they left entirely to the management of their steward. Robert Oastler lived at Fixby Hall, the Thornhill mansion, and was treated by the tenants as the virtual owner of the estate. When he died Richard, who had been articled to an architect, was appointed to succeed him, and took up his residence as steward at Fixby Hall.

Richard Oastler's father had been a strong churchman, of Wesleyan views, and a personal friend of John Wesley ; and Richard inherited his religious opinions. Through all his life he was intensely devout and maintained his churchmanship side by side with his Wesleyanism. He shared Wesley's Toryism ; and indeed his Toryism was, and remained, a part of his religion. But it also prescribed to him a high ideal of the duties of the squirearchy ; and, as the Thornhills' steward at Fixby, he conceived that the obligation of discharging these duties in their absence fell upon himself. His salary as steward was but £300, raised later to £500, a year ; but he was generous to tenants and kept open house at Fixby Hall. It is small wonder that his accounts fell into confusion, or that disputes arose about what expenses could rightly be charged to the estate. Oastler brushed his difficulties aside year after year by admitting as his own expenses which his employer would not agree to meet, and thus piling up against himself a growing burden of indebtedness to the estate. He must, I think, have been a very bad man of business, careless to a degree — especially after his mind had become so filled with the cause of the factory children that he could think of nothing else. At all events, this accumulating debt became his ruin when at length he and Thomas Thornhill fell out over politics. Thornhill had sympathised with Oastler's factory crusade, and had left him with a free hand, merely scoring up more claims against him year after year. But when it came to Oastler's incitements to the operatives to defy the New Poor Law, which Whigs and Tories had combined to pass, Thornhill changed his tune. He demanded that Oastler should give up his agitation, and discharged him when he refused. Then came the question of the debts, and in 1840 Oastler found himself Thornhill's prisoner in the Fleet.

That this was largely Oastler's own fault seems undeniable, even if Thornhill's conduct was unduly vindictive. Oastler maintained, in the spirit of his own Toryism, that Thornhill had no right to treat his Yorkshire estates merely as a source of income, without letting someone else play the Squire Bountiful to his tenants, if he would not live on them himself. He took up the role of squire on his employer's behalf, without any agreement that he was entitled to do so ; and Thornhill let him play the squire for many years without calling him to account. Old Robert Oastler had been Thornhill's close friend, as well as his steward ; and probably the squire shirked unpleasant explanations with the son. When at length they fell out, both were aggrieved. Oastler accused Thornhill of neglecting his duties as an aristocrat : Thornhill accused Oastler of squandering his money. The dispute was exacerbated because it coincided in time with the great Chartist uprisings in Yorkshire, for which Thornhill probably held Oastler's demagogy largely to blame. Thornhill probably thought it an excellent thing to keep Oastler mewed up in the Fleet, where he could do no harm. He did indeed end Oastler's kingdom, but only to make it the easier for O'Connor to reign in his stead.

Oastler became steward of the Thornhill estates in 1820, when his father died. Before that, he had given up architecture, and settled in business in Leeds as a commission agent. In 1816 he had married Mary Tatham, to whom he was devoted. They had two children, who both died in infancy. Oastler's business did not prosper, and he was in financial difficulties when he went to Fixby. He had already shown a tendency to mix politics with business. From 1807 onward he had been a fervent supporter of the movement against negro slavery; and in 1820 he had taken up with enthusiasm the popular cause of Queen Caroline against George IV. But the Queen Caroline episode was soon over; and for the next ten years Oastler made no public appearance except in connection with religious movements and the campaign for slave emancipation. Then, in 1830, he launched out suddenly on the crusade which was to make him famous.

The manner of his beginning was characteristically impulsive. In September 1830 he was on a visit to his friend John Wood, of Horton Hall, a prosperous worsted manufacturer of Bradford. Wood, a fellow religionist of Oastler's, was troubled in mind and conscience by the very bad conditions of overwork and cruelty to children which were prevalent in the Bradford mills, and he asked Oastler whether it had never occurred to him, when he was declaiming against negro slavery, that evils of a parallel sort existed nearer home in the Yorkshire factories. The same thought had, of course, occurred to many other people long before — it had been for many years, for example, one of William Cobbett's favourite themes. But apparently it had never occurred to Oastler — for there can be no doubt at all about the utter genuineness of his reaction. He had been too exclusively concerned with souls to see what was happening to the bodies of the factory children; and for the past ten years his work had lain near, but not actually in, the factory area. At all events, he listened with horror while John Wood told him about the working conditions in the Bradford mills. Wood was one of the best employers in Yorkshire; but he told Oastler that " in his own mill, little children were worked from six o'clock in the morning to seven o'clock in the evening, and that the only break off they had was forty minutes at noon; which break was ten minutes more than any other millowner allowed. In some mills in the neighbourhood the children were worked all the time without one minute of rest, being forced to snatch their food while they tended the moving machines." Wood gave him further details, and Oastler, aghast at what he had heard, dashed off that same day a vehemently worded letter to *The Leeds Mercury* — then the leading Whig-Liberal paper in the North — under the heading " Yorkshire Slavery " : " Let truth speak out, appalling as the statement may appear. The fact is true. Thousands of our fellow creatures and fellow subjects, both male and female, the miserable inhabitants of a *Yorkshire town* (Yorkshire, now represented in Parliament by the giant of anti-slavery principles) are this very moment existing in a state of slavery *more horrid* than are the victims of that hellish system — ' *colonial slavery* '. These innocent victims drawl out, unpitied, their short but miserable existence, in a place famed for its profession of religious zeal, whose inhabitants are ever foremost in *professing* ' temperance' and ' reformation ' and are striving to outrun their neighbours in missionary exertions, and would fain send the Bible to the farthest corner of the globe — ay, in the very place where the anti-slavery fever rages most furiously, her *apparent* charity is not more admired on earth, than her *real cruelty* is abhorred in heaven. The very streets which receive the droppings of an ' Anti-Slavery Society ' are every morning wet by the tears of innocent victims at the accursed shrine of avarice, who are *compelled* (not by the cart-whip of the negro slave-driver, but by the dread of the equally appalling thong or strap of the overlooker) to hasten, half dressed, *but not half fed*, to those magazines of British infantile slavery — *the worsted mills in the town and neighbourhood of Bradford ! ! !* . . . Thousands of little children, both male and female, *but principally female*, from seven to fourteen years of age, are daily *compelled to labour* from six o'clock in the morning to seven in the evening, with only — Britons, blush while you read it ! — *with only thirty minutes allowed for eating and recreation.* Poor infants ! ye are indeed sacrificed at the shrine of avarice, *without even the solace of the negro slave* ; ye are, no more than he is, *free agents* ; ye are compelled to work as long as the *necessity* of your needy parents may require, or the cold-blooded avarice of your worse than barbarian masters may demand ! Ye live in the boasted land of freedom, and *feel* and mourn that *ye are slaves*, and slaves without the only comfort which the negro has. He knows it is his sordid, mercenary master's interest that he should *live*, be *strong* and *healthy*. *Not so with you.* Ye are doomed to labour from morning to night for one who cares not how soon your weak and tender frames are stretched to breaking ! You are not mercifully valued at so much per head ! this would assure you at least (even with the worst and most cruel masters) of the mercy shown to their own labouring beasts. No, no ! your soft and delicate limbs are tired and fagged, and jaded, at only *so much per week*, and when your joints can act no longer, your emaciated frames are cast aside, the boards on which you lately toiled and wasted life away are instantly supplied with other victims who in this boasted land of liberty are HIRED — not sold — as slaves, and daily forced to *hear* that they are free."

Oastler's letter ended with a passionate plea for legislative protection, in the name of Christian love. Had not Christ said of the children — " Of such is the kingdom of Heaven " ? Surely the men of Yorkshire would fling off this " hellish bondage ", and set free, not only the negro slaves, but the factory slaves as well.

This letter did not at once appear. Edward Baines, the formidable editor of *The Leeds Mercury*, did not publish it for more than a fortnight, or without pressure. In the meantime Oastler was feverishly at work verifying what John Wood had told him, and discovering even worse horrors of the factory system. He found that the evils were not confined to the worsted trade, or to Bradford. They were much the same in the woollen mills — in Leeds and Huddersfield and Halifax, in fact throughout the West Riding and further afield. He began to accumulate appalling evidence of cruel beatings and lashings by overseers, to keep the weary children awake ; dreadful medical testimony about twisted and stunted bodies and warped minds, and dire reports of the poverty which compelled parents to expose their children to these horrors. He found sympathetic manufacturers who agreed with him, or half-agreed ; but he found many more who shrugged their shoulders and explained to him that the children were really quite well and happy, that hard work kept them out of mischief, and that, even if there were abuses, any attempt to mend them by legislation would make matters worse. Lower output would mean lower wages, and worse starvation : it would be fatal to interfere with parental responsibility or freedom of contract ; and in any case nothing could be done in view of foreign competition until the Corn Laws had been repealed, and the cost of production thus brought down to a reasonable level.

Oastler listened to these contentions with outraged fury : he wanted to know which came first — the claims of avarice or those of Christian decency and righteousness. His letter had created a considerable sensation, and had led to a prolonged newspaper controversy which spread from *The Leeds Mercury* to other papers, and he found himself called upon to substantiate his charges in face of a widespread desire to believe that they were not true. He found himself suddenly elevated to the leadership of the factory reform movement in Yorkshire, and involved in a terrific controversy which cut right across party allegiances in the great political struggle which was then beginning over the question of parliamentary Reform.

Oastler did not originate the factory movement, which had been active in Lancashire long before his visit to John Wood had aroused him to a sense of the importance of the problem of ' factory slavery '. The struggle had begun chiefly in Lancashire, where the cotton industry had adopted power-production and the factory system a long way in advance of the woollen and worsted trades of the West Riding. The elder Sir Robert Peel's Act of 1802, often called " the first Factory Act ", had been designed to afford some protection to the pauper apprentices who were then being transported in large numbers to work in the Lancashire cotton-spinning mills ; and Peel's second Act, of 1819, originally projected by Robert Owen, had also been confined to cotton mills, in which alone the factory system was at that date far advanced. But by 1830 the factory system, based sometimes on steam but sometimes still on water power, was spreading fast in the woollen and worsted and other textile trades besides cotton, bringing with it the same problems of overwork and extensive use of child labour to operate the new machines. The cotton trade, which had at that stage virtually no competitors except the native producers in the Far East, had by 1830 accepted the inevitability of some measure of legal regulation. The Act of 1819 had been followed by John Cam Hobhouse's Act of 1825, which had established a twelve hours day for young persons under sixteen, exclusive of an hour and a half for meals — thirteen hours and a half in all, with a nine hours day on Saturdays. These Acts were very imperfectly enforced, as there was no inspection save that provided by the local justices ; and the rule that no child should be employed under nine years of age was made inoperative by the lack of any general registration of births, and by the terms of the Act of 1825, which provided that the employer should be held blameless for employing children under the legal age when parents or guardians had mis-stated their ages. Nevertheless, the principle of regulation had been laid down and accepted in the cotton industry, and Oastler's first letter to *The Leeds Mercury* contrasted the protection accorded to the children in the cotton factories with the totally unprotected condition of the Yorkshire children. To have secured even the smallest amount of legal regulation was of some account ; for it caused a minority of scrupulous employers to obey the law and to be eager for its enforcement on their less scrupulous competitors. The support given by a number of Lancashire employers to factory reform was partly accounted for by the fact that, having accepted the principle of legal regulation, the better employers were disposed to press it further, in order to eliminate unfair competition. But it was also of account that the cotton lords had little to fear from foreign competition, whereas the employers in the woollen, worsted, linen, and silk trades were much more afraid both of the loss of foreign markets and of competition in the home market from the cheaper substitute, cotton cloth.

In 1830, when Oastler began his campaign, John Cam Hobhouse, the sponsor of the Act of 1825, was actually promoting in cooperation with Lord Morpeth, one of the M.P.s for West Riding, a further Bill, designed to extend regulation to all the textile trades. This Bill of 1830 proposed to establish for all textile factory workers under eighteen years of age a maximum working day of eleven and a half hours, *plus* an hour and a half for meals, with a day of eight and a half hours on Saturdays. The Bill was sponsored by a number of employers in Lancashire and a few in Yorkshire, and seemed at first to have fair prospects of success. But during the early months of 1831 the Halifax and Glasgow employers organised a big movement against it, demanding that its provisions should be confined to the cotton industry. Hobhouse and Morpeth took fright at the strength of the opposition, and, fearing to lose the whole Bill, agreed to limit it to cotton factories in the same way as previous Acts had been limited. They justified the course they had taken partly by urging that it was necessary if the Bill was to be saved, and partly by the contention that the main pressure for it had come from the cotton districts, where alone the workers were at this date at all effectively organised. John Doherty had organised the cotton spinners into a ' Grand General Union ' in 1829, and this Union, with the support of friendly employers, had been mainly instrumental in pressing for further legislation. The Yorkshiremen, on the other hand, were in 1831 only beginning to create any sort of ' General Union ' ; and Oastler's movement was still too young to have played any effective part in shaping the course of events.

Hobhouse's action in agreeing to drop his proposal to extend legislative protection to the woollen and worsted trades had an immediate influence on the course of the factory movement. Up to that point, Oastler and his friends had been concentrating their energies mainly on canvassing employers and Members of Parliament in support of Hobhouse's Bill ; but the defection of Hobhouse and Morpeth convinced them that nothing would be done to end ' Yorkshire Slavery ' until the workers themselves took the matter in hand. On October 20, 1831, Oastler published in *The Leeds Intelligencer* a letter addressed " to the working classes of the West Riding ", in the course of which he wrote : " For the future your course is plain. Let no promises of support from any quarter sink you to inactivity. *Consider that you must manage this cause yourselves*, nor think a single step is taken so long as any constitutional effort is left untried. Establish, instantly establish, committees in every manufacturing town and village, to collect information and *publish facts*. The public, generally, do not know what it is ; then tell them how it has gone on destroying the health and morals of the people. . . . Tell how the factory system beggars the industrious domestic manufacturers ! Count, if you can, the hundreds of respectable families who have been driven from comfort and independence by the all-powerful operation of this monopolising system ! Point to the poor rates, and show how it has filled the ranks of the paupers, and never forget that these ' liberal factory masters ' are not quite so ' liberal ' as the tyrannical slave holders. . . . On every election for Members of Parliament, use your influence throughout the empire to prevent any man being returned who will not distinctly and unequivocally pledge himself to support a ' Ten Hours a Day and a Time-book Bill '."

This appeal was the real beginning of the Short Time Committees, which were thereafter to be the main continuous agents in the campaign for factory reform. Oastler set out to organise these Committees on a basis which would allow of collaboration between operatives, friendly employers, parsons and dissenting ministers, physicians and other middle-class reformers alive to factory evils, irrespective of party allegiances or differences in religious outlook. In this spirit he entered in 1831 into the ' Fixby Hall Compact ' with the Huddersfield operatives, as the basis on which the campaign was to be conducted. At first, Oastler had proposed that he and the workmen, on account of their political differences, should work separately, but on parallel lines. " They thought differently. After a good deal of conversation, we agreed to work together, with the understanding, that parties in politics, and sects in religion, should not be allowed to interfere between us. That agreement has never been broken."

It was at this stage that Michael Thomas Sadler, the Tory M.P. for Newark, became an important figure in the factory movement. Sadler, a Leeds man and an old friend of Oastler's, had denounced the evil social effects of the factory system as far back as 1829 in his book on the Irish problem, and had made himself known as a strong opponent of the ' Malthusian ' doctrine of ' surplus population ' and the subsistence theory of wages. In face of Hobhouse's defection Sadler, probably under Oastler's influence, now proposed to take up the factory question in Parliament, and to introduce a Ten Hours Bill, applying to all the textile trades, and going a long way beyond what Hobhouse had originally suggested. Oastler then urged that Sadler, who was due to lose his Newark seat if the Reform Bill became law, should be adopted as factory reform candidate for Leeds, which was expecting to receive the right to elect two Members. This angered the Whigs, who accused Oastler and Sadler of trying to make party capital for the Tories out of the factory issue. Hobhouse wrote to Oastler describing Sadler's Ten Hours proposal as utterly visionary and impracticable in view of the state of parliamentary opinion, and also objecting strongly to any attempt to make factory reform an election issue. Hobhouse's own Act, limited to cotton factories, had just become law ; and he was very discouraging about the prospects of anything further being done. In these circumstances the newly founded Short Time Committees transferred their allegiance from Hobhouse to Sadler as the parliamentary spokesman of the movement, and Sadler was enthusiastically accepted as the prospective Tory Factory Reform candidate for Leeds as soon as the Reform Bill became law.

In March 1832 Sadler moved, in the still unreformed House of Commons, the second reading of the Ten Hours Bill, which was strongly opposed. Sadler, in order to avoid defeat, had to agree that the matter should be referred to a Parliamentary Committee of Enquiry, and the factory reformers were thereafter busy gathering evidence for this body, and also organising great demonstrations in favour of Sadler's Bill throughout the textile districts. Most notable of these demonstrations was the vast county meeting which Oastler gathered together at York in April 1832. Contingents, facing great hardships, marched to York from all the factory towns and villages, many walking as much as fifty or sixty miles there and back. Despite many difficulties — including the breakdown of the commissariat — the great meeting was held entirely without disorder ; and Oastler managed to assemble on the platforms many notables who agreed to give their support to the cause. Lord Morpeth, soon to be denounced as the arch-enemy of the factory reformers, presented in June the county petition in favour of the Bill. In August there was a similar great gathering in Manchester, which Sadler and Oastler addressed ; and they also set going in London a ' Metropolitan Society for the Improvement of the Condition of Factory Children ', with the Duke of Sussex as patron, and William Allen, Robert Owen's Quaker partner at New Lanark, as president.

All these events, it must be borne in mind, occurred while the Reform Bill agitation was at its height. In the autumn the House of Lords at last gave way, and the Reform Bill became law. A General Election followed at once ; and Sadler, standing at Leeds as a single-handed Tory Factory Reformer against two Whigs — John Marshall, a leading millowner, and Thomas Babington Macaulay — was beaten by a few hundred votes, polling 1596 to Marshall's 2012 and Macaulay's 1984. The Short Time Committees had to find a new sponsor to take charge of Sadler's Bill in the Reformed House of Commons.

To Oastler and his friends it seemed natural to seek such a sponsor among the Tories rather than among the Whigs or Radicals. The Rev. G. S. Bull, Vicar of Brierley, near Bradford, a militant parson — known to his enemies as ' The Bruiser ' — who had joined Oastler's crusade in 1831, and had become chief editor of its organ, *The British Labourer's Protector and Factory Child's Friend*, was sent to London to look out for a suitable successor to Sadler as the parliamentary protagonist of the cause. He lighted on Lord Ashley, later Earl of Shaftesbury, but then a young Tory M.P. sitting for the county of Dorset. Ashley, a devout Evangelical, agreed to take up the fight on behalf of the children, and to present to the new Parliament a revised version of Sadler's Ten Hours Bill ; and the Short Time Committees in both Yorkshire and Lancashire, under Oastler's influence, agreed to accept Ashley's leadership.

This was naturally unpleasing to the Whigs, who saw in it yet another manœuvre designed to capture the factory movement for the Tory party; and after Ashley had given notice of his intention to reintroduce Sadler's Bill, Morpeth tried to get in his way with an alternative measure based on the much less drastic proposals which had emerged from the Parliamentary Committee of the previous year. In effect, the Whig Government had no intention of allowing the Ten Hours Bill to become law in face of the hostility of the main body of the manufacturers. But, in view of the widespread agitation in the North, and of the large body of influential support commanded by the factory reformers, it realised the impossibility of doing nothing. Accordingly, it tried to temporise. Wilson Patten and Morpeth moved in April that a new enquiry should be held into conditions in the factory districts, on the plea that Sadler's Committee had considered the evidence for, but not the evidence against, the Bill. In the ensuing discussion the forces were nearly balanced, and the Whig motion for further enquiry was carried by only one vote.

The new enquiry was to be of a radically different character from the old. It was to be, not a Committee of Members of Parliament before which witnesses would be summoned in London, but a Board of Commissioners, expert investigators who would themselves visit the factory districts and collect their evidence at first hand on the spot. It was to be an experiment in the new Benthamite technique of social investigation, which was being used simultaneously for enquiring into the Poor Law; and, appropriately, Bentham's pupil, Edwin Chadwick, was to be one of the Commissioners.

The factory reformers were furious at having their Bill side-tracked by the proposal for a new enquiry, and they entirely refused to believe that the Commissioners meant business. Accordingly, the Short Time Committees throughout the factory areas decided to boycott the Commissioners, and to refuse to tender any evidence. But in truth Chadwick and his colleagues did mean business, though not necessarily the sort of business that Oastler and his followers wanted. The Commissioners were appointed in April 1833, and by May they were already in Lancashire and Yorkshire, pursuing their investigations, and doing their best to persuade the Short Time Committees to revise their boycott policy. The factory reformers, however, would not budge. Instead of presenting evidence, they organised demonstrations. The Commissioners, first in Manchester and then in Leeds and Bradford, were met with mass processions through the streets, and especially with mass demonstrations of the factory children, who presented addresses, drafted by their elders, demanding the immediate enactment of the Ten Hours Bill.

Undeterred by this unfavourable reception, the Commissioners gathered what evidence they could. With a celerity unexampled in the annals of official enquiry, they presented their report to the Government before the end of June. The evidence laid before them, despite the boycott, confirmed in all essential particulars the assertions of Sadler and Ashley ; and the Commissioners concluded that the conditions of child labour in the factories were unquestionably bad for the physique and mind of the sufferers ; that the children could not be regarded as free agents ; and that the case for legislation had been made out.

Before the report was received, Ashley's Bill had come on for its second reading in the House of Commons. From its reception, Ashley reached the conclusion that there was no hope of its acceptance as it stood ; and, in agreement with Sadler, he decided to jettison certain clauses in the hope that the Government would accept the rest, including the ten hours day. The clauses to which the strongest objection had been taken had been those which laid upon the employer the obligation of obtaining reliable evidence of a child's age before engagement, and those which provided that employers guilty of repeated offences against the Act should be punished by imprisonment, and not merely by fines — which were apt to amount to a good deal less than the profit resulting from the offence. These two clauses Ashley now proposed to give up ; but when the news of this reached Yorkshire there was great anger. Both Oastler and Bull denounced the proposal as a betrayal of the cause ; and when John Doherty, who had been representing the Short Time Committees in London during the negotiations over the Bill, was sent down to Yorkshire to explain Ashley's point of view at a meeting on

Wibsey Low Moor called to press for the speedy enactment of the Ten Hours, the delegates strongly supported Oastler against Ashley. The mischief, however, had been done.

This lightening of the Bill did not reconcile the Government to acceptance of what was left. In July Lord Althorp, on its behalf, announced that he was prepared to go no further than a maximum day of twelve hours for workers between thirteen and eighteen years of age, and an eight hours day for children between nine and thirteen, with even less stringent provisions in the case of silk factories. In the ensuing division the Government beat the factory reformers by the big majority of 238 to 93. Ashley thereupon announced that he would proceed no further with his Bill, and the Government was left to carry through its own proposals. Althorp's Act, which was thereafter rapidly carried into law, is notable in the annals of factory legislation as the measure which first extended regulation to the textile trades generally, and provided for Government inspectors to supervise its execution. But the regulations which it laid down bitterly disappointed the factory reformers. They embodied, subject to certain delays before full enforcement, what Althorp had proposed earlier, and no more.

Thus ended this phase of the parliamentary struggle, in what the operatives regarded as sheer defeat ; for they had no belief that the new inspectors would take their duties seriously, or that even the weakened provisions of the Act would be enforced. There followed a revulsion of feeling which for more than two years swept the issue of factory reform by legislation right into the background. This was the time when a great wave of Trade Unionism swept over the country, and Robert Owen's doctrines of Socialism and Cooperation became the vogue. The Yorkshire operatives flocked into a great secret Trades Union which had its head-quarters in Leeds, and speedily became involved in a life-and-death struggle with the employers. John Fielden joined forces with Robert Owen in creating the Society for National Regeneration, which appealed to the operatives with a demand for the Eight Hours Day, to be won, not by legislation, but by direct industrial action, in the form of a concerted refusal to work beyond eight hours. Owen, seizing on the occasion, tried to unite all the Trade Union forces under the banner of a Grand National Consolidated Trades Union, which was to make a speedy end of the profit system, and replace it by cooperative or guild production, with Equitable Labour Exchanges to arrange for the mutual barter of the workers' products.

The Government promptly met these movements by a declaration of war on the Trades Unions. Melbourne wrote encouragingly to the Yorkshire masters who had announced their intention of discharging every worker who refused to renounce membership of a Trades Union. Early in 1834 the Yorkshire operatives were driven by a sheer starvation to give way, and to announce the dissolution of their Trades Union. The arrest and sentence to transportation of the six Dorchester labourers who had administered an ' unlawful oath ' in admitting members to a section of the Grand National Consolidated Trades Union was a further proclamation of the authorities' determination to wage relentless war upon the Unions. In one area after another employers presented the ' document ' demanding renunciation of Trades Union membership. The flimsy internal structure of the Grand National Consolidated Trades Union collapsed under the strain ; and in the course of the summer Owen announced its dissolution, and proceeded to reconstruct on an alternative basis of merely ' Moral Force ' his plans for the speedy establishment of a ' New Moral World '.

From these developments, a full account of which would be out of place in this study,[1] Oastler stood aloof, though many of his supporters took part in them. He was no more in sympathy with Owen's New Moral World than with Universal Suffrage ; and he stood aside until the great Trades Union campaign had met with utter defeat. Most of the leading figures in the factory movement took the view that the demand for an eight hours day was utterly impracticable, and that the only sensible course was to go on pressing Parliament for the Ten Hours Bill. Oastler and Bull, unlike Fielden, refused to associate themselves with the Society

[1] For such an account see my book *Attempts at General Union, 1829–1834*, first printed in 1939 as a contribution to *The International Review of Social History*.

for National Regeneration. Their policy was to work with the progressive employers ; and most of these were driven into sharp antagonism by Owen's Socialist schemes. Moreover, the Owenite movement was strongly hostile to the Churches ; and the driving force of the middle-class element in the factory movement came from the religious employers.

While the workers were making their great ineffectual push for the Cooperative Commonwealth, the Government was busy pressing through Parliament the Poor Law Amendment Act of 1834. To this measure, which was supported by the great majority of Tories as well as Whigs in the House of Commons, Oastler was quite as violently opposed as the handful of Radicals, headed by William Cobbett and John Fielden, who fought every step of its progress in Parliament. He was opposed to it, both as an " Old-fashioned Tory " and as a friend of the factory workers. As a Tory who believed in patriarchal government, he hated the new policy of centralised State control which was embodied in the proposal to create a central Board of Poor Law Commissioners — the ' Three Bashaws of Somerset House ' — to whose authority the new local Boards of Guardians were to be subject. In his view relief was a right of the common people, and the control of it ought to be in the hands of the aristocracy, their national leaders. He was no less opposed to the principles which lay at the basis of the new law — ' deterrence ', by making the conditions of poor relief as irksome and unpleasant as possible, and ' less eligibility ', which meant that the circumstances of the recipient of poor relief were to be made, irrespective of need, worse than those of the least favourably situated workers in ordinary employment. He detested the notion of forcing the destitute into workhouses, where the sexes would be segregated and families broken up, instead of giving outdoor relief to the needy in the good old alms-giving way. Oastler's energies were diverted for the time from factory reform to opposing the New Poor Law.

For the time being, however, the ' Three Bashaws ' were making no attempt to enforce the law in the industrial North, even after it had become an Act. Their attention was concentrated on the agricultural districts, in which the Speenhamland system of subsidising wages out of the poor rates had been extensively applied. Their immediate measures touched the factory districts in only one respect. In response to demands from the factory owners, the Commissioners began to take steps to move surplus labour from the agricultural counties to the industrial areas, wherever they could find factories ready to employ them. This policy was bitterly resented by the factory workers, who regarded it as an attempt to beat down wages by supplying the employers with cheap unorganised labour. Oastler joined in their protests, and used the occasion to denounce the entire spirit of the Poor Law Act, and to counsel organised resistance to its enforcement.

During 1834 and most of 1835 the agitation for the Ten Hours Bill was practically in abeyance. In the summer of 1835 Oastler made up his mind that the time had come to revive it. Despite the disapproval of some of his more respectable coadjutors, he attempted to do this by writing a series of letters to the unstamped Radical newspapers which were then widely read among the working classes. The regular stamped newspapers, he urged, did not reach the workers : the excessive tax on newspapers, levied in order to check the growth of the popular press, made them much too expensive for ordinary wage-earners to buy. If the workers were to organise a new factory crusade instead of wasting their energies in visionary schemes of cooperation, or Trade Union action, or parliamentary Reform, the approach must be made to them through the journals which they actually read.

Oastler's letters were effective in bringing about a revival of the factory agitation. But the next organised move for a Factory Bill came, not from Yorkshire, but from Lancashire, where in December 1835 delegates from the cotton spinners met Charles Hindley and other Lancashire M.P.s, and put forward renewed proposals for a Ten Hours Bill. Following up this meeting, a big delegate conference, organised by the spinners, was held in Manchester in January 1836, when delegates were appointed to go to London and endeavour, with the help of Hindley and Brotherton and a few other friendly M.P.s, to secure a favourable reception for a new

Bill. But the delegates, when they reached London, found that their first task must be to beat off an attack upon what Parliament had already agreed to grant. The Act of 1833 had conceded two years' delay before the full enforcement of the restrictions on child labour, for those under thirteen years of age, to eight hours a day — or rather to a maximum working week of 48 hours. Poulett Thomson, President of the Board of Trade and a strong opponent of the reformers, now proposed that this restriction should apply only to children under twelve years of age instead of thirteen.

This news created great indignation in the factory districts. Ashley opposed it in Parliament, and the Government won on a division by only two votes. This was as good as a defeat ; and when, in June, Hindley asked for leave to bring in a Ten Hours Bill, the Government met him with a promise that the Act of 1833 should be fully enforced. The parliamentary leaders of the campaign thereupon withdrew their own Bill and agreed to give the existing Act a fair trial, provided that it was effectively administered. But the threat to the twelve-year-olds had thoroughly roused the factory districts ; and the Short Time Committees from this time onwards resumed full activity in Yorkshire as well as Lancashire.

It was, indeed, generally admitted that the Act of 1833 was being extensively disregarded. The new Factory Inspectors were doing their best ; but many employers were openly announcing their refusal to obey the law, and benches of magistrates, consisting largely of factory owners, were refusing to convict offenders. Oastler set out on a campaign to further the cause of strict enforcement ; and in the course of this campaign he visited Blackburn, where a peculiarly flagrant case of refusal by the magistrates to administer the law had just occurred. The magistrates, he was told, had described the Act of 1833 as " Oastler's Law ", and had refused to have anything to do with it, contemptuously dismissing complaints that it was being infringed. Finding some of these magistrates in his audience, Oastler addressed himself to them personally : " You say that the law is mine ; I say that it is the law of the land, which you have sworn to enforce. . . . Now, if the law of the land, intended to protect the lives of the factory children, is to be disregarded, and there is to be no power to enforce it, it becomes my duty, as the guardian of the factory children, to enquire whether, in the eye of the law of England, their lives or your spindles are most entitled to the law's protection. If the King has not power to enforce the factory law, I must and I will strive to force even you to enforce that law." Oastler then turned to the general body of the audience and said : " If, after this, your magistrates should refuse to listen to your complaints under the Factory Act, and again refer you to me, bring with you your children, and tell them to ask their grandmothers for a few of their old knitting-needles, which I will instruct them how to apply to the spindles in a way which will teach these law-defying millowner magistrates to have respect even to ' Oastler's law ', as they have wrongly designated the factory law ".

It is not surprising that this speech created a great outcry against Oastler, who was denounced as a Luddite. He stuck by his words, and repeated them in a pamphlet, *The Law or the Needle*, which had a wide circulation. This, coupled with his incitements to resist the Poor Law, led to trouble with his employer, Thornhill, as well as to protests from many of the millowner supporters of factory reform.

Meanwhile, in view of the gathering strength of the agitation, there was growing up a middle party which favoured a compromise, on the basis of an Eleven Hours Bill. Baines, of *The Leeds Mercury*, sponsored this movement, which was strongly opposed by the main body of the reformers. Ashley, in Parliament, continued to press for the Ten Hours ; and in 1835 his motion was barely defeated by 119 votes to 111. The Whig Government, realising the need for further action, introduced in 1839 a Bill involving no new principles, but designed to promote better enforcement ; but when Ashley carried an amendment for the inclusion of silk mills, the Government withdrew the Bill. Ashley and Hindley successfully moved for a new Committee of Enquiry into the condition of the factory children, and Ashley and Brotherton subsequently secured the inclusion of the coal mines within its scope. This enquiry produced an immense mass of evidence about the intolerable conditions of juvenile and female labour, and led up both to Ashley's Act of 1842, forbidding the employment of women and children underground in coal mines, and to the Factory Act of 1844. Finally, in 1847, while Ashley had temporarily lost his seat in Parliament as a penalty for voting in favour of the repeal of the Corn Laws, Fielden succeeded in carrying the Ten Hours Bill, for which the reformers had been struggling so many years.

These later stages of the factory movement will not be discussed in this essay. Oastler was concerned in them, but he was no longer the leader. In 1837, when the Anti-Poor Law agitation was at its height, he stood at a by-election for Huddersfield as a Tory opponent of the law and friend of factory reform, and lost only by 50 votes, polling 290 against 340 for his Whig rival. At the General Election the same year he stood again, and lost only by 323 votes to 301. It was widely believed that he might have been elected if he had not ruined his prospects by saying roundly that, as a sound Protestant, he would vote for the repeal of the Catholic Emancipation Act if the chance occurred.

But his affairs were rapidly approaching a crisis. In 1838 Thornhill gave him the choice between dismissal and renunciation of his Anti-Poor Law campaign ; and he accepted dismissal. His angry supporters issued a placard reflecting on Thornhill's conduct and character ; and Thornhill, deeming him responsible, began proceedings against him for recovery of the debts accumulated during his stewardship. Oastler did not dispute the claims, but pleaded that he had spent the money on Thornhill's behalf, and ought to be exonerated in fairness, if not in law. But Thornhill was angry ; and Oastler, after two years of dilatory proceedings, during which he was mainly in London in connection with the case, was lodged in the Fleet Prison until he should be able to discharge his debt.

He remained there, as we have seen, for more than three years. His confinement was as little irksome as such a thing could be to a man of his energetic temperament and out-of-door habits. His supporters sent him endless presents, of food, money, and indeed all manner of useful things. He was visited by many distinguished people, and by a host of admirers previously unknown to him. From the beginning of 1841 until his liberation in February 1844, he edited from prison his weekly *Fleet Papers*, in which he mingled accounts of his troubles with attacks on the Whigs and the Poor Law, and demands for the Ten Hours Bill. But the pen was not Oastler's natural weapon. He was a speaker and organiser of immense energy, and not by instinct a writer. *The Fleet Papers* were bought by his admirers ; but they did not exert much influence.

Indeed, Oastler's main influence during these years was indirect. In 1842 his admirers, including a number of distinguished Tories as well as his working-class friends, started the Oastler Liberation Fund in order to collect the money to pay his debts. Meetings were organised all over the country ; and Oastler's supporters put them to a double use — to raise money on his behalf and to conduct propaganda for factory reform. A substantial sum was collected, and endeavours were made to persuade Thornhill to abate his demands. But Thornhill was obdurate ; and it was not until February 1844 that a few of Oastler's wealthy supporters advanced the balance of the sum required, and thus procured his release. He came out of prison while the agitation which accompanied the debates on the Factory Bill of 1844 was at its height, and attended a great reception held at Huddersfield in his honour. But confinement and trouble had told upon him, and his wife was also ill. He retired into the country to restore his health, and hers ; but the following year she died, and the blow was sore. He went to live at Guildford, in Surrey, upon a small income provided by his generous friends. He was not able to take much part, owing to ill-health, in the closing stages of the struggle for the Ten Hours Bill.

Thereafter his health improved. In 1850 he supervised the publication of a collected edition of his speeches ; and in 1851 he started a new periodical, *The Home*, in which, until 1855, he continued to expound his peculiar species of Tory philanthropy. In 1856 his Huddersfield friends raised a further testimonial on his behalf ; and he lived on, in modest contentment, until 1861, when he died at Harrogate and was buried in the county of his birth.

Richard Oastler was never a thinker. He lived by impulse, grounded upon tradition. His sympathies were intense, and his devotion and courage without bounds. As far as he had a philosophy, it was one of aristocracy, of patriarchal benevolence as the duty of the ruling class. As a description of his political attitude, his own account, in *The Fleet Papers*, of what he answered when the Duke of Wellington asked him to define a Tory cannot be bettered. " My Lord Duke, I mean ' a place for everything, and everything in its place '. ' A good day's wages for a fair day's work.' The King, happy, serene, and venerated in his palace, — the nobles, happy, secure, and honoured in their castles, — the bankers, merchants, and manufacturers, happy, secure, and beloved in their mansions, — the small tradesmen and shopkeepers happy, secure, and respected in their houses ; and the labourers happy, secure, and as much respected as the best of them, in their cottages. And I mean also, that they should all be enabled, humbly, reverently, and rationally, to worship the God of their fathers. That is what I mean by Toryism, my Lord Duke." And further, anent the Whigs and middle-class Liberals, " Call it by what party name you may, it is all *Malthusianism*, which impiously denies the right of the poor to live ".

Such was Oastler, the Factory King — the Tory of the old school who would have no truck with the Charter, but was nevertheless one of the makers of the Chartist movement. For his eloquence and energy both made the factory agitation the powerful thing that it became, and roused the North to that fury of protest against the Malthusian Poor Law which his enforced removal from Yorkshire in 1838 handed over ready-made to Feargus O'Connor as the instrument of the Chartist campaign.

NOTE

It is a common delusion that, in the struggle for factory reform during the second quarter of the nineteenth century, the Tories were the friends, and the Whigs the enemies, of the factory workers. It is said that the Whigs and Radicals attacked the landowning interest, and the land-owners retaliated by voting for factory legislation. But in truth party allegiance had very little to do with the matter : support and opposition cut right across party alignments, and there were protagonists of the factory movement on both sides of the House of Commons. For example, in the critical division of May 18, 1844, there voted for Lord Ashley's amendment 61 Tories and 78 Whigs and Radicals sitting for British seats, and also 22 Irish Members, of whom 2 were Tories, and the rest Whigs or Nationalists. Disraeli voted with Ashley, and Peel against him. Macaulay voted for the Ten Hours, and John Bright against. Lord John Russell was for, and C. P. Villiers against. Other supporters included Palmerston, and opponents Gladstone. It is true that on this occasion the Tories were in office, and Ashley's amendment was directed against the Tory Government's scheme for a twelve hours day. This caused some Tory defections ; but the essential point remains. There were Whigs and Liberals of the Cobdenite school who were inveterate opponents of factory reform ; but equally there were plenty of Tories who were no less set in opposition.

The delusion that the Tories were the friends of the workers and the Whigs their enemies over the factory issue has been greatly encouraged by the fact that the two best-known spokesmen of the Ten Hours movement — Lord Ashley and Richard Oastler — were both Tories, albeit their brands of Toryism were very different. It is the case that in Yorkshire the drive for factory reform came mainly from the Tories. Michael Sadler, the original sponsor of the Ten Hours Bill, was a Tory ; and so were many of Oastler's principal coadjutors outside Parliament. In Yorkshire, the Tories were apt to appear before the electors as upholders of factory reform against Whig and Liberal representatives of the manufacturing interests. In Lancashire, on the other hand, the Members of Parliament who did most to further the cause of the factory operatives were all either Whigs or Radicals. John Fielden, who finally secured the Ten Hours Act in 1847, was a Radical ; and both Charles Hindley and Joseph Brotherton, the next best friends of the movement who sat for Lancashire seats, were advanced Liberals. If Factory Reform was allied with Toryism in the Yorkshire woollen district, among the Lancashire cotton centres it was as closely connected with one sort of Radicalism as it was hotly opposed by another.

IV

Thomas Attwood

THOMAS ATTWOOD, the Birmingham banker who presented to Parliament the Chartist National Petition of 1839, is generally dismissed in the history books as a "currency maniac" who joined the Chartist movement solely for the purpose of pushing his ridiculous monetary ideas. This is a curiously lopsided view. It is true enough that Attwood did hold certain opinions about currency and its relation to national prosperity with a fanaticism which caused these opinions of his to intrude into all his sayings and doings ; but his views on monetary questions were by no means nonsense, and, quite apart from them, there can be no doubt that his devotion to the cause of the people was entirely sincere. He was never in any sense of the term a Socialist : he believed in a reconciliation of interests between the middle and working classes that would leave the capitalists in full possession of the economic field and at the same time ensure the labourer of a square deal and a decent wage. He was never a Chartist in any sense in which Chartism implied class-antagonism between employers and workers ; and because Chartism did speedily come to imply this he soon felt that there was no place for him in the Chartist ranks. But he was a sincere Radical ; he believed in Universal Suffrage and the rest of the main political demands of the Chartists not merely because he hoped to capture the moment for his currency projects, but also because he held firmly that the claims of the main body of the people to good living conditions came first, and that this claim would never be put first by the politicians until they were made directly responsible to the people at large.

Attwood's currency views came into the picture because he was convinced that bad monetary policy was the main source of popular misery, and that a good monetary policy would bring prosperity to middle and working classes alike — indeed to all classes except the fundholders and other parasites who lived on fixed incomes and not on the rewards of their labour and enterprise. As a banker, he might have been expected to sympathise with the financial oligarchy ; but it must be remembered that he was a country banker, interested much more in the financing of railways and industrial enterprises than in lending money to Governments or profiting by low prices which meant depression and unemployment in the industrial areas. Railways needed goods and passengers to transport ; factories did best when the people were well endowed with purchasing power. The banking company of Spooner and Attwood could hope to prosper if Birmingham prospered, and not otherwise. Thomas Attwood had no fellow-feeling with London bankers who wanted to make money scarce and dear : his sympathy was with the active *entrepreneurs* who were crying out for credits, and with the workers whose well-being depended, in his view, much more on plentiful openings for employment than on the cheapness of goods.

Attwood had been writing and speaking about currency reform for more than twenty years before the birth of the Chartist movement. It is true enough that his monetary ideas came first and his Radicalism later. In after years, his critics used to put it about that he had been a Tory in his youth ; but he always denied this, and it seems to be based only on the fact that he came of Tory stock. His father, Mathias Attwood, founder of the bank, was a Tory ; and so was his elder brother, Mathias, who became the head of the associated bank in London and sat in Parliament both before and after the Reform Act as a Tory M.P. Thomas may have been a Tory in childhood ; but from the moment when he first took part in politics he was certainly not on the Tory side. His early political activities were indeed undertaken mainly in support of the manufacturing interest. He attacked the Orders in Council in 1812 and the monopoly of the East India Company in 1813. But even at this stage he was working in close connection with the Birmingham artisans as well as with the manufacturers. It was the artisan population of Birmingham, and not the middle class, that

presented him with a valuable testimonial in 1813 in gratitude
for his efforts on their behalf against the Orders in Council.
He was even then working closely with George Edmonds,
later Town Clerk of Birmingham, but at that time the
principal leader of the Birmingham working men. Those
who accused Attwood of Toryism probably meant little more
than that he had never been a Whig. He was a business
man of Tory antecedents, who came into politics at all only
when he saw cause for intervention on a particular issue. He
was not a regular politician until, in January 1830, he founded
the Birmingham Political Union. He was a banker, and most
of his time was taken up with the affairs of a country bank
through a period during which country banking offered fully
as many dangers as opportunities. He had to face as a
banker the many crises and depressions of the years which
followed the Napoleonic Wars — years of steadily falling
prices and of appalling recurrent distress for the workers
and reversals of fortune for the bankers and industrial
employers and farmers alike. He became a regular politician
only when he had become convinced that nothing short of
Radical Reform would set things right ; and he ceased to be a
politician when Radical politics developed in such a way that
he had to choose between the workers and the middle class.
He would not choose either : he was convinced that he held,
in his proposals for currency reform, the means of satisfying both. But neither would listen. The Chartists were
antagonising the middle-class Radicals by their threats of
violence ; and the middle-class Radicals preferred the
abolition of the Corn Laws to monetary reform. Attwood
found himself left high and dry ; for though he favoured
Free Trade he was not prepared to make it ' the cause '. At
the end of 1839 he resigned his seat in Parliament, and retired
into private life — hardly to emerge again. He was ill as
well as disappointed ; and before long creeping paralysis
laid hold on him, making him more and more an invalid all
his later years. By the time of his death he was nearly forgotten, even in the city of which he had been for years the
uncrowned king.

Thomas Attwood was born at Halesowen, not far from
Birmingham, in 1783. He was the third son of Mathias

Attwood, already a prosperous Birmingham banker. Thomas was educated first at Halesowen Grammar School and then at Wolverhampton ; and at about the age of seventeen he entered his father's bank. In 1803, when the scare of invasion came with the rupture of the Peace of Amiens, he became a captain in the Loyal Birmingham Volunteers, and held his commission for two years, resigning it in 1805. In 1806 he married Elisabeth Carless, a member of a well-known Tory family, and set up house at Sparkbrook, then a village. Then and throughout his life Attwood had a passion for birds and animals, and was never so happy as when he could bring back from his journeys some new creature to inhabit his garden. He loved stocking fishponds, watching birds, going to see any strange or exotic animal. When his children began to grow, he was for ever bringing them home new pets, which delighted him fully as much as them. Apart from this love for animals he was careless about his surroundings ; and it is clear that, though a banker, he had no passion for money. He lived simply and gave largely of what he had to give. As soon as politics became his absorbing interest, he resigned from his bank, taking only a competence with him. Up to 1830 he was well-to-do. Thereafter his political activities put a heavy strain on his slender financial resources. He never was, or wanted to be, a rich man.

Birmingham in Attwood's young days was a town in which young men came very rapidly to the front. It was growing very fast, and thriving on war orders. But it had no municipal corporation, being still subject to a manorial jurisdiction, which had in practice lapsed largely into the hands of a body of Street Commissioners appointed under a special Act of Parliament. Feudal offices survived in the form of a High Bailiff and a Low Bailiff, who had, however, not many functions. The High Bailiff presided over all meetings of the townsmen, and was usually chosen from among the leading churchmen ; while the Low Bailiff summoned the manorial court leet, and was usually a Dissenter.

In 1811 Attwood, at the age of twenty-eight, was chosen as High Bailiff of Birmingham. This meant little in relation to municipal affairs ; but his period of office coincided with the agitation over the Orders in Council and the threatened war with the United States. This gave his function as summoner and chairman of town meetings an exceptional importance ; for the continental blockade and the trouble with America were reacting disastrously on Birmingham's industries, and employers and workmen alike were up in arms against the Government. Attwood, seconded by his partner, Richard Spooner, put himself at the head of the movement and was sent to London to press the views of his fellow townsmen upon the Ministers and upon Parliament. This mission, in which he achieved considerable success, brought him into contact with leading figures in the political world, and also raised him to a position of great popularity in Birmingham, especially among the artisans. The Orders in Council were greatly modified, though too late to avert the rupture with the United States ; and on his return Attwood found himself a hero. Led by George Edmonds, the artisans subscribed two hundred guineas, mostly in pence, to present him with a specially designed piece of silver celebrating his achievements. He added to their gratitude by taking up the issue of the East India Company's trading monopoly, as the question of renewing the Company's charter was coming up before Parliament. This meant further deputations to London ; and again Attwood was given the credit for the considerable modifications which Parliament decided to make.

On both these occasions Attwood was able to speak as the representative of the views of employers and workmen alike ; for on both questions these classes were united by a common interest. He thus entered politics as the champion of causes in which the ' industrious classes ' were at one against the Government and the monopolists ; and this beginning to his political career was both the foundation of his remarkable ascendancy in later years and a powerful factor in determining his own attitude.

Within two years of the East India agitation came the end of the long war ; and by 1816 distress was everywhere, and worst of all in those places which had thriven most upon war orders and upon export trade. Attwood seems to have played no leading part in the Radical agitations which con-

vulsed Birmingham during the next few years. There is no
record of him in the proceedings of the Hampden Clubs or
in the meeting which chose Sir Charles Wolseley as ' legislatorial attorney ' to represent Birmingham in the counsels
of the nation. Birmingham had at that date no M.P.s of its
own. It was merely part of the county area, and such of its
inhabitants as had votes voted at the elections for the county
in which their residence was situated. Wolseley therefore
was chosen outside the law, to represent the unrepresented.
Attwood, so far from taking part in the movement, can be
seen from his private correspondence to have been strongly
against it. In 1818 we find him writing from London that
" the poor wretches who clamour for Burdett and Liberty,
meaning Blood and Anarchy, are far worse in ignorance and
stupidity than our Birmingham mobs ". But, as against
this, he did not sign the Loyal Address which was sent up to
London by a number of leading Birmingham citizens in
support of the Government's action against the Radicals.
His political attitude in those days was probably a moderate
Liberalism, equally hostile to Tory reactionaries and to a
Radicalism already in full cry against the manufacturing
interest as well as against the placemen and pensioners of
the old régime.

This was the point at which Attwood came forward
publicly as the exponent of a programme of currency reform.
The famous Bullion Committee of 1810 had proposed a
return, as speedy as possible, to the gold standard ; and this
advice, rejected at the time by the Government, had become
acceptable now that the war was over, and prices, in face of
the general economic dislocation and the cessation of war
demand, were tumbling catastrophically of their own accord.
Ricardo, Huskisson, the younger Peel, and all the orthodox
financiers and economists were in full cry for a return to
gold as the standard of value — a course which meant, in
view of the scarcity of gold, the forcing down of prices to a
low level and an immense increase in the real burden of the
National Debt incurred during the war.

In 1816, when the distress was already deep and widespread, Attwood issued the first of the long series of pamphlets
on the currency in which he attempted to demonstrate the

utter wrongness of the policy followed by the Government, on the advice of the leading London bankers and economists, during the post-war years. It was entitled *The Remedy : or, Thoughts on the Present Distress.* He pursued his argument in 1817 with *Prosperity Restored : or, Reflections on the Cause of the Public Distresses*, and with *A Letter to Nicholas Vansittart* [the Chancellor of the Exchequer] *on the Creation of Money, and on its Action upon National Prosperity*, and in the following year with *Observations on Currency, Population and Pauperism, in Two Letters to Arthur Young*, with whom he had been corresponding extensively, and in substantial agreement, concerning the means of putting an end to the prevailing distress. To these pamphlets succeeded others, too numerous to mention, in which the same arguments were reiterated. Attwood sent his writings to leading Ministers and politicians, such as Peel, Liverpool, and Brougham, receiving always polite answers. From time to time he gave evidence before this Committee or that, and was induced to hope that he had shaken the mind of this or that politician. But the general line of official policy remained unaltered ; and in 1819 the younger Peel's Act was passed, and the restoration of ' cash payments ' by the Bank of England — that is, of the gold standard as a basis for currency and prices — was definitely decreed.

The gist of the doctrine put forward by Attwood in all these pamphlets and in numerous letters, public and private, was that the supply of the means of payment — that is, of money — ought to depend not on the stock of gold held by the Bank of England or available for coinage, but on the productive capacity of the people. His argument was that the supply of money, as long as it was based on the supply of gold, could not be stretched to cover the quantity of goods that the country was in a position to produce except by means of a very sharp fall in prices. Such a fall, however, so far from causing increased production, was bound to inflict heavy losses on farmers and industrialists, who owed debts on which fixed interest payments had to be made : so that they could not reduce their costs in correspondence to the fall in prices unless they reduced wages to a much more than corresponding extent. Wages so reduced, however, would mean an immense decline in popular purchasing power, which would be by itself enough to ensure general depression.

Accordingly, the consequence of a deflationary monetary policy would be disastrous. Employers, unable to cut their costs, in face of fixed charges, by enough to produce at a profit at the previous level of output, would discharge workers and contract production. At the same time they would reduce wages as much as they could, and thus curtail popular purchasing power. Real income would be transferred from the active business men and the workers to the fund-holding classes ; and at the same time its total amount would be reduced by wholesale unemployment.

The remedy, in Attwood's view, lay in maintaining the supply of money at a level high enough to make it worth the while of farmers and industrialists to employ all the available workers. If this were done, there would be no reason why prices should rise beyond a reasonable level ; for the costs of production would be actually lower with full employment than with fixed overhead charges spread over a smaller output. The reasonable level for prices was in effect that at which it would just pay employers to employ all the available supplies of capital and labour — neither more nor less.

Attwood was accused in his own day, and has often been accused since, of being a mere inflationist, who believed that additional wealth could be created, almost *ad lib.*, by the emission of additional paper money. In fact, he believed nothing of the sort. He held the entirely sensible view that the objective to be aimed at was what economists nowadays call ' full employment ' ; and he did not believe, with the orthodox economists of his own day, that this could be secured by compressing prices, wages, and other incomes to fit the requirements of the gold standard.

But neither did he believe in uncontrolled inflation. He wanted an alternative regulator, instead of gold, to be used in settling the amount of money to be put into circulation. At different times he proposed different methods of bringing about the right adjustment ; but his favourite device was that of varying the volume of money so as to hold the wages of agricultural labour stable at about 16s. a week. That is to say, he believed that, if the wages of the lowest paid type of common labour were held approximately stable at this level by monetary manipulation, other wages would be kept tolerably stable in relation to them, and thereafter the workers would get the benefits of increased productivity in lower prices which would add to their purchasing power, without the risk of being thrown out of work by accidental causes, such as a gold scarcity which might force down wages or employment without any relation to the changing productive power of the economic system.

In modern parlance Attwood was not an inflationist, but an advocate of a ' managed monetary system '. He wanted a criterion of monetary policy more closely related to the economic condition of the country than a gold supply which was altogether outside the control of anyone in Great Britain ; and he held that stability of internal economic conditions was much more important than stability of exchange rates between Great Britain and other countries — the thing which came first in the minds of London bankers concerned mainly with overseas investment and the financing of foreign trade. He proposed that the regulation of the supply of money should be placed in the hands of the National Debt Commissioners, who should be authorised to issue paper money up to the point at which the resources of the country were fully employed, and to reduce the issue whenever there was any sign of a rise in prices above the level required to secure ' full employment '. The actual regulation was to be done by buying Government stock with notes whenever it was desired to increase the issue of money, and by selling stock and cancelling the notes received in payment whenever a reduction in the supply of money was needed.

This view, reasonable as it must seem to many people to-day, ran full tilt against the presuppositions not only of the orthodox bankers and economists, but also of most of the leading Radicals of Attwood's day. William Cobbett, for example, was the inveterate opponent of all forms of paper money, which he regarded as a cheat upon the public in the interest of the ' rag merchants ' — the bankers who issued paper banknotes — and the Government financiers who were enabled by it to pay in debased paper for the goods needed for the continuance of an unnecessary war. Cobbett had been demanding for many years a return to cash payments as the sole basis on which Government expenditure could be kept within bounds and the authority of the Government restrained. Cobbett realised fully that a return to the gold standard would mean, unless it were accompanied by other measures of adjustment, an immense increase of the real burden of the National Debt. But he and his followers had their own remedy for this — an " equitable adjustment ", or, in other words, a reduction in the rate of interest on the Debt corresponding to the fall in prices brought about by the withdrawal of the paper money. This, they argued, would leave the real burden of the Debt unchanged ; whereas Attwood's proposals would open the door to an unlimited issue of paper money by the State, and would thus enable placemen, pensioners, and Government extravagance generally, to increase and multiply at the expense of the " industrious classes ".

In 1832 Cobbett and Attwood were to hold at Birmingham a debate — celebrated in its day — on the merits of their respective opinions on monetary matters. But already, in 1816, Attwood's views had brought him into sharp opposition to the main body of popular Radical opinion. The Radicals wanted to make it difficult for the Government to get funds, in order to curb official power and extravagance : Attwood wanted to make it easy for country bankers to lend, and for business men to borrow, in order to increase production and employment. Probably it was this divergence more than any other that held Attwood apart from Radical politics for fifteen years after the end of the Napoleonic Wars.

In the matter of the currency Attwood's views were overridden, and he fell out of politics for a while, though he continued to press his currency views from time to time upon anyone he could persuade to listen. Throughout the eighteen-twenties he was mainly occupied with his banking business. Spooner and Attwood were bankers and financiers to many Birmingham industrialists; and they were also active in connection with the railway promotions of the 'twenties and 'thirties. Attwood spent much time in negotiating arrangements connected with the proposed railway lines from Birmingham to London and from Birmingham to Lancashire — the forerunners of the London and North Western Railway. He was active before Parliamentary Committees in coping with the schemes of rival promoters — for example, in diverting as far to the east as possible the rival group which was projecting a line through the Midlands — so that it eventually followed a course mainly non-competitive with the London and Birmingham. He had also to visit the Continent on several occasions in connection with the establishment of factories there under the control of Birmingham industrialists ; and he became involved in an interminable lawsuit in Chancery, in which his cousin, John Attwood, was the principal, in connection with the purchase price of land containing valuable minerals which John Attwood had sold to a company of speculators.

These commercial and financial activities kept him fully occupied all through the 'twenties. But then, in January 1830, he suddenly appeared as a fully-fledged Radical politician by founding the famous Birmingham Political Union. The moment was one of high political excitement. Wellington and the Tories, having granted Catholic Emancipation in the hope of staving off worse evils, were tottering to their fall. The Whigs under Lord Grey seemed to be on the eve of a call to political power after their long exile. The King was dying.

Popular feeling ran high. No one knew either what a Whig Government would attempt, or what it would be allowed to do, if Grey were to assume office. But the emancipation of the Catholics, in response to Irish agitation, seemed to presage the destruction of the old order in politics, and the triumph of the Reformers who had been kept under for so many years. To Radicals everywhere, it seemed necessary to appeal, over the head of the unreformed House of Commons, to the people themselves ; for it was felt that the Whigs would go as far as public opinion forced them to go, and not one inch further. There was a stirring everywhere of Radicals and middle-class industrialists who wanted to challenge the old class-ascendancy. Moreover, trade was bad and worsening, and there was an undercurrent of acute working-class misery and discontent.

These were the circumstances under which Thomas Attwood took the initiative in forming the Birmingham Political Union. His chief collaborators were middle-class men like himself; but he had again George Edmonds to rally artisan opinion behind him and to enlist the support of the new generation of working-class leaders which had sprung up since his efforts of 1812 and 1813.

There were opponents too. A section of the Birmingham Radicals, headed by Joseph Parkes, who had been working for years past in the Reform cause, wanted to know why they should be called upon to hand over the leadership to Attwood, who had given them no help through the lean years, just when their prospects were becoming immensely more hopeful. Cobbett's followers and many others disagreed with Attwood's currency notions, which were, however, very popular among the small employers and artisans. Attwood and his friends found no difficulty in brushing the opposition aside. They founded their new Political Union by acclamation at an immense mass meeting held in January 1830; and Parkes and his followers had either to join or to submit to being ignored. They joined.

By the end of the year the Birmingham Political Union found itself occupying a big position in the struggle over the Reform Bill which had been introduced into Parliament by Lord Grey's Whig Ministry. The Bill was, indeed, much more drastic than any of the Radicals had expected. On its negative side, in its proposals for sweeping away the rotten boroughs dominated by Crown or landlord influence, it went nearly as far as the Radicals themselves would have proposed to go. It was so drafted as to enfranchise the growing industrial towns and effectively to shift the balance of representation between the industrial and the agricultural areas. But on the other hand its franchise proposals were limited to the middle classes, and it did not include the ballot. The workers, if they supported it, would be supporting a plan for placing political power in the hands of the employing class. They would be breaking the political monopoly of the old ruling class, but it was to be doubted whether they would find the new authority any more to their liking than the old.

To Attwood and to others who believed in the fundamental identity of interest between employers and workmen, there was no doubt that both classes would benefit; and he and his friends felt no hesitation in putting their whole weight behind the Bill. This did not mean that they were satisfied with it as it stood : they would have liked it to go further. The ' Petition of Right ' drawn up by the Birmingham Political Union in 1830 included demands for Triennial, or more frequent, Parliaments, for the abolition of the property qualification for M.P.s, for payment of M.P.s, and for " the right of every man to have a vote in the election of members of the House of Commons who is in any way called upon to contribute to either National or Local Taxation, direct or indirect, by which your Petitioners understood that, either all taxes ought to be taken off from those articles necessary for the subsistence and comfort of working men, or that all working men, who are compelled to pay such taxes, should have a vote in the election of Members of your Honourable House ".

The Birmingham Reformers wanted more than the Bill ; but they were fully prepared to support the Bill as a first instalment. Attwood, at any rate, fully believed at this stage that the middle classes, once put in power, would see the reasonableness and justice of extending a share in it to their natural allies, the workers ; and he swept the great majority of the Birmingham workers along with him in this conviction. The more sceptical London Radicals, organised in the National Union of the Working Classes, attempted to disturb this harmony by sending down Henry Hetherington to found a similar Union of the Working Classes in Birmingham. But neither Hetherington on this mission nor Cobbett, who also supported the Whig Bill, but came to Birmingham in order to warn the workers against Attwood's paper money heresies, could make any headway. Attwood, despite the recency of his entry into Radical politics, swept the main body of workers as well as the small employers behind him : the B.P.U. was not only the first, but also easily the foremost of the numerous Political Unions which were organised all over the country as the struggle for the Reform Bill mounted to its climax.

That story would be out of place in this study, except as it directly affects the Birmingham Reformers. It was in response to an address from them that Lord John Russell made his famous utterance, " It is impossible that the whisper of a faction should prevail against the voice of a nation ". But, if the nation spoke with but one voice, the Government used two. There went up in the Tory press and in Parliament a howl that the Government, in encouraging the Political Unions, was giving countenance to subversive and revolutionary forces which were threatening rebellion unless their dictates were obeyed. The Cabinet took fright, and issued in November 1831 a proclamation denouncing political associations.

At the moment when the proclamation appeared, the Birmingham Political Union was busy reorganising itself, on the basis of a plan drawn up by Charles Jones, for the next phase of the struggle. The plan provided for making it into a more disciplined force, with groups and sections under subordinate leaders who would be in a position to transmit orders from the Council to the rank and file, and to act on their own initiative in any emergency. On receipt of the proclamation, the Union abandoned its plan and reverted to a simple mass membership, which was believed to keep it well within the law. There should be no pretext for the Government to invoke against it the law relating to ' Corresponding Societies '. Its leaders were determined, as far as in them lay, not to move an inch outside the law in the endeavour to make the power of the people effective.

This insistence on strict legality had been placed by Attwood right in the forefront from the beginning of the campaign. The slogan of the Union, borne upon its banners and repeated by its founder on every critical occasion, was " Peace, Law, and Order " ; and from this he would sanction no departure under any pretext. Such measures as a run on the banks — Francis Place's famous " To stop the Duke, go for gold " — he was prepared to sanction as being within the law ; but he opposed the plan that the Radicals should refuse to pay any taxes until the Reform Bill had become an Act. Later on, in the Chartist agitation, he was to draw a similar line between the ' sacred month ' or general strike, as a strictly legal withholding of labour, and the threats of violence uttered by the ' physical force ' Chartists. He adhered to the letter of the law, not without warning the House of Lords and the Tories, in the course of the Reform Bill struggle, that if they stood out against the will of the people neither he, nor any other peaceful Reformer, could be responsible for the consequences.

Through the critical years of the Reform Bill struggle, Attwood was a personage of prime political importance. He was at the head of the greatest and most united popular movement in the whole country ; and, though his currency notions peeped out from time to time, they were for the most part kept in the background. Men were content to leave such differences alone until the political issue had been settled. Apart from the Reform question, Attwood and his fellow Radicals were mainly concerned at this time with contemporary events abroad — with the successful revolutions in France and Belgium, which they regarded as running parallel to their own endeavours, and with the crushing out by Russia of what had remained of the Polish nation after the Partitions. The Birmingham Political Union declared its solidarity with the continental revolutionaries, and expressed its deep sympathy with the Polish people. A Birmingham Polish Association was formed in 1832, with Attwood as one of its leading spirits ; and at the same time his brother Charles (1791–1875), banker and industrialist of Newcastle-on-Tyne, and founder of the important Northern Political Union, was stirring up the Radicals of Northumberland and Durham in the Polish cause. The two Attwoods belonged thenceforward to the extreme anti-Russian section among the Radicals ; and Thomas was soon to couple in Parliament his activities on behalf of Radicalism at home with demands for a strong British policy directed against Russian aggression. Marx did not invent anti-Czarism as a doctrine of the political left. It grew spontaneously and strongly as the consequence of the crushing of the Polish revolt.

In due course the Reform struggle ended, and the Reform

Bill became law. To the first Reformed Parliament Birmingham had the right to send two Members ; and there was never the smallest doubt that Attwood would be one of them. He and Joshua Scholefield, the nominees of the Birmingham Political Union, were in fact returned unopposed, after the Tories had tried vainly to find a candidate. If there were Whigs who disliked the Radical nominees, they kept quiet. In 1832 no one would have stood the smallest chance of beating Attwood and anyone whom the Birmingham Political Union chose to nominate as his colleague. His personal popularity was immense ; and his prestige as the founder of Political Unions stood high.

Historians are emphatic in their verdict that Attwood's parliamentary career was a failure, just as they are emphatic about Cobbett's or Fielden's, and for much the same reason. Despite the fundamental difference of approach, Attwood the ' currency man ', Cobbett the friend of the agricultural labourers, and Fielden the factory reformer, were all Radicals in a sense in which the Parliament elected in 1832 emphatically was not Radical. They all believed that the Reform of Parliament ought to involve a sharp break with the past, not merely in commercial policy or in the class-distribution of the sweets of power and influence, but in the condition of the people. This was the question which in their several ways they were all determined to press upon the new House of Commons ; but this was the question on which the House was determined not to listen to them. Attwood's habit of reiterating his monetary heresies on every possible occasion and at undue length was no doubt a powerful contributory factor in ensuring Parliament's inattention ; but much more fundamental was the determination of the great majority of Whigs and Tories alike that the drastic parliamentary Reform should not carry with it a social revolution. The atmosphere of the House was that of Lord John Russell's — " Finality Jack's " — declaration that the Reform Bill was to be regarded as final. The people must look for nothing more in the way of political rights ; and what had been conceded must be made into a means of consolidating the rights of property, and not of threatening them. Orthodox Political Economy must regulate the relations between rich and poor ; and orthodox Political Economy was equally emphatic in rejecting Attwood's currency schemes, Cobbett's demand that the poor should be maintained out of the yield of the land, and Fielden's plan for legislation to ensure humane conditions in the factories.

In Parliament, Attwood was bound to fail, unless he had behind him a popular movement in the country strong enough to compel the House of Commons to attend to him. It may seem that he had, in the Birmingham Political Union, just such an instrument as he needed. But in fact the Reform Act was no sooner law than the B.P.U. began to fall to pieces. There were differences of opinion about the expediency of carrying it on at all, now that the great object had been won. Attwood himself was strongly in favour of its continuance ; but his fellow M.P., Joshua Scholefield, took a different view, and dropped out, carrying with him most of the manufacturers and men of substance who had joined it in crying out for " the Bill, the whole Bill, and nothing but the Bill ". The Birmingham Political Union remained in existence and continued to meet from time to time, right up to the period when it was reorganised, and entered on a new lease of life, in connection with the Chartist movement. But between 1832 and 1837 it was but a shadow ; and it furnished no effective backing to Attwood in his parliamentary activities.

It did not take long for Attwood to find grounds for dispute with the Whig Ministry. Almost the first business of the Reformed Parliament was to approve measures for the coercion of Ireland. Attwood opposed these strongly, attributing Irish disorders to Irish distress, and urging that the remedy lay not in coercion, but in raising the Irish standard of living by fuller use of the country's productive power — with the conclusion, of course, that a sounder monetary policy would be the best way of bringing this about. In March 1833 he came to his main theme, moving for the appointment of a Parliamentary Committee to consider the cause of, and propose remedies for, the prevailing distress — a motion the easier for Ministers to combat because it was put forward at a time of rapidly improving trade. He mustered, with Tory aid, 160 votes for his motion, against the Government's 194; but the Whigs took no notice of him, and thereafter he was vehement in his denunciation of the Whig betrayal of the people. In May a great open-air meeting at Newhall Hill — the scene of all the mass gatherings of the B.P.U. — approved a Petition asking King William IV to dismiss his Ministers.

The following year, 1834, made him yet more bitter against the Whigs. He hated the ' Malthusian ' Poor Law Bill as heartily as Cobbett, and was unsparing in his denunciations of it. He hated too the Whig attitude to factory reform. He had voted for Lord Ashley's Bill in 1833, and opposed the whittling down of it by the Ministers. At almost every point, except the projected reform of the municipal corporations, he found himself ranged against the Whigs, and also against those Radicals who accepted the doctrines of *laissez-faire*. With these latter he agreed, indeed, about Free Trade ; and in 1833 the Birmingham Political Union sent to Parliament a Petition asking for the removal of all taxes on the food of the people. But here too the Whigs were against him ; they were no more ready to repeal the Corn Laws than to rescind the Currency Act of 1819.

By this time the Birmingham Tories, encouraged by Attwood's breach with the Whigs, had begun to organise their forces with the view to challenging his position. They formed, in 1834, the Birmingham Loyal and Constitutional Association, and began to look round for a candidate to put into the field against him. They found their man in Richard Spooner, his old partner in the bank and lifelong personal friend, who, at first a Radical, had by now turned Tory. When the General Election came, in the following year, Attwood was easily at the head of the poll, beating Spooner by nearly two votes to one ; and Scholefield again won the second seat. In 1837 he and Scholefield were again elected, against a different Tory candidate ; and this time Attwood won by an even greater margin. His personal popularity was unshaken throughout these years ; and he could still gather immense meetings together when he pleased. But there was no longer, as there had been up to 1832, a definite objective to strive for, and to make a foundation for continuous popular activity. This came only in 1837, when the B.P.U. was reorganised as the instrument for a new campaign, this time not in support of any Whig Bill, but against the combined forces of both the established political parties.

We have now come to the point at which Attwood took the step which flung him into the Chartist movement. It is important to observe that the new phase arose out of a renewed trade depression, which spread misery wide among the Birmingham operatives. In 1833 and 1834 Birmingham had been one of the principal centres of the great Owenite Trade Union agitation. Birmingham had been one of the strongholds of the Grand National Consolidated Trades Union and of Owen's National Equitable Labour Exchange; and there the Builders' Union had set about the erection of its new Guildhall, which was to be the centre of education in the principles of the New Moral World. Attwood, away in London and busy with his parliamentary affairs, had played no part in these developments, which he probably regarded as visionary and misguided. He still stood for reconciliation of classes — for a reformed Capitalism, and not for Socialism of an Owenite or of any other brand. But the Trade Unions were broken in the struggles of 1834; and hard upon their defeat came the depression, with the New Poor Law to make it press yet more severely on the unfortunates who could find no one to employ them. Attwood's remedy was still the old one — monetary reform; but he was convinced by now that no such reform could be looked for without Universal Suffrage. In that respect Whigs and Tories were alike — or rather the Whigs were the worse, because they represented the monied, as against the agricultural, interest.

The reorganisation of the Birmingham Political Union had nothing directly to do with The People's Charter, or with the negotiations of the London Working Men's Association with the Radical M.P.s which led up to the drafting of it. Attwood was not present — was not, I think, invited to be present — at these consultations. He did not act with any group of parliamentary Radicals; and Francis Place probably felt that he would spoil the harmony of the proceedings by insisting on talking about his currency projects. The

B.P.U.'s move was entirely independent — prompted by the prevailing distress. It was, however, in many respects different from the movement which Attwood had inaugurated in 1830. It was against the Whigs and against the *laissez-faire* Radicals as well. It still included a considerable middle-class element, but no longer the larger manufacturers, who had got what they wanted, and were as hostile to Universal Suffrage as the Tories. The middle-class element in the revived B.P.U. consisted of professional men — journalists and the like — and of small manufacturers who believed in cheap credit and were not far removed in economic status from the skilled artisans. Birmingham was predominantly a town of small masters, who felt, almost equally with their workers, the immediate pinch of bad trade. In such a place, though there were great employers whose relations with their workers were much like those of the cotton lords of Lancashire or the colliery owners of Durham and South Wales, there was no deep class-cleavage between the general run of small working master craftsmen and the skilled workmen whom they employed. Dependent largely on distant markets, the men of Birmingham felt keenly the ups and downs of world trade. But adversity had a tendency rather to unite them than to drive them apart. Attwood's currency schemes appealed to both groups, because they promised better prices, fuller employment, and the uplifting of the ' industrious classes ' as against the parasites and the fund-holders away in London, who dominated the new Parliament as much as the old.

The revived Birmingham movement of 1837 was based on an attempt to organise a National Petition for further Reform. In this Petition, five out of the six points of The People's Charter found a place. The demand for equal electoral districts alone was missing ; and this was not a point of substance, but merely of emphasis — for the Birmingham Reformers were in fact as keen as anyone else on the redistribution of seats. It is true that the B.P.U. originally demanded not Annual but " Triennial or more frequent " Parliaments, and that its claim was not for Universal Suffrage as such, but for " Household Suffrage, or Representation coextensive with Taxation " ; but as the latter phrase was explained as including indirect taxation, the demand for Universal Manhood Suffrage was implicit. There was even an influential section which favoured votes for women ; and the revived B.P.U. had as its auxiliary a numerous Birmingham Female Political Union, which in 1835 presented to Attwood a special Address.

Before this the B.P.U. had been endeavouring to press Attwood's currency schemes upon Lord Melbourne as the right means of remedying the general distress. A deputation headed by Attwood went to London, interviewed Melbourne and his Chancellor of the Exchequer, Spring Rice, and came back empty-handed. At once the question was raised : should the Birmingham Reformers start a national currency campaign, and make their National Petition centre mainly on. this issue, or should they aim first at political Reform, with currency reorganisation to follow as the logical sequel to the people's victory ? The advocates of the latter view — P. H. Muntz, Benjamin Hadley, and T. C. Salt — won the day ; and the B.P.U. came out definitely for Universal Manhood Suffrage, and, after Lord John Russell's " finality " declaration, issued a manifesto calling upon all Radicals to join forces behind this demand. Among the bodies which responded to this appeal was the London Working Men's Association, which was already at work trying to create bodies similar to itself throughout the country to demand the enactment of The People's Charter.

The Glasgow Reformers also responded ; and early in 1838 the B.P.U. sent John Collins as a missionary to the Clyde. Much enthusiasm was aroused, and presently Attwood himself, with several of his lieutenants, was in Glasgow addressing a monster meeting. The B.P.U. and the L.W.M.A. joined forces. The Birmingham men accepted The People's Charter, and the Londoners agreed that the National Petition, amended to include the full Chartist programme, should become the means of bringing the Charter before Parliament and the entire people.

From this point the Charter and the Petition ran together, and were unanimously endorsed by one great gathering after another convened under the auspices of the local Reform societies. These were of many differing complexions, and under many conflicting influences. Some looked mainly to Birmingham for leadership, and some to London ; but others were offsprings of the mass agitation against the New Poor Law, which, led at first by Richard Oastler and Joseph Rayner Stephens, was passing more and more under O'Connor's leadership since his move from London to Leeds and his establishment in 1837 of *The Northern Star* as the organ of the Northern discontent.

At the chief of these gatherings which endorsed the Charter and the Petition, delegates were also chosen to attend the great People's Convention, which was to meet in London early in 1839, and was to superintend the presentation of the Petition to Parliament and thereafter to direct the people what to do. The entire campaign was made to centre round this coming event. Attwood, both at the Glasgow meeting in May and on his return to Birmingham, had spoken of a general cessation of work, by masters and men alike, as the instrument which the people could use to make their power effective in the event of Parliament refusing their just demands. This was no new idea. William Benbow had been advocating the ' Grand National Holiday ' for many years and had published in 1832 his pamphlet under that title, linking the idea of a general strike with that of a National Convention of the productive classes. The project had appeared frequently in the course of the Trade Union agitation of 1833 and 1834. It now reappeared, not as a slogan of class-war, but invested by Attwood with the solemn respectability of a national and entirely peaceable protest by employers and men together against the misdeeds of a Government which left them to languish in the midst of potential plenty. The ' Grand National Holiday ' became the ' Sacred Month ' — a demonstration of ' Moral Force ' which was to be imposing because of its display of popular discipline and self-control. Other men had doubtless other ideas about what would happen when the ' Sacred Month ' was proclaimed. But Attwood at this stage seems to have felt no doubts. He was carried away by the magnitude of the Birmingham revival and of his reception in Scotland, impressed by the level-headed determination of Lovett and his London colleagues, sure that all would go well, as it had done in the struggle for the Reform Bill between 1830 and 1832.

The Chartist Convention met in London early in February 1839, and Attwood's troubles began. To his mind, the ' Sacred Month ' was the supreme expression of ' Moral Force '; but there were delegates at the Convention who evidently conceived it in a very different spirit, openly proclaimed their adherence to ' physical force ' doctrines, and threatened to scare away his middle-class supporters even before the great Petition was ready to be presented to Parliament. It had been arranged that he was to present it, and that John Fielden was to be his seconder. But what was he to do if the Convention went over to a ' physical force ' doctrine which he verily abhorred ? At the end of March we find him writing in consternation to T. C. Salt at Birmingham of the consequences of the " unhappy discords " which have broken out. " So long as Birmingham remains firm, true and united, acting under the law and in defence of the law, but permanently and inflexibly determined to use every possible legal effort to obtain from the justice of Parliament the objects of the National Petition, the cause of the people can never be said to be lost. . . . Undoubtedly the wild nonsense about physical force has done much mischief. . . . I assert with confidence, that if the bitterest enemies of the people had sat down in an infernal conclave to devise the means of injuring the people's cause, they could not, by any possibility, have devised more efficient means than by recommending the people to have recourse to physical force. . . . You know, my dear Salt, that I have never been a man of blood — never animated by guilty ambition. . . . The miseries of the people shall never be increased through me. If I am to die a premature death, I will face it in a good cause ; but I will not die the death of a fool, or of a scoundrel. I will leave an unstained name behind me."

This letter, when it was read out, provoked much dissension, even in the ranks of the Birmingham Political Union. The ' physical force ' party had its adherents even there. By May, when the Petition was at last nearly ready, Attwood and Fielden were demanding that the People's Convention should withdraw its threats of violence before they could agree to present it to the House of Commons. The Convention replied evasively to this demand; but Attwood was in a quandary. He could not refuse to present the Petition without throwing away the whole of his work during the past two years, and bitterly disappointing his 'moral force' followers throughout the country. Despite his misgivings, he went on with his task and, on June 14, 1839, at length made his speech requesting the House of Commons to take into consideration the National Petition.

After briefly reciting and explaining the terms of the Petition, Attwood went on to declare his personal attitude. " Although I most cordially support every part of the Petition, and am ready to support and verify every word of it, and although I am determined to use every legal means in my power to carry it into law, I must say that many reports have gone abroad of arguments that have been used, or that are said to have been used, in various parts of the country, which I disavow. I never, at any period of my life, recommended any principles except those of peace, law, order, loyalty, and union, and that, Sir, in good faith, not holding one face here, and another out of doors. . . . My determination is to do all that lies in my power, as a man, as a Christian, and as a gentleman, to work out the wishes of the petitioners. Having stated so much, I wash my hands of any talk of physical force or arms. I want no arms but the will of the people, legally, firmly, and constitutionally expressed. . . . I say, if the people go on, washing their hands from all threats and insolence, but go on firmly, honestly, and constitutionally, I am sure their demands will meet with respectful attention."

When, a month later, the House was at last ready to hear Attwood's motion that the Petition should be considered, it can hardly be argued that this respectful attention was accorded: 46 members voted for his motion, and 235 against it. Various speakers, from Hume and Fielden to Lord John Russell and Disraeli, took part in the debate; and the unkindest cut was made by Russell, who produced a placard signed by the members of the Chartist Convention, denouncing " the power and corrupting influence of paper money ", and declaring that the industrious classes are " defrauded by the fraudulent bits of paper, which our state tricksters dignify by the name of money, and are at this moment being robbed by that system of three-fourths of their labour ".

Immediately after the debate, Attwood wrote in a letter : " Here was an argument which I could not answer. When Lord John Russell, holding the placard in his hands, and reading its contents, triumphantly enquired, ' Of what use would my reform be when my own friends rejected its most important objects ? ', I was paralysed. I had created the General Convention. It was the offspring of my own brain. I was surrounded by enemies on every side, many of them interested against me, and all contending against me. At this very moment, out of my own camp, a mortal weapon was directed against my heart."

That the Chartist Convention should have passed, apparently without dissent, a resolution directly in opposition to Attwood's cherished currency projects shows how completely the men of Birmingham had by that time lost control. The original delegates sent from Birmingham to the Convention had all resigned or gone away by April ; and new men, who were not adherents of Attwood's currency views, had taken their places. Instead of the great Convention of representatives of both masters and men that Attwood had dreamed of, there was left a gathering mainly working-class, in which the only remaining middle-class members were the loudest advocates of ulterior measures. Attwood had been slow to accept these unpalatable facts ; but Lord John Russell's hit went home. The Birmingham riots also seriously upset him ; for some of his oldest political associates had been responsible for calling in the London police and for the arrest of Lovett and Collins for defying the ban on public meetings in the Bull Ring after the Convention had moved to Birmingham. The Newport Rising of November 1839 was for Attwood the last straw. His hopes of winning the Charter by a grand display of ' Moral Force ' had evaporated. In December 1839 he resigned his seat in Parliament and announced his intention of retiring into private life.

At this point Attwood's public career practically ended.

His health was bad, and he retired for two years to Jersey in the hope of recovering his strength. In 1841 his fellow townsmen made him a presentation in recognition of his public services ; and two years later, when he had come back from Jersey apparently recovered, sixteen thousand of them signed a requisition urging him to return and lead a new movement. This was after the triple collapse of 1842 — after the defeat of the great Chartist strikes in the North, the rejection of the second National Petition, and the breakdown of Joseph Sturge's attempt to reunite the middle and working classes in the Complete Suffrage movement. Attwood attempted to come back, and to organise a new National Union ; but the magic of his name and presence had departed. Only a faithful few adhered to him : the National Union was stillborn. He went back into private life, except for an occasional letter on currency questions to the newspapers. His wife had died in 1840, shortly after his resignation ; and in 1845 he married again. Soon serious illness returned upon him — a creeping paralysis which, beginning in the fingers, gradually incapacitated him for work. He lived on until 1856 ; but he had ceased to count, and even in Birmingham he had been largely forgotten. A memorial was raised there after his death and a statue erected ; but the subscriptions for it were not easily gathered. If Attwood had died in 1832 his memory would have lived much better ; for men would have remembered his successes instead of forgetting his failure. As it was, the Chartists regarded him as a deserter, and the middle-class Radicals as a man who had played with fire, and got burnt. As for his currency notions, they were buried under the piles of new gold from California and Australia which increased the supply of money as effectively as his regulated currency would have done. Not till the twentieth century did anyone bother to look again for the truth in his ideas about the right relation between money and productive power. And even now, when many of the things he said are being said again, there are few who know he said them. He is still Attwood, the currency crank who took up with the Chartists in order to further his crack-brained notions. An intelligible verdict but a most unjust one !

Personally, Attwood was tall and slim ; and most men and women deemed him handsome. He was devoted to his wife and children and very ready to put himself about in the service of his friends. He was a devout churchman, at a time when the Church of England was not popular in Radical circles ; and he was an acute business man, very good at making money for others, but very little interested in keeping it for himself. Undoubtedly, he liked popular applause and enjoyed the devotion of his followers, and correspondingly missed it when it was withdrawn. He was like Robert Owen in that, believing absolutely in his panacea for the ills of society and finding it rejected by those in authority, he appealed to the people and became a Radical leader half in spite of himself. He was unlike Owen in that defeat and humiliation led him to give up the struggle. Owen would have been quite unperturbed by any such quip as Lord John Russell's. He would simply have continued to expound, as before, the principles of the ' New Moral World '. Attwood was more sensitive ; he accepted failure and, by doing so, narrowed his niche in the temple of fame, where the successes get the most conspicuous monuments, but the next best are for the failures who are unaware that they have failed.

V

John Frost

JOHN FROST, of Newport in Monmouthshire, lived to be ninety-three ; but historians would hardly have kept his name in memory but for the events of a single night. His name is known, because he was the reputed leader of the ' Newport Rising ' of 1839, and because that affair, small in itself, has been magnified by renown and conjecture till it appears in history as the British Revolution that was quelled at the first onset, and thereafter failed to happen. But it is very doubtful whether Frost was the real leader even of this local rising, and more than doubtful whether the Newport affair was part of any widely organised project of revolution. These questions I shall discuss later. Let us consider, before we come to them, what manner of man Frost was, and what he had done before he found himself charged with High Treason as the leader of the Chartists in arms.

John Frost was born at Newport on May 25, 1784. His father, an innkeeper in the town, died while he was a child ; and he was brought up by his grandfather, who was a working craftsman, a bootmaker. One account has it that he was sent to school at Bristol, another that he picked up such education as he got from his grandfather. At all events he abandoned bootmaking, and after his grandfather's death was apprenticed to a woollen draper at Bristol, and thereafter served, about 1805, as shopman to a merchant tailor in London, where he made his first contacts with Radicalism. Probably in 1806, he returned to Newport a convinced Radical, and set up on his own as a draper, in a shop which he leased from an uncle. He was already a great reader, and a keen student both of Tom Paine and other Radical writers and of his favourite authority on constitutional matters, Blackstone.

In 1809 John Frost was admitted a burgess of Newport, and three years later he married a widow, Mary Geach, a connection of his own, with whom he shared expectations from their common uncle, William Foster, who had been Mayor of Newport and was one of the town's most prosperous citizens. Mary Geach had two children by her first husband ; and eight children were born to her and John Frost between 1815 and 1826. Up to 1820 Frost appears to have attended strictly to business : at all events we have no record of any political activities of his during this period. He did well with his shop, and became a figure of some importance in the town.

In 1820 William Foster died, leaving his property to Mary Frost and her children, but pointedly excluding Mary's husband. In this year Frost began his political career by seconding the nomination of the Whig candidate for the Monmouthshire boroughs ; and he also became involved in a quarrel with Thomas Prothero, solicitor and Town Clerk of Newport, over the terms of Foster's will. This quarrel, of which it would be tedious to relate the particulars, speedily broadened out from a private into a public dispute. In 1821 Frost began his career as a writer of political pamphlets, accusing Prothero not only of sharp practice over the will, but also of corruption in connection with the affairs of the town. Prothero retaliated with an action for libel ; and between public and private matters Frost found himself in an awkward predicament. Prothero managed to saddle him with a debt for which he was very doubtfully liable ; and he arranged a collusive bankruptcy which left his property in the hands of his wife and family. Meanwhile, his attacks on Prothero's public conduct landed him in prison ; he spent six months in Cold Bath Fields Prison in London, and was bound over to keep the peace for five years. The curious can trace the detailed record of these occurrences in David Williams's careful *Life of John Frost* : they are important here only because they involved him in a bitter quarrel with Prothero and his younger partner, Thomas Phillips, who was the leader both of the old municipal oligarchy in Newport and of the local Whig Reformers.

In pursuit of his private and public quarrels Frost published at least thirteen pamphlets between 1821 and 1823, and became the spokesman of the general body of freemen of the town against both the landowning aristocracy and the Whig interest. But after his release from prison in 1823 he seems to have remained entirely silent for nearly seven years, during which he re-established his business fortunes and resumed his status as a respectable tradesman. He had not, however, given up his Radical convictions ; and the revival of the Reform question with the advent of the Whigs to power in 1830 caused him again to become active. In 1830 we find him pleading the cause of the agricultural labourers, whose revolt against intolerable conditions, most extensive in the Southern and Eastern Counties of England, had spread into South Wales. Frost, while deploring acts of violence, moved, at a meeting called for the purpose of rousing the respectable classes to take measures for the protection of property, an amendment asking for redress of the labourers' grievances. Not content with this, he bought up the printing press of Samuel Etheridge, his predecessor in the leadership of local Radicalism, and announced his intention of giving up business and devoting himself entirely to the cause of reform. He resumed his pamphleteering and, after joining hands for a time with his old antagonist Prothero in supporting the middle-class Reformers, proceeded in 1832 violently to denounce the Whigs as enemies of the people, and to advocate a thorough-going Radical policy, including Annual Parliaments and Manhood Suffrage. In this year he attempted to establish a local Radical paper, *The Welchman*, of which only one number appeared ; and he also embarked anew on his campaign against local corruption, as the defender of the claims of the freemen against the oligarchy which, under Prothero and Phillips, dominated the town's affairs.

Frost was, throughout these early ventures into politics, essentially a Cobbettite. His pamphlet style was plainly based on Cobbett's ; and, like his literary master, he waxed hot against the National Debt, high taxation, paper money, Whiggery, and the rest of Cobbett's aversions. He had a quite lively controversial style, and he enjoyed slanging matches with his enemies, Whigs and Tories alike. He had made himself the outstanding spokesman of advanced opinions, and the leader of the popular party among the freemen; and when, under the Municipal Corporations Act of 1835, Newport was equipped with its first elected Borough Council, it was no surprise when he was returned as a member of the new body. To this dignity he soon added membership of the first Board of Guardians under the Poor Law Amendment Act of 1834 — an office which he wanted not because he liked the Act, but on the contrary for the purpose of obstructing its administration. In the same year, 1836, he was proposed by the Town Council for appointment as a magistrate, in opposition to the nominees of the old municipal oligarchy, and was duly appointed by the Whig Government. At the end of the year he was chosen Mayor of Newport, and in this capacity, in 1837, he proclaimed the accession of Queen Victoria.

Thus John Frost, in his early fifties, was Radical Mayor of his native town, then rapidly growing in population and prosperity with the development of the coalfields in the Monmouthshire valleys. He had a long record of Cobbettite Radicalism behind him, was at enmity alike with Tory magnates from the county and Whig business interests in the town, and was regarded as the leader of the local Radicals in their attempts to prevent encroachments on the rights of the townsmen by the protagonists of either faction. In his new offices he plunged into further violent disputes with Thomas Prothero, whom he accused of appropriating harbour dues which were the property of the burgesses, and also with the principal landowner, Sir Charles Morgan. He was simultaneously engaged in vigorous controversy with the ironmasters and colliery owners of the neighbourhood over the administration of the New Poor Law, and had a further personal quarrel on his hands in connection with the affairs of his lawyer stepson, William Foster Geach, against whom Prothero and Phillips had made up a plausible allegation of unprofessional conduct.

It seems evident that these controversies made Frost unpopular with many of the middle-class Reformers who had hitherto supported him. In 1837 he was defeated when he stood for re-election for a second term as Mayor; and at about the same time he became connected with the Chartist movement, which was just then beginning to establish itself in the South Wales area. William Edwards, a local baker, founded a Newport Working Men's Association ; and at about the same period similar bodies were started in Merthyr, Swansea, Carmarthen, and other towns in South Wales. Frost does not appear to have been the prime mover in these developments ; but he was soon actively associated with the Chartist movement, and in 1838 he was elected to represent Newport, Caerleon, and Pontypool in the first Chartist Convention, which had been summoned to assemble in London in February of the following year.

Frost's position as a magistrate was of importance to the South Wales Chartists, because it enabled him to summon meetings and thus give them a status of legality. He was therefore, as well as for his own sake, welcomed eagerly into the Chartist ranks. Newport, growing in importance as a port for the shipment of coal from the inland mining valleys, was a dozen miles distant from the principal centre of the mining and iron industries ; and in general its life seems to have been curiously remote from the perpetual turmoils of the hinterland. A few miles away, at Blackwood, Ebbw Vale, Brynmawr, Nantyglo, Coalbrook Vale, Blaenavon, Rhymney, and Tredegar, and a little further afield at Dowlais and Merthyr Tydfil, bitter conflicts had been raging between coalmasters and ironmasters and their employees almost continuously for a generation. There had been strikes, riots, combinations and wholesale dismissals of those who ventured to belong to them — even hand-to-hand fighting between soldiers and workers, and many acts of violence on both sides. Working-class leaders had been executed and transported for their part in these affairs ; the entire area had a reputation for turbulence and oppression unequalled anywhere else in Great Britain. Yet of all this there was, up to 1838, hardly an echo in all John Frost's numerous writings and speeches. Newport was not a centre of Trade Unionism, open or secret, or of violent encounters between armed yeomanry or special constables or soldiers and the working people. Its feuds were more decorously conducted, by pamphlet and litigation ; and Frost, though he must have known all about the conflicts in the mining valleys, does not appear to have been mixed up in them at all. He was still, up to 1838, an ordinary Radical of the old school, adept at exposing civic abuses, at denouncing Tory presumption and Whig hypocrisy; and his followers were not primarily working men, but rather his fellow tradesmen and craftsmen of the borough, bent on asserting their rights against the claims of the notables.

Such was John Frost when he accepted nomination as a delegate to the first Chartist Convention and began to go about the mining valleys making speeches among his prospective constituents. At these meetings his favourite themes were still those of the old-style Radicalism — denunciations of the corruption of those in high places, of excessive taxes paid to maintain the pomp and pretensions of the governing classes, and so forth — seasoned with denunciations of the New Poor Law and with personal attacks on his long-standing antagonists — Morgan, Prothero, Phillips, and in effect all the leading Whigs and Tories of the neighbourhood. But at these meetings there were other orators much more eloquent than he — notably the young compositor, Henry Vincent, who had been sent out as a missionary by the London Working Men's Association to rouse the workers of South Wales and South-West England in support of The People's Charter. The upshot was that in January 1839 Frost received a letter from the Home Office enquiring whether he, a Justice of the Peace, had allowed himself to be nominated as a delegate to the People's Convention, and whether he had been present at a meeting held at Pontypool, at which violent and inflammatory language had been used. Frost replied with spirit to Lord John Russell, who was then Home Secretary, asserting his right to express what opinions he pleased as long as he faithfully performed the duties of his office. He denied that he, or anyone else at the meetings he had attended, had used " violent and inflammatory language ", and added pointedly, referring to the Reform struggle of 1830–1832, that " there was a time when the Whig Government was not so fastidious as to violent and inflammatory language uttered at public meetings ". He asked by what authority the Home Secretary assumed a power over actions of his unconnected with his office. " Am I to hold no opinion of my own in respect to public matters ?

Am I to be prohibited from expressing that opinion if it is unpleasing to Lord J. Russell ? . . . If these are to be the terms on which Her Majesty's Commission of the Peace is to be holden, take it back again, for surely none but the most servile of men would hold it on such terms."

Frost went on : " Is it an offence to be appointed a delegate to convey to the constitutional authorities the petitions of the people ? . . . Can it be a crime for a person appointed at a public meeting to get laid before the House of Commons a Petition, praying that the legislature will restore the ancient constitution of the country ? . . . Filling an humble station in life, I would yield neither to your lordship nor to any of your order in a desire to see my country powerful and prosperous. Twenty years' reading and experience have convinced me that the only method to produce and secure that state of things is a restoration of the ancient constitution."

There was much more in this strain, including a number of pointed references to the contrast between the Whig attitudes to the people before and after 1832, and to Lord John Russell's conduct in particular. But Lord John returned a smooth answer, and nothing was done at this stage to strike Frost's name off the Commission of the Peace.

This passage of arms sufficed to make Frost, previously unknown outside his own area, something of a hero when he took his seat in the People's Convention at the beginning of February 1839. He and Bailie Craig of Kilmarnock were the only Justices among the delegates, and had some honour on that account ; but Frost's standing with the delegates was the higher, because he had stood up manfully to the Whigs and held his own. He was entertained to dinner both by the West London Democratic Association, which belonged to the more extreme wing of the Chartist movement, and by the London Working Men's Association ; and on both occasions he used somewhat truculent language. At the first of these functions he said : " Here I am, a delegate and a magistrate ; and if Lord John Russell takes my name off, the people will put it on ". At the L.W.M.A. dinner he delivered an attack on the Bedfords — Lord John Russell's family — for the way in which their vast properties had been accumulated, and promised Russell that " within less than three months every collier in South Wales would know the history of Woburn Abbey and Tavistock Priory, and every victim of the New Poor Law should know what obligations had been attached to these vast estates when they were acquired ". Before this, in a speech made in the Convention itself, against J. P. Cobbett's motion that the delegates should pledge themselves to adopt none but strictly constitutional measures, he had said that " Reason would have no weight with the House of Commons : unless the Convention could make use of weapons other than reason no good would be effected for the people ".

These remarks were made to the accompaniment of further correspondence with the Home Office ; and in March 1839 Frost was deprived of his position as a magistrate. The Convention promptly, but vainly, petitioned for his reinstatement ; but, as he continued to use strong language, this was most unlikely to be conceded. He was, indeed, becoming more definitely associated with the left wing of the Chartist movement, as an active opponent of the ' moral force ' men, and an advocate of strong measures for making the Charter the law of the land.

Those who have read the journals and letters of Sir Charles Napier, who had at this time newly taken up his appointment as commander of the troops in the North of England, with a special mission to deal with the Chartists, will be aware that by March 1839 the upper classes were fully expecting a Chartist uprising in arms. Napier, who sympathised personally with the Chartist demands and hated both Whigs and Tories for their oppression of the people, was less certain. As a strong opponent of ' physical force ' doctrines, he was prepared to shoot down the Chartists if they did attempt a rising ; but he hoped to prevent an outbreak by a restrained show of force, and by no means credited the current notion that preparations had been made, under coordinated national leadership, for an appeal to arms. That the Chartists were arming was beyond doubt ; but in Napier's view their proceedings were sporadic and uncoordinated, and there were no national leaders in control of their campaign. Vague ideas of revolution were everywhere, mingled with the notion that the people must arm themselves in self-defence against the attacks of the rich ; but he doubted, and continued to doubt, whether they really meant to act on any extended scale. Certainly, he held, most of their leaders, from Feargus O'Connor downwards, had no such intention. Napier's great desire was to avoid bloodshed — to get over the dangerous times of bad trade, during which the workless were driven to desperation by the tyranny of the New Poor Law — and to hope that the trouble would die down, especially if the Government could be driven to do anything that would alleviate the sufferings of the people.

Napier, however, had an unusually cool head ; the common opinion among Ministers, squires, and industrialists alike was that revolution might break out any moment throughout the factory and mining areas. Napier had no doubt of his ability to quell it if it did break out ; but he dreaded the bloodshed. Most of the men with whom he had to deal officially had no such qualms : they wanted drastic action against the Chartists — the bloodier the better. Napier, away in the North, had nothing to do with South Wales, where conditions were even worse and industrial relations more bitter than in Lancashire or Yorkshire or on the Tyne or Clyde. Probably his mild firmness had a great deal to do with the prevention of even sporadic violence in the North during these troublous years. In South Wales there was no such wisdom as his in high places. Frost's language reflected but palely the bitter and passionate resentments of the men who had sent him as their representative to the People's Convention.

It was not, however, among John Frost's South Wales constituents but in the textile districts of Central Wales that the trouble came first to a head. Here, hatred of the New Poor Law was deep and angry, and the workers were in desperate poverty owing to the decline of the Welsh textile industries, aggravated by the depression of trade. There was drilling in progress, and fire-arms were stolen from local farmers. The magistrates decided to arrest the Chartist leaders, and sent for police from London to help them. The arrests, and the arrival of the Londoners, precipitated the conflict. The Chartists stormed the building in which the prisoners were confined, and released them ; and thereafter for some days the town of Llanidloes was in Chartist hands — until the military arrived, routed the mostly unarmed workers, and gave the employers their chance to exact a savage revenge. This was in late April and early May 1839, while the Chartist Convention in London was still busy about the presentation of the National Petition.

The Llanidloes affair had its repercussions elsewhere. It probably determined the action of the authorities in South Wales. At all events, in May they set about arresting Chartist leaders there also — including Henry Vincent, whose paper, *The Western Vindicator*, published in Bath, had become the principal organ of Chartism in both South-West England and South Wales. Frost was a regular contributor, parading his familiar Cobbettite doctrines ; but the strength of the paper lay in Vincent's articles, reporting his speaking tours and the progress of the movement throughout the districts covered by his journeys.

Many witnesses pay tribute to the power of Vincent's oratory, and to his immense hold on the people, men and women alike. He could sing as well as speak, a sure way to the hearts of South Wales audiences. His arrest profoundly moved the people, already stirred deeply by the Llanidloes struggle. Frost was sent post-haste from London to prevent sympathetic uprisings in South Wales ; for the Convention wanted to avoid all provocative action while the National Petition was still awaiting debate in the House of Commons. In South Wales, Frost made speeches designed to prevent an immediate revolt, but strongly enough worded — as they had to be, in order to achieve their purpose — to draw upon him a charge of seditious utterances. For the time being the Convention's purpose was served. The South Wales Chartists did not take up arms. In June, Frost was able to leave his own district in order to attend and address a great Chartist demonstration in Glasgow. But he had left behind him a placard on which the Government was in a position to base a second prosecution. He had proposed that, since the authorities were imprisoning the Chartist leaders, the workers should retaliate by seizing the bodies of some of their worst opponents, and holding them as hostages for the incarcerated leaders of the movement. " If others exceed the limits, if our leading men be imprisoned, no violence having been committed, why then we shall consider that a coal-pit is quite as safe a place for a tyrannical persecutor as a gaol for an innocent Chartist." This was highly seditious language, whether or not it was practically meant; and by June 1839 Frost had two serious charges hanging over him.

He was, however, not under arrest ; and at the beginning of July he returned to his place in the Convention to advocate ' ulterior measures ' after the rejection of the Chartist Petition by the House of Commons. He did not advocate the ' Sacred Month ', which he realised to be unworkable in view of the poverty of the people and the prevalence of unemployment in the factory and mining areas. But, if the ' Sacred Month ' were ruled out, what ' ulterior measures ' could the Chartists take, short of an attempt at violent revolution ? Neither Frost nor anyone else squarely faced the issue. When the Convention reopened in London on August 26, after a month's adjournment during which the delegates had been testing the state of feeling in the country, only a rump of the original membership remained. It had become clear to all that the ' Sacred Month ' was impracticable ; and in truth the only choice before the Convention was between dissolution and open rebellion. One party, headed by Peter Murray McDouall and Dr. John Taylor, and supported for the most part by Julian Harney, wanted to go on to the bitter end. But O'Connor and his followers realised the certainty of failure in face of Napier's skilful disposition of his forces, and the debate continued uneasily day after day, with no decided issue.

Frost was in the chair at the Convention during the most critical of these latter days ; and twice he was called upon to give his casting vote in face of an equally divided assembly. The question by then had become, should the Convention dissolve, with a view to the election of a new Convention as soon as a more favourable opportunity presented itself, or should it merely adjourn again, in the hope that things would speedily improve ? A special meeting was held on September 4, after an attempt had been made to get more delegates sent up from the provinces ; and on September 6 Frost gave his casting vote, at the end of a prolonged discussion, for adjournment in preference to dissolution. But this did not end the matter ; a few days later the question was voted on again, and this time Frost gave his casting vote in favour of dissolution. The great People's Convention, or rather what was left of it, came to an end on September 12, 1839. It ended with the issue still undecided between the advocates of rebellion and the advocates of awaiting a better opportunity.

During these last stages of the Convention, Frost, in accordance with his mandate from South Wales, had been doing his best to persuade the new Home Secretary, Lord Normanby, who had just succeeded Lord John Russell, to release Henry Vincent and other Chartist prisoners. He met with no favour, and had to return to South Wales to report both the dissolution of the Convention and the failure of his efforts on behalf of the prisoners. He continued, however, to make appeals to the local authorities — the Lord-Lieutenant and the county magistrates — to mitigate the severity of the conditions of Vincent's imprisonment ; and at the end of September he is found stating in support of his plea that " the agitation has now subsided ". At the same time he seems to have been engaged in an attempt to reorganise the South Wales Chartists on a new plan of ' tithings ' in each parish — that is, in groups of ten, each under a leader, who was to be responsible for transmitting instructions to and from his own group. It was alleged after the ' Newport Rising ' that this new organisation was undertaken with a direct view to armed revolt ; but, if this had been so, Frost would hardly have described the plan quite openly in one of his contributions to *The Western Vindicator*. What is clear is that, in face of the arrests, the new Chartist organisation in South Wales was meant to be more secret in its working than the old organisation based on the various local Working Men's Associations ; and to this extent it could be used to further the projects of the revolutionaries in the Chartist ranks.

It is also clear that, at the beginning of October, Frost was doing his best to dissuade the South Wales Chartists from any immediate appeal to arms. On October 3 he addressed a gathering of Chartists at the inn kept by Zephaniah Williams at Blaina, in Coalbrook Vale, and exhorted them to patience until he, as their head, issued the call to action. He told them that the rest of the country was not yet ready and that a premature outbreak would be fatal to the cause. Scotland and Lancashire and the West of England were preparing for action, but the time was not yet. Frost ended by saying that he proposed to offer himself as a candidate for Monmouthshire when Parliament was dissolved, and that he expected 30,000 men to march on Monmouth to support him on election day.

Frost's speech on this occasion — the last public gathering of the South Wales Chartists before the ' Newport Rising ' — does not read like the utterance of a revolutionary leader engaged in planning an armed revolt. It does, however, read very much like the troubled eloquence of a leader who, himself opposed to or realising the hopelessness of such a revolt, fears that his followers will forsake him and go their own way to disaster unless he covers up his counsel of moderation with a sufficient show of revolutionary language. It is pretty plain, not only from what Frost said on this occasion, but also from the speech made by his fellow leader, William Lloyd Jones, who was soon to stand with him and Zephaniah Williams in the dock, that revolutionary preparations were already afoot, and that the chance of an attempt at armed revolt was real. Frost was trying to stop the outbreak, either because he disbelieved in it altogether, or because he felt that the time was not ripe. Zephaniah Williams, it seems probable from the evidence, was also counselling prudence. The firebrand was William Jones, the young watchmaker whose speeches were rousing the mining valleys ; and behind Jones were other leaders, now mostly unidentifiable by name, who were the local organisers of the miners and ironworkers of Merthyr, Dowlais, Ebbw Vale, Blaina, Pontypool, and the rest of the barbarous townships in which the Guests and the Crawshays had pent up their human instruments of production.

The plausible conclusion is that the more militant local Chartists had been making their preparations for an armed uprising during the time while Frost had been away in

London at the Chartist Convention, and that Frost, on his return, found himself confronted with a revolutionary movement which it was beyond his power to control. There is plenty of evidence that for some time after the meeting of October 3 he continued to advise the men against a rising. He spoke in that sense in several of the most important centres ; and there were secret delegate meetings at which he presumably gave the same advice. But he was faced in the end with the choice between dissociating himself from the revolutionaries, at the cost of being branded as a traitor by many of his followers, and taking part in an armed movement which his judgement condemned as hopeless in the light of what he knew about the situation in other parts of the country.

There is much conflicting evidence about what was decided at the secret delegate gatherings of the Chartists which went on throughout October. It seems likely that finally Frost and those who agreed with him were outvoted, and that they then agreed to act with the more extreme party. But it is much more doubtful whether they agreed to take part in a real insurrection, or planned, as was stated at the trial, to set up an English Republic with Frost as President. The sole evidence for this comes from one witness, who very likely made it up in the hope of currying favour with the authorities. We do know, from a number of witnesses, that during the actual march on Newport Zephaniah Williams repeatedly assured those who were invited to join the march that there would be no bloodshed, and that the Chartists were only " taking a turn as far as Newport ". Whether this meant that Williams and his friends were expecting the soldiers in Newport to mutiny and join them or that they intended only to demonstrate in force and then retire from the town, it is now impossible to say. Probably some of the leaders meant one thing, and some another. Some intended the march on Newport to be merely a demonstration ; others regarded it as the opening move in a revolution.

At all events, throughout the mining areas secret preparations went on during October ; and at some stage Frost agreed to take part in the march on Newport. The general plan was that the Chartists should assemble in the hills at three main points on the evening of November 3, and then converge for a combined descent on Newport in the early morning. One contingent was to be drawn from Merthyr, Dowlais and Rhymney and the places near by; a second from Ebbw Vale, Bryn Mawr, Nantyglo, and Blaina ; and a third from Blaenavon, Abersychan, and Pontypool. From points of assembly up the valleys the three columns were to descend towards Newport, gathering recruits on the way ; and they were to meet at Risca for a combined entry into the town. They were to carry all the arms they could muster ; but, as we have seen, Williams and others were telling them, up to the last moment, that the arms would not need to be used.

The night of November 3 was dark and stormy. The Chartists were soon wet through ; and it is not at all surprising that their movements did not proceed according to plan. There were long periods of waiting for missing contingents ; and Frost, with the advance guard, spent hours of delay near the Welch Oak, only two or three miles from Newport. Finally, the order was given to advance, when the main body of Frost's and Williams's men had arrived, and also a few of Jones's from Pontypool. The main body of Jones's men from Abersychan and Blaenavon, reputed the most revolutionary centres, did not arrive at the appointed place of meeting until the affair at Newport was already over, and the other contingents were already in flight.

Frost, meanwhile, having decided to wait no longer for Jones, had descended into Newport with his men. The long delays had, of course, given the authorities in Newport ample time for preparation. There were only a handful of soldiers available, and most of them were engaged in guarding the workhouse, which was expected to be a special object of attack. In the town itself there were only thirty soldiers, under a lieutenant, who were posted at the Westgate Hotel. Here the magistrates had taken up their quarters ; and they had enrolled upwards of five hundred special constables, with whose help they secured the leaders of the Newport Chartists, and thus prevented any attack in the town itself. The few soldiers who were in the town had only arrived, in response to an urgent summons from the Mayor, a short time before the Chartists appeared on the scene.

Led by Frost, the Chartist detachments entered the town, and halted in the open space in front of the Westgate Hotel, where the thirty soldiers were now stationed. What happened next will probably never be known with any certainty ; for the evidence is conflicting. Someone among the Chartists shouted to the special constables gathered outside the door of the Westgate Hotel (the soldiers were still behind shutters inside a front room) either " Give up the prisoners " — *i.e.* the Newport Chartists who had been arrested and shut up in the hotel during the night — or " Surrender yourselves our prisoners " — *i.e.* a summons to the magistrates to surrender. The former sounds the more likely version, and at the trial only one witness was produced in support of the alternative allegation. Whatever was said, a special constable shouted back defiance, and a scuffle followed, in the course of which some Chartists seem to have penetrated into the hall of the hotel. At this point somebody let off a fire-arm, but whether it was a Chartist or a special constable who fired first remains unknown. More desultory firing followed, and some shots went through the shutters of the room in which the soldiers were still being held in reserve. Either the Mayor or the lieutenant in command of the soldiers — again the accounts conflict — thereupon ordered the soldiers to fire. The shutters were flung back, and a volley was sent into the middle of the crowd of Chartists gathered outside the hotel. The soldiers then fired again at the crowd, and also at the Chartists who had made their way into the hotel. On the average they fired but three rounds each ; the number killed by them is given variously at from ten to twenty-two. Probably the higher figure includes the wounded as well as the dead.

It appears that, at the first volley from the soldiers, the crowd of Chartists outside the hotel turned and fled. Either they had no stomach for a fight, or they were left leaderless because the most active Chartists were among those who had forced their way into the hotel. It seems likely that the presence of the soldiers came as an entire surprise. They were known to be in the neighbourhood ; but as we have seen, the main body was guarding the workhouse, and the small detachment at the hotel had arrived there only just before the Chartists. At all events, there was no resistance. The Chartist ' army ' turned tail, and its contingents began to make their way back to their native villages as best they could. Some of them, in their flight, fell in with William Jones and his contingent, just arriving on the scene ; and Jones, when he heard the news, is reported to have exclaimed " Damn me, then we are done ! " and retreated in order back into the hills.

Such was the ' Newport Rising ' — the nearest thing to an armed revolt that Chartism produced and, because it was the nearest thing, an episode magnified both by contemporaries and by subsequent historians. How small it was can be judged not only from the numbers of the slain — even if we accept the largest estimate — but also from the fact that the total of the claims arising out of it for damage to property came to less than £100. That so small an affair should have become as celebrated as the ' Newport Rising ' calls for some explanation ; but the explanation is easy to find. In 1839 a great many people in England — and especially in the upper classes — were expecting a Chartist attempt at armed revolution. When only the little ' Newport Rising ' actually occurred, it was natural to interpret it in the light of these fears ; and thus the largeness of expectation, rather than the smallness of the event, has determined its place in history.

There were at the time, and there are still, many versions of the story. One of the most popular has been that the aim of the Chartists was not to make a revolution, but only to set free Henry Vincent and his fellow prisoners from gaol. This version, however, is incredible. Vincent was in gaol, not at Newport, but at Monmouth, a long way away to the north-west ; and it cannot be credited that the Chartists, if they had meant to rescue Vincent, would have marched south on Newport instead of making west for Monmouth itself, by way of Usk. A glance at the map will put this point beyond a doubt. If the aim was to release Vincent, this must have been meant to be accomplished not directly, but by capturing Newport first, and then using the initial success as a means of rousing the entire countryside.

At the opposite extreme is the view that the ' Newport Rising ' was carefully arranged as a part of a general revolutionary movement throughout Great Britain, but that the rest of this movement somehow failed to come off. There is the oft-repeated story, produced by some of the Crown witnesses at the trial, that Frost had declared his intention of blowing up Newport Bridge, and thus preventing the Welsh mail from reaching Birmingham — its non-arrival to be a signal to the Midland Chartists to rise. This story was exposed as absurd at the trial. The Welsh mail did not go to Birmingham, except via Bristol, and the arrival of the coach from Bristol at Birmingham would be quite unaffected by what might happen at Newport. Probably there had been general talk about the stopping of the mail coaches acting as a sign to Chartists that revolts elsewhere had succeeded ; but this particular talk about Frost's intention to get the Birmingham coach stopped is clearly nonsense. Incidentally, he himself denied the story *in toto* in his later years, after his return to England, when admitting it would certainly have done him no harm.

It is much more a moot point whether the South Wales Chartists were acting in entire isolation, or did expect that their rising would be accompanied, or at all events immediately followed, by similar risings elsewhere. Much has been made of a circumstantial story, related by William Lovett in his autobiography, about a meeting of Chartist delegates held at Heckmondwike some time late in October, at which the delegates of the Lancashire and Yorkshire Chartists, headed apparently by Peter Bussey, were informed that the Welsh Chartists were preparing for a rising, and promised to cooperate. But Lovett's story, based not on personal knowledge — he was in prison at the time — but on information received from others, does not hold together very well. Its main point is to throw discredit on Feargus O'Connor for having first agreed to lead the rising, and then backed down, whereas O'Connor was certainly away in Ireland at the time when the alleged meeting took place. Moreover, Lovett's account appears to involve a meeting between Frost and the Northern leaders some time quite late in October ; but there seems to be little doubt that he was at this time in South Wales.

If there was any direct contact between Frost and the

Northern revolutionaries, it must surely have taken place earlier in October, probably about the 11th, when Frost was billed to speak at a Chartist dinner in Bury, Lancashire. It is quite possible that he did on this occasion confer with the Northern leaders ; but, if he did, he can hardly have made plans with them for an immediate rising, or why did he continue, after his return to Wales, to urge the South Wales Chartists to defer action ? Lovett's story also makes out that O'Connor sent emissaries to South Wales and to Yorkshire to endeavour to stop the rising ; but, if he did, this must surely have been earlier still, before his departure for Ireland on October 4 or 5. It seems more probable that the emissary who came to visit Frost was sent, not by O'Connor, but by Bussey or one of the other Yorkshire leaders. Lovett's version is that the emissary's task was to stop the Welsh from rising, that Frost told him it was much too late to prevent this, and sent him back to inform the Northerners that the Welsh revolt would go on according to plan, and that on receipt of the message Bussey and his friends decided to make their own plans for a rising a week later than the date fixed for South Wales. The news of the failure at Newport must, however, have damped Northern ardour — if the story is to be believed at all ; for no rising in either Lancashire or Yorkshire acutally occurred.

My reading of this confused account is that there had been talks in London, probably before the final adjournment of the Convention, about a concerted Chartist rising, and that probably Frost had taken some part in these talks. This would allow time for O'Connor's intervention with a view to stopping the appeal to arms before his departure for Ireland, and it would also plausibly explain Frost's behaviour. It is very possible that he had taken part in the discussion of plans for a rising until O'Connor, for whom he had a great admiration, dissuaded him, that he then changed his attitude and urged his South Wales followers not to rise, and that, when he found they were determined to rise in spite of him, he sent a message to Bussey in the hope that a simultaneous rising in Yorkshire might help to give the Welshmen a chance of success. This at any rate makes sense, and does not involve any perfidy, such as Lovett alleges, on O'Connor's part, or any irreconcilability in the dates. It is also quite possible that Frost and the Northern leaders met again in Lancashire on or about October 14, but without arriving at any agreed decision about a concerted rising.

The general conclusion seems to be that, whatever may have been said at the alleged meetings between Frost and the Northerners, the Welsh Chartists decided to rise on their own account, and without any firm assurance of support elsewhere. Nor is this difficult to believe ; for this same area in Monmouthshire and Glamorganshire had been the scene, only a few years before, of violent uprisings on quite as large a scale as the Newport affair, and it is highly probable that the surviving leaders of these earlier movements were also at the bottom of the later rising, and that Frost was merely a puppet in their hands.

This earlier revolt of the South Wales workers had taken place in 1831. From 1829 the coalfield had been suffering from severe depression. Wages were being cut heavily, and the men's grievances were aggravated by the prevalence of the truck system, under which the workers were paid largely, not in money, but in coupons which could be used only for buying goods, often at exorbitant prices, at shops kept by the employers or by foremen acting under their authority. This situation led, about 1830, to a rapid spread of Trade Unionism, and the local bodies were linked up into a ' Friendly Society of Coal Mining ', which in the spring of 1831 decided to become affiliated to the National Association for the Protection of Labour — John Doherty's attempt to build up from Manchester a General Union of all trades for concerted resistance to wage-reductions. The ' Friendly Society ' proceeded to organise mass demonstrations which marched about the coalfield demanding, at first with success, undertakings from the various masters that wages should be paid fully in cash, and truck abolished. In connection with this movement there occurred in Merthyr Tydfil, in June 1831, an affray which, beginning as a demonstration, developed into a pitched battle. The colliers, descending upon Merthyr much as Frost's contingents were to descend on Newport eight years later, wrecked the Court of Requests, in which were filed the accounts of debts owing by them, the company's truck shop, and other buildings, and then marched out of the town and stopped the ironworks in the neighbourhood. Reinforced by the ironworkers, the colliers then returned to Merthyr, where they found the magistrates assembled in the Castle Inn and defended by a detachment of Highlanders who were drawn up outside. Parleys followed. Guest, Crawshay, and other leading coalowners and ironmasters addressed the crowd, and asked it to disperse. Instead of doing so, the workers, directed in Welsh by a leader known as ' Lewis the Huntsman ', rushed in upon the soldiers and succeeded in disarming them. The magistrates and special constables inside the hotel thereupon fired into the crowd, killing at least fifteen persons and wounding sixty others. The workers withdrew to a distance, but did not disband. They retired with the arms they had taken from the military to a strong position about two miles away, and prepared to resist the expected reinforcements of soldiers.

On the following day there were further battles. The workers successfully ambushed two detachments of cavalry sent to the relief of Merthyr from Cardiff and Swansea. The Cardiff troop withdrew in fair order ; but the Swansea soldiers were surrounded and disarmed. The workers then released their prisoners, and marshalled their forces for an attack on Pennydarren House, where the remaining soldiers and special constables were assembled.

It was, however, decided to defer the storm of Pennydarren House for two days — presumably in the hope of getting reinforcements from further afield. This delay was fatal. More soldiers were brought in ; and the workers' army, when it at length advanced to the attack, found itself confronted with a much stronger force, and retreated. Dissensions then broke out among the workers, and men began to drift away. The soldiers, directed by the magistrates, advanced upon those who remained ; and the revolt ended in a disorderly flight. Its principal leader, Dick Penderyn, was caught and executed ; and the iron and coal masters promptly turned to the destruction of the men's Union, dismissing all who refused to renounce membership.

These reprisals did not end the revolt ; they drove it

underground. There followed at once the movement known as the ' Scotch Cattle '. Instead of trying to enrol the main body of the workers in open Unions, the remaining leaders adopted the plan of a secret terrorist organisation composed only of picked men. In 1832 the Scotch Cattle began a policy of beating and destruction of property directed against workers who undercut the established wage-rates, employers' agents who managed the hated truck shops, and other offenders against the claims of labour. The military were called in, and rewards were offered for the detection of the leaders of this movement ; but through the next two years the outrages, carried out by night by small groups of men with blackened faces, continued practically unchecked.

In 1834 a fresh wave of Trade Unionism swept over the whole country. In South Wales the old Union Lodges were re-formed and affiliated to Robert Owen's Grand National Consolidated Trades Union. But, as in other parts of the country, the employers retaliated by repeating their earlier tactics. All men who would not renounce Trade Union membership were discharged, and the Union was broken. The Scotch Cattle had ceased their depredations during this second period of Trade Union activity ; but on the break-up of the Union their forays were at once resumed.

It is against this background of violence, bred of the appalling conditions under which the South Wales workers laboured and lived, that the ' Newport Rising ' needs to be considered and interpreted. There was nothing more violent or revolutionary about the disturbances of 1839 than about these earlier affrays ; and it has to be borne in mind that the revolt of 1831 had gone successfully enough, up to a point, to give the leaders some reason to feel that they might do better at a second attempt. The only real difference was that the troubles of 1831 and the following years had been mainly local in origin and had arisen merely out of local grievances, whereas the movement of 1839 was, in form at any rate, part of a national agitation, with the aim of making The People's Charter the law of the land. The Newport affair occurred at a moment when a revolutionary attempt was at least half expected throughout the industrial areas. It therefore had the appearance of an abortive revolution and not, like the earlier movements, of merely local rioting. But I doubt whether the difference was of any great account in the workers' minds. In 1839, as in 1831, most of them were making their protest, as best they could, against almost unbearable conditions of oppression. They were not thinking about the Charter nearly so much as about truck and bad conditions, the breaking-up of their Union, and the new grievance of the Poor Law Act, with its ' Bastilles ' for immuring the victims of industrial depression.

These earlier movements make the events of November 1839 much more intelligible than they can be to historians who ignore them, and treat South Wales Chartism as an isolated episode. In the coal and iron districts of Glamorgan and Monmouthshire violence was endemic in the relations between masters and men. The northern factory areas and even the northern coalfields were homes of urbane civilisation compared with the South Wales mining valleys. No wonder Newport had its rising, however hopeless, whereas in Lancashire and Yorkshire and the North-East the workers decided, when it came to the point, to bide their time rather than embark on a hopeless revolutionary attempt !

In the foregoing account of the ' Newport Rising ' I have omitted all mention of one explanation that has been advanced, and even solemnly considered by some historians — that the affair was fomented by Russian agents and paid for by Russian gold. I have left it out, because there is no shadow of evidence for it, and it is too silly to be worth arguing about. David Urquhart, friend of Karl Marx and fellow hater with him of all things Russian, doubtless believed it when he put it about ; but Urquhart was capable of believing anything when he saw a chance of incriminating Russian agents. The entire story can be safely dismissed as the fantasy of a disordered mind. Not Russian agents, but sheer working-class misery and governing-class oppression, were responsible for the Newport revolt.

Frost, who had done his best to stop it almost to the last, paid the penalty for throwing in his lot with the revolutionaries when he realised that the thing was bound to happen, whatever he said. He, Zephaniah Williams, and William

Jones, captured after the flight from the Westgate Hotel, were first sentenced to death and then, after anxious debates and sharp divisions within the Cabinet, had their sentences commuted to transportation for life in view of the widespread campaign which was carried on throughout the country on their behalf.

They were tried in December 1839 by a Special Commission over which the Lord Chief Justice, Sir Nicholas Tindal, elected to preside. With him were Justices Parke and Williams, both certain to take a vindictive line against the prisoners. Parke had been prominent on the Special Commissions which had wreaked the vengeance of the governing classes on the agricultural labourers after the revolt of 1830–31, and Williams had been the judge responsible for the sentence upon the unfortunate Tolpuddle Martyrs in 1834. From such men the Newport Chartists could expect no mercy, but Tindal was a judge of a different order, and the hopes of the defence were in him. The Chartists throughout the country made a great effort to raise funds for the defence of the prisoners ; and Frost had on his side, against the Attorney General, Sir John Campbell, and the Solicitor General, Sir Thomas Wilde, who appeared for the Crown, two highly skilled advocates — Fitzroy Kelly and Frederick Pollock. Frost had, moreover, the enthusiastic aid of his solicitor stepson, William Foster Geach ; and, thanks to Geach's acumen, he and his fellow prisoners were very nearly acquitted on a technical flaw in the prosecution's procedure.

The flaw was purely technical — a failure to deliver the list of witnesses for the prosecution simultaneously with the indictment — but it had important consequences, even though the trial was allowed to proceed. Frost and his companions were charged with high treason — with levying war against the Queen ; and it was therefore necessary for the prosecution to prove that the march on Newport had been more than a riot, and had been intended as the opening move in an insurrection. There was no dearth of witnesses to assert this ; the question was, how far could their evidence be believed. The Crown witnesses were all too apt, in their eagerness to save their own skins, to assert too much, and to be tripped up, and betrayed into contradictions, by the cleverness of the defending counsel. There was, however, no real doubt that some persons had planned a real insurrection, and that Frost, even if he had tried to stop it, had thrown in his lot with it when he found that it could not be stopped. What is surprising is not that the prisoners were convicted, but that there should ever have been any doubt about the result of the trial. Yet there was great doubt; and at the end the Lord Chief Justice, in his summing-up, gave the jury a plain instruction that he favoured an acquittal, not because he held them guiltless, but because he considered that their crime had been something less than the high treason of which they were accused.

The jury, however, composed of good haters of the Chartists, was in no mood to draw fine legal distinctions. It convicted Frost and his fellow prisoners without a question; and there was nothing for it for Tindal but to pronounce sentence of death. The question that remained open was whether the sentence could stand at all in face of the technical objection raised at the beginning of the trial. This was a point on which the court had reserved judgement; and in January the fifteen judges of the Court of Exchequer met to hear counsel and consider the point. With characteristic legalism they decided by a majority that the objection raised by Frost's counsel was valid in law, and then went on to decide that the objection had not been raised at the correct time (Geach had only hit upon it after the trial had begun) and that it could not therefore invalidate the verdict.

The death sentence therefore stood. Protests, and demands for clemency, poured in upon the Cabinet from all over the country. But the Cabinet refused to relent until the Lord Chief Justice himself put in a plea against the exaction of the extreme penalty. Upon this the Cabinet gave way, and the sentences upon the prisoners were commuted to transportation for life. For three weeks before this, they had been in the condemned cell, expecting execution. When the Cabinet changed its mind, they were hurried out of the country with all possible speed.

John Frost spent the next fifteen years of his life — from his fifty-sixth to his seventy-first year — as a convict in

Tasmania. He had a bad voyage, in the course of which he rejected a proposal to take part in a plot for seizing the ship and making for South America. On arrival in Tasmania he seems to have been well treated. He was not compelled to wear convict dress, and was made a clerk in the office of the commandant of the penal settlement at Port Arthur. he wrote home to his wife a long reassuring letter about his condition. This was published in *The Times* and as a pamphlet, and led to an outcry that the Chartist prisoners were being pampered.

But Frost's relative good fortune was not to last. In his letter, intended only for his family, he had made a personal attack on Lord John Russell. For this he was put on trial under instructions from home, and sentenced to two years' hard labour under the cruel conditions then prevailing in the penal settlement. He must have had a magnificent constitution, for he not only endured this without losing his health, but said that he was at this period stronger than he had ever been before.

At the end of the two years Frost became an indentured warehouseman in a grocery store at Hobart. There he stayed for three years, under a bad master, before getting his ticket of leave. Then for eight years he earned his living as a schoolmaster. During this period his daughter Catherine came out to join him ; his wife wished to come, but he was still hoping to be able to return home, and unwilling for her to face life in a penal colony, or to sever her links with England. At last, in 1854 he got the news that the Aberdeen Government had pardoned him on condition that he lived outside Great Britain.

Frost was now seventy ; but he and his daughter left for the United States, where he stayed for a year, first in California and then in New York. During this period he published a pamphlet, *A Letter to the People of the United States*, mainly an exposure of the savage conditions of convict life, but containing also an attack on the British governing class as " the curse of the world ". In 1855 he was included among the political offenders pardoned at the close of the Crimean War, and was at length free to return to his native country. He settled down with his wife and family at

Stapleton, near Bristol, and lived on there for another twenty-two years. His wife died a year after his homecoming, and most of his children died or married ; but his daughter Anne lived with him for the rest of his life.

Frost was welcomed back by the remaining Chartists on his return to England. There were demonstrations in his honour in Newport and in London, and he announced his intention of resuming his place in public affairs. He lectured up and down the country, sometimes giving his audiences recollections of the early Chartist days, but more often speaking of the horrors of the system of transportation and demanding complete reform. He also amplified the pamphlet which he had issued in America into *A Letter to the People of Great Britain*. But his lectures seem to have been soon given up ; and Frost, like Robert Owen, turned in his old age to Spiritualism. He planned to write his life, but never did — or at all events no such writing of his is known to exist. He died on July 27, 1877, in his ninety-fourth year, many years after Chartism had ceased to be more than a memory.

The ' Newport Rising ' was a small affair ; and its leader was a small man, not only in stature, but in importance too. If Frost had not been the leading figure in the ' Rising ', there would have been little to make him more memorable than many other local protagonists of Chartism whose names are now forgotten. He was neither original in his ideas, nor possessed of any remarkable qualities of leadership, nor particularly interesting as a person. He was an honest enough Radical, more of the old Cobbettite school than of the new Chartist generation ; and his Radicalism stood the test of more than fourteen years' deportation, and remained with him to the end of his life. But there was not much ' to ' him ; and even martyrdom did not make him look like a great man.

To this day, the part which Frost actually played in the events which cause his name to be remembered retains its uncertainty. Was there a plan for a national Chartist uprising after the rejection of the National Petition of 1839, and, if so, was Frost privy to it, or even one of its chief instigators ? Did the colliers and ironworkers who marched on Newport during the night of November 3, 1839, believe that they were the advance guard of the British Revolution ; and, if so, who was responsible for making them hold this belief ? If there was a national plan, why did nothing happen in Lancashire or Yorkshire, where the main strength of the Chartists lay ? If there was no such plan, what possessed Frost and his associates to take up arms upon their own lonely account ? Were there *agents provocateurs* at work, or ' Russian agents ', as David Urquhart and his friends asserted, or merely fools ? I have done what I can to answer these questions ; but some are unanswerable, despite the efforts of historical students to sift out the truth. Probably some of them will remain without answers that can be proved correct.

There are, however, as we have seen, good reasons for being sceptical about the more sensational versions of the story. The ' Russian agents ' version can be safely dismissed : there is hardly a shred of evidence for it, and it is, on the face of the matter, obvious nonsense. The question whether there was a national plan of insurrection, and the ' Newport Rising ' was the only bit of it that even began to be translated into practice, is much more difficult. Plainly, many people wanted to believe that there was a national plan ; for, after all the Chartists' talk of ' ulterior measures ', after all the violent language that had been used, the subsidence of the movement, without an appeal to force, had the quality of an anti-climax, and the human mind prefers sensational to humdrum interpretations — at any rate when the danger is past. Moreover, even historians prefer history to make sense ; and the Newport affair, unless it was part of a wider plan, looks silly.

Suppose the Chartists had captured Newport, what could they have done ? Suppose they had, thereafter, marched on Monmouth, where their most popular leader, Henry Vincent, was in prison, what could they have done ? Suppose they had captured every town and factory in South Wales, or even made themselves complete masters of the Principality, what could they have done ? They could have done nothing, unless the English Chartists had risen too, and had met with a similar success. Surely, then, argue the rationalists, they must have expected the English Chartists to rise, or have

believed that they were actually rising, or they would never
have started on their ill-fated march. Alas, the historians
are more rational than history. Men do behave as idiots, not
only individually, but together. Leaders of men do lead,
even when in retrospect their acts of leadership appear merely
futile.

In this case there may have been a national plan — of
sorts — adumbrated during the last days of the Chartist
Convention, but never fully worked out or agreed on. But,
if there was, one would have expected some evidence of it
to survive. There were men alive afterwards who would
have run no risk from disclosing it — men who would surely
have known of its existence, and were safe enough in the
United States or Australia to have boasted of their part in it
with impunity in later years. None did so boast : no one
said a word that made the ' Newport Rising ' look less hopeless in its inception. There were plenty of vague hints and
surmises, but nothing more. I may yet be proved wrong ;
but the absence of any evidence makes me feel pretty sure
that there was nothing that deserves to be called a plan, and
that the ' Newport Rising ' was as local in its inspiration, or
nearly so, as it appears. It was, in effect, the outcome of the
same inhumane conditions in the South Wales collieries and
ironworks as had produced the Merthyr Rising of 1831 and
the violence of the secret ' Scotch Cattle ' during the succeed-
ing years. This suggests strongly that its inspirer was not
Frost, but some successor of Dick Penderyn whose name
history does not record, or some group of leaders who were
themselves the victims of the desperate oppression of the
Guests and Crawshays — the real rulers of the narrow
mining valleys whence the half-savage colliers and ironworkers made their ill-fated descent upon Newport. Eight
years earlier these same men had disarmed a body of High-
land soldiers and routed two troops of cavalry sent against
them by the forces of law and order. True, they had thereafter failed and broken when the soldiers were heavily reinforced. But their first adventure in rebellion had been
successful enough at the outset to encourage them to try
again. Frost was their leader only in the sense that, as their
delegate to the Chartist Convention, he did not hang back

when, against his advice and judgement, they decided upon their course. He felt responsible to them, and he paid the penalty of putting his loyalty before his interest or his judgement. He was an honest man, according to his lights, though not a great one.

VI

Joseph Sturge

JOSEPH STURGE, the 'Quaker Chartist', was born at
Elberton, Gloucestershire, on August 2, 1793. His
father was a fairly prosperous farmer and grazier, with
a family of twelve, of whom Joseph was the fourth. His
parents were both Quakers whose family associations with
the Society of Friends went back to the seventeenth century ;
and the neighbourhood of his birth was a stronghold of
Quakerism. Joseph was bred, lived, and died a devout
member of the Society of Friends, though he antagonised
many of his fellow members, and drew down on himself the
anger of many of the elders, by taking an active part in
politics. His offence was doubtless deeply aggravated by
the side he took, and by his readiness to work with ' infidel '
Chartists and enemies of the rights of property ; for the
Quakers were a well-to-do group, and inclined to extreme
conservatism in their attitude to public affairs, as well as
very strict about their communications with the ungodly.
But the Society had, even apart from the prejudices of its
members, in the early nineteenth century a strong prejudice
against any activities that might involve Quakers in the turmoils of party politics, and thus disturb that personal
' quiet ' which seemed to them essential to living a good life.
In business, indeed, they were deeply involved, and they felt
fully justified in taking part in such speculative affairs as the
promotion of canal, and later railway, enterprise. They
served on boards of commissioners for paving, lighting,
watching, and draining the new industrial towns, though
some of the stricter members felt qualms about activities so
likely to involve them in party strife. They were drawn to
take part in certain great crusades resting on a moral basis
— against the slave trade and later against slavery itself, and
for the prevention of war — although they could not forward

these causes without coming perilously near to political action. But, when it came to members of the Society of Friends actually standing for Parliament, or associating themselves with political movements which directly touched constitutional issues or the wider questions of economic and social structure, most of the older generation of Quakers held up their hands in horror, and even the younger Quakers did not enter into such affairs without anxious communing with God, and considerable fears of the effect on their morals and their prospects of eternal salvation.

Joseph Sturge was one of the leading offenders against the quietist tenets of the older school. Though he never succeeded in entering Parliament, he made several attempts and helped to secure the return of others of whose personalities and policies he approved. He served first on the Board of Street Commissioners, which was the main civic body in Birmingham before its incorporation as a borough, and thereafter as an alderman on its Town Council. He had a hand in starting several Radical newspapers ; he played his part in the Birmingham Political Union during the Reform Bill struggle ; and, what was worst of all, he accepted all the Six Points of The People's Charter, and was ready in furtherance of his political principles to join hands with working-class agitators tainted with atheism as well as sedition.

These were grave offences ; and many times at Meeting, Joseph Sturge had to listen to those whom the spirit moved to comment adversely on his backslidings. He took all such admonishments quite without resentment, and with a readiness at all times to avow his own fallibility and unworthiness. But he never took any notice of them, so as to alter his conduct. He prayed for reassurance, and received on every occasion the answer that he was right. He was indeed, by universal testimony of those who knew him, a very positive person, untroubled by any visible doubts concerning the correctness of his opinions. By his own account he was, in youth, " peppery " by disposition ; but in manhood he reserved this quality for his protests against cruelty and injustice, and kept a strong restraint over his temper in his public dealings. He was intensely humane, and a hater of every sort of oppression. And he had a remarkably practical mind, which moved instantly from the recognition of an abuse to devising means of removing it. Cobden said of him when he was sixty-three : " It is really refreshing to see Sturge's inexhaustible energy. He could run a dozen young men off their legs. No sooner is he back from his visit to Russia [in an attempt to stop the Crimean War] than he enquires if there is nothing to be done ! I have sometimes wondered what such men would do, if the world's crimes and follies did not find them plenty of employment in the work of well-doing."

Sturge's career would indeed have been impossible except to a man of great physical endurance as well as moral courage. He had a strong body, which could stand very great strains, and an exuberant energy which he never frittered away on trifles. Some of his doings have no doubt a certain absurdity ; and his habit of rushing off and doing a thing the moment he thought of it occasionally played him false. But much oftener it served him well : certainly, without it he could not have accomplished half so much.

Joseph Sturge had very little formal education. From the age of seven he spent three years running wild on the farm of his grandfather, Marshall, in Warwickshire. From ten to fourteen he was sent to school, first at Thornbury and then at the Quaker school at Sidcot, in Somerset. Then, at fourteen, he started work on his father's farm ; and, still in his teens, was set up on a small farm of his own at Awre, close by the Severn estuary. During these years of farming he also went about a good deal with his father to various agricultural markets, gaining knowledge which was to stand him in good stead later on ; and he began to take part in various religious activities, joining an ' Endeavour Society ' formed for mutual improvement by a group of young Bristol Quakers, and a little later becoming fired with zeal in consequence of a missionary visit to the neighbourhood by William Forster, father of the Liberal statesman, and thereafter his lifelong friend. Under this influence he became secretary to a Thornbury branch of the British and Foreign Bible Society, which he helped to found, and began to take an interest in the anti-slavery movement.

Farming, however, was not Sturge's bent, and in 1814 he accepted an invitation from a friend named Cotterell to join him in setting up in business as a corn-dealer at Bewdley, in Worcestershire. He moved to Bewdley, and in the following year his favourite sister, Sophia, joined him there to keep house for him. Two years later his father died, and two years afterwards his mother ; and thereafter he gave a home at Bewdley to a number of his brothers and sisters. His partnership with Cotterell had ended, and he was in business on his own account until, in 1822, his younger brother, Charles, joined him as a partner.

Joseph Sturge had begun business as a corn merchant at a very difficult time. Up to 1813 corn prices had been soaring ; but the bumper harvest of that year had brought them down sharply, and thereafter the general tendency was downward, but with very big fluctuations from harvest to harvest. The average price of British wheat per quarter, according to the official returns, fell from 126s. 6d. in 1812 to 65s. 7d. in 1815, rose again to 96s. 11d. in 1817, and fell away to 44s. 7d. in 1822. Fluctuations of this magnitude necessarily made the business of dealing highly speculative; and on several occasions Sturge found himself on the brink of ruin owing to sudden movements in the price. He did his best to keep his household expenditure down to a minimum which would leave him, even in bad times, money to spare for good causes. But he had anxious moments, and suffered from doubts whether so speculative a business could be reconciled with the requirements of his religion. But the bad times passed, and on the whole his affairs prospered. In 1822 he moved his headquarters from Bewdley to Birmingham, in order to be nearer to the centre of affairs. He had his wharves at Gloucester, managed by his elder brother, Thomas ; and his brother Charles gradually took more of the dealing out of his hands, leaving him free to devote an increasing part of his time to public affairs.

Before his removal to Birmingham Sturge had been active in the cause of peace as well as in the anti-slavery movement. In 1818 he founded a Worcestershire branch of the Peace Society, which had been started in London, mainly by the Quaker philanthropist, William Allen, two years earlier. In

Birmingham he soon began to take an active part in Quaker
' politics '. In 1824 he was concerned in a movement which
resulted in the expulsion of a number of rich Quakers from
the Meeting on account of laxity ; and two years later he
became secretary of the Birmingham branch of the Anti-
Slavery Society, which, after a period of inaction following
the abolition of the British slave trade in 1807, had begun
hesitantly to raise the question of the abolition of slavery
itself throughout the British Empire. In 1827 he became a
total abstainer in consequence of his observation of the evils
of drunkenness ; and thereafter his firm refused to take part
in the trade in corn to be used for malting or distilling. He
did not, however, advocate prohibition : he held that the
matter should be left to be dealt with by persuasion, without
the intervention of the State.

In 1830 Sturge was elected to serve on the Board of Street
Commissioners, who then had most of the government of
the town in their hands ; and in the following year he and
one of his brothers braved the criticism of their fellow
Quakers by throwing in their lot with Thomas Attwood's
Birmingham Political Union, and taking a decided stand for
parliamentary Reform. Sturge defended his conduct in a
letter published in the newspapers, in which he argued
strongly that there was nothing in the principles of the
Society of Friends which could prevent its members from
" joining their fellow countrymen in a peaceable cooperation
for the recovery of their political rights ". He contended
that nothing could " more effectually tend to secure peaceful
obedience to the laws at the present awful crisis, and during
the still more fearful times which we have reason to dread,
than the influence of an association comprising the great
bulk of the lower and a large portion of the middle classes,
and binding its members to such a line of conduct as this "
— *i.e.* the advocacy of parliamentary Reform by means of
peaceful and constitutional agitation. At about the same
time he took up more actively the question of slavery. The
old Anti-Slavery Society, under Fowell Buxton's leadership,
had not gone beyond the advocacy of very gradual measures
for the extinction of slavery. Sturge, on the other hand,
wanted a campaign for the complete and immediate outlawing

of slavery throughout the British possessions ; and he joined hands with James Cropper of Liverpool, George Stephen, and others to form in 1831 the so-called ' Agency Committee ', in order to start a popular campaign in favour of this policy. This campaign led up to the Emancipation Act of 1833, passed in the first session of the Reformed Parliament ; but the Act allowed a period of negro ' apprenticeship ' which retained during a transitional stage many of the characteristics of slavery. Sturge was strongly hostile to this part of the Act, and he and his friends carried on the agitation. In this campaign he was closely associated with James Cropper, whose daughter he married in 1834. His marriage was happy, but within a year his wife died, and his sister, Sophia, came back to keep house for him. Her influence on him, right up to her death in 1845, was very great ; and she was his constant supporter in his increasing activity in public and political affairs.

At this time Sturge, leaving the details of the corn business more and more to his brother, was busily engaged in the promotion of railways. He was a director of the London and Birmingham Railway, and became involved in a controversy about Sunday trains, which he opposed both on sabbatarian principles and in the interests of the workers, who needed their day of rest. But the anti-slavery movement absorbed his greatest energies. He became convinced that it would be impossible to get Parliament to accept the need for complete and immediate emancipation of the West Indian negroes unless someone went to the West Indies and collected on the spot full evidence of the ill-treatment that still prevailed, and of the survival of virtual slavery in spite of the Emancipation Act. In 1836–7, accompanied by a fellow Friend, Thomas Harvey of Leeds, he toured the West Indian islands, collecting evidence ; and on their return they published a book, *The West Indies in 1837*, marshalling the facts, and Sturge also gave evidence before a Parliamentary Committee of Enquiry. He and his friends formed the Central Negro Emancipation Committee, to press for a revision of the law; and in 1838, aided by the eloquence of Brougham and Daniel O'Connell, the emancipators forced the Government to pass a Bill giving additional protection to the negro ' apprentices '.

The various islands, pressed by the Home Government, thereupon one after another fully emancipated the ' apprentices ', and slavery in the British possessions was brought finally to an end.

Sturge, however, was by no means prepared to rest content with these victories. He immediately began to advocate a further crusade, with the object of getting slavery abolished throughout the world. In 1839 he was one of the founders of the new British and Foreign Anti-Slavery Society, set up with this purpose ; and in the following year, thanks largely to his efforts, the first World Convention of the opponents of slavery was got together in London.

This gathering was important, not only for its direct influence, but also because it was the occasion of the first important struggle in Great Britain over the question of women's rights. The original proposals drawn up by the London Working Men's Association, on which The People's Charter was based, had included Votes for Women. But this proposal was dropped in the Charter as impracticable ; and no articulate protest seems to have been made. At the Anti-Slavery Convention the question was one not of the parliamentary franchise, but of the right of women to sit as delegates. Certain American societies had included women delegates ; but the Convention by a large majority refused to accept them, and Sturge sided with the majority. The episode had a considerable influence on the growth of the movement for Women's Rights, especially in the United States ; but on this issue Sturge was unregenerate. He had freed himself of the old Quaker quietism as it applied to men ; but, though his sister was his constant political counsellor, he could not shake off his prejudices against women taking a direct part in public affairs.

Sturge was actively engaged in his work for the abolition of slavery during the period when the Chartist and Anti-Corn Law movements came simultaneously to the forefront of public attention. In 1838, shortly after being chosen as an alderman of the newly created Birmingham Town Council, Sturge attended the Anti-Corn Law Conference in Manchester, at which plans were made for the creation of the National Anti-Corn Law League. He joined that body, and was thereafter up to the end of his life a close friend of both Cobden and Bright, with both of whom he corresponded continually about public concerns. But in the following year, 1839, his preoccupation with the Corn Laws was interrupted by the series of events which arose out of the first Chartist Convention. The Chartist delegates, after meeting at first in London, moved in May 1839 to Birmingham ; and there in July occurred the sequence of riots which first brought the Chartists into serious conflict with the law. The Birmingham magistrates, alarmed at the presence of the Convention in their midst, and at the excited meetings which were taking place in the Bull Ring, asked for the dispatch of some of Peel's new London police to help in keeping order. The London police, then widely regarded as a new instrument of centralised bureaucratic government for the oppression of the people, were intensely unpopular ; and in July there were serious riots in the town, and the Chartists accused the London ' Peelers ' of having provoked the disturbances by their violent and unconstitutional conduct.

Sturge, on several occasions, did his best to preserve the peace by appeals to the people to do nothing outside the law. When some of the popular leaders had been sentenced for their part in the riots, he organised a petition for their release ; and in the following year he protested strongly against the measure which set up a local police force on the London model and placed its control in the hands, not of the Town Council, but of Whitehall. Meanwhile, in 1839 he had been made chairman of the committee appointed by the Town Council to investigate the charges of brutality and violence made against the London police. To the report of this committee, which censured the Birmingham magistrates for their action in calling in and subsequently complimenting the ' Peelers ', Sturge appended a personal note, in which he asserted his pacifism and protested against the arming of the police with lethal weapons. To this question he returned some years later, when the Government had agreed to hand over the control of the police to the local authorities, by moving unsuccessfully on the Town Council that they should carry no arms.

Apart from these activities, Sturge took no part in the

Chartist agitation of 1839. But when, at the end of that year, Thomas Attwood, ill in body and upset by the dissensions in the Chartist ranks and by the appeals to ' Physical Force ', resigned his seat in Parliament, a large number of Birmingham citizens invited Sturge to stand for the borough. He accepted the invitation, and put forward an election address which contains his earliest declaration of his political faith. The address began by saying that he belonged to no party, inasmuch as he considered the Christian rule of doing to others as we would they should do unto us to be of universal application. He then went on to declare himself in favour of the complete separation of Church and State, universal free trade and the abolition of all taxes on the necessaries of life, a great extension of the suffrage and the abolition of the property qualification for M.P.s, shorter Parliaments and Vote by Ballot, the abolition of capital punishment, and the extinction of slavery throughout the world " by moral and pacific methods ". He further called for a national declaration that war must be regarded as inconsistent with true national safety, and stated that, while he believed in Sunday rest for all employees, he was opposed to its enforcement by law. On the subject of the New Poor Law, then the great question of the day, he went no further than to condemn its harsh administration by the Commissioners and the local Boards of Guardians.

This address makes it clear that Sturge was at this time by no means a Chartist. He did not declare for Manhood Suffrage, which was in the forefront of the Chartist demands. He urged only ' Shorter ', and not ' Annual ', Parliaments ; and he said nothing about either equal electoral districts or payment of M.P.s. Moreover, his attitude towards the New Poor Law was by no means that of the Chartists, who were deeply committed to an unyielding agitation for its repeal. He was, in effect, a moderate Radical — very much more moderate than Attwood and the other leaders of the Birmingham Political Union.

In the event, the B.P.U. put its own candidate, G. F. Muntz, into the field, and Sturge withdrew, with the result that Muntz was elected by a good majority over the reactionary Tory, Sir Charles Wetherell. He was probably not sorry; for at this point the Anti-Slavery movement was again coming to occupy most of his attention. He had been deeply distressed by the failure of the Christian Churches in the United States, and even of the American Quakers, to make a solid stand against the continuance of slavery; and he made up his mind to tour the United States in the hope of winning over American support. Before he left England on this mission, he found time to make vigorous protest against Great Britain's policy in the Chinese Opium War; but for a large part of 1841 he was absent from England, travelling about America in company with the poet, John Greenleaf Whittier, on his self-appointed mission. His account of his visit was embodied in his only considerable book, *A Visit to the United States in 1841*, which was published the year after his return.

When he came back from America in August 1841, he found the Chartist forces in disorder. The riots in Birmingham and in the North and the abortive ' Newport Rising ' had scared many of the middle-class supporters of Radical Reform; and ' physical force' and ' moral force ' men among the Chartists were busy with mutual recriminations. William Lovett and the moderate leaders of the Birmingham Political Union, as well as many other Chartists, had broken with O'Connor, whose followers were trying to reorganise the left wing of the movement in the National Charter Association. Sturge conceived the idea of rallying the ' moral force ' section of the Chartists and of uniting it with the main body of middle-class Reformers in a national movement. Edward Miall, the leader of the advocates of church disestablishment, had recently started *The Non-conformist* as the organ of the movement, and had published therein a series of articles entitled *Reconciliation between the Middle and Labouring Classes*. Sturge reprinted the articles, with a preface by himself, in which he said that, while he had been devoting his energies to the campaign against slavery, it had sometimes been pressed upon him that the sufferings of his fellow countrymen had a prior claim on his attention; and he added, " I freely acknowledge that the Patriot and the Christian fail in the discharge of their duty if they do not, by all peaceable and legitimate means, strive to

remove the enormous evil of class-legislation ". He therefore appealed to his readers to give earnest attention to
Miall's proposals, which included an unequivocal advocacy
of ' Complete Suffrage ' — that is, Manhood Suffrage — as
an undeniable right of all men not disqualified by crime or
by the receipt of public money.

Thus began the Complete Suffrage movement, launched
originally by Miall's articles, but associated chiefly with
Sturge's name. Sturge's leadership began when he raised
the issue at an Anti-Corn Law Convention which he attended
in Manchester in November 1841. He there persuaded a
majority of the delegates, at a meeting over which Francis
Place presided, to endorse the ' Complete Suffrage ' plan, and
to authorise him and William Sharman Crawford, who
became the movement's parliamentary spokesman, to draw
up what came to be known as the ' Sturge Declaration '. It
was in the following terms :

Deeply impressed with the conviction of the evils arising from
class legislation and of the sufferings thereby inflicted upon our
industrious fellow subjects, the undersigned affirm that a large
majority of the people of this country are unjustly excluded
from that full, fair, and free exercise of the elective franchise to
which they are entitled by the great principle of Christian equity
and also by the British Constitution, " for no subject of England
can be constrained to pay any aids or taxes, even for the defence
of the realm or the support of the Government, but such as are
imposed by his own consent or that of his representative in
Parliament " [Blackstone's *Commentaries*].

This declaration was put about, and was extensively signed
up and down the country, especially by members of the
Anti-Corn Law League and by Chartists of the ' moral
force ' school. A Complete Suffrage Union was established
in Birmingham, and in the early months of 1842 many
similar bodies were founded in other towns. Preparations
were begun for a representative National Conference which
was to be held at Birmingham at the earliest possible date.

The Complete Suffrage Conference was held in April
1842. To it came, of the Chartist leaders of 1839, William
Lovett, Henry Vincent, John Collins, who had been Lovett's
collaborator and fellow prisoner, Dr. Wade, Vicar of

Warwick, R. J. Richardson of Manchester, Bronterre O'Brien, and several others who had been delegates to the original Chartist Convention. R. K. Philp of Bath, Arthur O'Neil the 'Christian Chartist', the Rev. Patrick Brewster of Paisley, then a leading figure in Scottish Chartism, and James Williams of Sunderland, gave their support. The Free Traders were also strongly represented. John Bright was there, and Archibald Prentice of Manchester, the historian of the Anti-Corn Law League. There was a plentiful attendance of dissenting ministers, of many denominations, and a sprinkling of churchmen, in addition to Dr. Wade, including Thomas Spencer, uncle of the young Herbert Spencer, who became himself secretary of the Derby C.S.U.

Miall in his articles, and Sturge and Crawford in their declaration, had concentrated on the issue of the suffrage, to the exclusion of the rest of the Chartist Six Points. But the Conference of April 1842 proceeded, by large majorities, to endorse in turn all the points of The People's Charter. This was not what Sturge, in calling the Conference, had hoped for or expected. He had meant, while accepting Manhood Suffrage with only a change of name, to present on other points a modified programme which would clearly dissociate the Complete Suffrage Union from O'Connor's National Charter Association. In particular, he did not want either Annual Parliaments or Payment of Members to be included in the Complete Suffrage programme. But he was overruled; and Lovett, at the head of the Chartist delegates, wanted to go yet further, and to insist that the Conference should accept the Charter by name. He was persuaded to water down his resolution, so that it proposed only that The People's Charter should be taken into consideration at a future Conference; and his motion, in this form, was seconded by Miall, who in his speech warned the delegates of the danger of wrecking the movement by pressing their claims too far. In the end, Lovett agreed to accept an amendment which provided that the Charter should be considered together with other proposals; and in this form his resolution was unanimously endorsed.

All this time O'Connor and his followers had been

denouncing the Complete Suffrage movement on every possible occasion. It was, *The Northern Star* argued, merely a dodge of the Anti-Corn Law League to capture the working classes, and secure their support for Free Trade, with every intention of leaving them in the lurch, as in 1832, as soon as the middle classes had got what they wanted. The Chartists who had associated themselves with the C.S.U. were vehemently attacked, and O'Connor tried to defeat Sturge's movement by summoning a rival Chartist Conference to meet in Birmingham simultaneously with the C.S.U. gathering. Actually, both Conferences did meet ; and there is no doubt that the main working-class following was with the National Charter Association. The C.S.U., by comparison, was a middle-class body, reinforced by moderate working-class leaders who had broken away from the O'Connorites without carrying with them any mass working-class following. Hatred of the New Poor Law and resentment at industrial oppression still dominated the factory districts, where O'Connor had his support. Complete Suffrage was not a hunger movement, but a respectable rallying of those who were democrats in principle.

But the adoption of the Six Points by the Complete Suffrage Conference altered the situation. O'Connor could hardly persist in denouncing all adherents of the C.S.U. as traitors now that they were making demands identical with those of his own National Charter Association. In 1842 there were two rival Petitions, each embodying the Six Points, circulating throughout the country for signature. The C.S.U., which did not aim at vast numbers, was ready first. Before the end of April, Sharman Crawford had presented its Petition, which was promptly rejected by 226 votes to 67. In May Thomas Slingsby Duncombe presented the rival, and much more extensively signed, Petition of the N.C.A. It was rejected in its turn by 287 votes to 49. What was to happen next ?

What did happen was the great strike movement in the factory areas known to history, rather misleadingly, as the " Plug Plot ". It was not really a plot : it was a spontaneous uprising of the factory workers in face of intolerable distress. The Chartists did not organise it : they only attempted to get control of it when it had broken out. Nor were they united even in this. While great mass meetings in various parts of the country — especially in Lancashire, which was the storm-centre of the strike — were passing resolutions in favour of remaining on strike until the Charter had become " the law of the land ", Feargus O'Connor's *Northern Star* was denouncing the strike as a manœuvre of the Anti-Corn Law League to divert attention from the Charter, and discredit the Chartist leaders. O'Connor became a fervent apostle of ' Moral Force ', and confusion grew worse confounded than ever.

The great strikes of 1842 were in fact the last mass movement of bitterness and hunger among the workers of the North. Trade, after some improvement, had become suddenly much worse, and the employers were everywhere demanding reductions in wages. The detested Poor Law Commissioners had by this time successfully installed their Boards of Guardians over a large part of the factory districts, and the Guardians were offering the unemployed the alternative of starvation or imprisonment in the workhouse ' Bastilles '. The result was a wild and desperate revolt which arose spontaneously, under no more than local leadership, in one place after another ; and the only leaders available were the Chartists, who alone possessed even the shadow of a national organisation or a common programme.

Under the economic conditions of 1842, mere strike action stood not the smallest chance of success. The hunger revolt could hope to achieve anything only if it became a revolution. That was what some of the Chartists, headed by Peter Murray McDouall, tried to make of it. But the Government's soldiers, spread about the disaffected areas, were much too formidable to be conquered by a leaderless and planless uprising. If the Chartists had been united, and O'Connor had placed himself at their head, there might have been at least a widespread rising in arms. But, with O'Connor at first denouncing the strikes and later but half-heartedly supporting them, and with the Chartists split into a ' physical force ' party, a ' moral force ' party, and a large middle party, which did not know which it was, defeat was certain. The strikes lasted through August, and then in September

the strikers drifted back to work — those who could get it —
or bowed their necks to the hard yoke of the ' Three Bashaws
of Somerset House '.

Sturge and his followers, advocates of ' Moral Force ' to
a man, watched disconsolately the terrible events of the
summer of 1842. Then, as the great strike movement collapsed, they had to make up their minds what to do about
the Complete Suffrage movement. The violence of the
summer had hardened the hearts of a large section of the
middle classes more than ever against the Charter ; and it
was clear that, if the Complete Suffrage Union were to
declare its adhesion to the Charter, a large part of its middle-
class following would drop away. On the other hand, would
the ' moral force ' Chartists — Lovett and his friends, and
the working-class moderates generally — agree to accept the
substance of the Charter without the name ?

Sturge worked on, in the hope that they would ; but
he had now to reckon, not only with Lovett and Vincent
and the ' moral force ' Chartists generally, but also with
O'Connor and what was left of the National Charter Association. The strike leaders had largely been arrested ; and
McDouall, the leading advocate of revolution among the
Chartists of the N.C.A., had fled to France. But there
remained O'Connor, Julian Harney, and a number of others
who had now to consider the future of their section of the
movement in face of the defeat. It seems clear that
O'Connor's policy, at this state, was to make every possible
endeavour to capture Sturge's movement and reorganise it
under his own leadership on a slogan of ' Moral Force '.
During July or at the beginning of August, he and his friends,
instead of continuing their denunciations of the Sturgeites,
had changed their tactics, and begun to laud Sturge as a true
friend of the people.

At this point Sturge had been adopted as Complete
Suffrage candidate for Nottingham, where his opponent was
John Walter, the proprietor of *The Times*. Now Walter, a
Tory, was also a vehement enemy of the New Poor Law and
a friend of Richard Oastler, whereas Sturge, as we have seen,
was not opposed to the New Poor Law, but only to the
harshness with which it was being administered. Sturge on

the other hand was a strong Free Trader, whereas Walter was a Protectionist.

This by-election at Nottingham was therefore a fine mix-up. Whereas the Anti-Corn Law Leaguers were hot for Sturge, a section of the Chartists, followers of Oastler and Joseph Rayner Stephens, were equally hot for Walter as an Anti-Poor Law man. O'Connor, as the enemy of Free Trade and of the Poor Law, might have been expected to throw his weight on Walter's side ; but then, Walter was a strong opponent of the Six Points, which Sturge had by this time accepted in their entirety. O'Connor and his group, already veering round to ' Moral Force ' and class-collaboration before the outbreak of the strikes, came down vigorously on Sturge's side ; and, much to Sturge's Quaker embarrassment, these allies, headed by O'Connor himself, poured into the constituency to campaign on his behalf, and came to blows with the followers of Oastler and Stephens. In the event, the contest was close. On August 4 John Walter was declared elected by 1835 votes to Sturge's 1801 ; but a few months later the election was declared void on account of bribery practised on Walter's behalf. The constituency had, indeed, a bad name for corruption ; and Sturge had fought it only on the understanding that no money was to be paid out in order to get votes for him, and had repeatedly emphasised this point in the course of his campaign. When Walter was unseated, he refused to stand again, and in April 1843 Thomas Gisborne, a moderate Radical, won the seat against Walter's son.

The Nottingham by-election, which created great excitement at the time, was over before the big strike movement began. In relation to O'Connor, this may be said. It clears him of having suddenly abandoned ' physical force ' tactics because he took fright at the strikes. He had in fact changed his policy earlier, probably as soon as the fate of the National Petition had been decided. His declared line was to give the middle classes a chance of proving their sincerity, and of showing what they could do. His hostility to the strikes is explicable on this basis, though his fantastic charges against the Anti-Corn Law League, of having fomented the strikes, are not. At all events, it is clear that from the moment of the collapse in the North O'Connor's policy was to capture the Complete Suffrage movement.

He was aided in this by the very natural desire of the Chartists who had already joined forces with Sturge to secure a better representation of the working classes at the coming Complete Suffrage Conference, at which the Charter was to be taken into consideration together with other Radical plans. It had been agreed that, at the next Conference, at least half the delegates should be working men — a harking back, this, to the composition of the National Political Union in the days of the Reform Bill — and that steps should be taken to secure the election of delegates at meetings to be held throughout the country. As the law stood, these delegates could not be sent up to the Conference as representatives of the local branches of the C.S.U. — for this would have come under the ban of the Act prohibiting ' Corresponding Societies '. The delegates would have to be elected at mass meetings ; and these meetings the followers of O'Connor proceeded to pack wherever they could, in order to get their own men chosen. In the confusion of the months just after the big strikes, no one quite knew who was a follower of O'Connor, and who of the old ' moral force' leaders ; and O'Connor found it a simple matter to get a good many of his nominees elected.

Consequently, when the Complete Suffrage Conference met at Birmingham in December 1842, O'Connor and his National Charter Association followers were present in force. This is not to say that they were in a majority ; for the ' moral force ' Chartists of the working class were there too, in addition to the Anti-Corn Law Leaguers and Sturge's more personal adherents. Sturge and his friends, in the hope of side-tracking Lovett's demand for the endorsement of the Charter by name, had caused to be prepared a ' Bill of Rights ', embodying all the Six Points ; and this they proposed should be taken by the Conference as the basis of discussion. This proposal greatly aggravated Lovett, who had not been consulted ; and he and O'Connor, inveterate enemies as they were, joined forces in demanding that the Conference should accept The People's Charter.

The result was a foregone conclusion. Any proposal

backed jointly by Lovett and O'Connor was bound to command a majority. The name of the Charter carried for most of the working-class delegates so powerful an appeal that they were bound to vote for its acceptance, regardless of consequences. But to the minority, who were prepared to accept the substance of the Charter, the name was anathema, especially in view of its recent association with the violent proceedings in the North. When the Conference, moved by Lovett's and O'Connor's appeals, had endorsed The People's Charter by a majority of more than two to one, the Complete Suffrage movement was virtually dead. Sturge's pacifism would not allow him to accept a name which had been associated with so many acts of violence ; and many of the middle-class delegates, without sharing his pacifism, would have nothing to do with a name so closely identified with the ideas of class-war and violent revolution. Sturge, and most of the delegates who had voted against the Lovett-O'Connor resolution, retired to another room to consider their future course of action, leaving the ill-assorted victors in possession of the field.

The victors, however, were quite incapable of working together. Lovett and O'Connor hated each other, not merely personally, but on principle. Their joint victory meant, in effect, that the Lovett party was squeezed out, and that O'Connor on the one hand and Sturge on the other were left to organise their several forces as best they could. The attempt at unity through ' Complete Suffrage ' had failed. O'Connor went away, and reorganised the National Charter Association ; Lovett faded into obscurity, with his National Association for the Political and Social Improvement of the People ; Sturge resumed his attempt to mobilise the ' moral force ' men in a rump C.S.U. based mainly on his middle-class supporters. After 1842 there was no one Chartist movement : there were only factions, each claiming to represent the true Radical tradition, and none having behind it the mass following necessary for commanding the respect of the governing classes.

The Complete Suffrage movement did not perish immediately as a result of the Conference of December 1842. The capture of the Conference by the O'Connorites did not carry with it the capture of the local Complete Suffrage Unions ; and Sturge remained in possession of the Birmingham C.S.U., which was the centre of organisation. He continued in fact to tour the country in 1843 on behalf of ' Complete Suffrage ' — and in 1844, when Joshua Scholefield, who had represented Birmingham as a Radical since 1832, died, Sturge was put forward by the C.S.U. as his successor. But the leaders of middle-class Radicalism in Birmingham had lost their earlier solidarity. The respectable ' Liberals ' put forward William Scholefield against him ; and as a result of this split Richard Spooner, Attwood's Tory partner, captured the seat with 2095 votes, against 1735 for Scholefield and 946 for Sturge. After that, the C.S.U. declined rapidly, both in Birmingham and elsewhere. The attempt to build a bridge between the middle and working classes by accepting the Six Points without their collective name had definitely failed.

While the Complete Suffrage movement was active, Sturge was often accused of being really an agent of the Anti-Corn Law League, entrusted with the task of seducing the workers from their allegiance to the Charter. The charge was quite untrue : in fact, even at the beginning of the movement Sturge had lost faith in the League. At the outset, he had been one of its most enthusiastic and uncompromising members. Cobden, writing of the constituent meeting held in Manchester in 1838, said of him that " a few words from him did more than anything to determine us to adopt for our principle ' the total and immediate repeal ' of the Corn Law ". Cobden added, " I remember how little the great majority were prepared for anything so strong and uncompromising, and how gladly nine-tenths of us would have avoided the question at the time ; but I believe it was our friend who, fresh from the experience of the Anti-Slavery struggle, pointed out the necessity of taking our stand on the rock of abstract truth and justice ; and I must say we found it our rock of safety during our seven years' struggle ".

But Sturge had altered his tone after his tour in the United States in 1841. He had come back not only prepared to advocate Manhood Suffrage, but also convinced that it was useless to expect other reforms until the people had been given votes. He wrote to Cobden soon after his return :

" I have been drawn to the conclusion that it is not only hopeless to expect justice for the labouring population from the representatives of the present constituencies, but that the infatuated policy which now guides our rulers will be persisted in, until they plunge millions into want and misery, if not bring them into a premature grave. I therefore think that the time is arrived when every friend of humanity, of whatever class, sect, or party, should endeavour to obtain and secure for the people a just and permanent control over their own affairs." Sturge had come to hold that Free Trade would not be won until the Charter, or something very like it, had prepared the way.

He had, however, especially from 1843 onwards, a second ground of disagreement with the Free Traders. After the passing of the Emancipation Act of 1833 he had, as we have seen, directed his energies to the abolition of slavery all over the world. As an instrument for this purpose he had come, since the foundation of the British and Foreign Anti-Slavery Society in 1839, to believe in a policy of boycotting slave-made goods. He therefore advocated, besides personal measures of abstention from consuming such goods, their exclusion from British markets by means of prohibitive tariffs or positive prohibition. But the Free Traders in general were violently opposed to this policy, which they regarded as a form of unwarrantable State interference with the free flow of exchange. The dispute came to a head at the second Anti-Slavery Convention held in London in 1843. Sturge and his friends wanted both to take measures against American cotton from the slave States and to maintain the almost prohibitive duties on foreign-grown sugar, which the orthodox Free Traders were bent on sweeping away. There was a direct clash between Sturge's principle of moral boycott and the Manchester School's principle of *laissez-faire*. This quarrel alienated him from the Anti-Corn Law League on the one side as much as his disapproval of ' Physical Force ' held him apart from the National Charter Association on the other.

Thus isolated — for the Liberals in 1846 lowered the duties on foreign sugar in face of a combined Tory-Abolitionist vote, while the Chartists rapidly resumed their hostility to the middle classes after the collapse of the C.S.U. — Sturge retreated from politics to crusading for the causes in which he had a purely moral faith. He had much to do with the summoning of the first General Peace Convention, which met in London in 1843. He was a vice-president ; and the plan seems to have arisen out of contacts which he had established with the Boston Peace Society during his visit to the United States. For the rest of his life, work for international peace and arbitration was his most continuous public activity. He was an assiduous attendant at successive World Peace Conferences — at Brussels in 1848, Paris in 1849, and Frankfurt in 1850. He fought hard against the American war threat of 1845, and made a quite astonishing private attempt to act as go-between, on behalf of the Frankfurt Conference, in the war between Denmark and Schleswig-Holstein in 1850, when he succeeded in interviewing both the Statthalter of Schleswig-Holstein and the Danish Prime Minister. Again in 1853, when the Crimean War was immediately imminent, he went post-haste to Russia as the emissary of the Society of Friends, and succeeded in holding a long discussion with the Czar, Nicholas, who is said to have been moved to tears by his Christian eloquence. In his last years, when the Indian Mutiny broke out in 1857, he laid all his plans for making off to India in the hope of restoring peace, and was only kept back with great difficulty on account of his failing health. In the last year of his life, 1858, he was president of the Peace Society, and was eagerly getting ready to preside over its Conference when death came suddenly upon him.

But, though Joseph Sturge devoted most of his energies during his latter years to such issues as peace and the abolition of slavery, he had not quite done with politics in a wider sense. In 1847 he allowed himself, at the entreaty of Edward Baines, the owner of *The Leeds Mercury*, to be adopted as Radical candidate for Leeds, the other candidates being the Whig manufacturer, James Marshall, and the Tory banker, William Beckett. His intervention arose on this occasion mainly out of the active part which he had taken in current controversies about popular education. The main question then at issue was that of State-aided as against voluntary education, with special reference to religious teaching. In 1845 Sturge had resigned his membership of the (mainly Nonconformist) British and Foreign Schools Society, on the decision of this body to accept State aid for the maintenance of its schools. ·Sturge, Baines, and many other Radical Dissenters argued that aid of this sort would inevitably interfere with the freedom of religious teaching, and that if the Dissenters accepted State aid for their, nominally, undenominational schools, they would have no good case for opposing similar aid to Church, or even Roman Catholic or Jewish or Mohammedan, schools. In Sturge's view, religion and education were inseparably bound up together ; and in view of this the only safe principle to follow was that of strict voluntarism and refusal of all State grants. If State money was to be accepted at all, he argued, it would be best for the State to take over the schools altogether : all the evidence from the past went to show that the voluntary principle and the State, or compulsory, principle could not be mixed without disaster.

This was the issue, then a very live one, on which he allowed himself to be adopted at Leeds. But he fought the contest, necessarily, on a wider programme, laying great stress on his advocacy of peace and international arbitration, and also urging the need for Radical measures of parliamentary Reform. He was left at the bottom of the poll, the Conservative coming in first and the Whig winning the second seat by 2181 votes to Sturge's 1980. He was invited to contest more than one seat in his later years ; but the Leeds election of 1847 was his last attempt to enter Parliament.

Sturge's belief in the voluntary principle in education had, before 1847, taken practical shape in his work for the people of Birmingham. In 1845 he opened the Severn Street Sunday School, " chiefly for the purpose of affording instruction in reading the Scripture and in writing to youths and young men from fourteen years of age and upwards ". Out of this at first small experiment arose quite large developments. A Women's School was started in 1848, and presently it became necessary to separate the adult from the youths' department ; and on the model of the Severn Street establishment, with its Sunday morning classes held before the hour of church or meeting, there arose in the Birmingham area numerous Adult Schools, many of which remain active to-day. Sturge was not the founder of the Adult School movement, which goes back a good deal further ; but he made Birmingham its principal centre, and one of the chief means of spreading the influence of the Society of Friends beyond its immediate circle of members and adherents.

From this educational venture Sturge went on to others — notably the reformatory for delinquent boys which he started at Stoke Prior in 1853. He was also active in the promotion of movements for the provision of parks and playing-fields ; and in his own city, which was remarkably backward in having no public open spaces even in the 'fifties, he rented and threw open to the public, especially to the children, a large open space known as ' Sturge's Field '. His philanthropy also manifested itself in other directions. Set on showing the possibility of growing sugar profitably with the aid of negro peasant proprietors, he bought an estate in Montserrat, and devoted much care to the attempt to establish a model negro community.

In yet another matter he mingled philanthropy with his work in the cause of peace. During the war with Russia, a British fleet visited the Baltic and bombarded the coasts of Finland, destroying much property, especially timber, and reducing considerable populations to destitution. Sturge was deeply shocked at this act of barbarism — as he was then by no means alone in regarding it — and having collected funds, mainly from his fellow Quakers, he set out in 1856 for Finland, bent on making some sort of material restitution to the Finns by relieving the sufferers. By this expedition he did much to restore Finnish friendship for Great Britain ; and he also made himself the pioneer of a form of international relief work for which the Society of Friends has been notable in more recent times. Nor should it be forgotten that he was sixty-three years old when he set forth for Finland bent upon this work of mercy.

Sturge was, indeed, from first to last indefatigable in his pursuit of good causes. Having at his back, thanks largely to his brother's devoted service, a solid foundation of business prosperity, he could afford to spend largely upon good works, not only in money, but also in personal effort. He was a man to whom many turned when they needed either money, or that resistless optimistic energy which is indispensable for making those in authority attend to causes which have no obvious popular appeal. He could stand up courageously too for unpopular causes, as well as for causes in which the main body of the public was not interested. In 1850, when the Pope's action in appointing Roman Catholic bishops and dividing up Great Britain into Roman Catholic ecclesiastical divisions caused an immense public agitation against Popery, Sturge appeared at a public meeting called in Birmingham in support of the agitation, and made a speech in which, much as he hated Popery, he defended the Pope's action in the name of religious liberty, and succeeded in deflecting the meeting from its original purpose. Two years before this, he had warmly defended the Continental Revolutions of 1848 ; and at the time of the Indian Mutiny, when the outcry against native atrocities was at its height, he spoke out boldly about Indian grievances.

Throughout his life Sturge was entirely fearless. He walked into the middle of a great crowd assembled for a prize fight, and tried to persuade the combatants to separate. He braved Russian winters, and went to and fro between armies, without considering questions of personal danger or privation. In this, his powerful physique helped him greatly : indeed, without it he could not have attempted a tithe of what he did. His weakness was that, with all his ready sympathy, he looked much less at causes than at effects, and never penetrated below the surface ills of the society which he so ardently desired to reform. To his mind, moral reformation was the clue to everything : he wanted to cure misery wherever he saw it ; but he seldom paused to enquire why it was there. He had, in effect, the essential qualities of the great philanthropist, but lacked those requisite for the successful political reformer. Though he took part in politics, he could never quite shake off the old Quaker feeling that he was thereby endangering his immortal soul.

VII

Thomas Cooper

THOMAS COOPER, the 'General' of the Leicester Association of Shakespearean Chartists, died at eighty-seven, and was sixty-seven when he published his autobiography. He was then, and had been for fourteen years, an itinerant preacher, a Baptist by persuasion, but ready to preach anywhere and to anyone his simple message of Christian faith and holiness. In doctrine, he was by then a very different person from ' Thomas Cooper the Chartist ', as he had proudly insisted on calling himself on the title-page of his best known poem, *The Purgatory of Suicides*, which had a great renown in its day. Unconsciously no doubt, in this late-written autobiography he toned down his past : so that no one, reading it and knowing nothing else about him, would get a correct picture of him as he had been in his Chartist prime. He was, indeed, ready enough to confess his past sins. He told fully the story of his days of unbelief, when, under the spell of Strauss's *Life of Jesus*, he had become a Secularist writer and lecturer, noted for his attacks on Sabbatarians and dogmatic ' believers ' of every sort. Such confession was part of his stock-in-trade ; but it was much harder for him to remember aright his political past as a ' physical force ' Chartist and an ardent supporter of Feargus O'Connor during the second period of Chartism, when, under O'Connor's leadership, the main body of provincial Chartists were seeking to reconstruct the movement after the defeat of 1839. The amiable old missionary confessed readily enough his religious sins ; but he could not help making himself out as having been, politically, a good deal more dove-like than he had been in fact. Fortunately, we have both the records of his speeches and writings and other persons' impressions of him as means of correcting his own expurgated version of his past.

187

Cooper served two years in prison for his part in the Chartist troubles of 1842. Like others, he came out of prison chastened in spirit — a convert from the ' physical force ' to the ' moral force ' school. He worked for a time with Lovett at his National Hall, took a leading part in attacking O'Connor's Land Scheme and O'Connor personally, and then, after another eight or nine years' activity as a Radical, was suddenly converted back — in the middle of one of his lectures — to the Bible Christianity which he had so often denounced. He then transferred his energies for the rest of his life from the political to the religious platform, and went about the country incessantly preaching till he was nearly eighty, and could do no more.

I say " converted back " because Cooper was a preacher in his youth as well as in his old age. His conversion in 1856, at the age of fifty-one, was not his first experience of grace. He had been converted first, in the course of a Primitive Methodist revival at Gainsborough, where he was brought up, at the age of thirteen or fourteen, and again, more durably, by the Wesleyans in 1829, when he was twenty-four. But after five years as a Wesleyan local preacher, he had quarrelled with the Wesleyans, and in his Chartist days had moved gradually over to a sort of Secularism. He had then for years enjoyed himself greatly in exposing the follies of the orthodox ; but he had carried over into his Chartism much of the revivalist fervour and method of his ' ranting ' youth. Like Stephens, he used about politics strong language which was the familiar instrument of revivalist preaching ; and I fancy that, like Stephens, he was often unaware how much like incitements to violence his fervent political utterances sometimes sounded. He was righteously indignant when he was accused of having incited to arson his audiences at Burslem in 1842 ; but, though he was acquitted on this particular charge, his fiery speeches may not have been without their effect in rousing the people of the Potteries to unlawful acts. He was no doubt speaking the strict truth when he said that he had adjured the people to observe law and order ; but such adjurations may well be of less effect on the actions of an excited crowd than the vigorous denunciations of the high and mighty by which they are often accompanied. Moreover, Cooper was, by his own assertion, at that time a ' physical force ' Chartist : if he did not tell the people to burn anything, as I am sure he did not, his reasons were prudential rather than grounded on any objection of principle to an appeal to force as the means of righting the people's wrongs.

Thomas Cooper was born at Leicester on March 30, 1805. His father, of Yorkshire Quaker descent, was a dyer, working on his own, and given to wandering. He had worked in London, and as far afield as India ; and a year after Thomas's birth the household moved to Exeter, and he set up his dye-shop there. Three years later the father died ; and Thomas's mother then returned with him to her native Gainsborough, in Lincolnshire, and established herself there as a dyer, conducting the tiny business unaided and eking out her scanty earnings by making for sale work-boxes and other sundries and hawking them round the neighbouring villages where she solicited custom.

Young Thomas was from the first an infant prodigy. At the age of three he had not merely learned to read, but was teaching this accomplishment to a boy of seven. At the age of eleven he was working as a pupil-teacher — getting no fees, but free schooling — in a private school at Gainsborough, and had launched out on that prodigious career of self-improvement which he records in his autobiography. He read everything he could lay his hands on ; and his memory was remarkable. From this passion for learning — the most sustained passion of his life — he was diverted for a time between the ages of thirteen and fourteen to religion ; and by the time his enthusiasm had cooled, he found himself called upon to set about earning a living. He went to Hull, intending to go to sea, but shrank back at the last minute, appalled not by the perils of the calling, but by the dreadful language used by the seamen. He went back to his mother, and was apprenticed to a cobbler instead. From 1820 to 1827 he worked regularly as a shoemaker, but without passing through a proper apprenticeship ; and he says in his autobiography that throughout this period — that is, until he was twenty-two — he never earned more than ten shillings a week.

Most of this time, after he had learnt the rudiments of his trade, he was working at home in his mother's cottage, cobbling away in his corner while she minded her vats. While he made or mended shoes — and indeed at all hours — he read. At sixteen he joined a Mutual Improvement Society and Adult School founded by his friend, J. F. Winks ; and this led him on to more systematic studies. He taught himself Latin, Greek, Hebrew, French, and presently Italian and German. He learnt by heart *Paradise Lost*, several plays of Shakespeare, and a number of works about Grammar and Christian Evidences. He rose at dawn and walked abroad in the fields, reading : he read all day and as long as he could afford light ; and he stored away an immense mass of poetry and prose, fact and fable, in his remarkably retentive memory. Nothing was too exacting for him ; he set himself the most impossible tasks, and accomplished them — until in 1827, when he was twenty-two, his health broke down.

This was not his first illness. He had smallpox when he was five, and was scarred by it, and very ill for a long time. But he was worse now, with a real breakdown brought on by overtaxing his strength. After a long interval he tried to resume his shoemaking, but found the task beyond his power. His mother, struggling hard to get a bare living, could not afford to keep him. With the aid of friends he was enabled to set up for himself as a schoolmaster at the age of twenty-three ; and into this new task he threw himself with immense intellectual energy. He wanted to fire his scholars with all his own passion : nothing less would suit him than to teach them the wonders he had learned. They must master Latin and become enthusiasts for Shakespeare. He had ideas for them quite beyond those of the small traders and craftsmen at Gainsborough whose children they were.

In the midst of this enthusiasm Cooper underwent his second conversion, and became a Wesleyan preacher. He abandoned his cane and his hard work, and felt himself filled with a spirit of universal love. Once, when he suffered a backsliding and lost his temper with one of his scholars, he suffered agonies of self-reproach. But grace returned. He kept on with his school, with modest success, pursued his reading indefatigably, adding ever new branches of learning to his store, and spent many of his week-ends in preaching, not only in and round Gainsborough, but as far afield as Lincoln, where in 1829 he met his future wife. Till then, he tells his readers, sex had not entered his life : there had been no room for it — a circumstance perhaps not un-connected with his illnesses, and connected with his studious habits not quite as he supposed. In 1831 he became engaged, and in 1834 he married — most happily, though I can find no record of any children being born.

Shortly before his marriage, he had left Gainsborough and taken over a school in Lincoln, with the help of his wife's relatives. He was glad to move ; for he had quarrelled with the Wesleyan Superintendent, whom he attempted unsuccess-fully to remove from office, and his local preaching had been brought to a stop. His wife and her family were ardent Wesleyans, and at Lincoln he resumed his religious work. But the quarrel pursued him : he was soon at loggerheads with the Lincoln Superintendent, who, he says, was poisoned against him by his Gainsborough colleague. Where the blame lay, I do not know : Cooper was very sure he was wholly in the right. At all events, he was so angry that he shook the dust of Wesleyanism from his feet, and plunged instead into teaching at the newly formed Lincoln Mechanics' Institute.

A new phase soon followed. Cooper developed a passion for music. He took the lead in founding the Lincoln Musical Society, and quickly developed it to a high pitch of excellence. Then came another quarrel ; he was accused of playing the dictator, and withdrew in anger to seek a fresh sphere for his abounding energy. He found it in journalism. In 1836 he began to write regularly for *The Stamford and Lincoln Mercury*, first as local reporter, but soon more ambitiously, and dangerously, as a contributor whose strength lay in candid and often highly critical articles about the leading figures in the cathedral city. These made him enemies ; but his articles sold the paper, and presently the proprietor invited him to move to Stamford and undertake full-time journalistic work. In 1838 Cooper closed his school and, together with his wife, went to live at Stamford in the house of the proprietor of *The Stamford and Lincoln Mercury*.

There seems to have been a misunderstanding. Cooper had understood that the proprietor-editor had meant to retire, and to go and live in the country, leaving the editor-ship and the house to him. But his employer did not go ; and in the following year, 1839, they parted. Cooper, with very little money and a great many books, went to London to seek his fortune. Like many before and after him, he went with an unfinished romance in his bag ; and, having during his years in Lincoln worked hard on the Liberal side for the sitting M.P., Bulwer Lytton, he had an idea that the famous novelist might be prepared to do something for him in return. He sought out Lytton and presented his manu-script. Lytton received it, making polite noises, did nothing about it, and, when Cooper called again, handed it curtly back.

The Coopers had hard struggles in London during the next few months. Cooper pawned his books, came near destitution, picked up odd shillings here and there, princi-pally by hack work for Lumley, the publisher, who set him copying in the British Museum, and was near the end of his hopes when he was appointed editor of *The Kentish Mercury*, on condition of going to live at Greenwich, whither he moved early in 1840. But this appointment did not last long ; and he was again in difficulties when he applied for, and was given, a post on *The Leicestershire Mercury*. Towards the end of 1840 he moved to Leicester, his birthplace, which he had quitted when he was but one year old, and settled down to his job of reporter and odd-job man to the local Whig-Liberal newspaper.

Of Cooper's political opinions up to this time we know little, except that he had been an assiduous worker for Bulwer Lytton during his years at Lincoln. The Chartist excite-ments of the years before 1840 seem hardly to have affected him ; and, to judge by his own account, he had when he went to Leicester no conception at all of the conditions under which the workers were living in the industrial dis-tricts, of the oppressions of the New Poor Law, or of the forces of revolt which had brought the country to the brink of revolution in 1839. These things seem not to have reached his imagination in any degree until residence in Leicester and actual first-hand observation of the wretchedness of the stockingers' lives brought them forcibly to his notice.

Cooper's conversion to Chartism, like his other conversions, happened suddenly. In the course of his duties as reporter on *The Leicestershire Mercury* he was sent to write a notice of a Chartist meeting. The Chartists had a small meeting-room in the town; and on this occasion the speaker was John Mason, a shoemaker like Cooper, and a well-known Chartist lecturer from Tyneside.

Cooper's first reflection on Mason's lecture was that there was nothing new in it. The Chartist programme was simply the old Radical programme, which had been popularised in earlier days by Major Cartwright and Henry Hunt. He comments that he had imbibed a belief in universal suffrage from papers lent him by Radical brushmakers in his youth. " Of all the ' Six Points ' of the ' People's Charter,' there was but one I did not like : the Ballot. And I do not like it now." Cooper in fact was a Radical on principle, but of the school which opposed the Ballot on the ground that it would encourage political dishonesty more than it would prevent political intimidation. Apart from the ' Six Points ', he found Mason's speech temperate and well argued ; and the only point at which he expressed and aroused strong feeling was when, in his peroration, he adjured his hearers not to be led away by the middle-class propagandists of the Anti-Corn Law League, not because Corn Law repeal was wrong, but because, if it were to be granted without the Charter, the middle classes would again desert and betray the workers, as they had deserted and betrayed them after 1832.

" ' Cheap Bread ! ' they cry. But they mean ' Low Wages ! ' Do not listen to their cant and humbug. Stick to your Charter ! You are veritable slaves without your votes."

Cooper was evidently impressed ; but what impressed him much more than Mason's speech was what befell him after the meeting. It is best told in his own words.

" As we passed out into the street, I was surprised to see the long upper windows of the meaner houses fully lighted, and to hear the loud creak of the stocking-frame.

" ' Do your stocking weavers often work so late as this ? '
I asked some of the men who were leaving the meeting.

" ' No, not often : work's over scarce for that,' they
answered ; ' but we're glad to work any hour, when we can
get work to do.'

" ' Then your hosiery trade is not good in Leicester ? '
I observed.

" ' Good ! It's been good for naught this many a year,'
said one of the men. ' We've a bit of a spurt now and then.
But we soon go back to starvation ! '

" ' And what may be the average earning of a stocking
weaver ? ' I asked. ' I mean, when a man is fully employed.'

" ' About four and sixpence,' was the reply.

" ' Four and sixpence,' I said ; ' well, six fours are
twenty-four, and six sixpences are three shillings : that's
seven-and-twenty shillings a week. The wages are not so
bad when you are in work.'

" ' What are you talking about ? ' said they. ' You mean
four and sixpence a day ; but we mean four and sixpence
a week.'

" ' Four and sixpence a week ! ' I exclaimed. ' You
don't mean that men have to work on those stocking-frames
that I hear going now, a whole week for four and sixpence.
How can they maintain their wives and children ? '

" ' Aye, you may well ask that,' said one of them, sadly."

Cooper was deeply stirred by this revelation, which seems
to have come to him entirely as a surprise. He contrasted
these wretched wages with those of labourers in Lincolnshire villages, earning twice as much, and with his own ten
shillings as a shoemaker still new at the trade — earnings
which he had hitherto thought meagre enough. He made
up his mind to find out for himself whether what he had been
told was true ; and he speedily found that it was, and that
the truth was even worse on account of uneven employment
and the ruthless administration of the New Poor Law. This
was Cooper's conversion to the Chartist cause.

The stockingers of Leicester and Nottingham were,
indeed, together with the handloom weavers of Lancashire
and Yorkshire, the most downtrodden of all the victims of
the Industrial Revolution. In the Northern textile areas

there were, side by side with the starving weavers, new classes of workers — mule-spinners, powerloom weavers, and workers in other new crafts based on the factory and the machine — whose conditions, bad as they were, tended slowly to improve with the development of the new industrial system. But the handloom weavers and the stockingers, still working mainly in their own homes or in small workshops under the domestic system, were helpless victims of the forces of economic change. These men with whom Cooper spoke were of the kind who had been Luddites in 1811 and in the bad years after the peace ; who had flocked into Doherty's National Association for the Protection of Labour and Owen's Grand National Consolidated Trades Union in the early 'thirties ; who had been beaten, and worse oppressed for their pains, whatever form of resistance they had tried. They were now Chartists, setting upon The People's Charter their hopeless hope.

Cooper became one with them, converted by the sight and imagination of their misery into a supporter of the Chartist cause. His mind busied itself at once with plans ; he became so full of their grievances that his position on the respectable Whig *Leicestershire Mercury* soon became impossible. He tried to promote a combination of men and manufacturers to secure both the Charter and the repeal of the Corn Laws ; but here in Leicester mutual hatreds of employers and employed were much too strong. The reward he got was his discharge from his position on the newspaper. He made preparations to leave the town, and again seek his fortune elsewhere.

At this point some of the local Chartists approached him and proposed that he should take over the editorship of their little paper, *The Midland Counties Illuminator*. A salary of thirty shillings a week was offered ; but there was much doubt whether the Chartists could ever afford to pay it. Nevertheless Cooper accepted, and also began lecturing to the local Chartists on Sunday evenings — startling them somewhat by opening and closing his meetings with prayer. But his thirty shillings were not fully forthcoming after the first week ; and he thereupon persuaded them to hand the paper over to him entirely — existing debt and all.

Cooper had ambitious ideas. He borrowed twenty pounds, found a new printer, rented an office in the High Street, and set out to make a splash. From his new office he sold *The Northern Star* and other Chartist literature, as well as his own paper ; and presently he was selling bread and running a coffee-house as well. The Leicester Chartists elected him as secretary in place of their previous leader, John Markham ; and he began an energetic campaign of open-air meetings, propaganda visits to surrounding villages, and processions of unemployed workers through the streets. Cooper had the art of publicity ; he speedily made Chartism in Leicester into a movement commanding wide popular support.

At this stage, early in 1841, there was an important by-election at Nottingham, where John Walter, the Tory opponent of the New Poor Law, was standing against a Whig. The Chartists backed Walter, and Cooper and Markham went over from Leicester to speak for him. Cooper reports himself as saying to Walter on this occasion, " Don't have a wrong idea of why you are to have Chartist support. We mean to use your party to cut the throats of the Whigs, and then we mean to cut your throats also." He adds that Walter laughed, " but he understood that the jest was an earnest one ".

John Walter was returned, only to lose his seat at the General Election three months later. On this occasion Cooper occupied himself at Leicester, where the Tories, though they had no intention of contesting the seats of the two Whig members, wanted to make a show of opposition up to the date of the poll. They therefore approached Cooper, and offered to pay Chartists who would attend at the hustings and hold up their hands in support of the dummy Tory candidate. Cooper agreed to this. " Your money," he said, " will do our poor fellows good." Accordingly, a number of Leicester Chartists attended and duly held up their hands. But not all the local Chartists approved of this action ; and it was the beginning of a rift which widened later into an open dispute.

In the meantime, Cooper had encountered difficulties over *The Midland Counties Illuminator*. The printer, either on political grounds or in the fear that his bills might not be paid, refused to go on producing the paper ; and Cooper could find no one else who would undertake to print it in a similar style. He had to give it up ; and in its place he began to issue a small halfpenny sheet, *The Chartist Rushlight*. This in turn soon gave place to *The Extinguisher* — a title based on an incident at the hustings, where a political opponent had managed to clap a large tin extinguisher on Cooper's head. In the following year, 1842, *The Extinguisher* was replaced by *The Commonwealthsman* ; but before the year was out the editor's imprisonment put an end for the time to his journalistic ventures.

At the General Election of 1841, Cooper himself appeared at the hustings as Chartist candidate for Leicester, and also at Loughborough. He maintained that at Leicester he had the largest show of hands ; but the Mayor declared that the Whigs had the majority. His next adventure in parliamentary politics was in the autumn of 1842, when there was a further by-election at Nottingham, in which Joseph Sturge stood as Complete Suffrage candidate against John Walter. Cooper and Feargus O'Connor supported Sturge, whereas Joseph Rayner Stephens spoke for Walter on account of his hostility to the New Poor Law. In this contest Cooper began to play his part in the Complete Suffrage movement, and a further rift opened between him and those Chartists who continued to denounce Sturge as an emissary of the Anti-Corn Law League, who was said to have been detached from the Cobdenites with a mission to wean the workers away from the Charter.

This, however, is to anticipate. From the beginning of 1842 Cooper had begun to put into force new ambitious schemes for the reorganisation of the local Chartist movement. In place of the small meeting-room which had hitherto been large enough to hold the Chartist gatherings, he secured the lease of a large hall, already known as the Shakespearean Room, and began to organise big indoor meetings, as well as an adult school and other educational activities. Some of the old Chartists who disapproved of his methods soon seceded and went back to the old meeting-room. Cooper then organised his own following as ' the Shakespearean Brigade of Leicester Chartists ', and began to assume the title of ' General ' which had been jokingly conferred on him. His methods, indeed, had much in common with those which were later associated with the Salvation Army. He found two local Chartist poets, William Jones and John Bramwich ; and together they produced a Chartist song-book which achieved a wide popularity. He led his hunger-marchers through the streets in growing numbers as trade grew worse and worse ; and his shop became the centre of a wide range of activities — including the giving of bread on credit to many hungry stockingers — an act of generosity which he could ill afford.

Cooper was at this time a strong partisan of Feargus O'Connor. This put him in opposition to the followers of Lovett and also to Bronterre O'Brien, who had just quarrelled with O'Connor and broken away from his leadership, and was giving his support to Joseph Sturge's newly founded Complete Suffrage Union. John Markham and the anti-Cooper section of the Leicester Chartists, on the other hand, were backing Lovett and O'Brien and upholding the ' moral force ' doctrines which Cooper and O'Connor denounced as ' Moral Humbug '. When the Markham party got O'Brien to speak in Leicester, the Shakespeareans invaded his meeting and voted Cooper into the chair. The proceedings ended with the passing of a vote of no confidence in O'Brien ; and later, when Henry Vincent paid a similar visit to Leicester, Cooper's supporters howled him down. Roused by Cooper's revivalist methods, Leicester acquired a reputation as a stronghold of ' physical force ' Chartism ; and Cooper and his supporter, J. R. Bairstow, were chosen as delegates to the Chartist Conference which was summoned to meet in Manchester on August 16, 1842.

This was not a ' Convention ', but a special Conference which had been called in haste in order to consider what action the National Charter Association ought to take in view of the great strikes which had broken out in the North of England. Throughout the industrial districts, 1842 was a year of deep depression and acute hunger. Unemployment was everywhere, and employers in one trade after another were seeking to enforce the acceptance of heavy reductions in wages. The second National Petition had been rejected in May, and there had been angry meetings at which ' ulterior measures ' had been proposed, but given up as impracticable in view of the state of trade. Then early in August, without any central direction, strikes broke out almost simultaneously in many parts of the country, from the Clyde and Tyne to Lancashire and the Staffordshire Potteries. In Lancashire, where the strikes were most extensive, crowds of strikers marched from mill to mill drawing the plugs of the boilers in order to enforce a complete stoppage of work. Hence the name commonly given to the movement — the " Plug Plot ". The Chartist leaders in Lancashire immediately tried to turn the strikes, which had begun as a protest against wage-reductions, into a mass demand for the Charter ; and the Executive of the National Charter Association assembled in Manchester and attempted, under the leadership of Peter Murray McDouall, to assume command of the movement.

At this point O'Connor, who was not a member of the N.C.A. Executive, on which he had refused to serve, made one of his sudden changes of front, and allowed the strikes to be denounced in *The Northern Star* as having been fomented by the Anti-Corn Law League for the purpose of discrediting the Chartists. O'Connor had just been supporting Sturge against Walter at the Nottingham election, and was for the moment attempting to work with the middle-class Radicals. He probably realised that the strikes were foredoomed to failure on account of the depression, and feared that Chartism, if it were identified with them, would be involved in their defeat. But O'Connor was wary enough not to burn his boats finally. He allowed William Hill, the editor of *The Northern Star*, to fulminate against the identification of the Chartists with the strike movement ; but he himself waited to see which way the cat would jump.

Cooper set out on August 9 on his journey to Manchester to attend the Chartist Conference. On the way he spoke to a big meeting at Birmingham, harangued striking colliers at Wednesbury and Bilston, and addressed stormy meetings in Stafford, where, seeing police taking notes of what he was saying, he hastily turned his speech into an ironical defence of the established order. As he reported to his Leicester supporters : " I showed how excellent it was to have a ' sweet little silver-voiced lady ', and pay one million and a quarter yearly to support her and her establishment. I demonstrated that loyal Chartists knew the land would be ruined if the Civil List were not kept up ; and that working men would weep their eyes sore if Adelaide were to be bereft of her £100,000 a year. I denounced any ragged shoemaker (Stafford, like Northampton, you know, my brave Shakespeareans, is a famous shoemaking town) as a stupid fellow, if he dared to talk about his aged grandmother being in a bastille, and vegetating on skilly, while the Dowager had three palaces to live in."

From Stafford Cooper went on to the Potteries, which he found on strike and in an uproar. In the Pottery towns he addressed a number of big meetings, culminating in a huge open-air gathering at the Crown Bank, Hanley, where John Richards, the veteran leader of the local Chartists, proposed, and Cooper seconded, a resolution that all work should cease until the Charter had become the law of the land. According to his own story, he repeatedly adjured the crowds at these meetings to observe absolute law and order during the strike ; but pistols were fired off among his auditors during the Crown Bank meeting, and, to use his own words, he " began to apprehend that mischief had begun which it would not be easy to quell ".

Cooper's main business, however, was in Manchester, at the Conference ; and after the Hanley meeting he tried to get a gig to take him to Whitmore, the nearest station on the railway to Manchester — the Pottery towns not being on the railway at that time. No conveyance was to be had ; and finally, guided by two local stalwarts, he set out to walk by night to Macclesfield, in order to pick up the Manchester coach on the following morning. His guides lost their way, and presently he found himself in Burslem, which, for fear of arrest, he had particularly meant to avoid. There he was arrested, and taken before a magistrate, who was in bed at an inn. He avowed his identity, but was finally allowed to go, and walked on to Crewe, where he picked up the train for Manchester, and found John Campbell, the Secretary of the National Charter Association, also on the train. As they approached Manchester, and saw that no smoke was ascending from the factory chimneys, " Campbell's face changed, and with an oath he said ' Not a single mill at work ! Something must come out of this, and something serious too ! ' "

While Cooper had been journeying by stages from Leicester to Manchester, events in the North had been moving fast. On August 12, 1842, a Conference of 358 delegates from the factory areas had met in Manchester, and had decided to convert the strike into a strike for the Charter. On the 15th, a further session had called upon the workers throughout the country to join the strike. This was the situation when Cooper reached Manchester ; and he and his fellow delegates had to make up their minds about the Chartist policy in relation to the strikes. Excitement naturally ran high ; and despite the opposition of William Hill, Richard Otley of Sheffield, and, surprisingly, George Julian Harney, there was a big majority in favour of giving the movement full support. Cooper made a fiery speech on the side of the N.C.A. Executive, which, headed by McDouall, was all for supporting the strikers. Cooper, to use his own words, " told the Conference that he would vote for the resolution because it meant fighting, and he saw it must come to that. The spread of the strikes would and must be followed by a general outbreak. The authorities would try to quell it ; but the Chartists must resist them. There was nothing now but a physical force struggle to be looked for. The Chartists must get the people out to fight ; and they would be irresistible, if they were united."

This speech brought O'Connor to his feet, to deprecate all talk about fighting, and to tell the Conference that the question before it was that of supporting the strikes, and not that of making civil war. Otley and Harney dwelt on the impracticability of expecting half-starved operatives to fight trained soldiers, and opposed the general strike on the ground that it would mean fighting. But many more speakers supported Cooper's attitude ; and O'Connor, seeing which way the wind was blowing, came down on the side of the Executive, and gave his blessing to the strike policy. The N.C.A. Executive thereupon issued a flaming manifesto, calling for a general strike throughout Great Britain in eight days' time, and urging the workers to keep the peace — until the strike had become general. The manifesto ended, " Strengthen our hands at this crisis ; support your leaders ; rally round our sacred cause ; and leave the decision to the God of justice and of battle ".

This call to battle not unnaturally led to orders for the arrest of the Chartist leaders, who had however dispersed before it was issued. Cooper, with Bairstow, returned to Leicester, where a decision to join the strike had been followed by conflicts between the workers and the police, and the movement had already collapsed before his return. He was busy getting up a protest against the action of the magistrates in breaking up the popular demonstration, when he was arrested on a charge that he had, in his address at Hanley a fortnight previously, been guilty of inciting the people to arson.

Great scenes of violence had, in fact, occurred in the Five Towns on the very evening of Cooper's departure for Manchester. In Hanley, Longton, Fenton, and other parts of the Potteries rioting had occurred on a large scale. Houses had been sacked and burnt down, including those of obnoxious clerical magistrates and colliery agents. This rioting was chiefly the work of the colliers, who marched in from the surrounding villages and occupied the towns. Soldiers were called in, and on the following day there was fighting in the streets of Hanley, when the colliers tried to unhorse the cavalry, and the troops fired, killing one member of the crowd and wounding others. Not for some days did the soldiers finally get the upper hand.

Cooper, after his arrest at Leicester, was taken to the Potteries and charged with arson, on the ground that, though he had not been present at the riots, having left for Manchester before they began, he had been guilty of inciting the crowd to violence by his speeches. That he had been in fear of arrest even before the riots is plain ; for he had left the town in a borrowed hat and cloak donned for purposes of disguise. But he maintained, both at his trial and later, that he had been so far from inciting his hearers to disorder that he had again and again urged them to be scrupulous in keeping the peace. His own comment, in his autobiography published thirty years afterwards, was this : " I see how rash and uncalculating my conduct was. But the demagogue is ever the instrument rather than the leader of the mob. I had caught the spirit of the oppressed and discontented thousands, and, by virtue of my nature and constitution, struck the spark which kindled the combustion."

From August to October 1842 Cooper was in Stafford Gaol, awaiting trial, and in company with a large number of other Chartists in a similar plight. Long before he was tried, the great strikes had collapsed. The strikers were no match for the soldiers and yeomanry when it came to deeds of violence ; and they had no power to prolong their resistance in face of the imminence of sheer starvation. The more violent the initial outbreak, the sooner the men drifted sullenly back to work ; but, even where there were no serious riots, the strikes were speedily broken. McDouall, who had been their fiercest supporter on the Executive of the National Charter Association, and had drafted the manifesto issued after the Manchester Chartist Conference, fled to France as soon as the collapse became evident, and was made by O'Connor and his followers the principal scapegoat of the defeat. The notion that the strikes had been instigated by the Anti-Corn Law League as a means of bringing pressure on the Government for the repeal of the Corn Laws, and at the same time of side-tracking the Charter, was revived ; and the Chartists who had most strongly supported the strike policy were denounced as tools or victims of the League.

Cooper was out of all this. His trial came on in October, before the Lord Chief Justice, Sir Nicholas Tindal, who had shown himself a friendly judge in the case of John Frost three years before. Cooper had made up his mind to conduct his own defence, and in preparing it he was helped by William Prowting Roberts, the Bath Chartist solicitor, who was soon to become famous as ' The Miners' Attorney '. Cooper was charged together with a number of other prisoners ; but it was clearly essential to his defence that he should be tried alone, as much of his case depended on his ability to prove his absence from the scene of the riots. For this purpose, his detention and appearance before a magistrate at Burslem stood him in good stead, as it enabled him to prove that he had left Hanley well before the riots began. Even so, he may be regarded as fortunate, in view of the state of public opinion, in having been brought in ' Not Guilty ' by the jury, after the judge had summed up on his side.

But acquittal on this particular charge was not the end of Cooper's troubles. He was immediately re-arrested on a charge of sedition ; and there could be little doubt that he would be convicted on this accusation. He succeeded, however, on Roberts's advice, on getting his case postponed to the next assizes, and he was admitted to bail, and thus enabled not merely to return home, but to play his part in the Chartist proceedings which followed the collapse of the strikes. He went back to Leicester, where he was feted at a public reception ; and he promptly threw himself into the preparations for the Complete Suffrage Conference which Joseph Sturge and his followers had summoned to meet in Birmingham in December 1842.

Cooper's vacillations in connection with the Complete Suffrage movement up to this time have been recorded already. He had begun by advocating union between the middle and working classes, but had then, under O'Connor's influence, taken up an attitude of strong hostility to the middle-class Radicals, on the ground that they were trying to win the people away from the Charter. He had veered round again, with O'Connor, to support Sturge against Walter at the Nottingham election of August 1842 — immediately before the strikes. Now, in face of the collapse of the strike movement, he and his fellow Chartists had to re-define their attitude.

At this stage the policy of O'Connor, which Cooper faithfully followed, was to endeavour to pack the Complete Suffrage Conference, not merely with Chartists, but with Chartists in sympathy with himself. It had been arranged that the delegates to the Conference should be elected, in order to conform with the law, at public meetings, and as far as possible so that from each place one delegate should be sent to represent the electors, and a second the non-electors. The consequence was a three-cornered fight to capture the representation between the Sturgeites, the O'Connorites, and the dissident Chartists of the schools of Lovett and O'Brien. In some places the division of the representation between electors and non-electors was observed, in others ignored. At Leicester Cooper's Shakespeareans succeeded in packing the electors' meeting, as well as the non-electors'; and the same thing happened in a number of other areas.

The result was that the Complete Suffrage Conference which met at Birmingham in December 1842 contained a substantial majority of Chartists — counting O'Connorites, O'Brienites, and Lovettites together. Cooper, chosen as one of the four delegates for Leicester, counted as one of O'Connor's following. The big question before the Conference was whether it should pledge itself to The People's Charter by name, or to the Bill of Rights, also embodying the famous Six Points, which the Sturgeites had drafted in the hope of getting the Conference to commit itself to the Chartist programme without accepting the name. On this issue the Lovettites and O'Brienites, as well as the O'Connorites, were arrayed against the Sturgeites. James Williams of Sunderland, seconded by Cooper, tried to achieve a compromise by proposing that both the Bill of Rights and the Charter should be received by the Conference, and that both should be made the basis of a National Petition to Parliament. But passions on both sides ran too high for this solution to be accepted. Lovett was outraged because he considered that the Sturgeites had gone behind his back in bringing forward the Bill in place of the Charter without consulting him; and the O'Connorites were for the most part no less intent than Lovett in pressing for acceptance of the Charter. The amendment in favour of the Charter was carried; and the Sturgeites withdrew from the Conference, to pursue their deliberations alone. A few Chartists, headed by Henry Vincent, went with them.

The majority, who remained behind, were a discordant body. Lovett and his friends were acutely hostile to O'Connor, and determined to pursue only ' moral force ' methods, whereas most of the delegates still held, despite the collapse of the strikes, to some brand of ' physical force ' doctrine. Cooper and J. H. Parry, the lawyer, an adherent of Lovett's, in the hope of holding the rival groups together, moved a resolution asserting the desire of the Chartists to conciliate and not to oppose those who, while favouring the principles of the Charter, were not disposed to pursue the methods of advocacy which Chartists approved. This proposal provoked warm opposition ; but finally an amendment, put forward by O'Connor, and saying much the same thing in rather different language, was carried. But though O'Connor and Cooper showed in this their desire to keep the cooperation of the ' moral force ' party, the rival groups soon fell again to quarrelling. Cooper asked Lovett whether he was prepared to merge his own ' moral force ' organisation with the National Charter Association ; and when Lovett refused there was more recrimination, and Lovett and his friends followed the Sturgeites out of the Conference.

The O'Connorites, left alone, then fell to discussing their future plans. Cooper submitted a scheme of organisation based on the holding of an Annual Chartist Convention, to be elected by public meetings in the localities. The Convention was to appoint officers, who were to form an Executive Committee and to hold quarterly sessions in different centres. There was to be a paid secretary, and the other officers were to receive payment for work done during the sessions. The Annual Conventions were to appoint general lecturers to tour the country (on the model of the Owenite missionaries) preaching the principles of the Charter. Members of the association were to pay a penny a week as a contribution to the centre ; and the itinerant lecturers were to be instructed to advocate temperance as well as the Charter.

This plan was ordered by the remaining delegates — now reduced from well over three hundred to a rump of 37 — to be submitted to the localities with a view to its adoption at a further Conference to be held in April 1843. But in fact the next Conference was not held until September 1843 ; and by that time Cooper was in prison and O'Connor had decided to bring forward an alternative plan of his own — the famous Chartist Land Scheme.

Cooper returned to Leicester from the Complete Suffrage Conference to find the local Chartists in considerable difficulties. In order to meet the expenses of his coming trial he persuaded them to hire the Amphitheatre and put on a series of performances of *Hamlet*, with himself in the title part ; but it does not appear that the venture realised any substantial sum. His trial for sedition came on in March, at Stafford ; and again he elected to be his own advocate. He spoke for ten hours, and felt very pleased with himself when he had done ; but, though he successfully rebutted the accusation of incitement to arson, which was again brought up against him, he was declared guilty, together with others, of seditious conspiracy, the question of sentence being left to the Court of Queen's Bench in London. Bail was again granted, pending the further hearing of the case ; and Cooper managed to address a number of Chartist meetings in Northampton and other Midland towns before he was called up to receive judgment. In May he delivered another monstrously long harangue to the judges of the Queen's Bench, but was sentenced to two years' imprisonment.

Thus, in May 1843 Cooper was removed for two years from direct participation in the Chartist movement. But he had no mind to be idle during his incarceration. While he had been in gaol the previous year he had occupied his time in story-writing, and had also begun, in blank verse, what he intended to make his magnum opus, a long poem entitled *The Purgatory of Suicides*. These activities had been set aside on his release; but now the great question was whether during the next two years he would be allowed access to books, pens, and paper, and enough privacy to continue his work. He arrived at Stafford Gaol with a large case of books, of which he firmly refused to give up the key ; and, when he found that he was to be treated as an ordinary prisoner, and deprived of the means of study and self-expression, instead of sitting down under this discipline he proceeded to make the life of the prison governor a misery until his claims were met. He eluded the turnkeys and got into the governor's room, where he demanded better food and access to his books ; he attended the prison chapel, and disturbed the service by laying hands on the chaplain and demanding that, as a Christian minister, he should intervene on his behalf. He tried other devices, and was subjected to punishments which seem, however, to have been mild in relation to his offences.

These methods were unavailing ; but presently, with the help of a fellow Chartist who was in the prison awaiting transportation, Cooper managed to get pens and paper and to smuggle out of the prison a letter to the Radical M.P., Thomas Slingsby Duncombe — a letter in which he announced that he had prepared a Petition to Parliament for better treatment, and that he proposed to place this in the hands of the prison governor, with a request that he should forward it to Duncombe for presentation. He asked Duncombe, if the governor failed to act on his request, to raise the matter in the House of Commons.

Cooper then put his Petition into the hands of the governor, asking him to show it to the visiting magistrates and to send it on to Duncombe. The governor at first rejected it, and tried to find out where Cooper had got pen and paper ; but Cooper refused to tell him, and threatened him that he would find himself in trouble if Duncombe did not receive the Petition. Thereafter, day after day, he badgered the governor to tell him whether his wishes had been complied with ; and at length he was told that they had. Duncombe, in fact, did get Cooper's Petition, after some weeks' delay, and at once asked the Speaker whether it was in accordance with the constitution for the magistrates to delay a prisoner's Petition to Parliament. The Speaker replied that it was not ; and the magistrates, in a panic, promptly sent for Cooper, and gave him all the conveniences for which he had asked. He was given good food and a place to work in, and he was allowed to write to his wife — a privilege previously denied him.

Thenceforward, Cooper had the goodly supply of books which he had brought with him. He resumed his reading, and set to work to write as well. He finished off the collection of stories which he had begun the year before, and went on seriously with *The Purgatory of Suicides*, which he had begun composing anew in the Spenserean stanza, and committing to memory, before he had been allowed writing materials. During his two years he wrote the whole of this formidable poem, and also, he says, developed for a time " a passion for Hebrew " which threatened, until he overcame it, to engulf all his other interests. He had, moreover, even amid these preoccupations, plenty of time to think; and before he came out of prison his religious views had undergone a considerable change.

As we have seen, Cooper had severed his active connection with the Wesleyans in 1835. But he says that, at any rate up to 1841, he regarded himself as still a Wesleyan. In Leicester his Chartist contacts had some effect in shaking his religious opinions ; but it was mainly while he was in prison that he became a sceptic, though not an atheist. It was not until after his release from prison in 1845 that he was able to read Strauss's *Life of Jesus*, which deeply influenced him, and led him to become a Secularist lecturer and to denounce the entire supernatural element in religion.

On his release in May 1845, Cooper did not return to live in Leicester. For a second time he went up to London to seek his fortune, armed on this occasion with his completed poem and his volume of stories. He sought out Duncombe, who gave him an introduction to Benjamin Disraeli — then deeply interested in Chartism, as he had shown in *Sybil*, which had been recently published. Disraeli introduced Cooper to several publishers, who in turn politely declined his poem, and then to Harrison Ainsworth, the novelist, who sent him to John Forster, of *The Examiner*, through whom he reached Messrs. Chapman & Hall. All these publishers told him that poetry was a drug in the market ; and he was near his wits' end when he met McGowan, the former printer of *The Kentish Mercury*, who was now printing *The Northern Star* for O'Connor.

Now, Cooper during his time in prison had come to feel about O'Connor very differently from what he had felt in 1842. He had gone to gaol as an O'Connorite, an advocate of 'Physical Force'. He came out, like many others, a 'moral force' Chartist, and found O'Connor advocating neither 'Physical Force' nor 'Moral Force', but a Land Scheme which seemed to him crazy nonsense. Moreover, he had not escaped denunciation from O'Connor for his part in the events of 1842 ; and O'Connor had rejected in favour of the Land Scheme the plan of Chartist reorganisation which he had drafted. Consequently, he had made no approach to O'Connor after his release ; but now McGowan told him that O'Connor was repentant of having denounced him, and eager to make friends. Cooper was persuaded to meet O'Connor, who offered him handsome apologies and, anxious to re-enlist him among his followers, offered to pay the cost of having his poem printed by McGowan. Cooper was flattered by O'Connor's praise of his verses, and accepted the offer ; and McGowan began to set the poem up in type.

It remained, however, to find a publisher. This need was at last met by an accidental encounter with John Cleave, the Radical bookseller who was a close friend of Hetherington and Lovett. Cleave put Cooper into touch with Douglas Jerrold, who showed his poem to Charles Dickens and arranged for its issue by a small publisher, Jeremiah How. How issued Cooper's stories, under the title *Wise Saws and Modern Instances*, as well as *The Purgatory of Suicides*, before the end of 1845, and also engaged him to write a Christmas book in verse. *The Baron's Yule Feast*, however, was finished too late for the Christmas market, and appeared early in 1846.

Cooper, having found his publisher, made haste to shake off his obligation to O'Connor, by getting the printing contract transferred to How. He was soon engaged in a bitter quarrel with O'Connor over the Land Scheme, and, as a convert to ' Moral Force ', was invited to become one of the lecturers at the National Hall, which Lovett and his friends were trying to make the centre of a new Chartist movement on purely moral and educational lines. He was also invited by Douglas Jerrold to tour the country and write for his new weekly paper a series of descriptive articles on the condition of the people of England.

Cooper seemed now to be fairly set up as an author. *The Purgatory of Suicides*, on the title-page of which he described himself as ' Thomas Cooper the Chartist ', had a remarkably good press, and was widely admired. It does, in fact, contain a good deal of writing of no mean order. In it, Cooper, proclaiming his faith in the people and his hatred of oppression, sets out to ask whether, in face of the tale of man's miseries and defeats, life is yet worth living, and seeks the answer in a review of famous suicides of history, ranging through the ages from the ancient world to Castlereagh and

Sir Samuel Romilly and displaying a vast accumulation of miscellaneous lore.

Cooper's poetical style is diffuse, and does not lend itself to quotation; nor is an estimate of his merits as a poet at all essential to my purpose. It is enough to say that his verse was good enough to be admired by Dickens, Carlyle, Wordsworth, and other literary notables, and to enjoy a considerable vogue. He wrote much more after 1845 — novels, stories, and verses, including a second ' epic ' of his old age, *The Paradise of Martyrs*, in addition to his educational and didactic works. But none of his later books either equalled in merit, or rivalled in popularity, his " prison-rhyme ", as he called it, *The Purgatory of Suicides*. None, at any rate, except his autobiography, on which I have drawn plentifully in writing this study.

As we have seen, Cooper in 1845 had quarrelled with O'Connor and begun to lecture at Lovett's National Hall. But he had not yet broken with the main Chartist body. He was elected as one of the delegates for London to the Chartist Convention of 1846; and immediately after his election he wrote a letter to the newspapers, announcing that he proposed to move eight resolutions highly critical of the proceedings of the Chartist Executive and of O'Connor personally. His resolutions demanded a complete separation of the direction of the Land Scheme from that of the Chartist body, an explicit repudiation of ' physical force ' doctrines, a declaration of the Convention's " resolve to seek the establishment of The People's Charter as a statute of the realm solely by peaceable, moral, and constitutional means ", and an affirmation " that this Convention regards Feargus O'Connor as unworthy of the confidence of Chartists, and hereby earnestly warns British working men of the folly and danger of union with him ".

These resolutions aroused a storm of indignation among O'Connor's still numerous following. Cooper had become convinced that O'Connor was using the funds received from the public for the Land Scheme to support *The Northern Star*, which had declined seriously in circulation; and he made no secret of his belief. He openly accused O'Connor of dishonesty, and, when he was refused admission to the columns of *The Northern Star*, returned to the charge in *Lloyd's Newspaper*. The charges did not shake the faith of the main bodies of Chartists throughout the country. Resolutions from local Chartist Associations, expressing full confidence in O'Connor and abhorrence of Cooper's treason, poured into the office of *The Northern Star*; and Cooper, who was the Secretary of the Veteran Patriots', Exiles', Widows' and Orphans' Fund, formed to raise money in aid of the dependents of the Chartist martyrs, found himself counter-accused of all sorts of dishonesty. He promptly resigned his office, with the remark, " I hereby discharge myself, hoping that some true sheep may be found, who will permit himself to be sheared, and succeed as cheerfully as I have done, for the benefit of the sufferers ".

The Chartist Convention met in August at Leeds. At the outset, Cooper called for an account of the state of the membership and funds of the National Charter Association; but no statement was forthcoming. Cooper persisted in his demands for information, until Ernest Jones, then a newcomer to the movement and a devout admirer of O'Connor, rose and moved his expulsion from the Chartist body. O'Connor appealed to Cooper to withdraw his resolutions; but Cooper persisted, and was thereupon expelled by vote of the Convention. He refused to leave the meeting, and a stormy scene was only ended by the chairman adjourning the Convention to the following day. Cooper attempted to gain admission to the resumed session, but was prevented by stewards, and had to content himself with addressing a crowd outside the place of meeting.

This ended Cooper's connection with the National Charter Association, and in effect with Chartism itself. Thereafter for a number of years he was essentially an independent. He was associated with the People's International League in 1847 and 1848, and there, in common with many Chartists who had broken with O'Connor, established links with Mazzini and other leaders of the foreign exiles in London. But he held aloof from the Chartist revival in 1848, despite various attempts to draw him in. "Experience," he wrote in his autobiography, " had rendered me a little wiser than to suffer myself to be mixed up again with any plot, however plausible : so I kept out of them all. . . . As I had nothing to do with the monstrous ' National Petition ', or the meeting on Kennington Common, or the ' glorious 10th of April ', or any of the ' monster meetings ' of that year, I am cut off, happily, from the later Chartist history of violence and failure."

The tone of this statement indicates the sharpness of Cooper's breach with the Chartists after 1846. He did not even keep up for long his association with the Lovett group, with which he had temperamentally little in common. He was finding for himself a new vocation as a popular lecturer on both religious and ' lay ' subjects, speaking sometimes on ' Christian Evidences ' in the spirit of Strauss's ' Higher Criticism ', and sometimes on literary and historical subjects. In 1847 William Johnson Fox, who was then in charge of the South Place Institute, fell ill, and Cooper took his place. In the following year he lectured regularly at the Owenite John Street Institution, and published an anti-O'Connorite pamphlet, *The Land for the Labourers*. In 1849 he resumed journalism, editing a journal called *The Plain Speaker* in conjunction with T. J. Wooler, the former editor of the famous *Black Dwarf*. In *The Plain Speaker* appeared his *Letters to Young Men of the Working Classes*, in which he mingled Chartist ' moral force ' opinions with adjurations to temperance and educational effort. In this year he also went extensively about the provinces lecturing. His range of subjects was immense. To quote his own words, he lectured during this and the following years on these among a number of other subjects : " the Lives of Luther, Mahommed, Cobbett, Paine, Kosciusko, Raleigh, William Tell, Rienzi, Howard, Oberlin, Neff, Bernard Gilpin, Latimer, Washington, Sir William Jones, Dr. Johnson, Major Cartwright, William Godwin, Louis Philippe, George Fox, Rousseau, Voltaire, John Knox, Handel, Haydn, Mozart, Mendelssohn, Beethoven, Defoe, William Pitt, Columbus, Sir Isaac Newton, Cortez, Pizarro, Thomas-à-Becket, Sir Robert Peel, Sir Charles J. Napier, Wickliffe, Calvin, Sir Thomas More, Wesley, Swedenborg, Pythagoras, and Beau Brummell — and on Negro Slavery, Church Establishment, Taxation and the National Debt, Mental Cultivation, the Age of

Chivalry, the Middle Ages, the Wrongs of Poland, the Gypsies, Athens under Pericles, Conquests of Alexander the Great, Ancient Egypt, the Histories of Italy, Switzerland, Hungary, etc., Pio Nono and the Italians, Genius of Pope, Dryden, Scott, Cowper, etc., the Peterloo Massacre and Henry Hunt, Monarchy, Aristocracy, Democracy, Early English Freethinkers, Philosophy of Lord Bacon, Philosophy of Locke, Gulliver's Travels, Astronomy, Geology, National History, the Vegetable Kingdom, the Baltic Nations — and many other subjects ". He kept unimpaired his tremendous thirst for acquiring and imparting information.

Cooper's connection with *The Plain Speaker* did not last long. At the beginning of 1850 he branched out with a new paper of his own. *Cooper's Journal* revealed him as still a Chartist of sorts, interested in continental revolutionary movements, but more in attacks on religious dogmatism and clerical obscurantism. He made vigorous onslaughts on the people who wanted to prevent the workers from holding Sunday meetings ; but he was very friendly towards the attempts of the Christian Socialists to promote working men's associations on a cooperative basis. Walter Cooper, one of the chief working-class members of the Christian Socialist group, was his cousin : accounts of the progress of the Association of Working Tailors and other Christian Socialist cooperative enterprises were given prominence in his *Journal* ; and several active Christian Socialists were among his frequent contributors. At the same time he continued his regular lectures at the John Street Institution, and added lectures at the Owenite-Secularist Hall of Science, in the City Road.

He also pursued his story-writing. A novel, *Captain Cobbler, or the Lincolnshire Insurrection : a Story of the Reign of Henry VIII*, was published in parts in connection with *Cooper's Journal* ; and when this was finished he set to work on a novel about Chartism, suggested to him by Messrs. Chapman & Hall. This he finished in 1852 ; but the publishers rejected it, and he cast it aside, and wrote another, *Alderman Ralph*, which duly appeared in 1853, and was followed, two years later, by *The Family Feud*.

Meanwhile, in 1851, he had toured most of Great Britain

and Ireland on an immense round of lectures, and in 1852 had come back to London in order to resume his lecturing there. He left the John Street Institution, but continued to lecture regularly at the Hall of Science until 1856, when his connection with the Secularists came to an abrupt end. He was billed to lecture on " Sweden and the Swedes " ; but on the platform he was suddenly moved to declare instead his conversion to the truths of Christianity.

This, from a well-known Rationalist lecturer, and before such an audience, was a sensational event. Thomas Cooper had the press of his life, and was at once involved in a series of debates with his namesake and fellow Secularist, Robert Cooper, with whom he had often been confused.

Conversion was, for Cooper, very awkward in a worldly sense. He had lost the power to lecture, and forfeited the support of his familiar audiences. For six months he was tongue-tied ; but thereafter he hired the Hall of Science on his own account, and began lecturing there in support of Theism. He was, however, plainly uncomfortable in his new role ; for he was still quite uncertain how far his own conversion was to carry him, or in what sort of God he believed. In his extremity he accepted work as a copyist in the office of the Board of Health, and laboured away there, copying documents for a very small remuneration, from the latter part of 1856 to the early months of 1858. During this period he also contributed articles on the condition of the working classes to John Henderson's short-lived paper, *The People*.

He was, however, mainly engaged during this interval in wrestling with himself. By 1858 he had arrived at an assured faith in a simple Bible Christianity, and at a belief that he knew what work God was calling on him to do. That year he set out on a course of itinerant preaching which lasted almost continually for eight years. He sold up his home and, accompanied during the earlier years by his wife, wandered homeless over the country, preaching the gospel to every creature. In 1859 he joined the Baptists ; but he did not limit his activities to any particular denomination. It was no matter where or to whom he preached, as long as he was spreading the good news.

Eight years of this wandering life led to a serious breakdown, and for a long time Cooper lay ill in the house of friends. His admirers raised an annuity for him, in the belief that his day was over. But in 1867 he was on the road again. His wife died in 1870, and thereafter he wandered less, and began to gather his discourses into little volumes, which had a wide sale. *The Bridge of History over the Gulf of Time* appeared in 1871, followed by *Plain Pulpit Talk* in 1872, and *God, the Soul, and a Future State* in 1873. In 1872 he also published *The Life of Thomas Cooper*, now the only book of his that is read, and in 1873 *The Paradise of Martyrs*, a long poem in which he versified in the Spenserean stanza his Christian faith, as he had put his Chartism into *The Purgatory of Suicides* thirty years before. In 1877 appeared his collected *Poetical Works*, followed by two more little booklets based on his sermons — *Evolution* (1878) and *Atonement* (1880). Finally in 1885 he published *Thoughts at Fourscore*, at once a supplement to his autobiography and a gathering of his reflections on the changes in morals and manners which he had seen in his time.

Needless to say, Cooper revealed himself in these latter-day writings as a strong anti-Darwinian and as a critic of the manners and morals of the new generation. The working men, he complained, had no longer the old seriousness of mind, the energy in the pursuit of knowledge, the earnestness which had marked such men in his younger days. He heard them talking, not about the soul or universal suffrage, but about sports and pastimes ; most of them seemed careless about the higher things of both this world and the next. What he omitted to notice was that this change in interest was largely a product of changed conditions. The main body of the working class was no longer perpetually near the verge of starvation, nor conscious of intolerable daily oppression. If it had forgotten The People's Charter, that was because the Charter had always been primarily " a knife and fork question ", and the edge had been taken off the old urgency of revolt. As for the passion for self-improvement which Cooper and many of his intelligent contemporaries had felt, that too had become less keen with the growth of public elementary education and the advent, with greater national wealth, of a less exacting code of conduct. Cooper deplored all this, as many other old Puritans deplored it. To him, the England of the 1880s seemed wretchedly slack and soft. It looks ' tough ' enough in retrospect to-day.

As for the man himself, he was obviously vain and given at once to self-righteousness and to occasional self-abasement. He grew up with a sense of being thwarted at every turn. Feeling in himself a great capacity for knowledge, he passionately wanted from childhood to become an educated man. He wanted to get to Cambridge University, and to emulate the great scholars who had risen from the humblest ranks in life. Probably thwartedness was responsible, more than anything else, for turning him into a Chartist ; and, having become one, he discovered in himself an undoubted capacity for demagogic leadership. But his heart was never really in politics : it was in education and moral instruction. These cravings he was able to satisfy first as a Rationalist lecturer and later as an itinerant preacher. Cooper's Chartism was only an episode ; but men of his stamp, who were drawn into Chartism by forces of both repulsion and attraction, cannot be ignored when we come to make up the final balance-sheet of that curiously many-sided and symbolic movement.

VIII

John Fielden

I T was John Fielden, the Radical master cotton spinner, who in 1847 introduced into Parliament the Bill which became the Ten Hours Act. In Parliament, he had struggled and voted for the Ten Hours for fifteen years — ever since his first election as M.P. for Oldham in 1832. Outside Parliament, he had been working for factory reform much longer still — from 1816, when he and his brothers petitioned Parliament in support of the factory movement led by Nathaniel Gould of Manchester, and in a less public capacity, from a still earlier date. Though Lord Ashley had been from 1833 the parliamentary leader of the factory reformers, it was fitting that Fielden should be made, by Ashley's temporary absence from the House of Commons, the spokesman of the movement on the occasion of its victory. It was not fitting that his reward should be defeat at the General Election which followed within a few months — defeat at Oldham, which he had represented ever since the Reform Act, and had held without difficulty even when he was supporting The People's Charter and calling upon the people to resist the New Poor Law with all their might.

John Fielden, the most faithful of all the Radicals, had grown to wealth with the rise of the cotton industry. He was not quite a self-made man ; for his father, Joshua Fielden, a Quaker of the old school and a Tory, had founded the business which, in the hands of John Fielden and his brothers, expanded into one of the greatest cotton spinning and manufacturing concerns in the country. Joshua Fielden, the father, had been a yeoman farmer who, after the manner of his time, had combined farming with woollen manufacture under the domestic system. He and his family and servants had produced woollen cloth on the handloom and carried it o market at Halifax, until he had realised the opportunities

218

presented by the new and developing cotton manufacture. In 1782 he left his old home, Edge End Farm, and set up a cotton ' manufactory ' at Laneside, Todmorden, in three converted cottages. At first the work was done wholly by hand ; but soon the spinning jenny replaced the wheel, and the carding engine was introduced. Joshua Fielden began building accommodation for his new machines ; and the famous Waterside Factory, the first of many to be controlled by the Fieldens, was gradually erected and enlarged. In these early days Joshua Fielden used to fetch his weekly supply of cotton from Manchester, and there deliver his woven goods, by means of a cart, which he and one of his five sons accompanied to market. The sons all went to work in the factory when they reached the age of ten ; and John Fielden many years afterwards used his own early experience in support of his case for legal restrictions on the hours of labour. " I well remember being set to work in my father's mill when I was little more than ten years old; my associates, too, in the labour and in recreation are still in my memory. Only a few of them are now alive ; some dying very young, others living to become men and women ; but many of those who lived have died off before they attained the age of fifty years, having the appearance of being much older, a premature appearance of age which I verily believe was caused by the nature of the employment in which they had been brought up. For several years after I began to work in the mill, the hours of labour in our works did not exceed *ten* in the day, winter and summer, and even with the labour of those hours, I shall never forget the fatigue I often felt before the day ended, and the anxiety of us all to be relieved from the unvarying and irksome toil we had gone through before we could obtain relief by such play and amusements as we resorted to when liberated from our work. I allude to this fact, because it is not uncommon for persons to infer that, because the children who work in factories are seen to play like other children when they have time to do so, the labour is, therefore, light, and does not fatigue them. The reverse of this conclusion I know to be the truth. I know the effect which ten hours' labour had upon myself ; I who had the attention of parents better able than those of my companions to allow me extraordinary occasional indulgence. And he knows very little of human nature, who does not know that, to a child, diversion is so essential, that it will undergo even exhaustion in its amusements. I protest, therefore, against the reasoning that, because a child is not brought so low in spirit as to be incapable of enjoying the diversions of a child, it is not worked to the utmost that its feeble frame and constitution will bear." [1] Fielden went on to say that he knew from his own experience that the greatly increased speed at which machinery was run had added largely to the strain upon the factory children, and concluded that a limitation of the hours of labour to ten a day was by no means a sufficient protection.

This is a powerful indictment of the factory conditions both of the eighteen-thirties and of the period, more than thirty years earlier, when John Fielden had worked as a child. Moreover, he had no doubt that the conditions had grown progressively worse. The hours of labour were no fewer, and were quite often more ; and the amount of exertion called for in each hour had seriously increased. He himself had been employed under relatively favourable conditions, not only because he worked in his father's mill, but also because things had been better there, even in his father's day, than in the great majority of factories. But he had suffered enough, even so, never to forget what he had gone through, and to keep for the rest of his life a lively sympathy for those who were subjected to similar, and greater, suffering.

As Joshua Fielden's sons grew up, and his business expanded, specialisation was introduced. Each son became a specialist in a particular department ; and John, the third son, who had most often gone with his father to market, took over the buying and selling side of the concern. This gave him wide contacts, and a knowledge of many firms and branches of the cotton industry. He was made a partner in his early twenties ; and on his father's death in 1811, he and his brothers succeeded to full control of the rapidly growing business. Well before this they had all become ardent Radicals — " arrant Jacobins ", their father called them. But their Radicalism did not find much scope till the closing

[1] *The Curse of the Factory System*, 1836.

years of the Napoleonic Wars, or cause them to become prominent until the years of severe distress which followed the conclusion of peace. John Fielden's public career as an opponent of factory cruelty began in 1816, when he and his brothers supported Nathaniel Gould's plea for factory legislation, and Fielden Brothers presented to Parliament a Petition asking Parliament to adopt effective measures of regulation. This was the movement which led up to the elder Peel's Factory Act of 1819 — the real beginning of factory control by the State. Fielden also showed his Radicalism in the same year by opposing the younger Peel's Bill for the restoration of the gold standard, and by demanding that, if prices were to be cut down by a reduction in the supply of money, there should be an ' equitable adjustment ' — the then equivalent of a Capital Levy — to scale down the interest on the National Debt in correspondence with the change in monetary values. Fielden also declared himself at this point a strong opponent of ' paper money ', and thus began his long association with William Cobbett, who was to be later his colleague as Member for Oldham in the Reformed Parliament, and to become connected with him privately as well as in public life when Cobbett's son, James Paul, married his daughter.

During the years after 1815 there was a very rapid growth of the cotton industry, in spite of the bad general conditions of trade. In particular, a great many new master manufacturers set up in a small way, with the aid of credit supplied by the country banks, and attempted to establish their position by taking on unemployed weavers at very low wages, in the hope of undercutting the larger manufacturers. This led among the latter to an outcry against unfair competition, and to a general lowering of wage-rates. In the hope of checking this tendency, a number of the larger firms became converts to the advocacy of a legal minimum wage, feeling confident of victory over the interlopers if wage-cutting were prevented. There was a considerable movement of this sort in 1819, when after the revival of 1818 the cotton trade sank into renewed depression ; and John Fielden was one of the leading advocates of wage-regulation. But the Government gave the movement no encouragement ; and before long it faded away as trade revived. The collapse of 1825 again caused a widespread development of the wage-cutting policy ; and in 1826 Fielden took the lead in a renewed campaign for the establishment of a minimum wage. On this occasion, despairing of help from the Government, the manufacturers who favoured wage-regulation put forward an alternative plan. Fielden and his supporters wanted the local Poor Law authorities to agree to maintain out of the poor rates workers who could not get employment at certain standard wages which the more reputable masters promised, subject to this undertaking, to observe. This proposal received quite extensive support ; but the Poor Law authorities hung back, and before any decisive steps could be taken the starving handloom weavers resorted to widespread machine-breaking in a desperate attempt to check the growth of the power-loom. The power-loom riots of 1826 proved fatal to the minimum wage movement ; and thereafter, though Fielden continued to advocate minimum wages established either by law or by agreement among the masters, the movement disintegrated. The workers had lost hope of getting any sort of wage-legislation passed by Parliament, and the more enlightened masters had lost hope of achieving what they wanted by voluntary agreement. The idea was not given up ; but during the next few years the workers turned their attention to the attempt to secure ' equalisation of wages ', which meant in effect a minimum wage, by Trade Union action. This was largely the impetus behind John Doherty's National Association for the Protection of Labour set up in 1830 ; and once again, in this campaign, the workers had Fielden Brothers' energetic support.

By this time the struggle for the reform of Parliament was reaching its height ; and in 1831 Political Unions modelled on Thomas Attwood's organisation at Birmingham were being founded all over the country. John Fielden presided at the meeting which formed the Todmorden Political Union, and gave his full support to the movement, though he personally favoured a more radical measure than the Whig Reform Bill. When the Reform Act became law in 1832, he allowed himself, though he had no ambition to be in Parliament, to be nominated as Radical candidate for Oldham, in partnership with his friend, William Cobbett, and largely in the hope that his nomination would help towards securing Cobbett's election. During the year he published what seems to have been his first pamphlet, *The Mischiefs and Iniquities of Paper Money* ; and Cobbett wrote a foreword to it.

At the election of 1832 Fielden and Cobbett had Whig candidates, as well as a Tory, against them ; but they romped home by enormous majorities, Cobbett getting 677 and Fielden 645 votes against 150 for the next highest candidate. In the Reformed House of Commons Fielden voted steadily for every Radical proposal. During the session of 1833 he seconded Cobbett's famous motion for the removal from office of Sir Robert Peel, voted for the Ten Hours Bill, the Ballot, the repeal of the Septennial Act, the imposition of taxes on property, and the revision of the Corn Laws, and opposed civil and military sinecures, naval impressment, compensation for slave-owners in the West Indies, and coercion in Ireland. He also supported Attwood's motion for an enquiry into the prevailing distress, though he was totally hostile to Attwood's currency proposals. This record for his first session as an M.P. he maintained throughout his parliamentary career. He was the most constant of Radicals, always to be found among that small band which was Radical in economic as well as political matters, and was as ready to vote for factory legislation as against the forces of aristocratic privilege.

His Radicalism caused him, during this same session, to oppose the Government's proposal to vote a sum of money for furthering popular education through Dr. Bell's National Society for the Education of the Poor in the Principles of the Church of England and Joseph Lancaster's undenominational (*i.e.* mainly nonconformist) British and Foreign Schools Society. But he opposed, not because, like Cobbett, he was against State action in the educational field, but because he wanted a national system of education under public control. Quaker by descent, he had early become a Unitarian, and had taken a leading part, in 1824, in founding the first Unitarian Chapel in Todmorden ; and he was in full sympathy with the Radical Dissenters who were opposed to all forms of control over education by the Established Church.

In 1833 and earlier, Fielden had given his support to the Ten Hours movement. But it had been his view that ten hours' labour, though it might be the least that it was of any use to ask Parliament to establish as a legal maximum, was too much for children and adults alike. He was as disappointed as Oastler with Althorp's Factory Act of 1833 ; but whereas the main body of the middle-class factory reformers set to work, after the defeat of their immediate hopes, to reconstruct the agitation for the Ten Hours Bill, Fielden took a different line. Trade Unionism was then sweeping over the country under the inspiration of Robert Owen ; and in the autumn of 1833, in connection with the creation of the Grand National Consolidated Trades Union, the Northern factory operatives became active in a movement for an eight hours day, to be secured, not by legislation, but by direct industrial action. Robert Owen was at the head of this movement ; and its most active organiser was John Doherty, the principal founder of the Cotton Spinners' Grand General Union of 1829 and of the National Association for the Protection of Labour the following year. The N.A.P.L. had by this time broken down ; but its old Lancashire supporters rallied to a new body, the Society for National Regeneration, which Doherty and Owen persuaded a Conference of delegates to set up at Manchester in November 1833. Fielden took an active part in this society, which became the instrument of the agitation for the eight hours day. Branches were established throughout the textile districts of Lancashire, Yorkshire, and the Midlands ; and a fierce quarrel broke out between its supporters and the leaders of the Ten Hours movement. The latter argued that the Regenerationists were ruining the cause by demanding too much and by alienating the support of the respectable factory reformers, such as Lord Ashley, and of the friendly employers, who were not for the most part likely to join Fielden in advocating a mass strike against themselves. G. S. Bull and others strongly attacked the Regenerationists ; and the controversy was vigorously maintained until the eight hours movement and the National Regeneration Society were alike snuffed out by the defeat and destruction of the Grand National Consolidated Trades Union in the summer of 1834.

Even before this collapse, Fielden had become involved in another Radical campaign on behalf of the workers. In 1834 came the new Poor Law Bill; and he again joined forces with Cobbett in vehement and angry opposition to the united policy of the Whig and Tory parties. From the very introduction of the Bill he and Cobbett threatened the Government that the attempt to put the New Poor Law into operation would be met by fierce popular resistance. " I tell you ", said Fielden in the House of Commons, " that the introduction of this new law in my constituency will meet with resistance, and I do not mind telling you frankly that, if such resistance takes place, I would lead it. If matters have come to such a pass that neither the sheriff's baton nor the constable's bludgeon can maintain public order against the aggressors, it is our duty to resist, and I am prepared to take upon myself a share of the responsibility." Fielden's line of argument against the ' Malthusian Bill ' is best summarised in a Petition from the inhabitants of Oldham which he presented to the House of Commons some years later, in 1839 :

That the New Poor Law was passed on the authority of Commissioners whose reports were so voluminous that no man could read and digest them in less than two years of diligent reading ; and that several volumes, even of these reports, on which the bill was founded, were not printed for the use of members till after the bill was passed. That the provisions of the bill itself are unconstitutional, inconvenient, and unjust ; and that the powers given to Commissioners under it have been, as might be expected, acted upon in a manner so arbitrary, and so shocking to humanity, that the country ascribes to those who procured it to pass the wicked intention that the powers should be so used, but the unmanliness of shrinking from avowing it by direct enactment. That, under this law, thousands of human beings have been driven from their native homes in the south of England into the north to seek employment in manufactures, and, having worked in disappointment, have pined to death, or wandered forth again, without home or means, outcasts in the world ; and that, this experiment of the Poor Law Commissioners and hard-hearted Guardians having failed, no redress to the sufferers is offered, except the mere unblushing avowal that the scheme [*i.e.* of moving labourers from the south to the north] is a failure, and is to end.

In the House of Commons, only a handful of members was ready to vote with Cobbett and Fielden against the Poor Law Bill, and for a time there was little organised resistance to it in the country. Cobbett, who had been trying to stir up the agricultural labourers against it, died in 1835 ; and at first the Poor Law Commissioners made no attempt to apply the Act in the Northern manufacturing districts. Fielden, meanwhile, had become actively involved in a last effort, in connection with the cotton weavers' Petitions of 1834 and 1835, to persuade Parliament to agree to the establishment of a minimum wage. Early in 1835 he and Cobbett were re-elected without opposition as M.P.s for Oldham. In June, on Cobbett's death, his son, John Morgan Cobbett, fought the seat as a supporter of his father's and Fielden's policy ; but Feargus O'Connor, who had lost his Irish seat in consequence of his quarrel with Daniel O'Connell, intervened as a third candidate, and thus enabled the Tory, J. F. Lees, to win by a narrow majority. Cobbett's death left Fielden much more lonely in the House of Commons. Hitherto, he had accepted Cobbett as his political leader ; and he had no ambition himself to lead. He could only plod away steadily, advocating good causes in a strong Lancashire accent which the House of Commons did not appreciate, and trying to make up by earnestness for his lack of natural eloquence. He was no orator, and he knew it ; and he was entirely without that confident egoism which contributed so much to Cobbett's power. But he held on his way, doing what he could. In 1836 he published his most ambitious pamphlet, *The Curse of the Factory System*, in which his coming fight over the introduction of the New Poor Law into the Northern Counties was plainly foreshadowed.

In this booklet Fielden argued the case for legislative restriction on the hours of labour not only of children, but of adults as well. He had already returned to advocating the Ten Hours Bill, as the most that could be hoped for from

Parliament ; but he made no concealment of his view that a ten hours day was too long to be consistent with humanity. He was also strongly opposed to the attempts then being made by the new Poor Law Commissioners to transfer labour in bulk from the agricultural South to the manufacturing districts. This policy, he pointed out, was instigated by the less scrupulous employers as a means of supplying them with cheap labour, and was reacting disastrously on wages. Fielden argued forcibly that such a result was contrary to the interests of the general body of manufacturing employers ; for the undercutting to which it led destroyed the purchasing power of the people, and thus deprived the employers of an adequate market for their goods. As for the fears of foreign competition, he cited his own experience as a good employer producing largely for foreign markets against the view that a living wage would destroy Great Britain's export trade. At the same time, he said plainly that he would sooner lose trade and money than countenance oppression, and cited abundant evidence to show both that wages were being excessively beaten down by unscrupulous masters, and that factory conditions of overwork and underpayment were having a disastrous effect on the health and physique of the workers.

At the General Election of 1837, Fielden was easily re-elected for Oldham ; and General W. A. Johnson, a fellow Radical and Cobbettite, captured as his colleague the seat which the Tories had won, thanks to O'Connor's intervention, in 1835. About this time the Poor Law Commissioners, having completed their work in the agricultural South, set seriously about the task of enforcing the principles of the Act of 1834 in the manufacturing districts. The object of the Commissioners was to rearrange the old poor law parishes into Unions, each to be administered by a Board of Guardians responsible to the central authority for carrying out the terms of the Act, and above all else for constructing the new workhouses, in which the approved methods of ' deterrence ' and ' less eligibility ' were to be applied, and for refusing all outdoor relief to the able-bodied, at least until the workhouses were filled to overflowing with their unfortunate victims.

Fielden had announced his intention of fighting the Commissioners ; and he meant to carry out his promise. The Commissioners, well aware that a warm reception awaited their endeavours in the factory areas, moved cautiously and by stages. They made no attempt to enforce at once, in the North, the prohibition of outdoor relief. They sought, first, to get the new Guardians elected by the parishioners and installed in office ; and secondly, to get the new workhouses built and made ready for the immuring of the destitute. Only when these steps had been successfully taken could they hope to be able fully to enforce the " principles of 1834 "

Fielden, on the other hand, was determined to prevent, if he could, the election of the Guardians, and, if they were elected, to prevent them from carrying out their work. In 1837 the Poor Law Commissioners, in their report, had to announce that in Oldham, Huddersfield, and other areas in Lancashire and Yorkshire it had proved impossible to get Boards of Guardians elected. This was the year in which was passed the Act providing for the public registration of births, marriages, and deaths ; and the duty of undertaking this registration was to be in the hands of the Boards of Guardians and their officers in the parishes. The Commissioners fastened on this Act, which was welcomed by the factory reformers as a means of securing better enforcement of the regulations fixing a minimum age of employment — for prior to it there was no easy way of determining children's ages, and thus deciding how far they were under the protection of the law. The Commissioners accordingly tried to get the Boards of Guardians elected by entrusting them in the first instance with registration duties only, without handing over to them the administration of poor relief. They saw that, if they could once get the new Boards installed and at work, the task of imposing the new Poor Law principles would be immensely simplified.

Fielden and his followers fought hard against this manœuvre, trying to prevent the Boards of Guardians from being elected at all. But not even in his home area was Fielden able to prevent the election of a Board. The Todmorden Board of Guardians was duly elected ; and in

August 1838 the Commissioners ordered it to take over the administration of the Poor Laws, though still without insisting on the immediate abolition of outdoor relief for the able-bodied. This was, indeed, the general policy of the Poor'Law Commissioners wherever they expected serious opposition. They tried to get a Board of Guardians elected for the new area, consisting of a Union of parishes, which was to be the future unit of administration ; and they tried to insert the thin end of the wedge by making the new Board responsible, at first, only for the registration of births, marriages, and deaths under the Act of 1837. Having accomplished this, they next handed over the administration of the Poor Laws, but omitted to make an order prohibiting outdoor relief to the able-bodied. By this gradual introduction of the new principles they hoped to disarm opposition, and to be able to get the new Boards of Guardians established in office without serious popular disturbances.

The anti-Poor Law party was fully alive to the purpose of these manœuvres. It had been seeking, ever since 1834, to stop the importation of blacklegs from the South of England into the industrial districts ; and it now attempted, first, to make it impossible for Boards of Guardians to be elected at all and, if that failed, to prevent them from taking over Poor Law administration. The history of this struggle can be traced in the annual reports of the Poor Law Commissioners.

Thus, in the Todmorden area, the opponents of the New Poor Law, having failed to prevent the Guardians from being elected, decided to do all they could to render their proceedings abortive. Fielden Brothers, under John Fielden's inspiration, issued in 1838 notices of dismissal to all their workpeople, announcing their readiness to re-engage them as soon as the recently elected Board of Guardians agreed to resign. The inhabitants were also invited to assemble for a meeting of protest outside the premises where the first meeting of the Guardians was to be held. The Guardians, forewarned of this project, cancelled their meeting and assembled in secret elsewhere. The attempt to enforce their resignation failed ; and after a time Messrs. Fielden were compelled to reopen their works.

On this occasion John Fielden issued a placard, addressed to the Board of Guardians. He wrote : " To oppose force to force we are not yet prepared ; but if the people of this and the surrounding districts are to be driven to the alternative of either doing so, or surrendering their local government into the hands of an unconstitutional board of lawmakers, the time may not be far distant when the experiment may be tried, and I would warn those who provoke the people to such a combat of the danger they are incurring. . . . I cannot help adding, as a point worthy of your most serious consideration, that your real difficulties may only commence when the period arrives for the relief of the poor being administered by your Board, and the officers acting under it. Supplies will be required, the rates will have to be collected, and, after having disregarded the entreaties of your brother ratepayers, this may be much more difficult to accomplish than you expect, even with the threatened force at your back. You have heard that tithes could not be collected in Ireland ; and if you persevere you may have the satisfaction of knowing that rates cannot be collected in England."

The Poor Law Commissioners reprinted these passages, with severe comment, in their report for 1838–9, and added that the overseers in the parishes of Todmorden and Longfield were refusing to supply the Guardians with any funds, and that accordingly it had not been possible to introduce the new system of relief into these parishes.

This was not the end of the story. The parish overseers of Todmorden and Longfield, in which the Fieldens' principal works were situated, persisted in their refusal to collect and hand over to the new Board of Guardians the amounts demanded in payment of poor rates. The Guardians, by way of retaliation, proceeded to present the defaulting overseers to Quarter Sessions for failure to discharge their lawful duties. The county justices thereupon ordered a distress to be levied on the goods of one of the defaulting overseers ; and constables were sent for from Halifax to execute the levy. Further proceedings followed, at the end of which a *mandamus* was issued from the Court of Queen's Bench to order the overseers to obey the law.

When, however, the constables from Halifax attempted

to levy the distress, they were met by mass opposition from the people of Todmorden. When their approach was known, the bell was set ringing in Messrs. Fieldens' factory, in order to summon the people to the defence ; and the constables were beaten off with their purpose unaccomplished. According to the report of the Commissioners, " the two officers were stripped of their clothes, and otherwise brutally treated, and had great difficulty in escaping with their lives into the adjoining township of Stanfield ; and here a further riot took place, accompanied by some destruction of property, and an attack upon the building in which the Guardians were accustomed to meet."

The magistrates thereupon announced their intention of swearing in special constables ; but before this could be done a further riot followed. The houses of the Chairman and other members of the Board of Guardians were attacked by a large crowd ; attempts were made to set fire to several houses, and a good deal of property was destroyed. The magistrates sent to Burnley for military aid ; but before the arrival of the soldiers the crowd had dispersed.

The principal leaders of the crowd having come from Fieldens' mills, the magistrates next used the soldiers to help them in making arrests ; and feeling ran so high that a force of infantry and cavalry had for some time to be stationed at Todmorden. In all some forty men were arrested and put on trial. One of them, who had the ill-fortune to be tried at Lancaster, was sentenced to nine months' imprisonment ; the others, tried at York, were found guilty, but were dismissed with a caution. The judge at York Assizes gave as his reason for this leniency that " there were parties far more deserving of punishment in reference to these transactions than the misguided men who then stood before him for sentence ". At Lancaster, the jury unsuccessfully recommended the prisoner to mercy, on the ground that he had been " influenced by others ". But no attempt was made to take any steps against John Fielden for his part in the affair.

These events happened during the winter of 1838–9, while the Chartist troubles were blowing up, and great meetings were being held all over the country for the election of delegates to the People's Convention. At Todmorden, the presence of soldiers was for the time being effective in preventing further riots; but the popular feeling had been so plainly shown that the Guardians, though they remained in office, made no attempt to enforce the New Poor Law in the Todmorden area, and the Commissioners in London refrained from making any order prohibiting outdoor relief in the parishes concerned.

Fielden, during this year of struggle, was fighting the new forces of bureaucracy on another front as well. When the Police Bill of 1839 proposed to empower the justices to levy rates for the payment of professional police forces, Fielden fought the Bill in Parliament, demanding that the ratepayers should be given control over the new police and over the appointment of their officers. This was also the year of the first Chartist Petition; and the Chartist Convention relied on Attwood and Fielden to present the Petition and argue the case for it in Parliament. It was Attwood, rather than Fielden, who took the lead in demanding that the Convention should repudiate ' physical force, projects before the Petition was presented; but, in any event, the objection was waived, and both Attwood and Fielden spoke in favour of the acceptance of the Petition as a basis for parliamentary examination. When it had been rejected, and the Convention proceeded to consider ' ulterior measures ', Fielden advocated the preparation of a second and more widely signed Petition, and, when his advice was rejected, stood aside from the Convention's further proceedings.

He did not, however, relax his Radical zeal. In 1840 he opposed in Parliament the renewal of the Poor Law Commissioners' tenure of office for a further period of years; and early in 1841 he moved in the House of Commons a motion for the repeal of the Poor Law Act of 1834. He had, he said, " from the introduction of the Bill into the House in 1834 to the present time maintained that there was no necessity for such an Act, and that what was called the abusive administration of relief to the poor under the law as it then stood was not caused by the poor themselves, nor by any defect in the law, but was the effect of excessive taxation, of alterations from time to time in the currency, of corn laws to make food dear and to sustain rents, of laws to repeal the tax on property, and raise the revenue by taxes on every article that ought to be consumed by the poor, and, lastly, of the Bill of 1819, which, by contracting the currency, doubled the pressure of taxation on the people, and withdrew from thousands the means which they would have otherwise had of employing the poor, and paying them wages adequate to their proper maintenance. . . . Where labour was scarce and wages low, the labourer had a right to more relief out of the provision made for him by the Poor Law, than where work could be had in plenty, and was properly paid for; and those resident among the poor were the best judges of the merits of every applicant. It was absurd to attempt, by a Central Board sitting in London, to lay down any regulation that could operate justly towards either the poor or the ratepayers, or to carry into effect any uniform practice of administration by means of a self-acting test."

Needless to say, these arguments did not prevail; and the mandate of the Poor Law Commissioners was renewed for a further period of years. But Fielden, if he did not convince the House of Commons, was saying what satisfied his constituents; and at the General Election of 1842 he and General Johnson were re-elected unopposed at Oldham. The Commissioners, however, encouraged by the renewal of their mandate and by the Chartist defeat of 1839, were emboldened to take more drastic action in the Northern Counties. In August 1841 they issued a general prohibition of outdoor relief to the able-bodied, save where exceptional leave was granted; and in February 1842 they embodied this and other principles of the New Poor Law in their first set of General Rules applicable over the whole country.

At Todmorden and in the surrounding districts the fight went on in spite of these rules and orders. With Fielden's encouragement the inhabitants refused to pay the poor rates, and the Guardians were unable to collect the money they wanted for building workhouses. The struggle lasted in all for more than forty years; it was not until John Fielden had been dead for nearly twenty years that the Poor Law of 1834 was fully enforced in the areas dominated by the Fielden mills.

After 1841, the struggle over the Poor Law settled down

into a persistent guerrilla warfare. Chartism, after flaring up momentarily in a new revolt during the distresses of 1842, rapidly lost its hold on the main body of the workers ; and in the industrial districts of Lancashire and Yorkshire the emphasis shifted back again to the movement for factory reform. Fielden supported in Parliament the Chartist Petition of 1842 ; but thereafter he devoted his main attention to the Ten Hours struggle, which was about that time energetically resumed. In 1842 deputations went up from the factory districts to interview Peel, and to lobby Members of Parliament ; and in the following session Sir James Graham introduced a Government Bill by which it was proposed to limit the hours of children of from eight to thirteen years of age to six and a half hours a day — to be worked continuously either in the morning or in the afternoon. For young persons of between thirteen and eighteen and for women up to twenty-one, there was to be a twelve hours day, and hours on Saturdays were to be limited to nine. The Bill also contained clauses dealing with the education of factory children ; and over these there arose a keen controversy, the Dissenters objecting to the control which it was proposed to place in the hands of the Church.

The factory reformers fought the Bill as utterly inadequate, especially because it proposed to allow work in factories from eight years of age ; and, faced with their opposition as well as that of the Dissenters, the Government withdrew the Bill. Charles Hindley, the lifelong friend of the children, then proposed to bring in a Ten Hours Bill, which was to include a limitation of the hours during which factories employing women and children would be allowed to remain open for work. But, on a Government promise of a further Bill the next year, Hindley withdrew his motion.

Accordingly, in 1844 Graham produced a new Bill, very much like the Government measure of 1843, but extending protection to all women, irrespective of age. The factory reformers organised great meetings all over the North to demand a Ten Hours Bill ; and in March Ashley actually carried in the House of Commons a Ten Hours amendment. There followed a confused series of divisions in which the Government and the reformers were alternately victorious, so that the Bill became a patchwork of conflicting decisions. Graham thereupon withdrew it and brought in a new Bill on the old lines. Ashley again moved his Ten Hours amendment ; but the Government having made the vote a question of confidence he was heavily defeated, and the Bill became law in its original form. Fielden, of course, acted closely with Ashley throughout these proceedings.

The Act of 1844 was followed by a renewed agitation in the factory districts, running side by side with the campaign of the Anti-Corn Law League. Many M.P.s who favoured Free Trade in corn were induced to promise that they would vote for the Ten Hours Bill as soon as the Corn Laws had been repealed, and the manufacturer had thus been placed in a fair position to compete with his rivals abroad.

In January 1846 Ashley, supported by Fielden, reintroduced the Ten Hours Bill ; but the factory issue was overshadowed by that of the Corn Laws. Ashley, though he had been elected to Parliament as a Protectionist, voted with Peel for Free Trade in corn ; and, with his customary conscientiousness, he felt that he had no right to keep his seat in face of his change of attitude. He retired from Parliament, and did not return until he was elected for Bath at the General Election of the following year. In the meantime, Fielden had taken over the leadership of the Ten Hours movement in the House of Commons. Ashley toured the Northern Counties, and Richard Oastler Scotland, in support of the agitation ; and in January 1847 Fielden moved the first reading of the Bill in Parliament. Helped by the votes of those who had promised to support it as soon as the Corn Laws were repealed, it passed the House of Commons in March 1847, and received the Royal Assent in June. After a campaign which had been practically continuous for sixteen years, the advocates of the ten hours day had at last won their victory, though there were troubles still to come over its effective enforcement. The employers attempted to evade the new law by working shifts of women and young persons, thus imposing longer hours upon the adult male workers. They introduced the ' relay ' system, starting batches of workers at different hours, and thus making effective inspection nearly impossible. These practices led to renewed agitation in the factory districts. Oastler and Joseph Rayner Stephens returned to lead a new crusade ; and the reformers challenged the employers' action in the law courts. But in 1850 the judges decided that shifts and relays were fully in accordance with the law of 1844, which that of 1847 had only amended and not repealed. Ashley introduced a fresh Bill, designed to make these practices unlawful ; but, faced with strong parliamentary opposition, he agreed to compromise upon a working day of ten and a half hours, on condition of getting the law properly enforced, and shift working stopped. This led to an outcry against Ashley in the factory areas. Oastler and the Fieldens denounced him as an apostate, and there was a renewal of mass meetings in the North. But the Bill legalising the ten and a half hours was passed under the auspices of the Whig Government ; and so the legal position remained. The agitation gradually died away in the 'fifties, and, though the Factory Acts were gradually extended to a number of additional trades, no further major change was made until 1867.

John Fielden had no part in these later developments. His last public act was his successful sponsorship of the Ten Hours Act of 1847. At the General Election of that year he and John Morgan Cobbett, who stood as his colleague, were both defeated at Oldham, and Fielden thereupon retired from public life. He died two years later, at Skegness, and was buried in the cemetery of the Unitarian Chapel at Todmorden, which he had helped to found. His brothers and successors in the firm of Fielden Brothers carried on the fight both against the New Poor Law and for the full enforcement of the Ten Hours Act ; and at the next election, in 1852, his son-in-law, J. M. Cobbett, won back the seat which he had lost. John Fielden had been very faithful, even to the end ; and his tradition lived on after him in the constituency which he had represented and in the town which his enterprise had raised to prosperity.

John Fielden was neither a commanding parliamentary figure, nor a popular leader able to move large masses of men by his eloquence. He was entirely devoid of political ambition, and took part in public affairs, not because he wanted to, but because he had a strong sense of duty to the workers whom he employed and a keen awareness of the evils of the rising capitalist system. In politics, he remained to the end more a Cobbettite than anything else. He was always ready to support any democratic cause; he voted and spoke on behalf of every proposal made during his fifteen years in Parliament in the interests of the common people. He was entirely devoid of self-seeking, egoism, and self-importance — too much lacking in these qualities for parliamentary success. His nickname, ' Honest John Fielden ', was thoroughly deserved; for he allowed nothing to deflect him from the advocacy of causes which he believed to be fundamentally just. But the House of Commons paid little attention to him ; and to the end he felt much happier in the North, among his own workers, than in the atmosphere of parliamentary debate. Without being a Chartist, he gave full backing to The People's Charter ; and as a great employer, he stood out persistently against his fellow employers who were interested only in getting rich quickly. He had as deep a reservoir of human sympathy as Oastler or Stephens ; and, as the chief proprietor of some of the largest spinning and weaving factories in the world, he never allowed himself to be blinded by self-interest to the spectacle of suffering which even his own mills presented to him. Unlike most men who have endured hardship in their youth, he never forgot what hardship meant, or felt for a moment that what he had gone through was good enough for others. Moreover, he was no mere philanthropist, but a democrat as well. Sometimes, indeed, he used language reminiscent of Oastler's — and of Cobbett's — exhortations to preserve the old institutions of England ; and again and again, in his attacks on the New Poor Law, he urged all those who wished to prevent revolution to rally their forces against it. Fielden was never a ' physical force ' Chartist, or any sort of a revolutionary ; but he was a persistent Radical and a believer in the sound judgement of the common people and in the right and capacity of ordinary men to manage their own affairs. He was in his fifties when the Charter was drafted — at an age when most men of affairs who have been Radical in youth have shaken off their ideals and settled down to take the world as they find it. John Fielden never did settle down : he fought his battle to the end on the side of the oppressed. His homely speech and manner failed to impress Parliament ; and to the Chartist masses he was always a friendly ally, and not a leader. Because of these facts, his memory has been obscured, and no one has yet thought it worth while to write his Life. History for the most part ignores him : even Radical history has passed him by with a bare mention. Yet he, if anyone, for faithfulness, honesty, and persistence in well-doing, deserves to be remembered among the people.

IX

James Bronterre O'Brien

JAMES O'BRIEN, who took to himself the additional name
'Bronterre', was endowed by Feargus O'Connor with a
further title — 'The Chartist Schoolmaster'. His right
to the name was that, more than any other of the leaders of
Chartism, at any rate in its earlier phases, he set out to
equip the movement with a positive social programme and
to define its general aims in intellectual terms. Ernest Jones
and, up to a point, Julian Harney can also be regarded as
having endeavoured to formulate a theory of Chartism, or
rather of the international proletarian movement of which
they held Chartism to be a particular manifestation. But
these attempts came later, when the Chartist movement had
already lost its original impetus ; and they were made very
much under the influence of Karl Marx and other continental exiles, such as the Blanquists, who had found harbour
in England. On the other hand, O'Brien's attempt was
independent both of Marx and of Blanqui, and was much
more closely related to the actual conditions and movements
out of which it arose. This is not to say that O'Brien was
uninfluenced by continental doctrines and examples : far
from it. But he took his models directly from the great
French Revolution — from Robespierre and from Babeuf
— and endeavoured to translate the democratic and equali-
tarian doctrines which had gone down to defeat in France
into terms of the political needs of the Great Britain of his
own day. He was also influenced deeply by Owenism,
though he dissented from certain of Robert Owen's doctrines,
and by Cobbett and Henry Hunt, who were his first masters
in the art of political agitation.

In effect O'Brien, at the very beginning of Chartism, was
seeking to find a theoretical basis for it as a class-movement
of the British workers — a movement expressing in action

the emergence of the working class as a claimant to political power, and thus fulfilling the democratic tendencies inherent in the Revolution of 1789.

These ideas O'Brien nowhere set down systematically. The only book of his in which they find more than incidental expression — *The Rise, Progress, and Phases of Human Slavery* — is in fact no more than an unfinished series of newspaper articles, written as late as 1849 and published in *Reynolds' Political Instructor*. These articles were gathered together, with a good deal of editing, and issued in book form in 1885, by some admirers of O'Brien. They represent his later thought, as it developed after he had lost his belief in the efficiency of ' physical force ' Chartism, and was trying to find a new social basis for the movement in an extensive programme of social and economic reforms.

For O'Brien's earlier version of Chartist philosophy it is necessary to turn to his long articles in *The Northern Star* and other periodicals, to reports of his speeches, and, more particularly, to the comments accompanying his translation of Buonarotti's book about Babeuf's *Conspiration des Égaux*, and to remarks scattered through his unfinished *Life of Robespierre*.

O'Brien himself always attributed to his poverty his failure to write down his ideas in any systematic way. He planned great works, which he never finished, or even began. Certainly he was poor — all through his later years very poor — and in continual difficulty over providing for his wife and family. But it is to be doubted whether his poverty was the root cause of his inability to finish what he had begun or projected. Though it be true that what prevented him from going on with his *Life of Robespierre* much beyond the first volume was the seizure for a debt of the library which he had accumulated for that purpose, and though he would probably have finished this particular book had he not been thus prevented, I find it difficult to believe that he would not have begun upon others and finished them, had there not been some obstacle in his own mind. I doubt if O'Brien, at any time after his release from prison in 1841, had it in him to do any sustained piece of literary work. He was, or he had become, a journalist and a lecturer rather than a writer of books. Moreover, he had become by then a deeply disappointed and disillusioned man. His poverty and the lack of appreciation of his qualities, after the plaudits showered upon him a few years before, rankled in his mind, and helped to make him incapable of sustained creative effort. But I think the poverty affected him not so much directly as because it was to him the token of his rejection by the people.

For a brief space of time, from his emergence as the ' schoolmaster ' of the ' physical force ' Chartists to his being shut up in prison in October 1840, O'Brien held a great popular position among the leaders of Chartism. He was the outstanding writer on O'Connor's *Northern Star*, and O'Connor did not weary of singing his praises. He was an enormously successful speaker — not a mob orator after the fashion of O'Connor or Stephens, but something very different, a lecturer who could keep great audiences listening with sustained interest and enthusiasm to elaborate discourses seldom less than three, and sometimes as much as five, hours long. He was acclaimed as the intellectual leader of Chartism, and saw himself as the Robespierre of the coming British Revolution. And then, quite suddenly, all these things were taken from him. His quarrel with O'Connor caused him to be vilified by most of those who had been previously his most ardent admirers ; and, though he had lost his faith in ' Physical Force ', he was quite unable to come to terms of real fellowship with the ' moral force ' men who had been his principal opponents. He was left high and dry, with almost no following ; and the disappointment was bitter to a man, naturally ambitious, who had staked everything on the success of the democratic cause, and now saw the movement in which he had believed dying, not nobly, but foolishly and meanly amid the sectarian quarrels of its leaders.

Disappointment did not cause O'Brien to abandon his beliefs. His convictions were too deeply rooted for any such apostasy. He went on teaching his gospel of democracy, dismally conscious all the while that he was no longer greeted with the old applause. In 1848, for a little while, he hoped again. But he could find no assured place for himself either then, or in the attempted reconstruction of Chartism after the defeat of that year. He became, in his own phrase, an 'eclectic', standing apart from Chartism in its later stages, sympathetic, but sceptical and aloof. He had, in fact, no message capable of moving the new generation. His thought was a curious mixture of agrarian democracy and protest against the developing abuses of capitalist monopoly. But in the Great Britain of the eighteen-fifties agrarian democracy was out of date, and it was still too soon to rouse the people against monopoly capitalism. O'Brien's ideas fell between two stools ; and there were few who listened to him.

James O'Brien was the son of a wine and spirit merchant, established at Granard, County Longford. His father failed in business, went to the West Indies in the hope of retrieving his fortunes, and died while his son was still very young. The boy, born in 1805, was admitted in 1818 to Lovell Edgeworth's model school at Edgeworthstown, which had been opened two years before. He became principal monitor, and was noticed in his schooldays by Maria Edgeworth and by Sir Walter Scott. In 1822, probably with help from the Edgeworths, he was sent to Trinity College, Dublin, where he distinguished himself, winning the Science Gold Medal in 1825. After six years in College he began, in 1828, to study for the Bar in Dublin. Having graduated early in 1829, he transferred himself to London, and entered at Gray's Inn with a view to practising at the English Bar. But almost at once he became involved in politics. He had come to London, full of democratic sympathies which he had already formed, just as the struggle for parliamentary Reform was entering upon its most critical stage. " My friends ", he wrote later, " sent me to study law ; I took to Radical Reform on my own account. . . . I soon got sick of law, and gave all my soul to Radical Reform." He met 'Orator' Hunt and William Cobbett, joined the London Radical Reform Association, and soon, under Hunt's chairmanship, made his appearance as a speaker in the Radical cause.

1830 was the year in which William Carpenter, with his *Political Letters*, opened a new round in the struggle for the freedom of the press. Carpenter's *Letters*, issued nominally as separate pamphlets, were designed to evade the stamp

duty then imposed on newspapers, with the deliberate intention of making them too expensive for the poor to buy.
O'Brien, under signature " Bronterre ", wrote three long
articles for the *Letters*, and thus laid the foundations of his
reputation as a journalist. His first article, on Irish affairs,
advocated the repeal of the Act of Union, but also raised the
class issue, by asserting that the opposition to repeal was
based, not on a desire to unite the two countries, but rather
on the determination of the governing classes to preserve
their power to exploit the Irish people. The second article,
written in terms implying the sense of a great crisis near at
hand, was largely Owenite in its general tone, without fully
committing its author to Owenite doctrines ; and the third
was a sympathetic account of Owenism, leading up to an
insistence on the need for radical Parliamentary Reform as
the next step towards the realisation of Owen's social
objectives.

These three articles gave O'Brien a standing in Radical
circles. William Carpenter was put in prison for publishing
his *Political Letters* unstamped ; and his friend, Henry
Hetherington, decided to carry on this fight by publishing an
unstamped periodical openly, in defiance of the law. This
was the famous *Poor Man's Guardian*, which appeared regularly as a weekly newspaper from 1831 to 1835. Hundreds
of persons were put in gaol for selling it, and Hetherington
himself, as responsible publisher, served several terms of
imprisonment, until in 1834 the Tory Lord Chancellor,
Lyndhurst, astonished everybody by affirming that it was,
after all, not important enough to be regarded as a newspaper,
and was therefore lawfully published without a stamp.

During most of this period, O'Brien edited *The Poor
Man's Guardian* for Hetherington. Early in 1831 he had
accepted the position of editor of *The Midland Representative
and Birmingham Herald*, a new Radical paper published in
Birmingham. He had moved to Birmingham, and taken an
active part as speaker and writer on behalf of Attwood's
Birmingham Political Union. But in June 1832 *The Midland
Representative* was amalgamated with *The Birmingham
Journal*, which R. K. Douglas edited ; and O'Brien's job
was gone. Returning to London, he was associated for a

few months with Henry Hunt and William Lovett in working for *The True Sun*. But when Henry Mayhew, who had at first edited *The Poor Man's Guardian*, resigned in November 1832, O'Brien took his place, and quickly made the *Guardian* the leading ' unstamped ' paper of the day, with a circulation which stood for a time at 16,000.

For the next few years, O'Brien was working closely with Henry Hetherington. In February 1833, in addition to editing the *Guardian*, he began to issue, through Hetherington as publisher, his own paper, *The Destructive, and, Poor Man's Conservative*, with the motto " While we desire to be destructive of evil, we are still more zealous to be conservative of good ". Presently, Hetherington issued yet another paper, *The Twopenny Dispatch* ; and of this also O'Brien took editorial charge. In December 1833, as the Owenite Trade Union movement began to gather force, *The Destructive* turned into *The People's Conservative and Trade Union Gazette*, only to disappear in the general eclipse of the Trade Unions in the course of the following year. *The Poor Man's Guardian*, despite its vindication in the law courts, also lost favour, and was discontinued at the end of 1835. *The Twopenny Dispatch*, on the other hand, prospered ; and in September 1836 Hetherington enlarged it and reissued it, at 3½d., as a stamped weekly, under the title of *The London Dispatch and People's Social and Political Reformer*, still under O'Brien's editorship. The newspaper tax having been reduced in that year to 1d., it seemed worth while to try out the effects of conformity with the law.

But the *Dispatch* was too dear at 3½d., and in 1837 O'Brien found himself again out of a job. Meanwhile he had begun, in 1836, to write for John Bell's *London Mercury*, and had started a penny paper of his own, containing articles without news, in order to escape the tax. To this latter he gave the title, *Bronterre's National Reformer* ; and he endeavoured to make it an organ of advanced Radical theory, and an instrument of publicity for the books which he was planning to write. But he could not make his *National Reformer* sell without news. Only eleven issues appeared ; and O'Brien lost on the venture such money as he had, and became involved in debt. He did, however, issue in 1836 his translation of Buonarotti's book on *Babeuf's Conspiracy*, with a prefatory Life of Buonarotti and an address to his English readers, in which he set out his reasons for translating the book. It contained, he said, " one of the best expositions of those great political and social principles which I have so long advocated in the *Poor Man's Guardian* and other publications, and which I am still endeavouring to inculcate through the columns of *Hetherington's Twopenny Dispatch.* The application of these principles I deem to be of paramount importance to the human race. Society has been hitherto constituted upon no fixed principles. The state in which we find it is the blind result of chance. Even its advocates do not claim for it any other origin. The right of the strongest — the only right acknowledged by savage man — appears to be still the fundamental charter of all ' civilised ' states. . . . The means are different, but the objects and end are the same. What the savage or uncivilised man does *individually* and *directly*, by the exercise of mere personal prowess, the civilised man (so called) does *collectively* and *circuitously*, by cunningly-designed institutions. . . . [Buonarotti] shows that to correct the evils of this latter state, without at the same time retrograding to the former, was the ground problem sought to be resolved by the first French Revolution, and . . . I was so forcibly struck by the coincidence of Buonarotti's ideas with my own, that I immediately resolved to translate the book."

At the end of his address to his readers, O'Brien announced that he had a number of works in preparation, and hoped to publish them at an early date. They included a *Life of Robespierre* and also *A Real History of the French Revolution*, *A History of the English Commonwealth*, and *An Essay on the Existing State and Future Prospects of Society*. None of these works, except the opening sections of the first, was ever published. *The Life of Robespierre* began to appear in weekly numbers at 3d., and in monthly parts at 1s., and the first volume was published in book form before the end of 1838. At least one part intended for the second volume also appeared ; but at this stage O'Brien's books and furniture were seized on account of his debts, and the book had, for the time, to be given up. The blow was heavy ; for in

1836 and again in 1837 O'Brien had visited Paris in order to collect materials for his writings, and he had brought back a considerable number of important notes and documents, as well as books. The work thus painfully interrupted was never resumed : O'Brien wrote no more, except incidentally, about Robespierre or the French Revolution until he published together his verse elegy and his brief prose dissertation on Robespierre in 1859.

O'Brien's political attitude up to this time — that is, up to the birth of the Chartist movement—can best be studied in his contributions to *The Poor Man's Guardian* and to *Bronterre's National Reformer*. He was writing regularly for these and other journals from the end of the struggle for Parliamentary Reform, through the period of aggressive Trades Unionism which followed, and, after the collapse of the Grand National Consolidated Trades Union, up to the emergence of Chartism in London and of the widespread Anti-Poor Law movement in the industrial districts. His attitude throughout this troublous period was two-sided. On the one hand he was continually telling the Trades Unionists and the Owenites that their social schemes were impracticable without the conquest of political power ; and on the other hand he was insisting to the parliamentary Reformers that Reform would not be of any good to them unless it were accompanied by fundamental changes in the basis of society. *The Poor Man's Guardian, The Destructive*, and O'Brien's other papers were enthusiastic about the development of Trades Unionism and Owenite Cooperation, and gave very full reports of current Trade Union and Cooperative affairs. O'Brien's leading articles gave ardent support to these movements as means of securing to the workers the full produce of their labour and of ending capitalist exploitation. But he had also from time to time to deprecate the tendency of Trades Unionists and Owenites to ignore the need for Universal Suffrage as a means of securing their economic rights. To suggest that they could establish the Cooperative Commonwealth before they had won their political rights was, he said, like telling people to swim without going into the water. He said to the workers, " The Trades Unions will, if rightly supported, work out your political salvation " ; and he stressed the point that the working classes had to gain the capacity to act together by direct experience of their economic struggles against wage-reductions and the Whig Poor Law. But he also insisted that the Trades Unions would have to be brought into politics, and taught to fight for Universal Suffrage, before there could be any hope of their achieving their economic ends.

The Poor Man's Guardian especially was, under O'Brien's and Hetherington's control, an exceedingly lively and unsectarian paper, giving an excellent all-round picture of current economic and political movements, and allowing free expression in its columns to all sections of the working-class agitation, from Lovett to Oastler, and from Owen to Henry Hunt. Its philosophy was one of using the day-to-day struggle as a means of educating the working classes for wider political and social ends ; and it insisted, not on dogmas, but on the need for sustained effort and comprehensive organisation in both the industrial and the political field. How much of the credit for this should be assigned to O'Brien, and how much to Hetherington, must remain uncertain ; but assuredly their close collaboration during these years was more fruitful than what either of them did after they had parted company.

The collaboration lasted until 1837, when it ceased abruptly in consequence of a dispute between two rival groups among the London Radicals. In 1836 Lovett, Cleave, Hetherington, and their closest political associates formed the London Working Men's Association ; and in July of that year O'Brien, together with a few other middle-class sympathisers, was elected an honorary member. Both the first draft of The People's Charter and several of the earlier manifestos of the L.W.M.A. were published in full in *Bronterre's National Reformer* ; and for a few months O'Brien seemed to be working in the fullest harmony with Lovett and his colleagues. But early in 1837 a quarrel began. Daniel O'Connell had been among the Radical M.P.s who had entered into relations with the L.W.M.A. and had taken part in the preliminary stages of preparing The People's Charter. But in 1837, in connection with the trial of the

Glasgow cotton spinners, O'Connell associated himself with a violent attack on Trade Unionism, directed especially against the alleged malpractices of the Dublin trades. O'Brien, who had been a strong upholder of the Trades Unions during the struggles of 1833–4, retaliated with a vigorous attack on O'Connell, of whose temporising Irish policy he also disapproved. Together with Julian Harney and other left-wing members of the L.W.M.A., he was carpeted and censured for bringing the name of the L.W.M.A. into the controversy without its official authority.

This episode led to a severance of O'Brien's relations with the L.W.M.A., and with Hetherington's newspapers. Instead, he strengthened his connection with John Bell's *London Mercury*, of which he became joint editor. The *Mercury* was at this time the organ of a movement which aimed at linking up the various bodies working for Radical Reform under the auspices of a Central National Association, run chiefly by Feargus O'Connor and a certain J. B. Bernard, an eccentric landowner with a devotion to currency reform. Bernard, aided by O'Connor, was then trying to promote a united movement of farmers and workers on the basis of a combination of Universal Suffrage and a scheme of public credits to the producers. O'Brien joined forces with Bernard and O'Connor, and spoke at the inaugural meeting of the Central National Association. Bernard acquired the owner-ship of *The London Mercury*, and put in O'Brien as joint editor ; and for a few months the new body made a con-siderable stir. But Bernard soon got tired of meeting the losses of *The London Mercury* and withdrew his support. O'Brien then ceased to be joint editor ; and Bell, after struggling on for a little while alone, sold the paper to Hetherington, who merged it in his *London Dispatch*.

During his association with the Central National Associa-tion — his first collaboration with Feargus O'Connor — O'Brien seems first to have put forward a plan which was during the next few years to be closely connected with his name. He proposed that the advocates of Universal Suffrage should, in as many constituencies as possible throughout the country, nominate people's candidates at the hustings, and get them elected by show of hands. The persons thus chosen were then, without proceeding to the poll and being defeated because of the narrow franchise, to present themselves at Westminster at the opening of Parliament and take their seats as the real representatives of the people. For this purpose, they were to arrive in London accompanied by a sufficient force of their unrepresented constituents to ensure that their claims could not be ignored. With this backing, they were simply to occupy Parliament and to defy the unrepresentative legislators chosen by the votes of the small minority of the people to whom the franchise had been conceded by the Reform Act of 1832.

There was nothing novel in this proposal. It was based on the scheme for the election of 'legislatorial attorneys' which had been attempted by the Reformers just after the Napoleonic Wars. But O'Brien was able to urge it with renewed force now that the Act of 1832 had produced a new Parliament hardly more representative of the people than the old. In fact, a half-hearted attempt was made to apply O'Brien's policy at the General Election of 1837, by the nomination of 'hustings' candidates in a number of places. O'Brien himself proceeded to Manchester, and was successful, at the hustings, in securing a show of hands in his favour. But he did not go on to the poll ; nor was his plan of a simultaneous march on London and a forcible occupation of the House of Commons pursued.

By the end of 1837 the Central National Association had collapsed. Bernard, the financier of the movement, had withdrawn his money ; *The London Mercury* had died ; and O'Connor, scenting mass trouble in the factory districts, had left London for Yorkshire and began at Leeds his agitation against the New Poor Law, and his new Radical journal, *The Northern Star*, for which O'Brien soon began to write many of the leading articles on current affairs.

O'Brien's connection with *The Northern Star* lasted from the beginning of 1838 to his imprisonment in the spring of 1840 ; and during this period he was much the most influential journalist in the Chartist ranks. In addition to his regular articles for O'Connor's paper, he began in October 1838 to edit *The Operative*, a London paper owned and controlled by representatives of the metropolitan Trade

Unions. In both these papers he delivered strong attacks on the advocates of ' Moral Force ' as the sole method of working for the Charter or for political and social reform. Francis Place, who was strongly hostile to him, said of his writings during this period : " O'Brien wrote long and well-adapted papers to the notions which had been carefully instilled into each of the vast number of working men who took an interest in public matters. His purpose being what it has always been, the destruction of all property in private hands, all profits, all interest, all accumulation, and thus to bring down the middle and upper classes and to elevate the working class to one common level, which he asserted would be for the advantage and comfort of all. This taking doctrine he handled with much dexterity : it was highly acceptable to those to whom it was addressed. . . . They were gravely misled . . . but the writings of O'Brien tended to increase the sale of the paper [*The Northern Star*], helped to make O'Connor a great man in his own conceit, enabled him to pay Hill [the editor] and O'Brien money enough to induce them to go on vigorously. . . . From their proceedings subsequent to the time now treated of no doubt can be entertained that these men fully expected to see all that they promised accomplished."

O'Brien and O'Connor were in fact during this period in the closest political association. O'Brien's writings were just what O'Connor needed to give weight to the reporting of *The Northern Star* ; and O'Brien was happy in the belief that he was helping to give form and direction to the great proletarian uprising in the North of which O'Connor had constituted himself the leader. When the People's Convention met in February 1839, O'Brien, thanks to his oratory as well as to his writings, had been nominated as a delegate by a number of areas, including London. He took the field promptly against the leaders of the L.W.M.A., by opposing the choice of Lovett as secretary and proposing instead, not one of the left wing, but Hadley or Salt, who were delegated by the Birmingham Political Union and were even further to the right than Lovett. Presumably he realised that there would be no chance of carrying the election of anyone belonging to the ' physical force ' school, and preferred the

Birmingham men, who under Attwood favoured the notion of a peaceable general strike, to Lovett, his and O'Connor's chief opponent among the London Chartists. But Hadley and Salt both refused to stand, and, in O'Connor's absence, Lovett was elected. Thereafter, almost at once O'Brien was sent as a missionary on behalf of the Convention to the Southern Counties. He went on a propaganda tour in Sussex, Hampshire, and the Isle of Wight, creating local Chartist associations and trying to stir up a popular movement in readiness for ' ulterior measures ' should the House of Commons reject the National Petition. In April 1839 he went on a similar tour in Lancashire ; and on his return at the beginning of May he was foremost among those who advocated the removal of the Convention from London, where it would always be subject to the danger of arrest, to Birmingham, where it would have a large popular following at hand, and be much less exposed to attack by the forces of the Government. He served as reporter to the committee appointed by the Convention to prepare an address to the people on the subject of their immediate attitude while the fate of the Petition was still in suspense. His colleagues in preparing this report were O'Connor, Frost, Lowery, and Fletcher — a predominantly ' physical force ' group. They advocated that, despite the efforts of the Government to stir up the middle and upper classes against the people, the Chartists should " rigidly obey the law " and refuse to be led by spies or irresponsible persons into a resort to physical force. But at the same time they were to see to it that their opponents kept the law. " Bear in mind that you have the same right to arm that your enemies have, and that if you abandon that right your liberties are gone for ever." The Chartists were to avoid parading their arms, for fear of giving a handle to their enemies. But at the same time, " Fail not with those arms to resist any and every unconstitutional attempt to suppress your peaceable agitation by physical violence ".

These were intentionally equivocal words. They were closely related to O'Brien's plan whereby the unrepresented people was to elect its own representatives, and ' ulterior measures ' were to be employed to force their acceptance upon the Government. This plan the Convention adopted in May, soon after its removal to Birmingham; but O'Brien, fearing that its publication might give the Government an excuse for arresting the delegates, now proposed that it should first be circulated privately among the local Chartist groups, and issued publicly only after assurance of their support had been obtained. To this the Convention would not agree, and the plan was published at once.

The proposal to consult the local Chartist groups was, however, adopted; and it was decided that the delegates should return to their constituencies with a view to ascertaining the willingness of the people to resort to ' ulterior measures '. O'Brien, on O'Connor's proposal, drew up a series of resolutions, which the Convention approved, defining the policy to be followed during the period of ' simultaneous meetings ' now to be inaugurated. The people were to pursue strictly lawful methods and to refrain from taking any arms to the meetings, and the Chartist leaders were everywhere to consult the local authorities about the arrangements before the meetings were held. But it was added, " should our enemies substitute war for peace, or attempt to suppress our lawful and orderly agitation by lawless violence, we shall deem it to be a sacred duty of the people to meet force with force, and repel assassination by justifiable homicide ".

On this basis the Convention adjourned in order to consult the people. O'Brien accompanied O'Connor on a speaking tour in Yorkshire and Lancashire, and then went on to Glasgow and to an extended tour of the Scottish centres. On his way back he addressed meetings at Newcastle and in other North-East Coast areas and again in Yorkshire and Lancashire. He was still engaged on this round of meetings when the People's Convention reassembled, and was absent when, after the House of Commons had rejected the National Petition, the Convention decided to call a general strike.

This decision, however, caused him to hurry back to his place in the Convention; and on July 19, 1839, he moved that the strike decision be rescinded. On the basis of what he had seen in Scotland and the North, he was fully convinced that the strike had, at that stage, no prospect of success.

With trade very bad and unemployment everywhere prevalent, a general strike was impracticable, and would certainly fail to command Trade Union support. A partial strike, which alone could be got, would be a disaster. He wished to say to the people, " If you strike universally, you strike success-fully ; but, if partially, fatally ". The people, he was sure, was not ready ; and it was the duty of the leaders in these circumstances to have the courage to make their decision afresh, in the light of the facts. Moreover, the general strike would be widely regarded as the prelude to a revolution, and this was, up to a point, his own view ; but he did not wish to be rashly precipitate.

This speech was effective in getting the strike order post-poned, while a further committee of the Convention con-sidered anew the attitude of the people towards the proposal. This committee's report on the state of opinion and prepared-ness in the country was decisive ; and on August 6, on the motion of O'Brien and O'Connor, the general strike was definitely called off. Thereafter, O'Brien was the prime mover in the proposal that the Convention should dissolve itself. There was, indeed, clearly no point in continuing the sittings. The delegates had plainly to choose between the policy of admitting defeat for the moment and trying again later on, and that of going underground with a view to preparing for insurrection. O'Brien proposed that, in order to keep within the law, the local Chartist associations should be advised to form themselves into electoral bodies, with a view to carrying out his plan of promoting ' hustings ' candi-dates at the next General Election. But the rump of the Convention rejected this scheme, and issued instead a ' Valedictory Address ' quite empty of clear guidance.

Before the Convention came to this inglorious end, O'Brien had been first arrested on account of one of his speeches during his tour and then speedily released on bail. Early in October he was arrested again, but was a second time let out on bail. During his lecture tours in the spring and summer he had been endeavouring, with O'Connor's blessing, to raise funds for a Chartist daily, to be published in the South of England as a counterpart of *The Northern Star* ; and in the autumn he and William Carpenter joined hands over this project, and founded *The Southern Star*, which first appeared in January 1840. But in February O'Brien had to go north to Newcastle to stand his trial for sedition, and Carpenter was left as sole editor. The paper struggled on until the following year ; but O'Brien had no further connection with it — nor did his wife apparently receive anything from his share in the profits, which, it had been agreed, should be paid over to her in the event of his imprisonment. Probably there were no profits ; at all events there arose an acrimonious dispute, which did the paper no good.

At Newcastle O'Brien conducted his own defence, and succeeded in so discrediting the testimony of the Crown's witnesses as to secure an acquittal, and to prevent the conviction of a number of other Chartists who were charged with similar offences. But he had still to stand a second trial at Liverpool for another speech. Until the case came on, he continued his lecturing and writing. He was not so fortunate in Lancashire as he had been in the North-East. The indictment was based this time not on a single speech but on the whole of his doings during his tour in Lancashire the previous summer. O'Brien again defended himself ; but he and his co-defendants were found guilty by the jury, and he was sentenced to be gaoled for eighteen months and to find sureties for his good behaviour for a period of three years thereafter.

O'Brien's imprisonment was of course part of the general drive against the Chartist leaders which followed the ' Newport Rising ' of November 1839. There were complaints at first that he was being ill-treated in gaol, and Petitions were made early in 1841 for his release on grounds of ill-health. These were refused ; but from a fairly early stage he was allowed books, and it does not appear that he suffered from any exceptional ill-treatment. He had, however, the knowledge that he had left his wife and family ill-provided for. O'Connor, on behalf of *The Northern Star*, had agreed to pay Mrs. O'Brien £1 a week for as long as her husband was in gaol, and this was duly paid ; but with next to nothing coming in from other sources, the household was in serious difficulties.

O'Brien's financial prospects were not brightened when,

in July 1841, he found himself, still in prison, at loggerheads with O'Connor over the policy to be followed at the General Election. O'Connor urged Chartists to vote for the Tory candidates in order to take their revenge on the Whigs. Although he was an opponent of the Anti-Corn Law movement, as an attempt by the manufacturers to draw the workers away from dealing with their real enemies, and held that the Corn Laws should be repealed only by a People's Parliament which would at the same time reform the currency and prevent the land from falling into the usurers' hands, O'Brien was by no means prepared to side with the Tories. " Our business ", he wrote in reply to O'Connor's appeal, " is to disavow both factions alike. . . . As to the new *hocus-pocus* policy of promoting Chartism by inundating the next House of Commons with Toryism, I cannot find language capable of expressing my contempt for it." He held that the only sound course was to go on making Chartists until Chartism had become powerful enough to " extinguish both parties together ".

This was strong language to one who had been his immediate political leader. But he was anxious to avoid a breach if he could. He wrote to O'Connor : " I will not be angry with you. So pray don't be angry with me. . . . We must tie you down rigidly to principle. We must show you that, while we honour you as our undoubted chief and champion, we are ready to throw *even you* overboard the moment you attempt to substitute expediency for principle."

At this General Election, O'Brien, still in gaol, was nominated as ' hustings ' candidate for Newcastle-on-Tyne, and obtained the show of hands in his favour. The representation of the borough was shared between a Whig and a Peelite Tory ; and apart from his intervention there would have been no contest. He did not go to the poll ; and a curious situation thus arose. O'Brien maintained that the action of the returning officer in declaring the sitting Members elected without a poll was illegal, and that he was entitled to the seat. But he had of course no means to contest the point at law.

In his address " to the electors and non-electors " on

this occasion, O'Brien described himself as " a Conservative Radical Reformer in the just and obvious meaning of these words ". He advocated the enactment of The People's Charter, and then went on to define his economic programme : " I am also for the perfect inviolability of private property. I consider the public has no more right to invade or appropriate the property of individuals (without their consent) than individuals or fractions of the people have to invade the property of the public. I shall therefore oppose all schemes of confiscation or agrarianism, and resist everything in the shape of sumptuary laws. . . . Any attempt to do away with the present monstrous inequalities of wealth and condition, otherwise than by the natural effects of just legislation, would but injure the rich without benefiting the poor. . . . At the same time, I hold it to be perfectly just and competent for the legislature to interfere with any and every species of private property, where such interference is required by the public interest, provided always that the parties interfered with be fully indemnified by compensation. . . . I am opposed to every species of monopoly, whether of wealth, power, or knowledge."

This last point O'Brien went on to develop at length. He was against corn laws, money laws which conferred exclusive privileges on corporations of bankers, and all restrictions on trade and industry, especially " when imposed to create monopolies for particular interests ". Parallel to these measures, which would reduce prices, he demanded a reduction of the National Debt, in order to prevent the fall in prices from enriching the usurers. He proposed a publicly owned National Bank, a drastic revision of the tax system, the abolition of all restrictions on the liberty of the press, and the severance of all connections between Church and State.

This programme, put forward as early as 1841, is a fair summary of the political policy which O'Brien advocated consistently for the rest of his life. It is obvious that his sojourn in gaol had made him much less revolutionary ; he had indeed evidently drawn from the events of 1839 the moral that revolution by force was impracticable. His insistence on the rights of property, which he combined with an intense belief in the necessity of land nationalisation, indicates rather a change of emphasis than a change of view. O'Brien had never been a believer in expropriation. He had supported with enthusiasm Owenite schemes of Cooperation and Trade Union plans for taking industry into the hands of the producers. But he did not favour the seizure of private property, but rather its conversion in certain cases into public property under the rule of law. He held that the State ought to own the land, as the natural birthright of all men ; but he wanted the State, not to farm it, but to let it out to those who offered the highest rents for its use, and he was quite ready to pay compensation even to the landlord, provided that the State retained the unlimited right of taxing what he received. In short, O'Brien was not a Socialist in the modern sense of the word, but a Radical social reformer who directed his shafts at monopoly in all its forms. Later, he came to lay more stress on the need for extending public ownership to great companies which had got into their hands the control of basic utilities, such as railways, gasworks, waterworks and canals, and even large-scale corporate businesses in general. But he continued to base his case against these bodies on the ground that they were anti-social monopolies, and did not, to the end, attack private enterprise as such, or deny the right of compensation where a real, as distinct from a monopolistic and artificial, right of property was to be taken over by the public. In practice, this view carried him a long way in the direction of modern evolutionary Collectivism ; but I doubt if he himself ever realised how far he had travelled along that road.

O'Connor did not break with O'Brien on account of the latter's attack on his election policy. On the contrary, upon his release from gaol in September 1841, *The Northern Star* appealed for the raising of funds in order to buy O'Brien a printing press, with the aid of which he could issue a newspaper of his own. A national fund was in fact instituted ; but not much money came in. O'Brien, in bad health after his time in prison, resumed his lecturing and writing, but not with his old success. He was accused, with what justice I know not, of appearing drunk at a meeting at Huddersfield in November ; and he seems about this time to have thought seriously of emigrating with his family, but to have been unable to raise the necessary funds. During the early months of 1842 he was lecturing in Scotland and Northern England ; and in the London Chartist Convention of April he represented Newcastle-on-Tyne.

But before the Convention met, a serious new quarrel had arisen in the Chartist ranks over Joseph Sturge's attempt to unite middle-class and working-class Radicals under the banner of Complete Suffrage. O'Brien was among those who gave early support to this movement ; and he attended the Complete Suffrage Conference as well as the Chartist Convention. This led to a new slanging-match between O'Brien and O'Connor, who denounced Complete Suffrage as a machination of the Anti-Corn Law League to draw the workers away from the Charter. There was a formal public reconciliation between the disputants at the April Chartist Convention ; but O'Brien continued his collaboration with the Sturgeites, and issued a pamphlet vindicating his conduct against O'Connor's attacks. He said that O'Connor's conduct in relation to the Complete Suffrage movement had been " most inconsistent, absurd, and mischievous " ; and he put in a spirited defence of the new policy. " I have never ", he wrote, " proposed a union or alliance with the middle classes ; and that for this obvious reason, that it is impossible to unite with men who will not unite with us. The middle classes, as a body, have shown no disposition whatever to recognise the justice and wisdom of our principles. . . . But there is a considerable and growing minority of the middle classes with which I deem a union not only possible but probable. . . . This portion is composed partly of good and wise men, whose probity and love of justice raise them above class-prejudices ; and partly of tradespeople and others in embarrassed circumstances who see no hope . . . while the laws are made only by, and for, the opulent portion of society."

The controversy of which this was the beginning soon ended all friendly relations between O'Brien and O'Connor. Later in the year, after the collapse of the great strike movement in the North, O'Connor changed his attitude to the Complete Suffragists, and for a time gave his support to

Sturge. But the hopes of collaboration broke down in December, when at the Complete Suffrage Conference Lovett joined hands with O'Connor to refuse to give up the name of the Charter, and the Sturgeites, though prepared to accept the Six Points, refused to swallow the name.

During this controversy over Complete Suffrage, O'Brien had lost his connection with *The Northern Star*, which abused him in unmeasured terms. But in July 1842, with such money as had been raised on his behalf, he acquired the editorship and part-ownership of *The British Statesman*, and announced that he proposed in its columns to advocate ' Whole-Hog Chartism — genuine Chartism, and no mistake! No factious politics, but real Democracy! " But in face of the dead set now made at him by *The Northern Star* and the O'Connorites in general, he could get no public large enough to keep the paper in existence. It died in 1843, much to the delight of *The Northern Star*. O'Brien also had difficulties over his lectures. When he went to speak at Leicester at the invitation of the anti-O'Connorite Chartists, the followers of Thomas Cooper attended in order to howl him down.

The quarrel with O'Connor became still more bitter in 1843, with the launching of the Land Scheme at the Chartist Convention of that year. O'Brien was not a delegate; but he attacked the scheme from the moment when it was first put forward, ridiculing O'Connor's calculations and suggesting that before long those who were unfortunate enough to acquire land under the scheme would be tied hand and foot in the bonds of the usurers, and the whole plan would be hopelessly insolvent. " But the strangest thing of all," O'Brien wrote, " is that the philanthropic Feargus should have dragged millions of people after him to torch-light meetings, demonstrations, etc., all attended with great sacrifice of time and money, and caused the actual ruin of thousands through imprisonment, loss of employment, and expatriation, when all the while he had only to establish a ' National Chartist Cooperative Land Society ' to ensure social happiness for us all, and when, to use his own words in last week's *Star*, he had discerned that ' political equality

can only spring from social happiness '. Formerly, he taught
us that social happiness was to proceed from political
equality ; but doubtless when his land-bubble has burst,
he will have the old or some other new creed for us."

After the collapse of *The British Statesman*, O'Brien was
left at a loose end, and in considerable distress. He managed,
from the wreck of his fortunes, to save enough for a new
venture. In October 1844 he moved with his family to
Douglas, Isle of Man, where he set up as a printer and
stationer and also ran a circulating library. His reason for
choosing the Isle of Man was that the stamp duty on newspapers did not apply there, and that he hoped to be able to
build up a circulation for a newspaper which he proposed
to start there free of tax, with the power to make use of the
distributive facilities of the Post Office, which were not in
England open to unstamped papers.

The National Reformer lasted, with an interval of some
months in 1846, for two years and a half. But O'Brien had
hard work all the time to make it pay its way. It was devoted
largely to polemics against O'Connor and to contributions
from disgruntled Chartists who had grown weary of
O'Connor's dictatorship and disapproved of the diversion
of all the remaining energies of the National Charter Association to pushing the Land Scheme. But these anti-O'Connor
Chartists did not make up a coherent group ; nor did O'Brien
succeed in rallying them under his own leadership. After
1846 the paper had to be reduced in size ; and a lecture tour
made by O'Brien in England early in 1847, mainly with the
object of pushing its circulation, had only disappointing
results. Later in that year O'Brien realised what assets he
had in the Isle of Man and returned to England, influenced
perhaps by the premonitory rumblings of revolution in
Europe.

He had still enough following to secure election as a
delegate to the Chartist Convention of 1848. He there
represented London, together with William Cuffay and
Henry Child. But he found himself from the first quite
out of sympathy with the proceedings ; for he disbelieved
entirely in ' Physical Force ', in O'Connor, and in the reality
of his fellow delegates' claims to represent the working class.

On April 9, the day before the Kennington Common meeting,
of which he disapproved as likely to lead to a violent clash
with the authorities, he attended a meeting of his constituents in Lambeth, and formally resigned his seat in the
Convention. It was deemed advisable, he said, that the
Convention's proceedings should be unanimous, and, as he
could not go with them, he had resolved not to throw the
apple of discord among them. He believed they were actuated
by the best motives ; but their conviction was different from
his, and had been so from the first. O'Brien, who had been
advised against going to the meeting, was howled down.
He had no further part in the events of 1848 — at least, none
that has attracted the chronicler.

He reappears in politics towards the end of 1849, with a
series of articles contributed to *Reynolds' Political Instructor*
— the series subsequently republished in book form after
his death, with many additions and changes, as *The Rise,
Progress, and Phases of Human Slavery*. These articles are
of considerable interest ; but, like much of his work, they
break off abruptly with the task less than half done. The
historical articles carry the story of slavery no further than
the reign of the Emperor Constantine, though they are
adorned with many more modern parallels. Having advanced
thus far, O'Brien stopped ; and the rest of the book, as
published in 1885 by Martin Boon, is made up of other
articles, mostly of later date, expounding O'Brien's political
and social programme. It is impossible to say whether the
earlier articles were actually written in 1849, or were a
fragment of one of the treatises which O'Brien had planned
to write in the 'thirties. Their principal interest lies in the
parallel drawn in them between the chattel-slavery of preceding epochs and the wage-slavery characteristic of modern
capitalist civilisations. " The only difference is, it is in the
one case slavery direct and avowed ; in the other, slavery
hypocritically masked under legal forms. . . . What are
called the ' Working Classes ' are the slave populations of
civilised countries. These classes constitute the basis of
European society in particular and of all civilised societies
in general. . . . The working classes, however general and
extensive an element they constitute in modern society, are,

nevertheless, but an emanation from another element, much more extensive and general, bequeathed to us by the ancient world under the name of Proletarians. By the term Proletarians is to be understood . . . every description of persons of both sexes who, having no masters to own them as slaves, and consequently to be chargeable with their maintenance, and who, being without future or friends, were obliged to procure their subsistence as they best could — by labour, by mendicity, by theft, or by prostitution. . . . We use the term . . . to denote every description of persons who are dependent upon others for the means of earning their daily bread, without being actual slaves."

On this class analysis O'Brien goes on to base an account of the perversion of Christianity, of which the mission was to abolish human slavery, into an instrument for sustaining wage-slavery instead. " For what did these Christian emancipations operate ; and what have been their consequences to humanity ? They turned well-fed, well-housed, comfortable slaves into ragged, starving paupers ; and their consequences have been to fill Europe with a race of Proletarians by far more numerous and miserable than the human chattels of the ancients, whose place they occupy in modern civilisation."

The logical consequence of this perversion, O'Brien argued, must be social revolution, or, as he now preferred to call it, social reformation. " Whether this reconstruction shall be effected peaceably in the way of social reformation, or emerge, like order out of chaos, from the throes of a violent convulsion, is a secret of the future, which time alone can disclose. It ought to be, it may be, and, we trust, will be a peaceful reformation. The times are favourable for such a change. The amazing revolution which has lately taken place in the arts and sciences, as applicable to the purposes of human economy, ought naturally to give birth to another revolution of a kindred quality in the political and social mechanism of society. This second social revolution — the transition from proletarianism and wages-slavery to real and universal emancipation — may be effected without the loss of a single life, or the sacrifice of a shilling's worth of his possessions by any man of any class."

On the basis of these ideas O'Brien, in conjunction with G. W. M. Reynolds and the old Owenite Socialist, Lloyd Jones, founded early in 1850 the National Reform League. New organisations for the regeneration of Chartism were at that time numerous ; but O'Brien differed from most of the projectors in that he refused to resign his membership of the National Charter Association, even though he disagreed with its policy. At this time and again later, he was invited to stand for election to the Chartist Executive ; but he refused. He continued, however, to regard himself as a Chartist and his new League as a complement, rather than a rival, to the National Charter Association. Together with Reynolds he gave lectures in 1850 under the auspices of the N.C.A. ; and he also took part with Julian Harney in the activities of the Fraternal Democrats.

The National Reform League never gathered to itself any large body of adherents. But it was an interesting and to some extent an influential body in the field of ideas. The seven (or sometimes eight) Propositions of the National Reform League, drafted by O'Brien, received wide publicity in pamphlet form, and were endorsed at meetings of both the Fraternal Democrats and the National Charter Association. They are much too long to quote in full ; but, briefly, they included the following : a new Poor Law, based on a uniform, centralised rating system, and designed to provide employment wherever possible, or decent maintenance, without degrading conditions, when work could not be found ; State purchase of land, and the location thereon of the unemployed poor ; a scaling-down of the National Debt in correspondence to the fall in prices since the wars during which it was mainly incurred, and the extinction of the remainder by means of taxes levied on property ; the gradual resumption by the State of ownership of land, mines, and minerals, and the use of the revenues accruing therefrom to the State to pay the cost of public services, to " execute all needful public works, and to educate the population " ; the initiation of a State system of public credit in order to encourage small-scale enterprise, and of a new National Currency " based on real consumable wealth and not upon the variable and uncertain amount of scarce metals " ; and the setting-up by the State everywhere of " public marts, or stores, for the reception of all kinds of exchangeable goods, to be valued by disinterested officers appointed for the purpose, either upon a corn or a labour standard . . . thereby gradually displacing the present reckless system of competitive trading and shopkeeping ".

To these seven points was added, by way of postscript, an eighth, which was in effect an omnibus of things left out. Under this head were included a sound compulsory system of national education for youth ; public ownership of railways, canals, bridges, docks, gasworks, waterworks, etc. ; and a more humane code of both civil and penal law. But these further reforms, it was announced, " will be easy of accomplishment when those comprised in the foregoing propositions shall have been effected ".

This was the gist of O'Brien's political policy. But he also gave endorsement to Robert Owen's propositions concerning the basis of ' Rational Religion ' and announced that the National Reform League was ready to collaborate with the National Rational League, founded on the principles of Robert Owen.

Soon after the creation of the National Reform League, G. W. M. Reynolds started *Reynolds' Newspaper*, and O'Brien wrote regularly for it during 1850 and 1851, and may possibly have had some share in the editorial responsibility. But he dropped off *Reynolds'* in 1851, and, giving up journalism, founded the Eclectic Institute and the Eclectic Club with premises in Denmark Street, Soho — an educational and cultural centre closely similar to Lovett's National Hall in Holborn. But his new Institute soon fell into difficulties ; and in 1852, after an abortive attempt to run him as Radical candidate for Westminster, his friends set out to raise a permanent endowment fund on his behalf — Ernest Jones being among those who served on the committee formed with this object. In that year we find him planning, without success, to start yet another paper ; and in 1853 a proposal to make him joint editor with Ernest Jones of *The People's Paper* led to a breach with Jones and the remnant of the official Chartists. In 1855 he came forward again in opposition to the Crimean War, which he denounced as a contest waged " for the benefit of the moneyed aristocracy ".

Thereafter, in poverty and in practical retirement from active politics, O'Brien suddenly took to writing political poetry. In 1856 he published his satirical *Sermons on the Day of the Public Fast and Humiliation for England's Disasters in the Crimea*, rapidly followed by his *Ode to Lord Palmerston* and *Ode to Louis Napoleon Bonaparte*. These were succeeded in 1857 by his *Elegy on the Death of Robespierre, with an Historical Sketch of the three Assemblies which made the Revolution of 1789*; and when he reprinted some of these writings in 1859, he added a prose *Dissertation on Robespierre* which pointed the morals he had meant to draw in the Life of his hero which he had left unfinished twenty years before. A further verse satire, *A Vision of Hell*, issued the same year, was a fierce onslaught on the British upper and middle classes, who were accused of " using Hell as a sort of artillery on the side of established power, to terrify poverty and ignorance into blind submission to arbitrary and wrongful rule ".

These verses have no literary merits, except trenchancy. *The Elegy on Robespierre* is based largely on Milton's *Lycidas*; and the satiric verse has no musical quality. O'Brien was but little past fifty when he wrote these latest writings; but they were the work of a man whose day was over. He was in fact ill and declining in health. In 1859 a renewed attempt was made to raise a Testimonial Fund on his behalf; and Charles Bradlaugh among others gave his help by lecturing for it. Aided by it, O'Brien managed to keep a house over his head for the remaining few years of his life. He died on December 23, 1864.

O'Brien's is not a cheerful story. He was a man of great oratorical power, considerable journalistic ability, and some learning and originality of thought. But his best work was done as editor of *The Poor Man's Guardian* when he was in his twenties; and thereafter, from whatever cause, his abilities ran largely to waste. Either he was ill, as well as poor, almost continuously from his release from prison in 1841, or there was something else seriously wrong with him besides poverty. He could write well, and even brilliantly at times; but he could make no sustained effort, and even as a journalist he could never make his papers sell.

To his merits as an orator, in the days of his greatness, tribute is nearly universal. Gammage is enthusiastic in praise of his lucidity, his power of satire, his wit, his masterly logic. All are agreed that he was able to hold vast audiences listening intently for hours on end while he expounded the basic principles of the Chartist doctrine, and that his most lengthy expositions were punctuated to the end by rapturous applause. It is also generally agreed that he was a pleasing companion, and free from any evident personal vanity. Gammage tells us that " in stature he was considerably above the middle size, of fine figure, though rather inclined to the stooping posture of the scholar. . . . Viewed when unpleasant thoughts were agitating his mind, he was certainly not the most prepossessing of men, but under the influence of pleasant sensations, there was no man more fascinating than O'Brien."

Intellectually the ablest of all the Chartist leaders, O'Brien set out at an early stage to provide the movement with a philosophy. Taking Robespierre and Babeuf as his masters, he sought to apply the lessons of the great French Revolution to the England of half a century later. Beginning upon this task amid the tumults of the Reform Bill agitation, the Trades Union upheaval of the early 'thirties, and the struggles against the Whig Poor Law and for Factory Reform, he set out on his task in the anticipation of a social revolution which somehow failed to happen. The failure did not alter his diagnosis of the fundamental social forces : that remained the same to the end. But, having been a revolutionary, he became a reformist, attempting to formulate both a theory and a practical programme of social transformation. He can be seen, in his later writings, struggling towards many of the conceptions of Social Democracy which were to become the theoretical foundations of modern evolutionary Socialism. But there was, in his day, no movement to aid him in working out his theories ; and he floundered, half realising that the struggle of the future would have to be waged against monopoly capitalism, and half-bogged in the concepts of a society of small-scale private enterprise. That he was a powerful thinker even his scattered and fragmentary writings make abundantly plain ; but he was never able to pull his thoughts together into coherence, or to resolve the contradictions of his devotion to revolution *à la* Robespierre and his sense that the further growth of capitalism required a solution different from his master's.

X

George Julian Harney

GEORGE JULIAN HARNEY was Chartism's *enfant terrible*
— a young enthusiast, addicted to flaunting the red
cap of liberty at public meetings, a revolutionary by
sentiment as well as by conviction. Under the influence
of Bronterre O'Brien, his political master in the early days
of Chartism, he steeped himself in the ideas and phrases of
the French Revolution, and inscribed ' Liberty, Equality,
and Fraternity ' upon his banner. He conceived it as the
mission of the working classes to complete the victory of
1789 by establishing the ' Social Republic ' ; and he chose
for himself the role of Marat, *l'ami du peuple*, in the coming
British Revolution. He liked to sign his own articles ' Ami
du Peuple ', or ' A Friend of the People ' ; and *The Friend
of the People* was the name which he gave to two of his short-
lived ventures in Radical journalism.

Harney had been imprisoned three times for selling
unstamped periodicals before he was out of his teens. In
his early twenties he was a recognised national leader of
left-wing Chartism ; and he shook the dust of British politics
off his feet before he was forty years old. After a long
sojourn in the United States he came back to England an old
man, and lived on, a forgotten figure, into his eighty-first
year, still holding his old Chartist principles, but quite out
of touch with the new Labour movement which had grown
up during his absence. Edward Aveling, who went down to
Richmond to interview him for *The Social Democrat* during
the last year of his life, described him as " a straggler of
1848 ". The name was apposite ; for the year of European
Revolutions meant much to Harney, the most internationally
minded among the Chartist leaders.

1848 meant much less to most of his fellow Chartists ;
for Chartism was, in its essential foundations, a purely

British movement. Whereas the Corresponding Societies of the 1790s had been the response of the British working classes to the great events in France, and even in 1830 the French and Belgian Revolutions had exerted a deep influence on British Radicalism, Chartism, as a mass movement, arose out of purely British conditions, and was for the most part led by men who had but a dim awareness of any affinity between their struggle and the contemporary movements among the workers on the Continent. It is true that Lovett's London Working Men's Association issued, quite early in its career, an *Address to the Working Classes of Europe, and especially to the Polish People*, in reply to an address received from the Polish Democrats, exiled after the suppression of the revolt of 1830. It is true that sympathy for foreign exiles and foreign popular movements was strong among the skilled artisans of London and the provincial towns, and that the memory of 1789 was continually refreshed by the reading of Paine's *Rights of Man*. But it is none the less true that Chartism, as a mass movement, arose out of peculiarly British conditions to which there was no near analogy elsewhere in Europe. Chartism became a mass movement because it gathered up into itself the hatred of the new Whig Poor Law of 1834, the revolt of the Northern factory workers against the hideous ' Factory Slavery ' which developing British capitalism claimed the right to impose upon the workers in the name of freedom of enterprise, and the resentment at the Whigs' desertion of those who had been their allies in the late struggle for the Reform of Parliament. The masses who shouted and marched against the hated ' Bastilles ' and the hated power-factories felt but dimly Harney's enthusiasm for continental revolutions; and even slogans of world-wide workers' solidarity meant little to them. They threw up leaders made in their own image, and concerned more with the immediate local struggle than with either theories or world-wide appeals. The British workers had their own most painful oppression to face ; and both political and economic conditions were too widely different in Great Britain and elsewhere to provoke similar mass reactions. Harney and Lovett, in their several ways, both wanted European revolution, and saw the affinity between their own struggles and those of the workers in other countries. The main body of the Chartists in the industrial areas were too much engaged with their own sufferings and oppressions to spare more than a cheer for continental victories — or, much oftener, for the victims of continental tyranny who were able to find asylum in Great Britain.

There was, of course, Ireland ; but Ireland was a special case. Its wrongs were not likely to be forgotten while O'Connor was leading the English Chartists ; and from the 1790s onwards there had been close connections between Irish Nationalism and Radicalism in Great Britain. But two things made against any close relationship in the Chartist days — Daniel O'Connell's strong hostility to Trade Unionism, and the fact that in many trades Irish immigrants were undercutting British workers, and showing small enthusiasm to join either Trade Unions or any political movements, except their own.

Chartism therefore developed, throughout its earlier phases, as a peculiarly British movement ; and Harney's perpetual harking back to the glories of the French Revolution and his desire to regard British working-class action as merely part of a world-wide proletarian uprising were apt to seem unrealistic, and to make little appeal outside a narrow circle of convinced revolutionaries. This became less true as Chartism itself shrank up in its latter days ; for the few who remained faithful were the most likely to respond to internationalist appeals. But at this stage Harney fell foul both of Ernest Jones, his principal colleague — and rival — in the leadership of the Chartist ' rump ', and of Karl Marx, in whose quarrels with fellow exiles he found himself a somewhat bewildered participant. From the Marxist point of view, Harney backed the wrong horse in the disputes which accompanied the break-up of the Communist League : he fell from grace in the eyes of Marx and Engels and became no longer their ally, but an empty ranter at whom they directed their gibes. They called him ' Citizen Hip-hip-hurrah ', in reference to his unfailing, but also undiscriminating, readiness to applaud all manner of revolutionary sentiments ; and Ernest Jones, their remaining stand-by, drove him out of the Chartist leadership. That was the end of him, in relation to British politics. He retired to Jersey, then the home of many exiles from continental persecution, and thereafter to the United States ; and when at length he came back to England his day was long past. He was the *enfant terrible* of Chartism : it was not his fate, despite his longevity, to become its ' Grand Old Man '.

George Julian Harney was born in Kent on February 17, 1817. His father was a sailor, who died while he was a child. After attending a dame school and one or two private schools, at which he says he did not learn much, he was sent in his eleventh year to the Royal Naval School at Greenwich, as an orphan, and was there trained for seafaring. He left school when he was fourteen, and went to sea, visiting Lisbon and Brazil. But he soon abandoned sailoring, and when he was nearly sixteen found employment as shopboy to Henry Hetherington, the famous editor and publisher of unstamped periodicals. Hetherington was then in the thick of his fight with the Government as publisher of *The Poor Man's Guardian*, which Bronterre O'Brien was editing for him ; and Harney threw himself enthusiastically into the struggle, and developed an immense admiration for O'Brien and therewith for the French Jacobins, who were O'Brien's revolutionary heroes.

The Poor Man's Guardian ran from 1831 to 1835, and Hetherington announced challengingly on its title-page that it was published contrary to the law. " Established contrary to Law, to try the power of Might against Right ", it was sold all over the country by literally hundreds of agents who were prepared to risk imprisonment in the struggle for the freedom of the press. Harney's first two spells in gaol were in London — one in Coldbath Fields Prison and the other in the Borough Compter ; and after serving these short spells he was ready for more. He was sent to Derby, to replace Hetherington's local agent who had been imprisoned there, and in 1836 was arrested and duly sentenced to six months in gaol, for selling various unstamped periodicals. When he was set free he returned to London, and joined forces with O'Brien, who was writing for a new militant journal, *The London Mercury*.

O'Brien was at this time working closely with Feargus O'Connor, who had recently broken with Daniel O'Connell and lost his seat in Parliament as an Irish member. Together, early in 1837, they formed a Central National Association, designed to serve as a rallying point for the forces of extreme Radicalism, and to unify the various local bodies under a common control. At about the same time, in connection with this movement, Harney and other left-wing Radicals founded the East London Democratic Association, and the leaders of this body, including Harney, joined the London Working Men's Association, which Lovett, Hetherington, Cleave, Vincent, and others had created the previous year.

A quarrel speedily followed. Daniel O'Connell was one of the Radical M.P.s who had met with the leaders of the L.W.M.A., under Francis Place's influence, in order to draft a reform programme which parliamentary and working-class Radicals could unite to further; and out of this collaboration arose the draft of The People's Charter. But in 1837 occurred the celebrated trial for conspiracy of the Glasgow cotton spinners; and O'Connell in Parliament delivered himself of a violent attack on Trade Unionism, based largely on denunciations of the malpractices of the Dublin Trade Societies. Harney, writing as a member of the L.W.M.A., promptly attacked O'Connell by letter, and a vigorous interchange of correspondence followed. Harney sent the letters to *The Times*, which published them; and the L.W.M.A. found itself in the awkward predicament that one of its members was publicly denouncing one of the M.P.s with whom it was supposed to be collaborating in the cause of the Charter. The publication of the letters was followed by the passing of a vote of censure on Harney by the L.W.M.A., and thereafter by his expulsion. His crime, in the eyes of his fellow members, was not that he dissented from O'Connell's views, but that he had taken the name of the Association in vain, by writing as a member of it without prior consultation as to the policy to be pursued in face of O'Connell's attitude. The result was that Harney and his friends, driven out of the L.W.M.A., changed the name of their East London society, which, rechristened as the London Democratic Association, proceeded to start a militant campaign in opposition to the more circumspect adherents of Lovett, Hetherington, and the rest of the respectable artisans who dominated the older body.

The London Democratic Association, largely under Harney's leadership, took the field in April 1838 with a thorough-going Radical programme. Harney was its secretary; and it set out, unlike the L.W.M.A., to enlist a mass following among the London workers. The L.W.M.A. began as, and remained, a select body, not seeking recruits except among those of whose loyalty and intelligent service its leaders could feel assured. It had no wish to enrol large numbers; but the Democratic Association, which continued to be strongest in East London and south of the river, found its recruits mainly among the worse paid workers, such as the weavers of Spitalfields, the dockers, and the large body of Irish labourers in the capital. It had soon several thousand members, whereas the L.W.M.A. had only a few hundreds. Harney and his friends attacked the Lovettites for their exclusive reliance on peaceful educational propaganda. This, they said, was well enough in its way; but " what our enemies will not give us out of respect for justice, they are not going to yield to us as a result of moral suasion ". They accused the L.W.M.A. of being a tool in the hands of the people's enemies, the middle classes, " whose endeavour is to concentrate, by the establishment of this and other such light delusions, the abilities and energies of the people, and then to nullify their effects ". They added, " Whatever the middle classes have ever taken in hand has turned out to the people's cost to be delusive and fraudulent : therefore, as the producing classes intend to regenerate their country, they must rely on themselves and on themselves alone ".

The Central National Association had appealed to the unrepresented of all classes : it had not spoken in these terms of proletarian self-assertion. But by the time the East London Democratic Association had become the London Democratic Association O'Connor had left London for Leeds, to found *The Northern Star* and attempt to put himself at the head of the movement in the factory districts, and the dissolution of the London group which had gathered round him had left the road free for Harney and his East London followers. J. B. Bernard, the chief financier of the Central National Association and of *The London Mercury*, had withdrawn, and the *Mercury* had ceased publication. O'Brien had transferred his activities to *The Northern Star*.

In effect, these changes made Harney the outstanding representative in London of the Chartist mass movement which had its stronghold in the North. But, small as the L.W.M.A. was, it, rather than Harney's L.D.A., continued to be regarded as the instrument of the London Chartists. The L.W.M.A. was the originator of The People's Charter and the inspirer of the Working Men's Associations which had come into being in many parts of the country. It corresponded ceaselessly with these bodies, as well as with Attwood's Birmingham Political Union, the Scottish Chartist Societies, and other groups of Radical Reformers whom there was hope of enlisting in the cause. When, out of this correspondence, there arose the idea of a People's Convention, to assemble in London early in 1839 and present a National Petition to Parliament, the L.W.M.A. seemed the natural body to undertake the work of organisation, and to nominate delegates to represent the London workers. Moreover, the L.W.M.A. was strong enough, on its home ground in Westminster, to carry its own nominees at the public meeting at which the delegates received their formal appointment.

Accordingly, at the People's Convention of February 1839, Harney represented not London, but three provincial towns in which the Chartist left wing was in the ascendant. These were Derby, where, as we have seen, he had been arrested for his part in the ' unstamped ' agitation ; Norwich ; and Newcastle-on-Tyne. During the months before the Convention met he was speaking at these and other places ; and the tone of his oratory can have left no doubt in his hearers' minds that he belonged to the ' physical force ' school. He said at Derby : " Believe me, there is no argument like the sword, and the musket is unanswerable. . . . We will make our country one vast howling wilderness of desolation and destruction rather than the tyrants shall carry out their infernal system. . . . I have given you to understand that the men of the North are armed. I trust

you to follow their example. Time was when every Englishman had a musket in his cottage, and along with it hung a
flitch of bacon : now there is no flitch of bacon, for there is
no musket : let the musket be restored and the flitch of
bacon will soon follow."

With these sentiments Harney came to the People's
Convention of February 1839. Back in London, he set
about founding a new paper to take the place of O'Brien's
London Mercury ; and *The London Democrat* duly appeared
in April as the organ of the L.D.A., of which he was also
secretary. He was soon at loggerheads with the majority of
the Convention over the procedure to be followed. When it
was decided that the delegates should split up in order to
go on deputation to Members of Parliament and solicit
support for the Charter, Harney refused, on the ground that
it was futile to expect the *bourgeois* Parliament to yield to
such methods of persuasion. By March he and the L.D.A.
were in full cry against the Convention for its indecision and
lack of force. At a public meeting held in London, Harney,
O'Connor, Frost, and other speakers used very strong
language in exhorting the people to prepare themselves for
the coming struggle. This led to a scene in the Convention,
followed by the resignation of three of the Birmingham
delegates — Salt, Hadley, and Douglas — whose places were
filled by newly elected delegates of more violent views.
Upon this, the L.D.A. resolved " That if the Convention
did its duty, the Charter would be the law of the land in
less than a month. That no delay should take place in the
presentation of the National Petition. That every act of
injustice and oppression should be immediately met by
resistance " ; and Harney duly presented its three resolutions to the delegates. When the Convention proceeded to
consider " ulterior measures " in May, Harney was again
to the fore. The principal " ulterior measures " proposed
by the special commissions which the Convention had set
up to consider what should be done if Parliament rejected
the National Petition included a run on the banks for gold
(an echo here of the Reform struggle of the early 'thirties),
abstinence from alcoholic liquors and all exciseable articles,
the buying of goods only from sympathisers with the people's

cause, the procuring of arms for popular self-defence — and a universal cessation of labour. These proposals, representing a compromise between the ' physical force ' and ' moral force ' schools, were severely criticised on both sides. The strict constitutionalists saw in them the prelude to civil war and accordingly rejected them out of hand. But Harney and the extreme left were also critical. Harney wrote in *The London Democrat* : " The only one of the plans here proposed which appears to me to be at all feasible is the ' National Holiday ', and this I am prepared to show means nothing less than insurrection. This is soon shown. I shall pass over all minor objections, and will even grant that which I feel assured would not be the case, viz. that it really would be a ' *national* holiday ', that is, a general strike of the *whole* of the working classes throughout the country ; and I ask, how are the people to subsist during the ' second week ' ? I presume I shall be answered that the people must provide themselves with a week's subsistence beforehand. This I assert would be, on the part of the people, an impossibility ; as this proposal would be no secret, the upper and middle classes would have provided *themselves* with a week's, aye, more than a week's subsistence. But not so with the people. The man who now earns a pound a week finds the whole of his wages bespoke before the Saturday night comes. How then is he to procure a week's provisions beforehand ? And if he could not, how could the man (and there are thousands such) whose wages are as low as *seven* and even *five* shillings a week ? The consequence would be that . . . [by] the Thursday, mad with hunger, they would attempt to take by force the food from those who possessed it. Then would come the deadly conflict between those who had and those who had not the food. And what would this be but insurrection and civil war ? " After more argument, in which Harney attacked the inconsistency of those who advocated a general strike but opposed the arming of the people, he went on to say that an unarmed people would inevitably be forced back to work by sheer hunger, and ended : " Let there be no blinking the question. These are not the times to be nice about mere words : the fact is that there is but one mode of obtaining the Charter, and that is by INSURRECTION."

What, then, was Harney's policy ? At the end of April, when the Government crisis seemed to make a General Election likely, he argued that the Chartists should everywhere nominate their own men and carry their election at the hustings. But " to elect representatives without enabling them to take their seats in the legislature would be the veriest farce imaginable. To complete the good work, it will be necessary that each representative should be furnished with a body-guard of sturdy *sans-culottes* some thousands strong." All these contingents were then to set out on a simultaneous march upon the capital. The ' millions of men ', with their representatives, would encamp for one night on Hampstead Heath, and the following morning march on London.

This proposal, in slightly varying forms, Harney put forward repeatedly. He wanted the simultaneous march, whether there was to be a General Election or not. His view was that the Charter would not be got except by fighting for it ; and he became more and more impatient of those ' physical force ' men who believed that there was a practicable stopping-point short of insurrection. This was the message which he carried round the country in May, when he went touring the provinces in order to test the state of popular feeling.

It is surprising that Harney was not among the Chartists who were arrested at this stage ; for he certainly went far beyond Vincent or others who were taken by the police in the vehemence of his appeals to the people. By the time the Convention reassembled in Birmingham at the beginning of July, after the great series of meetings throughout the country, he was in fact ' wanted ' by the authorities ; and he stayed in hiding in a house near the Bull Ring, with George Jacob Holyoake as his near neighbour. But soon he was off again to the North ; and later in the month he was arrested at Bedlington, in the colliery area near Newcastle, on account of a speech which he had made in Birmingham, and brought back to Birmingham to await trial. He was, however, soon released on bail, and was able to take part in the closing stages of the People's Convention. He was among those who, after the ' Sacred Month ' had been abandoned as

277

impracticable on the motion of Bronterre O'Brien, voted for the dissolution of the Convention.

It might have been expected, in view of his earlier attitude, that if there had been really at this stage a national plan of insurrection, Harney would have been in the thick of it. Indeed, it is some evidence against the view that there was such a plan that Harney, after the dissolution of the ' People's Parliament ', went off to Scotland and spent the next few months in a series of propaganda tours on behalf of the Scottish Chartists. This is the more remarkable in that the Scots, at a Convention of their own held in Edinburgh on September 1839, set up a separate organisation, pledged to pursue the demand for the Charter only by peaceful and constitutional methods. Stranger still, we find Harney, in March 1840, writing in *The Northern Liberator*, the Newcastle Chartist paper, urging the English Chartists to follow the example of the Scots by setting up a similar organisation. It seems reasonable to suppose that, having realised the impossibility for the time being of success by revolution, Harney had gone over to the view that constitutional agitation was preferable to the half-way measures which found favour with the majority of the ' physical force ' Chartists.

It should perhaps be mentioned at this stage that Harney's long immunity from arrest, followed by his release upon bail, brought some suspicion upon him among his fellow Chartists. He was accused of being a police spy and *agent provocateur*, who incited the people to rebellion only for the purpose of betraying them. But this suggestion, for which there is only very slender evidence, seems quite incredible in the light of his later career. It was, however, encouraged at the time by his sudden shift from insurrectionism to lecturing for the Scottish Chartists, and still more by the fact that, when his case at length came on for trial in March 1840, the Grand Jury threw out the bill against him. He had, indeed, been arrested not for any of his more inflammatory utterances, but for one of the mildest speeches he ever made ; and he was thus able to get off scot free. Even so, I cannot believe that there was really any substance in the charges made against him ; and that they were not seriously believed at the time is made plain by the fact that, though he continued to play an active and often highly controversial part in the later activities of Chartism, they do not appear to have been brought up against him.

In the course of his work in Scotland Julian Harney took to himself a wife, whom his friend, Holyoake, described many years later as " a Mauchline beauty of the Amazon type, whose heroism was notable ". Holyoake added, " in times of danger she would say to her husband ' Do what you think to be your duty, and never mind me ' ". She became a well-known figure, accompanying her husband to his meetings. Karl Marx and Friedrich Engels made fun of her in their letters.

On his return from Scotland as a married man Harney settled down in Sheffield, where he earned his living as the local correspondent of *The Northern Star*, then edited by Bronterre O'Brien. He there lived with Holyoake, who was just beginning his career as a leading exponent of Secularism. At the General Election of 1841 the Chartists put up a number of candidates in order to have the right to speak at the hustings and if possible get a favourable show of hands, but without any intention that they should go to the poll. Harney and Lawrence Pitkeithly were the ' hustings candidates ' for the West Riding of Yorkshire, where two Whigs, Lords Milton and Morpeth, were fighting two Tories. The West Riding had returned Whigs steadily since 1832 ; but on this occasion the Tories were elected after a close contest, in which many Chartists supported them in protest against the Whig Poor Law and the Whig refusal to grant the Ten Hours Day.

Harney was not a delegate to the Chartist Convention which met in 1842 and arranged for the presentation of the second National Petition. But he came back into prominence in June, when Samuel Holberry, one of the Sheffield Chartists who had been imprisoned for conspiracy and the administration of unlawful oaths after the troubles of 1839, died in prison. Holberry had been ill for some time, and a fellow prisoner, Clayton, had already died in gaol. Negotiations were already going on for Holberry's release when he too died. The Sheffield Chartists gave him a great public funeral, and Harney was the chief speaker. His oration was much less fiery than those of two years before : it was a solemn exhortation to his hearers to avenge the Chartist martyr by standing firm for the cause. " Swear, as I now swear, that neither persecution, nor scorn, nor calumny ; neither bolts nor bars, nor chains, nor racks, nor gibbets ; neither the tortures of a prison death-bed, nor the terrors of the scaffold, shall sever us from our principles, affright us from our duty, or cause us to leave the onward path of freedom ; but that come weal, come woe, we swear, with hearts uplifted to the Throne of Eternal Justice, to have retribution for the death of Holberry ; swear to have our Charter law, and to annihilate for ever the blood-stained despotism which has slain its thousands of martyrs, and tens of thousands of patriots, and immolated at its shrine the lovers of liberty and truth."

Not long after this came, provoked by the appalling distress brought about by the combined influence of severe depression and hard Poor Law administration, the great series of strikes in the industrial districts commonly known as the " Plug Plot ". The strikes were in the beginning entirely apart from politics ; but under the influence of the local Chartists, a delegate Conference representing the Lancashire strikers declared in favour of remaining out until the Charter had become the ' law of the land '. An emergency National Conference of Chartists was hastily summoned to meet in Lancashire in order to settle what attitude the Chartists throughout the country ought to take up towards the strikes ; and angry recriminations set in between the supporters and opponents of the attempt to convert the movement into a general strike for the Charter. McDouall and the Executive of the National Charter Association strongly favoured the attempt to use the occasion for carrying out the policy of the ' Sacred Month ', whereas others denounced the strikes as a manœuvre of the Corn Law Repealers, and urged that the manufacturers were well pleased to close their factories in view of the depression, and had deliberately brought about the stoppage by demanding impossible wage-reductions, in the hope of forcing the Government to repeal the Corn Laws as a means of alleviating the distress.

O'Connor blew hot and cold. Harney, as in 1839, took the line that a general strike could not possibly succeed unless it became an insurrection ; but on this occasion he went on to say that, from what he knew of the state of opinion among the Sheffield workers, he was convinced that an insurrection would fail, and that the main body of the workers was prepared neither to strike nor to fight for the Charter. He did not, however, succeed in persuading the special Chartist Conference which had been hastily summoned to meet at Manchester in order to determine the Chartist policy. The Conference voted in favour of an attempt to make the strikes general, and to continue them until the Charter became law ; and McDouall drafted for the Executive a fiercely worded manifesto adjuring all the workers to join the strike movement.

From the Conference Harney returned to Sheffield to pursue his opposition to the strike policy. In a speech to his Sheffield constituents, he said that he did not believe the majority of the trades were Chartists. Even if those present at the meeting were to vote for a strike, would the rest of the workers follow their lead ? Would they not rather drift back to work under the pressure of hunger ? Before he could call for a strike in Sheffield, he would need to be assured of two things — that the trades of Sheffield were Chartists, and that they would turn out of themselves for the Charter without being coerced.

Harney was essentially right. The strikes did not become general, and most of the organised trades held aloof. By the end of the month in which the trouble had flared up — August — nearly all the strikers had been driven to sue for work ; and the Government set about a policy of mass arrests of the Chartist leaders on charges of conspiracy and sedition. Harney, despite his opposition to the strike movement, was one of those who were arrested. But his luck held. Though he, in common with O'Connor and many other leaders, was found guilty on one — but only one — of the many counts in the indictment against them, the verdict was upset on a technicality by the Court of Queen's Bench, and once again Harney got off scot free.

Before the trial came on, Harney, out on bail, went as delegate from Sheffield to the Complete Suffrage Conference convened by Joseph Sturge to meet in Birmingham in

December 1842. He acted there as a supporter of O'Connor, joining loudly in the outcry against surrendering the name of the Charter in order to get middle-class support, even though Sturge and his party were prepared to endorse all the Six Points without the name. Indeed, from this time onwards, for a number of years, Harney was closely associated with O'Connor, and was brought by this association to a position of key importance in the Chartist movement. He was still only twenty-five years old ; but he had cast off some of his early extravagances, and was no longer given to sporting the Cap of Liberty, or making quite such revolutionary public utterances as in the salad days of the London Democratic Association. He still belonged, however, to the left wing of the movement ; and it is a delusion to suppose that his opposition to the strike policy of 1842 meant that he had become a convert to ' Moral Force ', or had abandoned his revolutionary hopes, even if he had been compelled to defer them.

O'Connor, after many hesitations, had given his vote for the general strike ; but after its failure he came round to the opinion that it had been all a trick on the part of the Anti-Corn Law League, and Harney, as the critic who had foretold what would happen, came into high favour with the Chartist leader. In 1843 he was made sub-editor of *The Northern Star*, and was also elected to serve on the Executive of the re-constituted National Charter Association, now almost wholly under O'Connor's influence.

From 1843 to 1850 Harney was in effect editor of *The Northern Star*, as Feargus O'Connor's lieutenant, and his fortunes were closely linked with O'Connor's. This was the period during which the Chartist Land Scheme, O'Connor's ill-starred attempt to give a new direction to the movement in face of its experience of political and industrial defeat, ran its course ; but there is no evidence that Harney took much interest in the scheme, though he necessarily gave it great prominence in the paper.

In 1843 O'Connor moved the headquarters of the National Charter Association to London, and the publishing office of *The Northern Star* followed a little later. Before the move, while the paper was still being issued from Leeds,

Harney received a visit from Friedrich Engels, who was then busy upon his book on *The Condition of the Working Classes in England*. This meeting was of considerable importance in determining Harney's future. Harney said, many years later : " I knew Engels ; he was my friend and occasional correspondent over half a century. It was in 1843 that he came over from Bradford to Leeds and enquired for me at *The Northern Star* office. A tall, handsome young man, with a countenance of almost boyish youthfulness, whose English, in spite of his German birth and education, was even then remarkable for its accuracy. He told me he was a constant reader of *The Northern Star* and took a keen interest in the Chartist movement. There began our friendship over fifty years ago. . . . He was largely given to hospitality, but the principal charm at his hospitable board was his own ' table talk ', the ' good Rhine wine ' of his felicitous conversation and genial wit. He was himself laughter-loving, and his laughter was contagious. A joy-inspirer, he made all around him share his happy mood of mind."

It was doubtless partly due to this meeting that Harney, after the removal of *The Northern Star* to London, came into close contact with the already numerous continental exiles who were to be found there. In 1844 Karl Schapper and the Pole Oborski took the lead in founding in London an international society, the Democratic Friends of All Nations, with which William Lovett was closely connected from the start. In the following year Harney and Thomas Cooper, then newly released from prison, organised a dinner to commemorate the formation of the London Democratic Association, and the Pole, Beniowski, and other exiles were invited as guests. This led to a second dinner, this time in commemoration of the foundation of the first French Republic ; and on this second occasion there was a big master of French, German, Italian, Polish, and other exiles. Cooper took the chair ; and Harney, the principal speaker, announced that " the word ' foreigner ' must no longer figure in our dictionary. We may belong to the English, French, Italian, or German branch ; but Young Europe is our common name and under her flag we challenge tyranny and inequality."

Engels reported this celebration at length in the *Rheinische Jahrbücher*; and out of it sprang, in March 1846, the Society of Fraternal Democrats — an international society, with secretaries for each of the main national groups. Harney was secretary for Great Britain, and virtually of the Society as a whole. The Cracow rising of February 1846 had given a fresh stimulus to sentiments of international solidarity : the National Charter Association called a public meeting in support of the insurgents, with O'Connor and Harney as the principal speakers. For months Harney filled *The Northern Star* with long accounts of the struggle.

The Society of Fraternal Democrats announced itself as " not being a society or party, but merely an assemblage of men belonging to different countries for the purpose of mutual information ". It had therefore no doctrinal basis, and no set rules. Even when, in 1847, some rules were introduced, there was no fuller declaration of principles than that contained in the Fraternal Democrats' motto, ' All Men are Brethren '. The Society did, however, in general endorse Harney's public declaration of the principles on which its members had come together.

" We renounce, repudiate, and condemn all political hereditary inequalities and distinctions of caste ; we declare that the earth with all its natural productions is the common property of all ; we declare that the present state of society which permits idlers and schemers to monopolise the fruits of the earth, and the productions of industry, and compels the working class to labour for inadequate rewards, and even condemns them to social slavery, destitution and degradation, is essentially unjust. . . . Our moral creed is to receive our fellow men, without regard to ' country ', as members of one family, the human race ; and the citizens of one common-wealth, the world."

This declaration is unqualified in its cosmopolitanism and advanced in its economic ideas. But the activity of the Society by no means satisfied Engels, though he rejoiced at its formation. In October 1846 we find him telling Marx that he has written to Harney to protest against the pacific tendencies of the Fraternal Democrats, and to advise him to keep in touch with Marx. In effect there was too much brotherhood and too little class-war for Engels about the doings of the Fraternal Democrats ; he wanted to turn them, and the Chartists, into a class-conscious proletarian revolutionary movement based on Marx's ideas. But the Fraternal Democrats included elements too divergent for this to happen easily ; and Marx and Engels set to work to win over those of the members who seemed most favourable to their views — notably Harney, who held a key position as British secretary and editor of *The Northern Star*. On the other hand, many of the continental exiles and of their English sympathisers found the Fraternal Democrats much too proletarian for their taste ; and these elements rallied round the People's International League, which Mazzini brought into being the following year (1847).

As continental revolution came nearer, the foreign exiles in London became more and more active, and the internationalists among the British Radicals made increasing efforts to stimulate a sense of solidarity among their followers. As Harney wrote, " The people are beginning to understand that foreign as well as domestic questions do affect them : that a blow struck at Liberty on the Tagus is an injury to the Friends of Freedom on the Thames ; that the success of Republicanism in France would be the doom of Tyranny in every other land ; and that the triumph of England's democratic Charter would be the salvation of the millions throughout Europe ".

By 1847 international affairs overshadowed all else. At the General Election, Chartist and other left-wing candidates appeared on the hustings — and some went to the poll — to fight the Government primarily on its international record. Harney went down to Tiverton to oppose Lord Palmerston, delivered at the hustings a formidable onslaught on his foreign policy, and was taken seriously enough to be answered by his opponent in a speech of several hours' duration. This was the election in which O'Connor won a seat at Nottingham — the one and only Chartist to enter Parliament definitely on the Chartist ticket. Harney, content with getting the proceedings at the hustings well reported, withdrew and did not go to the poll. Indeed, he probably had not the money ; and Tiverton was not a constituency in which he could have hoped to poll many votes — if any at all. His purpose was merely to make a demonstration ; and this he did.

Towards the end of the year Harney had his first meeting with Karl Marx, who came over from Brussels to deliver to the Fraternal Democrats an address on behalf of the Belgian *Association démocratique*. The two societies decided to enter into closer relations. In reply to Marx's address the Fraternal Democrats sent a long reply, probably drafted by Harney, explicitly appealing to the Proletarians of all countries to unite. " We are aware that it is to the veritable people, the Proletarians, the men whose sweat and blood are poured out daily under the slavery imposed upon them by the present system of society, we are aware that it is to them we must look for the establishment of universal brotherhood. It is the interest of landlords and money-lords to keep the nations divided ; but it is the interest of the proletarians, everywhere oppressed by the same kind of task masters, and defrauded of the fruits of their industry by the same description of plunderers, it is their interest to unite. And they will unite. From the loom, the anvil and the plough, from the hut, the garret and the cellar, will come forth, are even now coming forth, the apostles of fraternity and the destined saviours of humanity."

Marx, of course, had come to London, not merely to present the Belgian address to the Fraternal Democrats, but to attend the Conference of the Communist League from which emerged the celebrated *Communist Manifesto*. Thus, simultaneously with the exchange of addresses, a document of infinitely greater importance was being prepared. Marx was, moreover, trying to lay the foundations for an international Democratic Congress to be held in Brussels in September 1848 ; and we have Harney's letter to Marx announcing that this proposal had received the unanimous approval not only of the Fraternal Democrats, but also of the German Working Men's Association in London, and of the national and metropolitan Chartist Executives.

Preparations for this Congress went ahead actively, to the accompaniment of the first stages of the European Revolutions of 1848. Early in March we find Harney and Ernest

Jones both in Paris, together with Marx, who writes to Engels announcing the formation of a Central Committee, and also saying that Harney is ill. But thereafter the rise and fall of the European revolutionary movement swept the projected Congress aside.

Meanwhile, in view of developments in Europe, it had been thought wise to reorganise the Fraternal Democrats as a society with a purely British membership, but working in close conjunction with the foreign groups in London, as well as with such bodies as the Brussels *Association démocratique*. In effect, the Fraternal Democrats were to become the British section of the projected Democratic International.

Harney, on his return from Paris, can for a while have found little time to spare for the affairs of the Fraternal Democrats. As revolutions broke out in one part of Europe after another, the Chartists in Great Britain began to bestir themselves for a parallel effort. All over the country the excitement became intense, and there were sharp divisions of opinion about policy. O'Connor was busy organising a new National Petition, to be presented under the auspices of a Chartist Convention summoned to meet at the beginning of April; but there were many Chartists who held that the uselessness of petitioning had been amply demonstrated and that the right course was to proceed immediately to organise for a revolutionary outbreak. Drilling and arming went on all over the industrial areas on a much larger scale than ever before; and even those who acceded to the petitioning had to contemplate what was to be done when the House of Commons had again rejected the Charter.

At the Convention of 1848 Harney represented Nottingham — O'Connor's constituency; and he brought up a message from Nottingham Chartists that this was the last Petition to the existing House of Commons in which they would agree to take part. So strong was the feeling at the Convention in favour of ' ulterior measures ' that, despite O'Connor's insistence that only peaceful methods should be employed, the delegates proceeded at once to consider future action on the assumption that the Petition would be rejected. They decided to call, for the end of April, a National Assembly of one hundred delegates, to supersede the Convention and to remain in session until the Charter had become law — in other words, virtually a Provisional Government.

O'Connor was opposed to this move ; and Ernest Jones and Harney had to choose between participation in it and holding their positions on *The Northern Star*. Jones, by resigning from the *Star* and attending the Assembly, put himself at the head of the more advanced Chartists, though he was much less extreme than some. Harney, on the other hand, stuck to his editorship and was therefore not a delegate to the National Assembly. He had doubtless a difficult choice — between his livelihood and his position of vantage as editor on the one hand, and his left-wing opinions on the other — for there can be no doubt that he agreed with Jones rather than with O'Connor.

Meanwhile, there was the Petition to be presented — by a monster procession which was to assemble on Kennington Common and thence march to the House of Commons with O'Connor at its head. It seems clear that O'Connor meant this to be a vast, peaceful demonstration, and not the beginning of a revolution. But some of his lieutenants may have thought otherwise ; and the Government, and governing-class circles generally, terrified by events on the Continent, undoubtedly thought that it would be the signal for a revolutionary outbreak, and made the most elaborate preparations for meeting it by force. The old Duke of Wellington was put in command of a large body of troops stationed in London ; almost the whole of the upper and middle classes were enrolled as special constables, or posted to other defence services ; and the Duke devised the simple strategy of forbidding the procession to enter Westminster, and of holding the bridges against the assembled people, who would thus be safely shut away on the south bank of the river.

Harney was one of the speakers at the famous Kennington Common meeting of April 10, 1848. It is a matter of history how O'Connor, faced with the police prohibition of the march on Westminster, gave way and called upon the assembled multitudes to disperse quietly to their homes. As Ernest Jones seconded this advice, we must conclude that the Chartists in general — even those of the left wing — had decided that, in view of O'Connor's attitude and the vast preparations made by the Government, it was useless to defy the ban. Harney, while O'Connor and the leaders of the Chartist Executive were carrying the Petition to the House of Commons in a cab, stayed behind and addressed an Irish demonstration on Kennington Common. It is worthy of note that Captain O'Brien, the Irish leader, attended the Chartist National Assembly, though not as a delegate.

Early in May, the Chartist National Assembly met, displaced the O'Connorite Executive, and elected a new one, on a provisional basis, including Ernest Jones and P. M. McDouall, who had taken Harney's place as delegate for Nottingham. The Assembly then proceeded to overhaul completely the machinery of the National Charter Association, reconstituting it in groups of ten, each under a leader who was responsible to a group higher up — evidently a plan for making the N.C.A. into a body more capable than before of assuming the control of a revolutionary movement, and of undertaking underground as well as open work.

It is clear that throughout the rest of the year, whereas O'Connor was against any attempt at revolution, a large section of the Chartists was definitely preparing for an armed rising, and that, on two occasions at least, a definite date was fixed for the attempt — first for June 12 and then for August 15. Serious outbreaks actually occurred, with fighting between Chartists and soldiers, in many places in the North. But on this occasion the Government acted with greater promptitude than in 1839. The arrest of John Mitchel and other Irish leaders in March was soon followed by numerous arrests of Chartists. Ernest Jones, now the outstanding leader, was arrested early in June, after a speech in which he had adjured his hearers to be ready for June 12 ; and Fussell, Vernon, Sharpe, and Joseph Williams were among others who were lodged in gaol. McDouall and a number of London leaders soon shared the same fate, chiefly in connection with the postponed attempt at a rising in August. The left wing of Chartism was rendered almost leaderless until Harney, defying O'Connor, returned to the reconstituted Executive later in the year, with Thomas Clark and Samuel Kydd as his principal fellow members.

There is abundant evidence that police spies and *agents provocateurs* had a large share in bringing about the actual attempts at armed rising during the year. In one case after another they were shown to have played an important part in provoking local outbursts. But this does not prove that the Chartists themselves were not attempting to organise a revolution : the truth seems to be rather that the tactics of the authorities were to disorganise concerted plans by bringing local troubles to a head. Of course, the Chartists were not united. O'Connor was touring the country, trying to explain away the collapse both of his Land Scheme and of the National Petition, and doing his best to discourage revolutionary outbreaks ; and O'Connor had still a very large and devoted following. He had, however, by this time fallen out with most of the leaders ; and Harney's position on *The Northern Star* was increasingly precarious, especially as O'Connor was remarkably devoid of sympathy for or interest in the continental revolutions, and was continually objecting to the amount of space devoted to them in *The Northern Star*.

By the end of 1848 all prospects of a British Revolution had disappeared, and over most of Europe the revolutionary cause was going down to defeat. Harney became again intensely active in the Fraternal Democrats, watching anxiously each phase of the struggle and continually addressing meetings of protest and sympathy. The Fraternal Democrats underwent a further reorganisation in October 1849, after Harney, no longer able to say all he wanted in *The Northern Star*, had started a new paper, *The Democratic Review*, as a monthly organ of the international movement in London. In 1849 Harney also became active, with Thomas Cooper and others, in a renewal of the agitation for the removal of the newspaper stamp duty ; and by 1850 we find him, in *The Democratic Review*, supporting Walter Cooper, Thomas Cooper's cousin, in his attempts to establish self-governing workshops with Christian Socialist help. These new lines of action were not pleasing to Karl Marx, who wanted *The Democratic Review* to become the organ of his own form of international Socialism ; and in August 1849 we find Marx writing to Engels to say that Harney is showing signs of living on terms of friendship with the Free Traders.

But this was a momentary expression of annoyance rather than a considered judgement. Marx kept in close touch with Harney : more than a year later we find him writing again to Engels to explain that Harney has to be very careful of what he says in his papers for fear of arrest, but clearly still regarding him as an ally. Early in 1851 Engels writes to Marx explaining Harney's friendly attitude to the Cooperative Societies. " It seems that these societies are actually very numerous in Lancashire ; and Jones and his friends are afraid, if in one way or another they join in an alliance with the Chartists, the whole Chartist movement may fall into their hands. This circumstance explains more than one of the concessions which Harney has thought fit to make to them." It appears that Leach, also of the Chartist Executive, had as a Cooperator been defending the abstention of the Cooperative Societies from politics on the ground of this very fear.

This, however, is to anticipate. The collapse of the half-revolutionary movements of 1848 had left the Chartists at sixes and sevens. While Ernest Jones and Harney, through the National Charter Association, proceeded to formulate a largely socialistic programme as a new basis for the movement, other Chartists went off in a number of different directions. At this stage, in January 1849, Sir Joshua Walmsley, M.P. for Leicester, Joseph Hume, and a number of other middle-class Radicals attempted again something resembling Joseph Sturge's Complete Suffrage Union of 1842. They formed the National Parliamentary and Financial Reform Association, designed to unite Radical Free Traders and moderate Chartists on a programme of household suffrage. Finding that this by itself would attract no working-class support, the new Association proceeded in August to widen its programme to include a lodger franchise and the abolition of the property qualification for M.P.s. This would have brought a very large section of the workers into the electorate ; and the Chartists had to think again about their attitude to the movement. Even Harney wrote sympathetically of it in September 1849 in *The Democratic Review* : " Delusion apart, the new ' union ' [*i.e.* of the middle and working classes] amounts to this : the *bourgeoisie* will not unite with the proletarians for the Charter, but they cannot obtain their own pet measures of 'reform' without help; they, therefore, make certain concessions, use coaxing language, and talk vaguely of a future when, the new Reform Bill won, Universal Suffrage, or the entire Charter, may possibly have their support. The Chartists, though unwilling to abandon the measure for which they have so long struggled, are conscious that they have not the strength to achieve their favourite object, whilst struggling by themselves; they, therefore, accept the terms offered by their more moderate allies. The two parties, weak in themselves, acquire strength by their union, and may prove strong enough to carry the 'reform' they are agreed to support."

This, if it had stood by itself, would have sounded very like adherence to the 'Little Charter', as Hume's Bill of 1849 was called. But Harney went on to say that, while he did not intend to oppose the 'moderate Reformers', he had no faith in them. "To have the masses ready for all emergencies, it is necessary that the advocates of the Charter should stand by their own flag. So at least I mean to do; and by so doing I believe I shall best serve the course of veritable Progress." To this he added that neither the 'Little Charter' nor even the Charter itself would help the people, "unless the majority were prepared to elect men with heads to conceive, hearts to dare, and hands to execute those measures of social reform, which are essential for Labour's redemption from the tyranny of Feudalism and Capital". He ended: "Brother Proletarians! the demand for 'Reform' to be effective must be national, and, therefore, I would have you join in that demand; but take care that you make an important addition to the shout of the Drury Lane liberals; let your cry be 'Vive la Réforme — Démocratique et Sociale!'"

In other words, Harney recognised in 1849 that Chartism had ceased for the time being to be a mass movement of the people, and wanted it to continue as a proletarian spearhead for organisation and propaganda; and he was ready to support union with the middle class for limited reforms on opportunist grounds, until the chance of something better returned.

On this basis he continued his collaboration with Marx and Engels through the Fraternal Democrats. In April 1850 he joined with them and the French Blanquists in forming in London the Universal League of Revolutionary Communists, which thus defined its object — " to overthrow all privileged classes, to subject these classes to the dictatorship of the proletariat by means of sustaining the permanent revolution till the realisation of Communism, which must be the final form of organisation of human society ". But this revolutionary League never existed except on paper ; and Marx abandoned it within a few months. It was, indeed, one of the victims of the split which took place in the Communist League in September 1850, and led to the departure of Marx and Engels from that body.

Meanwhile, Harney's association with the continental revolutionaries had led in May 1850 to a final breach with O'Connor and to his resignation of his connection with *The Northern Star*. There had been growing difficulties with O'Connor for a long time past. Harney was an ardent Republican as well as an international revolutionary, whereas O'Connor disliked all these things. He now had to choose between his salary and his principles ; and he threw up his livelihood, and set out to start a new weekly of his own, as a rival to the *Star*. It appeared in June 1850 under the challenging title of *The Red Republican* ; and in November Harney published in it the first English translation of the famous *Communist Manifesto* of 1848.

Harney defined his new paper's attitude in these words : " As regards the working men swamping other classes, the answer is easy — *other classes have no right even to exist*. To prepare the way for the absolute supremacy of the working classes . . . preparatory to the abolition of the system of classes, is the mission of the *Red Republican*."

In December 1850, however, *The Red Republican* changed its name to *The Friend of the People* — Harney's old *Ami du Peuple* pen-name, based on his admiration for Marat. It seems clear from Marx's letters that he was under threat of arrest, and that this accounted both for the change of name and for the less violent tone of the paper under its new title. At any rate, the change in no way interfered with his close relations with Marx and Engels. Engels sent articles to *The Friend of the People*, chiefly designed, as he himself wrote to Marx, under the guise of a commentary on current continental events, to discredit Mazzini and his adherents. But by February 1851 the correspondence of Marx and Engels about Harney begins to take a different tone. They were highly critical of Harney's attempt to preserve an attitude of impartiality in relation to the split in the Communist League, and of his keeping up friendly relations with Schapper, Willich, and the other leaders of the League group from which they had broken away. We find Marx reporting indignantly that Harney, unlike Ernest Jones, has spoken at a banquet organised by the rival faction, that he has written and spoken in praise of Louis Blanc and his ideas, and so on. Harney is accused of a tendency to admire " official great men ", of personal vanity, and of foolish theatricality in wearing a red ribbon and parading his revolutionism. Engels writes from Manchester wondering what he is to say if he sees Harney. Marx writes back an account of Harney's misdeeds in associating with such persons as Willich, and calls his erstwhile English collaborator an " ass ". " One cannot ", he adds, " let these improprieties pass without exacting vengeance." The vengeance of Marx and Engels took the form of alluding to Harney in their letters as ' Citizen Hip-hip-hurrah ', in allusion to his indiscriminate applause of revolutionaries of every brand and colour ; and they also exchanged disparaging remarks about Harney's wife, who was a faithful and too appreciative figure at the public meetings which he addressed.

Harney's quarrel with Marx — or rather, Marx's with him — did not at first involve any breach with Ernest Jones, with whom he continued to work closely in Chartist affairs. After his resignation from *The Northern Star* there arose a lively controversy inside the National Charter Association between Jones and Harney on the one hand and the Manchester Chartists, supported by the *Star*, on the other. The Manchester Chartists, backed by O'Connor, called a separate conference in January 1851 and repudiated the leadership of Jones and Harney, who went on with their official Convention, and there adopted an extensive social programme, and decided to organise a further National Petition, and to attempt to build up closer relations with the Trade Unions. The new programme called for the nationalisation of the land, the encouragement of cooperative associations, the repudiation of the National Debt, complete freedom of the press, public maintenance of the unemployed, and a number of secondary social reforms.

The Democratic Review continued, side by side with Harney's more ambitious journalistic ventures, until May 1850, when he announced its abandonment in view of his preoccupation with *The Red Republican*. This latter, after its conversion into *The Friend of the People*, lasted until July 1851, whereafter, for eight months, Harney was absent in Scotland, presumably either visiting his wife's relatives or organising for the Scottish Chartists, or perhaps both.

This temporary withdrawal from the centre of affairs followed negotiations between Jones and Harney for the establishment of a Chartist journal under their joint auspices. This project had broken down by February 1851 ; and Jones thereafter started *Notes for the People* as a rival to Harney's *Friend of the People*. In July we find Marx recording with pleasure that Harney's paper is losing circulation, whereas Jones's is going up. Harney then abandoned his paper and went away to Scotland ; but he revived *The Friend of the People* in February 1852, after his return.

At this point an opportunity occurred to purchase *The Northern Star*, which was nearly dead, from the printer ; and, to Jones's annoyance, Harney stepped in and bought it for £40. There ensued between the two protagonists of proletarian Chartism what Marx described in his letters as a " cockfight ". *The Northern Star* could not be made to pay ; and in August Marx records gleefully that MacGowan, the printer, has expelled Harney from the office and installed Jones in his place. But the *Star* did no better after this change : it expired finally in November 1852. Harney, meanwhile, tried again with *The Vanguard*, which lasted until 1853. In its final number Harney wrote : " Silenced by the force of inexorable circumstances, my devotion to the good cause will remain unchanged. I confess that in the miserable politics of this country and its still more miserable politicians

— of all factions — I feel not the least interest. Such hope as yet animates me finds support elsewhere."

Before this, in 1852, Harney had dropped off the Chartist Executive. He tried, in the same year, to re-start the Fraternal Fund for the relief of foreign victims of political persecution, and he also, jointly with George Jacob Holyoake and other disgruntled Chartists, including William Newton of the Engineers, took part in an attempt to create a new Universal Suffrage movement without using the name of the Charter. But this came to nothing ; and, in effect, as his parting words in *The Vanguard* imply, he was despairing of British politics, and disposed to confine himself to activities in connection with foreign revolutionary movements. In 1854 we find him speaking at Newcastle-on-Tyne on the occasion of a presentation to Garibaldi by the local democrats, but from 1853 he had to all intents and purposes severed his connection with the Chartist movement.

At this time Jersey was the home of a large body of French Republicans who had been ousted from France by Louis Napoleon's *coup d'état*. A branch of the *Commune Revolutionnaire* had been established in Jersey in 1852 ; and thence Victor Hugo, Felix Pyat, and other French exiles conducted their intrigues until the British Government, at the instance of Napoleon III, expelled them in 1855. Some time in this or the previous year Harney settled down in Jersey, where he soon equipped himself with a new journal, *The Jersey Independent*. In 1855 he published in Holyoake's *Reasoner* an article protesting against the expulsion of the refugees from Jersey, and in the same year he went to Guernsey, where Hugo had found refuge, to deliver to him an address from the International Association — the successor of the Fraternal Democrats as the organ of the sentiment of international solidarity among the remaining Chartists.

In Jersey Harney remained until 1862. Engels, on a visit there in 1857, wrote back to Marx a description of Harney in his new environment. " Thanks to a long, jet-black beard he has given himself a bizarre appearance, and is rather like the dirty Jew who transported us in his little boat from the steamer to land : it certainly becomes him better. . . . We passed some time together at a *café*, where he talked to me about the Constitution of Jersey ; nothing was said about old times. He appears, for the moment, to be thoroughly delighted to have abandoned high politics to find refuge in his little ' kingdom of the blind '. As a one-eyed man he is king of the opposition, with the leading grocer on his right and the leading tallow-chandler on his left. The battles are staged in Royal Square, where the grocer has delivered a knock-out to the chief editor of *The Jersey Impartial*, a Bonapartist spy named Lemoine : the outcome is a lawsuit which has lasted a year already. . . . For Harney, the entire history of Jersey is divided into two periods — that before and that after the expulsion of the toads [the French exiles]. The difference between these two parts of history is that in neither of them did anything happen."

Harney had not, however, entirely lost interest in English affairs. In 1858, when Ernest Jones at last abandoned his attempt to keep the Chartist movement in being on the old exclusive basis, and called a Conference to bring about collaboration between the working-class and middle-class reformers, Harney attended, and took part in the creation of the Political Reform Union — one of the forerunners of the successful Reform movement of the eighteen-sixties. He seems, however, to have taken no part in its subsequent activities — presumably because he was still out of the way in Jersey. There he appears to have stayed until, in 1862 or 1863, he made up his mind to emigrate to the United States.

Of what Harney did in America I have only the most shadowy notion. He received a public welcome from the Boston ' Liberals ' in 1863, and was thereafter successful in getting an appointment as a Civil Service clerk in the State House. According to his somewhat uncharitable friend, Holyoake, he soon began sending home articles highly critical of the United States and of American institutions — which Holyoake appears to have regarded as undemocratic conduct and in bad taste. He remained in the United States until 1878, when he returned to England and found employment on Joseph Cowen's Radical *Newcastle Weekly Chronicle*, which was a haven of refuge for quite a number of old

Chartist stalwarts. This connection he retained right up to his death at the age of eighty, in 1897, living in his last years at Richmond, Surrey, where Edward Aveling, Marx's son-in-law, found and interviewed him on behalf of *The Social Democrat* a few months before his death. In that same year a number of Socialists, mindful of his past services, clubbed together to present him with a purse of £200 ; for, whatever he had done in the United States, he had gathered no riches. He died at Richmond on December 9, 1897.

George Julian Harney shares with Ernest Jones the distinction of having been the first English Marxist, and the most determined to assert the cause of Chartism in proletarian terms. Of all the Chartist leaders, he had the largest and most continuous association with continental revolutionary movements, and the clearest notion of the essentially international character of the working-class struggle. He was, however, an enthusiast rather than a reasoner ; and his enthusiasm was apt to be somewhat indiscriminate in relation to foreign sufferers of every sort and kind. Gammage, the historian of Chartism, as well as Marx, commented on his vanity. Comparing him with Dr. John Taylor, Gammage wrote that he " assumed the same carelessness of manner as his colleague, but the effort was too palpable not to be noticed by the discerning portion of his friends, to many of whom it gave pain, while it afforded a subject for ridicule to his opponents. Vanity was one of his prevailing weaknesses. Perhaps at that time [1839] he might be somewhat excused, for he was little past his minority, a very dangerous time of life for a man even of the strongest mind to be elevated to greatness, and Harney's mind was not one of the strongest. We do not intend to cast a slight upon his talents, for they were considerable, but many men of respectable talents fall into the mistake of supposing themselves to be greater than they really are, and from this weakness Harney was not free. . . . The dark piercing eyes were shaded by a moody brow, and were never at rest, but constantly changing from one object to another, as though he distrusted all around him. About his life there was an appearance of strong vindictiveness, which pointed him out as a dangerous enemy, and experience only served to prove the correctness of the impression. It may, however, be said of him that to those whom he considered his friends no man could be more warmly or devotedly attached." Gammage goes on to say that Harney was a poor speaker, who would never have been able to hold an audience in normal times, but that he had stock enough of strong words to move the people in times of political excitement. The pen was, however, his real weapon.

In youth, Harney was of a " ruddy complexion, of medium height, grey eyes, and a plentiful shock of dark-brown hair ". He must have been a romantic figure, in his early Chartist days — romantic, and rather impracticable. As he grew older, he retained his own romanticism, but became, to his cost, less romantic in the eyes of the world. It ended in his disappearance from politics, at an age when most men are only beginning to make their influence felt. For Harney was still but forty when Engels gives us our last real glimpse of him, with his jet-black beard, burying himself in the petty affairs of Jersey, and no doubt between-whiles dreaming of the revolution *manqué*, and of his own return to leadership when the masses rose at last and proclaimed the Proletarian Republic.

XI

Feargus O'Connor

FEARGUS O'CONNOR was unquestionably the best-loved, as well as the most-hated, man in the Chartist movement. Not in one district alone, but all over England (much less, however, in either Wales or Scotland), he had an immense hold upon the people. He could not only, with his stentorian voice and his wealth of wit and scurrility, rouse huge audiences to enthusiasm : he could also make them do things, and enlist their unquestioning loyalty. With almost every other leader in the Chartist movement he had, sooner or later, a bitter quarrel which left abiding resentment behind. But with the people, who knew him, not personally and intimately, but as a platform figure and a writer adept at dramatising his own personality, O'Connor never quarrelled. When things went wrong, the blame was never his or the people's : the fault lay with the other leaders, who were being false to the cause and leading the people astray. Even amid the ruins of Chartism and the collapse of the Land Scheme in which many thousands had lost their money, O'Connor kept his popularity. When, after several years of confinement in a madhouse, he died in 1855, thousands followed his body to the grave, and there was mourning all over England for a lost leader.

The judgement of historians has differed markedly from the popular verdict. Hardly one of the historians of Chartism can write about O'Connor except in tones of acrimonious dislike. This is no doubt largely derived from the language used about him by his erstwhile colleagues, such as William Lovett, whose hatred of him comes out plainly in almost every reference. It is indeed abundantly plain that O'Connor was an impossible colleague. He would be lauding a man to the skies one week, and pouring vituperation upon him the next. His language about fellow Chartists with whom he differed was as extravagant as anything he ever said about Peel, or Melbourne, or Brougham, or Lord John Russell. Moderation in speaking was alien to his nature ; and the habit grew on him of writing very nearly as he spoke — using words and phrases as means of stirring the passions of his readers, never arguing but always vehemently asserting whatever he wanted to be believed, and always making his allusions highly personal and concrete, with the least possible admixture of abstract ideas.

These are qualities of the demagogue ; and O'Connor was a demagogue of the highest order. They are qualities consistent with leadership, but only if the demagogue remains fully conscious of what he is doing, and capable of making his demagogy the instrument of a clearly conceived policy. O'Connor's fatal defect was that he had no such policy in his mind. His ideas were a jumble. He did, I think, believe in a sort of democracy — a sort not inconsistent with his own leadership. He did believe, confusedly, in a happy state of peasant tillage — a state in which each man would own the land he tilled, and be in his own cottage unquestioned master of his family's affairs. But at or near that point O'Connor's thinking stopped short, and another quality — lively hatred of oppression — filled its place. He did truly sympathise with the ragged Irish peasant ground down by absentee landlordism, with the hapless handloom weaver engaged in a vain and wretched struggle against the might of the machine, with the miserable pauper torn from wife and children and shut up in the detestable degradation of one of the new Poor Law ' Bastilles '. His feeling for such sufferings as these was strong and genuine ; and this it was that made the wretched and the oppressed all over England look on him as their friend, and go on forgiving and loving him whatever he did amiss.

Men who were not themselves wretched and bitterly oppressed, but knew O'Connor well and had to work with him, had no such strong bond to make them go on loving him when they had found him out. There were in particular certain temperaments to which O'Connor's was so strongly antagonistic that from the first they revolted against him. This was true of Lovett, with his passion for truth and reason and his hatred of words that did not mean what they said. O'Connor's declamations outraged Lovett's sense of decency. He regarded O'Connor as the arch misleader of the people almost from the first moment of their contact. Moreover, Lovett and the little group which gathered round him in the London Working Men's Association had a rooted distrust of leadership itself, regarding it as inconsistent with their democratic principles. They wanted the working class itself to lead — collectively — through the association of its more intelligent members, who were naturally to be found for the most part among the skilled artisans — their own class. Perhaps they had been sickened of leadership by their experience of Owenite Trades Unionism, which the " Revered Father ", Robert Owen, had certainly led most unfortunately up the garden path. They wanted no more leaders to lead them astray : henceforth the people would guide itself by the light of its own intelligence. But whereas Lovett and his friends, in repudiating Owen's leadership, never lost their deep love and respect for him as a man, they had no use for O'Connor in any capacity.

O'Connor was, in fact, just the type of gentleman adventurer whom they wanted to keep out of *their* movement. It went down with the people when he described himself as " the direct descendant of the ancient Kings of Ireland " — which he did very often — and when he boasted to them about his own high doings ; and that the people liked this vainglory was an added offence in their eyes. They had no use for the ancient Kings of Ireland any more than for Queen Victoria. They disliked the gentry on principle — and no doubt disliked most of all self-styled gentlemen whose claims to ancient lineage rested on somewhat slender foundations. They hated O'Connor for pandering to just those irrational qualities in the people which they were patiently trying to uproot. But O'Connor knew what the people liked, and gave it to them good and plenty, without pausing to argue with Lovett and his friends about the consistency of his sayings with rational democratic principles.

O'Connor's appeal, as he was fond of saying, was to the ' fustian jackets ' — not to the small minority of skilled artisans whose economic position had for the most part been

improved, and not worsened, by the Industrial Revolution,
but to the immensely greater number of textile operatives,
miners, and factory workers in general who were feeling,
in the late 'thirties and early 'forties, the full brunt of intense
economic depression. He knew that these men and women
loathed the factories — either because they were shut up in
them for abominably long hours of toil, or because factory
competition was, year by year, taking away their means of
life at loom or stocking-frame. They loathed industrialism,
then in its most savage mood of self-satisfied imperviousness
to the appeals of suffering, and most religiously sure of its
mission to pile up profits to the glory of its God. O'Connor's
agrarianism offered them the hope of escape from their
hateful oppression — of escape into the blessed country
which they idealised from their own memories of childhood
or their parents' tales, and of an old age serene and bright,
at their own firesides, far from the terror of the Malthusian
' Bastille ' and the sniffing Workhouse Master and Overseer
of the Poor. That was why they — for all their poverty —
contributed their pence to O'Connor's Land Scheme ; and
that was why the other leaders, when they quarrelled with
O'Connor — on whatever ground — discovered that he, and
not they, could command the allegiance of the masses.

Madness is not easy to define, and it will always remain a
moot point at what stage in his career O'Connor began to go
mad. Probably not, in any certifiable sense, until after the
accumulation of troubles which the collapse of the Land
Scheme brought upon him. But in a wider sense there was
always in O'Connor a streak of madness. He lacked always
the power to relate means to ends, to count enough in advance
the consequences of his actions, to govern his own conduct
so as to make it consistently serve his purposes. He was
always irresponsible — up to a point ; and then he would
draw back suddenly, when he saw all too late whither he
was heading. For there was, side by side with the irre-
sponsibility, a fund of caution in him which his enemies
called cowardice. He would boast and bluster, giving his
followers an utterly false impression of what he was going
to do, and then he would alter his course with a jerk, regardless, and perhaps unaware, of the difficulties imposed on his

colleagues and lieutenants by his sudden shifts of front. That he was a coward I find ' Not Proven ' : that he often seemed to act as one, to those who were called upon to act most closely with him, is plain enough.

If the Chartist movement had been a winning, instead of a losing, cause, posterity might well have judged O'Connor very differently. He was a genial, jovial, friendly, sympathetic person, when things were going well. But with Chartism things could not possibly have gone well under any leadership. The middle classes, newly seated in power and rapidly coming to terms with the old governing class whose privileges they had invaded, were not going to have Universal Suffrage and the rest of the ' Six Points ' at any price. Household Suffrage — Hume's ' Little Charter ' — or something like it, might indeed have been carried much sooner than it was if the whole of the working class had been prepared to back the more Radical section of the middle class in agitating for it. But what a hope ! The main body of the workers did not want the vote as such : it wanted higher wages, shorter hours, better factory conditions, more assured employment, and release from Poor Law tyranny ; and not one of these things would the Radical middle class have agreed to offer it.

But, without middle-class support, the working class was in the last resort powerless. That Parliament should again, so soon, reform itself under working-class pressure was out of the question ; and this being so, there was no other way, short of insurrection, of making the Charter law. But insurrection was hopeless. It would have been quite possible for the workers, under united leadership, to make a formidabler evolt — to occupy whole districts, to burn the houses of many obnoxious persons, to destroy many factories. But for what ? They had no arms that could have withstood the soldiers, given time for the soldiers to arrive on the spot ; and there is not a shred of evidence that the soldiers would have been likely to act with them. Without a soldiers' rebellion, a Chartist revolution was impossible ; and, with Napier in command of the Northern District, a soldiers' revolt was utterly unlikely.

The basic truth was that, in the 'thirties and 'forties,

capitalism was a rapidly developing system which was in a position to increase the total wealth of the country at an unprecedented rate. Its possibilities, so far from having been exhausted, were immense ; and the leaders of capitalist industry possessed the ruthless confidence of men assuredly advancing towards new triumphs of productive technique. Anything which endangered these developments was, to their minds, anti-social and unprogressive ; and though many of them had democratic sympathies, they would stand for nothing that would check the speed of economic advance. They were right in saying that, if the workers would but abide patiently the passing of the immediate crisis, and await the blessings which would follow upon the repeal of the Corn Laws, much of the prevailing misery would disappear, and the real standard of living would rise — provided that they were allowed to have their way in opposing all artificial restrictions on the pace of economic advance. The old governing class, much as it misliked the manufacturing upstarts, was prepared to act with them wholeheartedly in opposing Radicalism. This meant that the Chartists, whose political proposals were openly put forward as means to economic ends, had to reckon with the united opposition of the old and new governing classes to any fundamental change. Against such a combination of forces they were powerless to achieve more than local and temporary successes. Force, in the last resort, was on the side of their enemies ; and they could be sure that, in the last resort, it would be used ruthlessly, by men who were well assured that God and the Spirit of Economic Progress were their unquestionable allies.

O'Connor was in the unhappy position of leading — for, much more than anyone else, he was the leader — a movement which could not possibly succeed either in getting the Charter or, what was more important, in enforcing the social changes of which the Charter was only the symbol to the main mass of its supporters. Many of these changes were to come, gradually and slowly, but not at the hands of the Chartists. They were to come, as by-products of the very industrial processes to which O'Connor, and those who thought with him, offered instinctive opposition. They were to come, not by means of a movement back to the land, but through industrialism itself, in the course of its triumphant conquest of world markets ; and, as they came, they were to lead the workers away from Chartism towards easier and more practicable methods of advance — through Cooperative Societies on the Rochdale Plan, Friendly Societies, and Trade Unions of skilled workers aiming at economic improvement through sectional monopolies of scarce kinds of labour. All through the latter years of Chartism the mass movement of the workers was breaking up into separate group movements, each with a limited aim ; and no quality in the Chartist leaders could have prevented this. It was inherent in the situation : it had to happen.

O'Connor's faults appear magnified by failure. But they were grave faults none the less. They included a total incomprehension of the new forces with which Chartism was called upon to deal. For O'Connor industrialism was just a great, ugly beast which he did not understand. He did not see that the powers of technical progress were irresistible, and that what mattered was who was to be their master. The idea of regenerating England by spade-husbandry, in the eighteen-forties, was visionary far beyond the wildest of Robert Owen's dreams. It was reactionary as well ; it turned O'Connor at times into an ally of Tory praise-pasts, and unfitted him utterly for telling friends from enemies among those whose fortunes were committed to the development of the machine.

Yet these very reactionary qualities in O'Connor's leadership helped, for a time, to heighten its appeal. They enabled him to speak comfortable words to the people, and to get straight to the hearts of the victims of economic progress. Between millennial Owen and reactionary O'Connor, who could both find a way to the people's imaginations, there were all the more reasonable leaders, who failed precisely at this point. There was nothing inspiring in the notion that conditions would slowly improve for the mass of the people as the benefits of increased production filtered gradually down — nothing at any rate that could inspire the ' fustian jackets ', as distinguished from the relatively well-to-do artisans who could afford to wait. The rationalist leaders of the intelligent portion of the productive classes had to make up for this deficiency by invoking the Rights of Man, and appealing to abstract principles of social justice. But there was an inevitable aridity about such appeals, unless they were plentifully seasoned with invective against the oppressors ; and, when they were, the invective, rather than the appeal to reason, was apt to go home to the main body of the audience. O'Connor, who could outvie the rationalists in invective, and offer hope, however illusory, into the bargain, was the natural tribune of the people.

If O'Connor was from the outset a little mad, he had every excuse. His father was Roger O'Connor, who was certainly more than a little mad. Like his son, Roger was much addicted to dwelling on his descent from the ancient Kings of Ireland — though his fortune came from a more respectable ancestry of London merchants, whose claims to ancient lineage cannot be verified. Roger, with his brother Arthur, subsequently a general in the French service, was an active member of the United Irishmen, and suffered several years' imprisonment for his part in their affairs. He was a strong sceptic, who declared Voltaire to be his God, and was the author of a very curious book, *The Chronicles of Eri*, which purported to be " translated from the original manuscripts in the Phoenician dialect of the Scythian language ", and to give the only true account of the early history of Ireland. These manuscripts were wholly imaginary — as imaginary as his own description, beneath the frontis-piece portrait, as " O'Connor Cier-rige, head of his race, and O'Connor, chief of the prostrated people of this Nation ! " The best known episode in Roger O'Connor's varied life was his trial and acquittal on the charge of robbing the Galway mail-coach with violence — a crime he was alleged to have committed, not for gain, but in order to recover certain love-letters addressed to Lady Oxford by his close friend, Sir Francis Burdett, who was in danger of being cited as co-respondent in a divorce suit on account of them.

For the purpose of this essay, it does not matter whether Roger O'Connor robbed the Galway mail or not, but only that he was the kind of man of whom such deeds were easily believed. He was, at all events, a roystering, free-thinking

Radical Republican with plenty of money and a complete disregard for respectable opinion.

Of Feargus's youth we know little, except tales told by himself ; and in relation to these we have to bear in mind that he was always a racy, rather than an accurate, narrator. That he was educated at Portarlington Grammar School seems certain, though he also referred to schooldays in England. It rests on his own authority that, on leaving school, he and another brother, Frank, went to live with his elder brother, Roderick, on an estate given by their father, and that he and Frank, considering themselves unfairly treated, stole two of their brother's horses, which they rode to Rathcoole and then sold in order to obtain money for going to England. They took boat, according to the story, at Dublin, and after various adventures arrived in London, where Frank, the elder of the two, sought out Burdett and demanded his help. Burdett, forewarned by Roger of their probable arrival, exacted a promise that they would return home, and gave them £50. They spent most of the money on the way ; but finally they embarked at Bristol, and were nearly shipwrecked on the voyage to Cork, into which harbour their vessel had to be towed.

Burdett next placed Feargus on a farm, which he stocked for him. But Feargus, according to his own story, preferred hunting to farming, and the farm did not prosper. He took to horse-dealing in a small way ; but presently he resolved to be a barrister, and entered at Trinity College, Dublin, and subsequently at King's Inn. He went through his course, and was duly called to the Bar. At this stage his father disinherited him ; for he could not be called without taking the oath of allegiance, which Roger regarded as inconsistent with the dignity of a descendant of the ancient kings.

Born in 1794, Feargus O'Connor must by this time have been in his middle twenties. As far as we know, he had taken no part in politics, though he had doubtless imbibed some of his father's revolutionary principles. His first known public speech was made at Enniskene, County Cork, in 1822, in denunciation of the iniquities of the landlords and the Protestant clergy. But he may before this have been involved with the ' Whiteboys '. In later years, when he was asked whether it was true that he had been wounded in a fight with the King's soldiers during the Whiteboy troubles, he would reply enigmatically, but so as to give his hearers the impression that the story was true. Thomas Frost, the Chartist journalist, reports him as saying that, just after the battle of Carriganimme, " curiously enough, there was a burnt hole, about the size of a bullet, in the skirt of my coat. I had been smoking a cigar, and some of the ashes had fallen upon it ; and, still more curiously, I had a sore leg at the time ". O'Connor went on to say that, having received friendly advice from a magistrate that he had better make himself scarce, he rode on horseback from Cork to Dublin, got thence to London, and remained in hiding for thirteen months, until the breeze had blown over, in a humble garret at No. 4 Northumberland Street, in the house of Major O'Flaherty.

O'Connor used to say that during this sojourn in London he was hard-pressed for money, and turned to writing for a living. At top speed he produced a novel, *The White Boy*, two tragedies, a comedy, and a farce. But publishers and managers fought shy of his compositions, and his brief career as an author was broken off as soon as he felt it safe to return to Ireland. He did, however, publish at about this period a pamphlet on the state of Ireland.

There is no further news of O'Connor's political activities until after the passing of the Catholic Emancipation Act of 1829. Thereafter, he set to work to organise the new electors of County Cork, with so much success that at the General Election of 1832 he was returned for the county at the head of the poll, defeating one of the official Whig candidates, and annoying greatly the county families which considered themselves to have a right to monopolise the seats. At this election, O'Connor ranked as a Repealer — a follower of Daniel O'Connell ; and in the new Parliament — the first after the Reform Act — he spoke mainly on Irish questions, in support of O'Connell's party. He voted, however, with the Radicals, whenever he was in his place in the House. Thus, in the session of 1833, he voted for a tax on property, against the house and window tax, and for Thomas Attwood's motion for an enquiry into the causes of the prevailing distress ; and he also actively supported Ashley's Factory Bill.

With O'Connell he was soon at loggerheads, favouring a much more aggressive Repeal policy than the ' Liberator ' was prepared to endorse. Despite this rupture, he held his seat at the General Election of 1835, only to be disqualified by a Parliamentary Committee for want of the requisite property qualification, though he seems to have been in possession of an estate worth some £300 a year. He is said next to have proposed to raise a volunteer brigade for service with the Queen of Spain ; but, William Cobbett dying in April 1835, he determined to offer himself as Radical candidate for the vacant seat at Oldham, in opposition to Cobbett's son, John Morgan, who was married to the daughter of John Fielden, the Radical cotton manufacturer who held the other seat.

O'Connor's intervention, though he got but a handful of votes, was enough to bring about John Morgan Cobbett's defeat by a majority of thirteen. William Cobbett's last days had been devoted largely to urging the working classes to offer united resistance to the Whig Poor Law Act of 1834 ; and it was on this issue that O'Connor claimed the right to contest the Oldham seat as his successor. He had already, in 1833, delivered to the National Union of the Working Classes, which was then the leading political society among the London workmen, an address strongly attacking the Whigs and expressing Radical sentiments, and had begun to build up connections with extreme Radicalism in England. He had fought the Poor Law Bill in Parliament, along with Cobbett and the handful of Radicals and old-school Tories who alone opposed it ; and, shut out from effective participation in Irish politics by his quarrel with O'Connell, he was ready to transfer his attention to Great Britain.

During the next year O'Connor was endeavouring to create in London a Central National Association designed to unite all the Radical bodies in the country upon a programme of further reforms. In this attempt he was soon associated with the Cambridgeshire Radical farmer, J. B. Bernard, who, like Attwood of Birmingham, wanted to combine Radicalism with currency reform ; with Allan Davenport; with Julian Harney; and with Bronterre O'Brien, who was then editing Hetherington's *Twopenny Dispatch.* It was in connection with this movement that he worked with Harney in forming the London Democratic Association, as a rival to Lovett's London Working Men's Association, of which he had been made an honorary member soon after its foundation in 1836.

At this stage O'Connor was advocating what he called " the Five Cardinal Points of Radicalism " as the basis for a renewed political agitation. But his Central National Association made no progress; and Bernard, who seems to have been the chief financial backer of the movement, soon withdrew. In 1837 O'Connor made up his mind that the real centre of popular agitation was to be found, not in London, but in the factory districts of the North. There the Poor Law Commissioners were just beginning to set up their new Boards of Guardians, to prohibit outdoor relief to the able-bodied, and to enforce the famous principles of ' deterrence ' and ' less eligibility '; and their efforts coincided in time with a deep depression of trade which was causing famine conditions throughout the textile areas. The crusade against the new Poor Law was evidently the key, at this stage, to the making of a mass movement for political reform; and the crusade against the Poor Law had to be run from the North. In November 1837 O'Connor, now established at Leeds, issued at 4½d. the first number of *The Northern Star.*

The Northern Star was a stamped newspaper, published at a price which put it a long way beyond the means of ordinary workers. It could not compete with unstamped papers, published at 1d. Nevertheless, it became almost at once by far the most important organ of the new movement of working-class Radicalism. For one thing, it was a real newspaper, whereas the ' unstamped ' had either no news at all, in order to escape the law, or very little, both in the hope of evading it, and because they had no money to spend on news-gathering and no space for its presentation. The *Star*, on the other hand, was big enough to report meetings at length and to give local news, and yet not to stint its readers of articles or of publicity for the doings of its proprietor.

O'Connor had soon a body of paid correspondents in the principal centres, and a staff of writers who presented the Chartist case with considerable literary skill.

O'Connor himself had no skill at journalism, and no taste for the editorial grind. Nor had he any intention of being rooted at Leeds, in an editor's chair. He acquired, as editor of *The Northern Star*, William Hill, a former Unitarian minister who was also associated with Owenite Socialism ; and as printer and manager another stalwart Owenite, Joshua Hobson. Bronterre O'Brien, a fellow Irishman from London, who had made his name as editor of Hetherington's *Poor Man's Guardian*, became his principal leader-writer.

Round Hill and O'Brien was collected an excellent team of writers belonging to the Radical left wing. Of ' Chartists ' it would still be premature to speak ; for The People's Charter was not published until May 1838, and by that time *The Northern Star* was already well established. The *Star*, in effect, began not as a Chartist organ, but much more as the expression of working-class protests against the Poor Law and demands for factory reform. It advocated Universal Suffrage and the rest of the Chartist demands, primarily as means to these ends. Only when the London Working Men's Association had published the Charter, and began to secure for it the support of Radical working men's associations in many other places, did *The Northern Star* take up the Charter, and substitute the ' Six Points ' for O'Connor's original five-point programme.

But, though O'Connor and *The Northern Star* were ready enough to accept the Charter as an immediate political objective, they were at no stage ready to accept the political leadership of the L.W.M.A. O'Connor, moving not merely between Leeds and London but all over the country, in the course of his agitation against the Poor Law, wanted, and knew that most of his hearers wanted, something much more immediate than the programme of political education of the masses propounded by Lovett and his friends. Lovett seemed to think that the masses ought to fit themselves for the rational exercise of political power in order to reinforce their claim to its possession : the O'Connorites, headed by O'Brien, argued that the only way of fitting the masses for political power was to let them take it, and then learn by using it. Both parties claimed the vote as a right; but whereas, for Lovett, a right implied a corresponding obligation, for O'Connor and O'Brien the entire question was one of power.

I do not mean that the Lovettites were prepared to postpone the demand for Universal Suffrage until the masses had been educated to use their votes aright. Far from it. But Lovett and his group did hold that, since the right to vote rested on man's claims as a rational being, it was incumbent on them to use only rational appeals in rousing the people to a sense of its rights. I do not mean that O'Connor did not appeal to the notion of human rights. He did. But, for him, the right was that of the oppressed to shake off their oppressors, by any means in their power.

This was the inwardness of the conflict between ' Moral Force' and 'Physical Force' as it had begun to develop in 1838, even before the People's Convention had met. It was not that Lovett repudiated the notion of an appeal to force. On the contrary, he gave his support to ' ulterior measures ', even to the extent of realising that they might mean civil war. It was not that O'Connor was ready to stake everything on the chances of insurrection. This was very far from being the case, as the event showed. The real difference, in 1838, was between those who held that the method of working-class agitation should be educational and rational, and designed to elicit the sympathy of men of good-will in other classes, and those who held that the governing classes would yield nothing except from fear, and that accordingly any and every method should be used to make the demand for Radical reform as formidable as possible in their eyes.

Thus, it was not that the O'Connorites were class-conscious, whereas the Lovettites were not. On the contrary, Lovett and his friends were acutely class-conscious, and very determined, if they could, to keep the control of the movement in working-class hands. It was the O'Connorites who did not care a button about a man's class as long as he was on the right side for the time being. O'Connor might denounce the middle classes in unmeasured terms, but he had no objection to middle-class helpers. It was Lovett who, very conscious of being an intelligent working man, was ready to collaborate with middle-class Radicals, but was also determined not to allow middle-class leaders to usurp the control.

Over these issues, never more than obscurely stated, a great struggle was being waged in 1838, even while O'Connor, Attwood, and Lovett, and their respective followings, having agreed to amalgamate forces behind The People's Charter and the Birmingham National Petition, were together preparing the arrangements for the People's Convention of 1839. In the great meetings which were held up and down the country in order to choose the delegates — forty-nine and no more, because the law banned assemblies of fifty delegates or over — the representatives of all the various schools of thought spoke from the same platforms, and sought to dissemble their disagreements. Thomas Attwood, insisting that strict obedience to law and order must govern all their proceedings, and proclaiming that he was an absolute ' moral force ' man, had yet persuaded himself that a ' simultaneous cessation of labour ' was something essentially different from a ' general strike ', and well within the bounds of legality and Moral Force. O'Connor, by way of concession, subdued his threats of ' Physical Force ' to generalities about the right of resistance to illegal oppression, and was quite ready to give ' Moral Force ' a trial, recently as *The Northern Star* had dubbed it ' Moral Humbug '. Lovett, poised between the two, affirmed with O'Connor the right of rebellion and with Attwood its inexpediency — save in the very last resort.

The meetings over, and the delegates chosen, the People's Convention met in London in February 1839. For what ? To present the People's Petition, and receive Parliament's verdict upon it. And then what ? It was certain, beyond a peradventure, that the House of Commons would reject the Petition out of hand. What was to happen then ? Was the Convention to proclaim itself as the supreme representation of the unrepresented — by far the greater part of the nation ? Was it to become a Constituent Assembly, to make new laws on behalf of the people ? Or was it simply to disperse, its work done, in order that those who had brought it together might in due time organise — another Petition ?

No one knew the answers to these questions ; and most of the delegates did not want to know the answers. There were some who, holding firmly to the ' moral force ' view in all events, were clear in their minds that the Convention ought to go away and come again another day. But these were a minority, and they were practically all of the middle class. Lovett and his associates were not among them, any more than O'Connor or O'Brien. Lovett was quite prepared for the Convention to turn into a Constituent Assembly of the people, if it could do so with the moral fervour of the main body of the people behind it. What he was not prepared for was an *émeute*, begun by a small body of revolutionaries, in the gambler's hope that the people would join in on the right side.

As for that, no more was O'Connor prepared for a gambler's throw. He knew well enough, when it came to the point, that if he could not frighten the governing classes into surrender, he could not beat them in arms. But he did not begin to say this to himself until the prospect of an armed rising faced him as an immediate possibility. He had not enough forethought to see whither he was heading until he found the precipice straight in front of him. Consequently, all through the early months of the Convention he was uttering threats, whereas Lovett was counselling prudence, though, if the issue had been squarely faced, Lovett would have been the likelier to declare for insurrection — on principle, while O'Connor would have declared against it — on expediency.

The trouble of the bluffer is that he can never say what he really means. He is always pretending, in the hope that his enemy will be deceived. In this process he very often deceives himself. It is difficult to feel formidable when you know you are bluffing ; and, in order to avoid this difficulty, you are apt to refuse to ask yourself whether you are bluffing or not. To a man of O'Connor's temperament such an evasion came easy. No one, least of all O'Connor himself, knew till quite late in the day whether he was in favour of an appeal to force or not.

O'Brien's position was quite different; for O'Brien, equally with Lovett, was a rationalist. O'Brien did favour ' physical force ' methods until, sent as an emissary of the Convention to test the people's preparedness in various parts of the country, he reached the unwelcome conclusion that the people were not prepared at all, and that to appeal to force would be to provoke inevitable defeat. On this basis, O'Brien proposed to the Convention the calling-off of the ' Sacred Month '. O'Connor supported him, but not because he had undergone a similar conversion by seeing the situation for himself. O'Connor had known all along, deep inside him, what the situation was ; but he had not faced it, until he had positively to decide. Up to the last minute he had bluffed on, without asking himself whether he was bluffing or not.

Consider O'Connor's successive attitudes during the Convention of 1839. On February 4, right at the beginning, he declared that the people would not have troubled to elect the delegates if it had thought that they could do no more than petition Parliament. In mid-March he was declaring that " millions of petitioners would not dislodge a troop of dragoons ", and warning the delegates that, if they dispersed without doing something more than petition, the people would reckon with them when they went back home. But a few days later, when it was proposed to issue a pamphlet, reprinted from articles in *The Morning Chronicle*, in defence of the people's right to arm, O'Connor moved that the matter be deferred. In the middle of April he was denouncing as cowards and traitors the out-and-out ' moral force ' men who had already deserted the Convention, and was talking of a general cessation of labour as the right answer to the expected rejection of the Petition. The workers were to " meet the cannon with the shuttle, and present the web to the musket ". Early in May he moved that the Convention remove to Birmingham, in order to be nearer its supporters and harder for the Government to arrest. At Birmingham he gave only hesitant support to the issue of the Convention's manifestoes threatening ' ulterior measures ', but a few days later he proposed that any serious attempt by the Government to arrest the delegates should be the signal for putting them into effect. At the same time he moved and carried a proposal to issue a strong warning to the people against carrying arms in public, or allowing dissension to arise at their meetings. In June, at meetings in the country during the Convention's adjournment, he was asserting that he was quite ready to subscribe to the doctrine of standing by the law, " and not give our tyrants the slightest advantage in attacking us in sections ; but should they employ force against us, I am for repelling attack by attack ".

On the resumption of the Convention's sittings at the beginning of July, O'Connor urged a return from Birmingham to London in order that the delegates might be at hand when Parliament debated the Petition ; and he also reported that his experience in the country had assured him that the Convention was now in a position to take a firmer stand, and to say to the Whigs " Either you must give us Universal Suffrage, or we will take it ". He supported the proposal, which was carried, to urge the people at once to start a run on the banks for gold, to abstain from excisable articles, to deal only with Chartist sympathisers, and to " exercise their constitutional privilege " of possessing arms. He also again supported the project of a general strike, in the event of the Charter being rejected.

But when, after the Petition had been rejected, the Convention met in order to decide upon its course of action, and a motion was carried calling a general strike for August 12, O'Connor was not present. When O'Brien, who had also been away addressing meetings in the country, moved on his return to rescind the vote, O'Connor moved an adjournment of the discussion pending a further meeting which all delegates should be imperatively urged to attend, and then, at the adjourned meeting, made a speech so full of *pros* and *cons* that no one could discover what he meant. But, in the end, he seconded O'Brien's motion. Finally, at the very end, in September, he was one of those who voted against the motion dissolving the Convention, which was carried only by Frost's casting vote from the chair.

This record explains itself quite easily on the assumption that O'Connor only took his fences when he came to them, and planned nothing ahead. It also disposes, incidentally, of the allegation that before the end of the Convention, O'Connor was at the head of a national plot for an armed rising, concocted among the members of the ' physical force' party. If O'Connor had favoured a rising, or been privy to plans for bringing one about, he would have voted for the dissolution of the Convention, and not against. It was a confused division ; but the leading ' physical force' men — Frost, Peter Bussey, Laurence Pitkeithly, Dr. John Taylor, Julian Harney, and William Cardo — all voted in favour of dissolving the sessions.

It is, indeed, plain on other grounds that, if there was a national plan for a rising in the autumn of 1839, O'Connor was not informed of it. O'Connor himself said later of Peter Bussey, the Bradford innkeeper, that " this fellow got up several committees, to be held in different parts of the country, to establish the best means for getting up a revolution, of which Feargus O'Connor was to be kept *in utter ignorance* ". Robert Lowery, who was a supporter of O'Connor in 1839, categorically told Gammage, the historian of Chartism, that " O'Connor knew nothing at all about it ; but he was the only man in England who could have prevented it ". The allegation that O'Connor first took part in a plan for insurrection, and then backed out at the last moment, seems to be based only on the evidence of David Urquhart, who had no connection with Chartism and was capable of believing any tall story that suited his book. Lovett repeated the allegation ; but he was in prison at the time, and did not profess to have first-hand evidence. Moreover, it is an undoubted fact that O'Connor went to Ireland on October 4 or 5, and did not return to England until the ' Newport Rising ' was over. It is really too much to believe that O'Connor, having first planned a rising and then repented of it, went away to Ireland a month before it happened and did not use his immense influence with the people to prevent the outbreak.

The evidence bearing on this point I have discussed already in my study of John Frost, and I do not need to repeat it here. I think there is no doubt that O'Connor was entirely ignorant of the plans for a rising in Newport or anywhere else. He was kept in ignorance, because the extreme ' physical force ' men were well aware that he would not support their projects. That version of the story makes sense : no other I have met with does.

The ' Newport Rising ' of November 1839, and lesser troubles elsewhere, determined the Government to put as many Chartist leaders as possible out of the way. O'Connor was naturally among those who were dealt with ; and at York in March 1840 he was convicted of seditious libel, and in May brought up to receive sentence — eighteen months' imprisonment in York Castle. He said at the time and after-wards that he was treated brutally in prison ; and so doubt-less he was — for the prisons of those days were not pleasant places, except for the few prisoners who were allowed to have rooms in the gaoler's house, have their own food sent in, and generally treat their prison as a hotel. It does not appear that O'Connor was treated nearly so badly as many others ; he was allowed to have his meals sent in from a hotel and to pay a fellow prisoner to clean his cell, and was given access to books and writing materials. According to his own story, he used the occasion to write a novel — which as far as we know has not survived. Personally, I doubt if more than a fragment was ever written. It may even have been the curiously rambling and incoherent serial which began, and never finished, in O'Connor's and Ernest Jones's periodical, *The Labourer*, in 1847. But it is also quite possible that it never existed at all, except in O'Connor's lively imagination.

O'Connor was in prison until September 1841. He said later that he had managed, by a trick, to smuggle out of York Castle an account of his prison experiences, hidden in the back of a mirror ; and the paper reached the office of *The Northern Star*, which published it under the heading " The Mirror of York Castle ". But the fact that he was able to publish many other articles in the *Star* during his imprisonment throws some doubt on this anecdote.

During O'Connor's enforced absence, the Chartist move-ment was endeavouring to reorganise its forces after the defeat of 1839. Attwood and his followers had dropped out ; Lovett, released in 1840, was preparing to launch his new National Association on purely educational lines ; the

Scottish Chartists had broken away and formed a ' moral force ' organisation of their own. But there remained a large body of Chartists, especially in the factory districts, who looked upon O'Connor as their leader, and eagerly awaited his return. *The Northern Star*, carried on without a break during his absence, kept him before the movement, and ensured him of a platform as soon as he was able to resume his activities.

Out of the measures of reorganisation carried out in O'Connor's absence emerged the National Charter Association, founded in Manchester in July 1840, by a delegate Conference, which rejected a plan, smuggled out of prison by O'Connor, for staking the whole fortune of the movement on an expensive plan for starting a daily paper. The local organisation of the N.C.A. was to be based on ' classes ' of ten, each under a leader, combined into wards, and then into larger town units. The main policy was to be that proposed earlier by O'Brien, of running ' hustings ' candidates at elections, and at a convenient season declaring that they, and not the House of Commons, truly represented the people. Corn Law repeal meetings were to be attended, and amendments moved in favour of the Charter. This constitution was later revised, in order to evade the law against Corresponding Societies ; but its essential character and policy were not changed. From 1840 onwards the N.C.A. was the main Chartist organisation.

In the middle of 1841 there was a General Election, and the N.C.A. tried out its ' hustings ' policy in a number of places. But the election caused a rift in the ranks. O'Connor wrote from prison urging all Chartists to vote for Tory candidates in order to give expression to their hatred of the Whigs. O'Brien, also in prison, but full of his ' hustings ' plan, which he held would be vitiated if Chartists voted for either Whigs or Tories at the poll, energetically opposed. There was a battle-royal between the rival prisoners in the columns of *The Northern Star*. But the quarrel did not, for the time being, end their connection, though it broke their friendship.

In September 1841 O'Connor came out of gaol and promptly set out on a great speaking tour, receiving ovations

from his followers, and castigating unmercifully, in each place
he visited, those Chartists who had ventured to disagree with
him. There was to be a new Convention, to present a new
monster Petition, early in 1842 ; and soon preparations for
it were in full swing. Thomas Slingsby Duncombe, the
Radical M.P. for Finsbury, who now began to be closely
associated with O'Connor, was to present the Petition, which
was far to exceed that of 1839 in the number of its signatories,
despite the defection of three of the main groups responsible
for the earlier petition — the Attwoodites, the 'moral force'
Scots, and the L.W.M.A. But these dissentients had not
merely seceded ; they were becoming active on their own
account. Numbers of them were rallying to the new Complete Suffrage movement, started at the end of 1841 with the
object of "reconciliation between the middle and working
classes ". Joseph Sturge, the Birmingham Quaker corn-
dealer, friend of Bright and Cobden, and hitherto active
supporter of the Anti-Corn Law League, was at the back of
it ; and soon supporting him were Lovett and many other
well-known Chartists, including — *mirabile dictu !* — Bronterre O'Brien, a convert from 'physical force' doctrines,
and a strong critic of O'Connor's tendency to back the Tories
against the Whigs.

From O'Brien, who had been among the most savage
critics of the Corn Law Repealers, this apostasy was unbearable ; and there was a quarrel of infinitely greater acerbity
than that of the previous year — and a resulting severance
of O'Brien's relations with *The Northern Star.* O'Connor
and his followers fulminated against the Sturgeites, and
redoubled their attacks on the meetings of the Anti-Corn
Law League.

The Convention met in April ; and the Petition, said to
have well over three million signatures, was presented — and
rejected — in May. This time there was no thought of
'ulterior measures'. The delegates went home to their
constituents, among whom distress was even deeper than it
had been in 1839. But what were the Chartists to do ?
Despite their three million signatures, they knew that for
the moment they could do nothing.

Their problem was solved for them, after a fashion, by

the great strikes which spread over the North and Midlands in August, in response to widespread wage-reductions enforced by the employers in face of the depression. The strikes were spontaneous ; the Chartists as a body had nothing to do with bringing them about, however active individual Chartists may have been among the factory workers. The question at once arose, what attitude ought the National Charter Association to take up ? The Chartist Executive, headed by Dr. McDouall, had no doubts. It wanted to turn the strikes into a general strike, to be continued until the Charter was made law. A Conference of strikers' delegates in Lancashire was persuaded to declare for this policy. But O'Connor, who was not a member of the Executive, took quite a different line. According to him, the Free Trade manufacturers had deliberately provoked the strikes by their wage-reductions, in the hope of forcing the Government to repeal the Corn Laws.

At a Chartist Conference, hurriedly assembled in Manchester, the issue was fought out. O'Connor, finding himself in a minority, swung round, and voted for the strike. But penniless men could not conduct a general strike unless they could turn it into an insurrection, and for that there had been no preparations, material or moral, among the Chartist leaders. As the strikers drifted back to work, starved into submission and cowed by numerous arrests, O'Connor could be heard upbraiding McDouall, who had fled to France, as the man who had been responsible for leading the people astray.

Meanwhile, before the strikes but after the defeat of the Petition, O'Connor had changed his tune about the Complete Suffragists. In July and early August he embarrassed Joseph Sturge, who was standing for Nottingham as Complete Suffrage candidate against John Walter, of *The Times*, by speaking for him and lauding him to the skies as a true friend of the people. In fact, the O'Connorites, after the defeat of their own Petition, had determined to do their best to capture the Complete Suffrage movement and convert it to the Charter. This policy was resumed after the defeat of the strikes, in preparation for the Complete Suffrage Conference which was to meet in December 1842.

I have told elsewhere the story of the break-up of the
Complete Suffrage movement after Lovett had joined forces
with O'Connor in refusing to accept the substance of the
Charter without the name, and the Sturgeites had thereupon
left the Conference. As those who remained — followers
of Lovett, O'Brien, O'Connor, and a host of miscellaneous
groups — could not work together, that was the end.
O'Connor was left, at the end of the calamitous year 1842,
to make what he could of those who remained faithful to
his leadership inside the National Charter Association.

He had, however, first, with fifty-eight other Chartists,
including Thomas Cooper and Julian Harney, to face his
trial for seditious conspiracy on account of his part in the
strike movement of 1842. It was a remarkable trial, in which
the judge, Baron Rolfe, behaved throughout with great
favourableness to the prisoners, and the Crown Prosecutors
also showed a reluctance to push their charges home with
any acrimony. The result was that O'Connor, who defended
himself, was convicted on only one of the nine counts included
in the indictment — broadly, that of inciting the workers to
strike — and that similar verdicts were returned in the case
of the other prisoners, some being acquitted altogether.
Moreover, when the case was carried to the Court of Queen's
Bench, a technical flaw was discovered, and none of the
prisoners was ever called up for judgement. Other Chartists,
who were tried in other parts of the country, were much less
fortunate. O'Connor, while paying tribute to the judge for
his fairness, boasted that his eloquence and skill in managing
the case had saved himself and his fellow prisoners. He
published a full report of the proceedings, interspersed with
many comments and dissertations of his own — among
them what purported to be a true account of the strikes of
1842, attributing their origin to the evil machinations of the
Anti-Corn Law League.

This trial before Rolfe took place at Lancaster in March
1843 ; and when it was over O'Connor was free to direct his
attention to the reorganisation of the scattered forces of
Chartism. He did a very curious, quite disastrous, but
entirely characteristic thing. For the Charter itself there was,
for the time being, nothing to be done. O'Connor tried,

by his personal influence, to swing his entire Chartist follow-ing over from agitating for the Charter to working for a grandiose plan for covering England with peasant holdings, to be acquired by purchase through a Chartist Cooperative Land Society, and to be tilled, by spade husbandry, by regenerated factory operatives, rescued from the dark, satanic mills, and converted into dauntless, self-dependent cham-pions of the rights of the people.

It is eloquent, both of O'Connor's personal influence and of the hatred of the factory system among a high proportion of its victims, that this scheme caught on. It attracted much more support than Robert Owen's attempt, through the Home Colonisation Society, to settle workers on the land under a socialistic scheme of really cooperative cultivation. Queenwood, the Owenite Cooperative Colony established in 1839, was in the thick of its accumulating troubles at the moment when O'Connor's rival scheme was launched. O'Connor had no use for cooperative tillage ; his plan was for peasant proprietorship. He appears to have been quite honestly convinced that a man with no previous agricultural experience, cultivating a small plot by the recommended methods of intensive spade husbandry, could not merely make a good living for his wife and family, but also, by his work in improving the productive quality of the land, could double its capital value in three years. In April 1843 he began to advocate his proposed Land Scheme enthusiastically in *The Northern Star* ; and the same year he issued in parts his book, *A Practical Work on the Management of Small Farms*.

This curious volume is a mixture of expositions of O'Connor's social and economic views, accounts (not easy to believe) of his own prodigious exploits as a practical farmer in Ireland, and detailed instructions for the preparation and care of land for certain crops, and for the management of the little holdings of from one to four acres on which he proposed to settle the surplus factory labour of Great Britain. His arguments are interesting. He held that the only possible way of raising wages was to remove surplus labour out of the manufacturer's reach, and thus compel him to offer a higher price. Given a free land system, with ready access to the land for anyone who chose to take up a holding, the workers would at last be able to bargain on equal terms. This depended of course on the correctness of O'Connor's assumption that the standard of life on his peasant holdings would be very much above that which the industrial workers could command under existing conditions ; but on this point his optimistic calculations of the yields obtainable under spade husbandry left him in no doubt. His practical estimates were worked out mainly in terms of potatoes and other root crops and vegetables ; but he also asserted that his peasant system would enable Great Britain to become self-sufficient in wheat and cereals generally. Incidentally, he advocated the repeal of the Corn Laws in conjunction with the institution of his new system, as they would be unnecessary, and in any case foreigners would be normally unable to compete with the high production of the free British peasant.

This remarkable doctrine was only a development of what O'Connor had been preaching earlier as a remedy for the woes of Ireland. In 1841 he had published in *The Northern Star* a series of *Letters to Irish Landlords*, written from his prison at York. He had there promised the landlords that, if they would let out their lands in small plots to peasant holders, with security of tenure, and would provide help in land improvement and instruction in the art of spade husbandry, their rents would be speedily raised to undreamed-of heights. In his adaptation of this plan to the needs of Great Britain, the landlord was dropped out as an active agent ; and it was proposed that the workmen themselves should club together and purchase land in the open market. The land would then be reconditioned and broken up into small plots, each equipped with the appropriate farm buildings and with a pleasant cottage, and the new cultivators would each be given a start with a small sum of money for buying stock.

Even O'Connor did not, at this stage, profess to believe that Great Britain could be regenerated and made into a land of happy, well-to-do peasant proprietors merely by this method. He wanted his scheme to be made general by legislation ; but he insisted that legislators would never attend to it until a practical demonstration had been given of its beneficial effects. " Without political power the system could never be made so general as to be of national benefit ; while, upon the other hand, I do not believe that any other inducement, save that of the practical result of the plan of small farms, ever will be sufficiently strong to produce such a public feeling as will bring into moral action such an amount of mind in favour of both changes, as neither minister nor party would dare to resist." O'Connor's general conclusion was that, while Chartists ought to go on working for the Charter, they ought to devote their main energies to getting his Land Plan into practical operation on a large enough scale to provide a convincing demonstration of its excellence.

This proposal to push the Charter into the background in favour of the Land Plan naturally caused a storm. O'Brien, the leading advocate of land nationalisation, fiercely attacked the scheme as both unworkable and inexpedient. He pointed out at length that O'Connor's calculations were fantastically optimistic, and that if the plan did succeed on any substantial scale, the effect would be to raise the price demanded by the landlords for further purchases of land, and thus enrich them at the workers' expense. He ridiculed the view that financiers would advance money on the basis of O'Connor's estimates of the value of the land ; and he concluded by saying that, if by a miracle the Plan were to succeed, so far from further-ing social progress, it would establish a solid body of ultra-conservative peasant owners who would block all radical change. " Every man who joins these land societies is prac-tically enlisting himself on the side of the Government against his own order."

Despite these and many similar warnings, the Birmingham Chartist Conference of 1843 was persuaded by O'Connor to approve the Land Plan, and to authorise O'Connor and W. P. Roberts, the two lawyers of the movement, and the new Executive to proceed to work it out in detail. O'Connor, who had hitherto refused to serve on the Executive, prefer-ring an irresponsible position outside, now agreed to serve, and to become treasurer, with T. M. Wheeler, of *The Northern Star*, one of his satellites, as secretary. In effect, the Chartist organisation passed almost completely into his hands — a change which was carried even further when, at the Conference of 1844, the headquarters of the N.C.A. were removed from Manchester to London.

The Land Plan had been approved in principle : the next thing was to knock it into a seemingly workable shape. But this involved serious legal difficulties. It would be necessary for the Plan to be organised by some responsible body which the law would be prepared to recognise. But how was this to be done ? An organisation designed to buy land and settle cultivators upon it could hardly be regarded as a Friendly Society ; and it could only get the status of a joint-stock company either by Act of Parliament or by special grant from the Government — neither of which was in the least likely. If it could not get recognition under either of these categories, it could only carry on as an unincorporated association, which the courts would refuse to recognise and would treat, at best, as a vast partnership and, at worst, as an illegal body. If it were treated as a partnership, every person who subscribed to it would become liable, without any limit, for all its debts ; if the courts pronounced it illegal, it might at any time be ordered to be wound up.

So formidable did these difficulties appear that the Chartist Conference of 1844 actually decided against going on with the Plan. But O'Connor persisted, in face of all conclusions against it ; and in the following year the Conference agreed to let matters proceed. The Plan was launched publicly in April 1845, with its legal status still undetermined ; and the body responsible for it was given the name of the Chartist Cooperative Land Society, with O'Connor virtually in complete control of its affairs.

After many more legal difficulties, the attempt to enrol the Land Society as a Friendly Society had to be given up ; and as an alternative O'Connor and Roberts determined to register it as a Company under the new Companies Act of 1844. It was provisionally registered in October 1846, and a few months later changed its name to the National Land Company ; but the particulars required for full registration were not forthcoming, and the question of the Company's legality remained undecided.

Meanwhile O'Connor and his friends went ahead, not without much further criticism from Chartist opponents of the scheme. In 1846 the critics were headed by Thomas Cooper, who published in *Lloyd's Newspaper* a series of resolutions for which he had been refused publicity in *The Northern Star*. These included a frontal attack on O'Connor's trustworthiness; and elsewhere Cooper bluntly accused O'Connor of taking the money subscribed for the Land Plan and using it to meet losses on *The Northern Star* and for other private purposes of his own. In addition to demanding O'Connor's removal from all positions of trust, Cooper urged that the Land Plan should be completely severed from the N.C.A., which should get on with its proper business of agitating for the Charter.

A furious controversy followed. O'Connor announced his intention of resigning his position as deputy-treasurer of the Land Society (W. P. Roberts was treasurer) until his honour had been vindicated. But resolutions of confidence in him poured in from all over the country, and presently his resignation was withdrawn. Cooper, in face of howls of execration, persisted in moving his resolutions at the Chartist Conference; but he was shouted down, and thereafter formally expelled from the Chartist body.

By 1847 the Land Society had got down to business, though its legal status was still insecure. O'Connor and Ernest Jones, a recent recruit to Chartism, started *The Labourer* as the monthly organ of the land movement; and in May the first estate bought on behalf of the Land Company was formally opened with a ceremony, including the recital of a poem written for the occasion by Ernest Jones. This was the Heronsgate, or Herringsgate, estate, near Rickmansworth, which was re-named O'Connorville and promptly filled up with settlers under the plan. Visitors to it can still find a relic of its past in the name of the local inn — ' The Land of Liberty '.

It was a part of Cooper's charges against O'Connor that Heronsgate had been acquired in his name, and not in that of the Land Company, or of its treasurer, W. P. Roberts. The answer made was that acquisition in the name of the Company was impossible, as it had still no legal status, and that the purchase had been completed in O'Connor's name because he had begun the negotiations and it was doubtful if Roberts would have been accepted by the vendor. This explanation did not still the criticisms ; but the Land Company went on its way in spite of them. It acquired five other estates — Charterville, near Minster Lovel, in Oxfordshire, where the original cottages and allotments can still be seen ; Lowbands and Snig's End, in Gloucestershire ; and Dodford and Mathon, in Worcestershire — though the purchase of Mathon was never finally completed.

Money came in at a remarkable rate, considering the poverty of most of the subscribers. The basis of the plan was that members should purchase shares in the company by instalments of anything from 3d. to 1s. a week. Each fully paid-up share was ultimately to entitle the holder to an allocation of one acre of land, with the necessary buildings and a cash advance of £7 : 10s. for purchase of stock and equipment. Those subscribers who were fortunate enough to get land were chosen by ballot ; and holdings were normally of from one to four acres, according to the amount subscribed. While in occupation of these holdings, they were to pay a yearly rent of 5 per cent, calculated on the capital cost.

On this basis some hundreds of households were settled on the estates bought by the Land Company. But at this stage there arose an outcry in the press against the scheme, not merely from Chartists who were hostile to it, but also from many other quarters, including Poor Law authorities which feared that the tenants, unable to subsist on the produce of their holdings, would become chargeable to the parishes in which the Land Company's estates were situated.

In connection with the Land Company, O'Connor had set up a Land Bank, into which some of the subscriptions were paid ; and this led to further attacks, as he appeared to have unquestioned control over the money. Nevertheless, contributions continued to roll in, and by November 1847 the total sum subscribed exceeded £80,000. But the legal status of the Company was still undecided ; and early in 1848, moved partly by newspaper controversies, but also partly, no doubt, by a desire to hit back at O'Connor for his attempt to stimulate a mass movement after the pattern of those on the Continent, the House of Commons ordered a

Special Committee to enquire on its behalf into the Land Company's affairs and to make a report.

By this time O'Connor had become a Member of Parliament. Amid all his preoccupations with the Land Plan he had not quite forgotten the other aspects of Chartism, albeit he seemed at this time to think them relatively unimportant. From the launching of the Plan in 1843, warfare had been intensified between the O'Connorites and the leaders of the Anti-Corn Law League. In this contest the O'Connorites were at a disadvantage, because they did not venture really to defend the Corn Laws. According to O'Connor, his small farms would be so efficient as to stand in no need of protection. In his book of 1843 he asserted that the Corn Laws ought to be repealed, but not until the Land Plan had been adopted. Elsewhere he argued that repeal should be further conditional upon an ' equitable adjustment ' of financial claims, in order to prevent the land of England from falling into the usurers' hands.

On this basis Chartists went about interrupting Anti-Corn Law meetings, and moving amendments in favour of the prior adoption of the Charter, or the Land Plan, or an ' equitable adjustment ' — an old phrase, this, of Cobbett's — according to taste. In the course of these interchanges O'Connor repeatedly challenged Bright and Cobden to public debate ; but the offer was not accepted until 1844, when rival demonstrations arranged at Northampton by the two parties were converted into a four-handed debate between Cobden and Bright on the one side, and O'Connor and M'Grath on the other. The debate was held at hustings erected in the open air ; and the common opinion seems to have been that the Free Traders had an easy victory. They had a simple case to argue : O'Connor, since he would not defend the Corn Laws, had a difficult one ; and intricate argument was not his forte. At all events all his enemies, Chartists and Free Traders alike, shouted out that he had been exposed ; and undoubtedly the League propaganda received an additional impetus from the debate.

This event, however, did little to shake the confidence of the main body of O'Connor's following. The Chartist leaders parted company with him, one after another ; but the Chartist rank and file remained for the most part faithful. When, in 1846, John Cam Hobhouse, on appointment as President of the Board of Control, had to stand for re-election at Nottingham, O'Connor appeared as a candidate against him at the hustings, but did not go to the poll. But a year later, at the General Election of July 1847, O'Connor stood against the two sitting Members, Hobhouse and Thomas Gisborne, who was a Radical of sorts. O'Connor was elected in company with the younger John Walter, the sole Tory candidate for the two seats. He did not actually run in partnership with Walter; but his campaign was directed almost exclusively against the Whigs, and was mainly agrarian in character, and undoubtedly he and Walter were supported mainly by the same anti-Whig voters.

Nevertheless, O'Connor's election was widely acclaimed as a great Chartist triumph; and added importance was attached to it because it coincided in time with the near approach of revolution over a large part of Europe. O'Connor, however, signalised his return, after twelve years' absence, to the House of Commons by moving, in November, neither the adoption of the Charter nor public endorsement of the Land Plan, but repeal of the Act of Union between Great Britain and Ireland.

The events of the early months of 1848 brought the Charter back right into the middle of the picture. With thrones and constitutions toppling all over Europe, it seemed incumbent on the Chartists either to make a national effort or to confess final defeat. Some of those who had dropped out because of hostility to O'Connor's control of the movement came back as delegates to the Chartist Convention of 1848, which was to present to Parliament the third, and last, monster National Petition on behalf of the unrepresented classes. A mass demonstration to present the Petition was fixed for April 10, to meet at Kennington Common and march in procession to the House of Commons, with O'Connor at its head.

O'Connor, meanwhile, was loudly announcing his utter loyalty to the Charter, of which he had during recent years seemed to take little account. " I would rather die than give up one particle of the Charter," he wrote in his national

appeal of April 1. He went on to proclaim that " our movement is a labour movement, originated in the first instance
by the fustian jackets, the blistered hands and the unshorn
chins ", and added " I would not give a fig for the Charter
if we were not prepared with a solid, social system to take
the place of the artificial one which we mean to destroy ; and
it was good that we did not succeed earlier with the Charter,
before we were ready with the new social system. . . .
The Charter and the Land. Those are our objects."

With this appeal went a plan for a British Republic, to be
based on peasant ownership and peasant democracy — and
doubtless with Feargus O'Connor cast for the part of
President. Did he not even say that his uncle, Arthur
O'Connor, who was aged eighty-five, was likely to be made
President of the coming French Republic, and remind the
people, oftener than ever, of his descent from the ancient
Kings of Ireland ?

The semblance of regained unity in the early months of
1848 concealed real differences as unbridgeable as ever. On
the one hand, there was a revival of ' physical force' resolutions and underground projects of insurrection — in which,
as usual, spies and *agents provocateurs* played a leading part.
On the other there were Chartists, such as O'Brien, who had
once been ' physical force' men, but were now not prepared
to countenance any threat of revolutionary activity. Between
these groups — the out-and-out ' moral force' men played
no part at all — was poised O'Connor, already full of the
growing troubles of his Land Plan, and very soon, despite
his boastings, to become fully conscious that his followers
were in no condition to challenge the might of the Government in arms.

The Government, on its side, made immense preparations
for combating a threatened uprising. It filled London with
soldiers, under the old Duke of Wellington, enrolled special
constables by tens of thousands, and determined to barricade
the Thames bridges in order to prevent the Chartist contingents from crossing the river. O'Connor, set on avoiding
a bloody conflict in which he knew defeat would be certain,
abandoned the march on Westminster, and bade the
assembled multitude on Kennington Common disperse

quietly to their homes, while he and the Chartist Executive
bore the Petition to Westminster undangerously in a few cabs.
The great day, April 10, which had been supposed to mean
revolution, passed off without anything at all happening;
and many people in all classes were prompt in drawing
the moral that, as an aggressive force in politics, Chartism
was dead.

Chartism had, nevertheless, ten years' existence, of a sort,
before it: O'Connor much less. He duly presented the
National Petition, claiming that it bore 5,700,000 signatures
— a number which the clerks to the House of Commons
reduced on examination to well under two millions. This
was, indeed, a very large number; but he spoke to a House
which, relieved of its fears of revolution, was in no mood
to take him or his cause seriously — the less so because the
shadow of the Land Company's difficulties lay across his
reputation.

In June the House of Commons, having disposed of the
Charter by handing it on to a Committee for examination,
turned to the affairs of the Land Company. A Select
Committee was set up to investigate allegations of irregularity
in its conduct; and by August this Committee had produced
six reports giving a practically complete narrative of the
Company's transactions. It found that the Land Company
was illegal; that its affairs were in complete confusion, and
that no proper accounts had ever been kept; and that it was
on the brink of insolvency. But it also found that, so far
from O'Connor having profited by the Company's money,
he had lost heavily, and it was in debt to him to the extent
of several thousand pounds. O'Connor's honour was
vindicated; but he was convicted of quite appalling carelessness and mismanagement. Finally, the Committee recommended that the Land Company, despite the illegality of its
doings, should be given powers to wind up its affairs in the
ways likely to be in the best interest of its misguided contributing shareholders.

This was the end of O'Connor's Land Plan, though not
of the settlements which he had founded. Some of these
lived on, as groups of tiny holdings in no respect unlike
others created without any political purpose. What ended

z   333

was the notion of regenerating England by means of spade culture. The Land Plan, and anything resembling it, ceased to figure in the Chartist programme.

The events of 1848 also ended the period of O'Connor's ascendancy in the Chartist movement. The next few years were full of faction fights between rival groups which claimed to inherit the true spirit of Chartism. A number of leading Chartists, including Ernest Jones and McDouall, had been imprisoned for their part in the troubles of 1848 ; and until they came out of gaol the National Charter Association languished. In July, 1849, the House of Commons at last voted on the Chartist Petition, which was rejected by 222 votes to 17. The Chartists had mustered 46 votes in the House of Commons for the Petition of 1839 and 49 votes for that of 1842 : now they could muster a mere 17. In 1850 O'Connor once more moved in Parliament a motion in favour of the Charter ; but the House was counted out. Radicalism was dying in Parliament as well as outside.

O'Connor's popularity had undoubtedly waned. After Ernest Jones's release from prison in the middle of 1850, the old leader soon found himself at loggerheads with the new, and with the Chartist Executive. O'Connor also quarrelled with Julian Harney, who had been the mainstay of *The Northern Star*. The *Star* had fallen heavily in circulation, and was now losing money.

In truth, O'Connor, after the collapse of his Land Plan, had no policy at all. One day he was in favour of joining forces with the middle-class Radicals, now organised in the Financial and Parliamentary Reform Association, on a basis of household franchise, widened to include lodgers. Another day he would denounce these same reformers as the enemies of the workers, and entreat the Chartists to have nothing to do with them. In 1851, without the sanction of the Executive, he called a Chartist Conference of his own at Manchester, where the local Chartists were discontented with the London leadership, and wanted the headquarters of the N.C.A. to be moved back to the North. But this gathering was quite unrepresentative, and achieved nothing. O'Connor was thereafter re-elected to the Executive at the regular Chartist Conference later in the year ; but he was no longer at the head of the poll, and had lost his grip on the movement. He was in effect already more than half mad.

For what purpose I do not know, at the beginning of 1852 O'Connor paid a rapid visit to the United States — where, if he had had time to look, he might have seen his thesis of the effect of free access to the land on wages illustrated under conditions more propitious than could exist in an old, settled country such as Great Britain. He returned in the course of the spring ; and in June he was involved in a scene in the House of Commons with Becket Denison, the Leeds banker who sat for the West Riding. He was removed by the Sergeant-at-Arms, pronounced insane, and lodged in Dr. Tuke's private asylum at Chiswick. There he remained until 1854, when, against doctor's advice, he was removed to his sister's house in Notting Hill. There, on August 30, 1855, he died.

When O'Connor was dead, old enmities were largely forgotten. He was given a great public funeral at Kensal Green, and most Chartists preferred to remember his virtues rather than his faults. *The Northern Star*, for so many years the principal instrument of his power, had perished well before him. It came into the market in 1852, when O'Connor was no longer capable of conducting it ; and Julian Harney bought it for a song, only to be compelled to give it up a few months later. It expired finally in November 1852.

The story of O'Connor's last years was tragic. As his disease grew upon him, he drank more and more heavily, and became more and more outrageously inconsequent in his views. He had always been fond of good living, and a notable *raconteur*, chiefly of his own experiences ; but in these years he grew incoherent in both public and private speech. His articles, which he was in the habit of dictating to his nephew, Roger, as he strode about the room, had the same quality as his speech. At no time after the failure of the Land Plan had he really any notion of what he meant.

But he must not be judged by his doings of these years. In his heyday he was undoubtedly a tremendous popular force. " Upwards of six feet in height, stout and athletic, and in spite of his opinions invested with a sort of aristocratic bearing, the sight of his person was calculated to inspire the masses with a solemn awe ", says Gammage. He had, moreover, a tremendous voice, admirably suited to speaking to great meetings in the open air. At indoor meetings, unless they were of great size, and in the House of Commons, this was a handicap ; for he could not easily subdue his tones to fit a small assembly.

O'Connor was, in fact, a great mob-orator, with a large fund of sympathy for the people, a great deal of egoism, especially in relation to his fellow leaders, and a very small stock of ideas. He was a thoroughly bad and rambling writer, addicted to imitating Cobbett, but quite lacking Cobbett's vigour of style. Except when he was vituperative he was, as a writer, very dull. As an organiser and leader he was ruined by his incapacity for collaboration. He wanted to be boss ; but he had no clear policy, especially at moments of crisis, when he said first one thing and then another, and always came down in the end on what he felt likeliest to be the winning side. He was, in truth, a disastrous leader ; but it is necessary to bear in mind that it is very doubtful whether any leadership could have enabled the Chartist movement to succeed. The governing classes — old and new combined — were too strong for it ; and it is difficult to lead well a movement which is fated to kick helplessly against the pricks.

XII

Ernest Jones

" The land it is the landlords' ;
 The trader's is the sea ;
The ore the usurer's coffer fills ;
 But what remains for me ?
The engine whirls for master's craft,
 The steel shines to defend
With labour's arms what labour raised
 For labour's foe to spend.
The camp, the pulpit, and the law
 For rich man's sons are free ;
Theirs, theirs are learning, art and arms ;
 But what remains for me ?
The coming hope, the future day,
 When wrong to right shall bow,
And hearts shall have the courage, man,
 To make that future *now*."

ERNEST JONES
From *The Song of the Factory Slave*

ERNEST CHARLES JONES, the Chartist leader, was born in Berlin in 1819, and died in Manchester in 1869. Engels wrote to Karl Marx on the occasion of his death that " he was the only educated Englishman among the politicians who was, at bottom, entirely on our side ". From the moment of his conversion to Chartism in 1846 he had laboured incessantly for the Chartist cause. Through the 'fifties he was its one remaining leader of any note ; and when Chartism was finally dead he continued his work in the cause of the people, living on to play an important part in the renewed Reform movement which led up to the Reform Act of 1867. He stood for Parliament repeatedly as a Chartist candidate : his last contest, as a Radical, was fought at Manchester in 1868 ; and at the time of his death he was preparing to fight there yet again. His funeral was a great and impressive gathering of the Radicals ; but others

337

who were not Radicals came too, to pay tribute to his memory — for he was a man whom all respected and many loved. He was a poet as well as a politician, and a novelist as well as a poet. A barrister by profession and born to wealth and high social standing, he threw away fortune and professional career in the cause of the Charter. He served two years in prison, and was gravely maltreated there. As long as Chartism was a living movement, he was abused and maligned on all hands — by many of his fellow Chartists as well as by his political opponents. Only when Chartism was safely dead were his utter uprightness and devotion generally recognised.

In political attitude, Ernest Jones was a Socialist as well as a Chartist. For many years he was deeply influenced by Karl Marx, with whom he was intimate. Later, he and Marx parted company when, amid the disintegration of Chartism, he had come to believe that no Reform could be brought about except by collaboration between the workers and the middle classes. Marx denounced his apostasy ; but it is clear from his letters that he did not cease to respect the man. Engels, who knew him well at Manchester, where he was settled during his later years, certainly respected him highly. Much more than any other Chartist leader he was a forerunner of modern Socialism. It was, indeed, his fate, entering the Chartist movement when it was already beginning to decay, to preach Socialism to the British working class at the time when it was least ready to listen. For in the third quarter of the nineteenth century British capitalism, with the markets of the world at its command, relaxed the extreme pressure upon the workers which had marked its earlier phases. Wages rose, and conditions improved, especially for the skilled craftsmen who were the natural leaders of the working class ; and as these turned aside from Chartism to build up their ' new model ' Trade Unions and their Cooperative Societies on the Rochdale plan, the spirit of rebellion died, and proposals for a radical reconstruction of society were brushed aside. This did not deter Ernest Jones from pursuing year after year his fruitless crusade ; but he had fewer and fewer followers, until at last the Chartist movement literally died out and left him alone.

It is a remarkable fact that no Life of Ernest Jones has ever been published, beyond a brief pamphlet, though of course his name figures prominently in books about the Chartist movement. There is no want of material. Jones left a diary, now preserved at Manchester ; he wrote much journalism, which largely chronicles his efforts for the Charter, and his stories and poems are full of material for the biographer. His life ought to be written ; but for the time being this brief essay must serve to remind the present generation of a Socialist pioneer who has not often been given his due.

There was in Ernest Jones's beginnings nothing to fore-shadow his career. He was the son of a cavalry officer, Major Charles Jones, who had fought under Sir John Moore and under Wellington in the Peninsula and, on retiring wounded from the service, had become equerry to Ernest, Duke of Cumberland and later King of Hanover, after whom his son was named. Ernest Jones was brought up and educated in Germany, where he lived until he was nineteen. His father had bought an estate, Rheinbeck, in Holstein, and there he was taught by German private tutors until he was enabled by the grant of letters of nobility by the King of Hanover to proceed to the exclusive College of St. Michael, at Lüneburg. In 1838 his parents brought him back to England, and he began his studies for the Bar. He lived the life of a young man of wealth and fashion, was presented to Queen Victoria, and, in 1841, married Jane Atherley at St. George's, Hanover Square. It was what he called in his diary " a dashing wedding " : his wife was the daughter of a Cumberland landowner, and related to the Stanleys, Earls of Derby. The couple settled down at 33 Upper Montagu Street, in the West End, to live the ordinary life of the well-to-do.

Ernest Jones had become an author long before this — at the precocious age of eleven. In 1830 his parents had published his juvenile poems — some written when he was eight — with a fulsome dedication to the King of Hanover. They are rather better than might be expected. In the year of his marriage he published his first tale, *The Wood Spirit, a Romance*, interspersed with songs and poems. The critics spoke very highly of it; but it is unreadable to-day. It belongs to a forgotten *genre*, of utterly unreal half-legendary romance, which was then popular. Its success started him on a career of literary journalism, which continued until it was interrupted by his entire absorption in the Chartist movement. Meanwhile, two sons were born to him and, in 1844, he was called to the Bar and set out to practise, attaching himself to the Northern Circuit. He went to live at Hampstead, in Rosslyn Hill; and there he wrote and published in 1845 his first considerable poem *My Life, or, Our Social State*. This too was enthusiastically reviewed, though it is possible to trace in it the forces which were making him into a Chartist — a deep sympathy with suffering, a sense of the hollowness of the society in which he had hitherto moved, and a passion against social injustice.

About this time he became acquainted, by chance, with Feargus O'Connor's paper, *The Northern Star*. He records in his diary how, early in 1846, he went to see the Chartist leaders, and threw in his lot with them. He was not a man to do things by halves. From that moment Chartism was the first thing in his life. He entered the movement as one of O'Connor's lieutenants, and speedily became prominent at the Leeds Convention of 1846, where he sided with O'Connor in the dispute over the Land Scheme which led to the expulsion of Thomas Cooper, another Chartist poet, from the ranks of the movement, then dominated by O'Connor.

Ernest Jones was a remarkable orator, with a great power of swaying large audiences. He had a very powerful, melodious voice, and his style was at its best when he was using the spoken word. To his oratory, more than to his poems, he owed his rapid rise to influence in the Chartist ranks, though he was doubtless also welcomed as the Chartist gentleman *par excellence*. Gammage, the contemporary historian of Chartism, who disliked him, paid tribute to his excellence as an orator:

Unknown previously to the working classes, he came into their ranks under the patronage of Feargus O'Connor. An aristocrat is always most acceptable to the working classes, even to Democrats, and the young sprig of aristocracy, promoted, as

O'Connor would say, to the ranks of the Democracy, was received with enthusiasm. He possessed exactly the qualities for captivating the crowd, with the single exception that, unlike his patron O'Connor, he was small in stature ; but his voice was stentorian, his delivery good, his language brilliant, his action heroic — and, above all, he had a concealed cunning, which had the advantage of bearing every appearance of the most extreme candour. In the art of flattery, no demagogue ever excelled him. He could, in a breath, transform a man who could scarcely string together five sentences in English into a clever fellow, and a most accomplished orator ; and, what was stranger, he could get him to believe it. He was ever as ready to face the frowns of the elements of Nature as those of the enemies of Democracy. He would speak on a wide heath, amid the howlings of the pitiless storm, and dash aside the umbrella that was held to shelter him.

As for Jones's cunning, my reading of his speeches does not bear out Gammage's remarks. Ernest Jones was not cunning ; he was not consciously flattering the people ; he believed in them with all the faith of the converted aristocrat. His eloquence was not studied, but natural ; but, whatever its source, it made him immediately a power in the movement. He went all over the country speaking ; and, as Gammage bears witness, he never spared himself. To the very end of his life, he was utterly regardless of the weather. He was never known to wrap himself up against a storm, or to pay the smallest attention to getting wet through. His unconcern in these matters killed him in the end ; but he must have had a magnificent constitution to endure the hardships which he put up with.

For his own part, he set, at this stage, more store by his poems than by his oratory. He records in his diary on October 8, 1846 : " To-day O'Connor saw McGowan about my Chartist poems. I am pouring the tide of my songs over England, forming the tone of the mighty mind of the people. . . . I thank God I am prepared to rush fresh and strong into the strife or struggle of a nation — to ride the torrent or to guide the rill, if God permits." His Chartist songs began to appear in many forms — in O'Connor's *Northern*

Star, in book form, in broadsides and little booklets. They were sung and read at many Chartist gatherings.

By the beginning of 1847 Jones was O'Connor's closest associate. He became co-editor of *The Northern Star* and induced O'Connor to embark with him on a new monthly magazine, *The Labourer*, to which he contributed prose stories and articles as well as poems. He became active as a sponsor of O'Connor's Land Scheme for settling discontented factory workers back on the land ; and he wrote a poem celebrating the foundation of O'Connorville, the Chartist land colony near Rickmansworth.

During this year, Ernest Jones fought his first parliamentary contest as candidate for Halifax. There were four candidates for the two seats — a Conservative, a Whig, Ernest Jones, and the Radical Edward Miall, editor of *The Nonconformist*, and an active member of Joseph Sturge's Complete Suffrage Union. At the hustings, Jones and Miall easily carried the day ; for there the voteless could shout as loud as any. But at the poll the Tory and the Whig won, with 511 and 507 votes, against 349 for Miall and 280 for Jones — a remarkably good poll, considering the fact that in those days no workman had the right to vote.

This was the General Election at which Feargus O'Connor was elected for Nottingham — the only man who ever found his way into the House of Commons as a Chartist candidate. Politically, Chartism was at the highest point of its influence, though industrially, as a mass movement of the workers, it had already began to recede. Ernest Jones's supporters had been confident enough to hope that he might be elected : the campaign at any rate gave him an assured standing among the Radical workmen of the North.

In the Chartist Convention of 1848 Jones represented Halifax, and played an important part. He was prominent in support of the resolution advocating nationalisation of the land, with a view to the settlement on it of the surplus population from the manufacturing districts. He took an active part in the arrangements for presenting to Parliament the monster Chartist Petition of that year, and in the famous Kennington Common meeting which was the last great rally of Chartism before its disintegration had become plain. It is well known how the Government, fearing riot, prevented the Chartists from marching through central London to the House of Commons and, having allowed their great gathering to reach Kennington Common, effectively guarded the bridges against them with many thousands of special constables enrolled for the occasion, and bodies of troops held near in reserve. It fell to Jones's lot to urge the crowd to disperse quietly, and not, in its unarmed and unprepared condition, to risk a conflict with the forces of the Crown. This went sorely against the grain with him ; for he had proclaimed himself not merely a Chartist, but a Chartist of the ' physical force ' school, ready to attempt the forcible seizure of power as soon as a chance presented itself. But he was well aware that the Chartists were not nearly strong enough, in face of the Government's elaborate precautions, to win their way by force ; and accordingly he counselled discretion against the angry protests of William Cuffay and other leaders of the extreme ' physical force ' party among the London Chartists. Eventually, the crowds dispersed quietly, and the Petition reached the House of Commons, not with a multitude escorting it, but under O'Connor's care, in three hansom cabs. Not many people realised that on that day the Government had finally laid the Chartist spectre ; but so it was. In that year of continental revolutions British Chartism had made its challenge to the established order ; and the challenge had been taken up. Up to the day of the Kennington meeting, the ruling classes in England had been really afraid of a Chartist revolution. Thereafter, they feared it no more.

Jones, however, did not realise how decisive the defeat had been. At the Kennington Common meeting he had announced himself, even while he counselled prudence, as a ' Physical Force ' Chartist ; and thereafter he set to work at once to help in organising the movement for a revolutionary attempt. These doings soon brought him into conflict with the police. Early in June, addressing a meeting of the London Chartists, he recommended a thorough reorganisation of the Chartist forces with a view to a renewed attack. " Rest assured ", said he, " that I shall not preach a miserable doctrine of non-resistance and passive obedience. But at the same time I shall preach the doctrine of manly firmness, and no heated impetuosity. . . . I verily believe that not a single blow need be struck, in this country, for liberty." But in the same speech he declared himself to be a " physical force" Chartist, denounced the "measures of the half-and-half men ", and urged his hearers to defy any ban the Government might attempt to place on the right of public meeting. The Government, he declared, " are not mad enough to put down public meetings, and, if they were mad enough to do it, I for one thrust defiance in their teeth, and dare them to disperse this assembly ".

Actually, after Ernest Jones had left the meeting in order to go to the North of England, where he was due to address a number of Chartist demonstrations, the police did break it up, and there was a conflict in the course of which a number of persons were taken into custody. Two days later, Ernest Jones was arrested in Manchester and brought to London to be tried for sedition, unlawful assembly, and riot. There were several other prisoners ; but the cases were taken separately. At Jones's trial, the Attorney General made a great point of his social standing and his profession as a barrister as aggravations of his offence. Serjeant Wilkins, who defended him, made all possible play with his successful efforts to prevent violence on the occasion of the Kennington Common meeting, where he had induced the crowd to disperse quietly. But he was convicted. While awaiting sentence, he addressed a long open letter to Chief Justice Wilde, in the course of which he offered a defence of his conduct. He wrote that he had been described as " a designing demagogue, an ambitious adventurer living on the people ", but that, on the contrary, he had " sacrificed domestic comfort and pecuniary resources to the cause " that he had embraced. " As to my being an adventurer, my position raises me above the necessity of struggling for wealth in the future, inasmuch as a considerable property is settled upon my family and myself, to the possession of which we must come at no very distant period. . . . But they call me a designing man, a designing demagogue. I will tell them I have never gained by the Chartist Movement. I have invariably refused all and every remuneration for my humble services in the

People's Cause : I have never, though repeatedly pressed to do so, accepted of one farthing for my lectures, either in town or country ; and it is only a few weeks since that, without solicitation, I have been unanimously elected a member of the Chartist Executive, and abandoned a situation of far higher emolument, to devote myself to the duties of that office. As a barrister, I have invariably refused to accept fees from the poor. . . . When I tell you, in addition to this, that my present means are very limited — indeed, painfully so — and that my opportunities of obtaining lucrative employment have been frequent, I think you will do me the justice to say that no mere adventurer, no designing demagogue, stands before you now."

Jones went on to put forward a vigorous defence of the right of public meeting, against the view that an assembly, lawful in itself, could become unlawful merely because great numbers attended it, or because the police apprehended that it might lead to a riot. Moreover, he argued, " the purpose of a public meeting is not merely to discuss a grievance, but to concert measures for its remedy ". Mere petitions, he wrote, went utterly unheeded. " These things, my Lord, have taught the people that petitioning is of use no longer, and they wish to demonstrate the public opinion by more apparent means. They, somehow, have an idea that a petition from a million of men, forwarded in stray thousands, on stray bits of paper, would be neglected, the same as such petitions have been before ; but that the same million of men presenting their petition in person would meet with some attention ; and at their meetings now they are publicly organising to this effect. A few men being in prison will not prevent this result, it will only accelerate it ; but, I trust, it will not irritate the petitioners."

From this language, not likely to endear him to the judge, Ernest Jones went on to a passionate defence of the Chartist cause : " Do not believe that we few men are the creators of British discontent or Irish insurrection. . . . Follow out the links of your political chain in alternate cause and effect : Monopoly and Destitution, Discontent and Crime, Taxation and Insurrection. Behold, how you have been niggardly with schools, which forces you to be profuse with prisons. Behold, how you have grudged the poor their rights, which makes you fearful for your own ! . . . Let the Government divide the waste lands among the people — they would support the entire pauper population, and thus relieve the artificial labour market, so that work would be obtained at fair wages by the unwilling idle. . . . Instead of building workhouses, erect Colleges of Agriculture : instead of emigration, promote home colonisation. . . . You think Chartism is quelled. Learn that it is more strong than ever. While oppression reigns, Chartism resists. While misery lasts, Chartism shall flourish ; and when misery ceases the Charter will be law."

Jones's eloquence was not calculated to save him. He was sentenced to two years of solitary confinement, and thereafter to be bound over to keep the peace for three years.

The Chartist prisoners of 1848 were treated with barbarous severity — so much so that the two who were sentenced with Ernest Jones both died in prison. He survived ; but he had very much to bear. His treatment, which was afterwards the subject of official investigation, in the course of which the main facts were admitted, is best described in his own words, written many years later : " I was kept for more than two years in separate confinement on the silent system, most rigidly enforced — so rigidly that for an involuntary smile I was sent for three days to a dark cell on bread and water. For the first nineteen months I was kept without books, pen, ink, or paper, and had to sit out that time in a cell, twelve feet by seven, locked up in solitude and silence, without even a table or a chair. To this cell (the day cell) were three windows, two without glass but with rough wooden shutters, through which the wind and snow and rain of winter blew all over the place. My night cell was of far smaller dimensions, 9 feet by 4 feet. Its window was unglazed — its shutters did not meet the window frame nor each other by one or two inches. There was an aperture over my bed 18 in. by 12 in., through which the snow and rain fell on me as I slept, saturating my clothes with moisture, so that often the water dripped from them as I put them on. The bed itself was a sack of straw with a piece of carpeting.

From this bed I had to go, when I rose at five in the morning, across two yards in my shirt and trousers only, to wash and dress in the open air, after getting wet through in the rain and snow while dressing, and sitting all day in my wet clothes in my fireless cell ; for during the first twelve months I was allowed no fire in my day cell. During the intense frost of the winter of '49, I had to break the ice in the stone trough in which I was compelled to wash, in the same water, frequently, that other prisoners had used. The diet was so poor, and often of so revolting a kind, that at last I was unable to walk across my cell without support, through loss of strength. Neither fork nor knife was allowed at meals, and I had to tear my food with my fingers. Bent to the ground with rheumatism, and racked by neuralgia, I applied for permission to have a fire, but this was denied me, as already stated, till the second year of my imprisonment. Then I became so weak that I was compelled to crawl on all fours if I sought to reach the door of my cell to knock for assistance. On one occasion I fell against the grate, and had a narrow escape of being burned to death. It will be remembered that in the year of 1849, the cholera raged so fearfully in London that in one day as many as 417 persons died. During the height of the plague, while suffering from bowel complaint, I was sent to a darkened cell, because I did not pick the oakum that was brought to me as my daily task. . . . During all this time, after the first few weeks, I was allowed to hear from my wife and children only once every three months. . . . Out of the four other political prisoners who were sentenced simultaneously with myself, two — Alexander Sharp and John Williams — died in prison after about six months' endurance of this treatment ; and the coroners' juries in their verdicts attributed their early deaths to the sufferings they had undergone, censured the treatment, and recommended its discontinuance — but it was continued, unaltered, notwithstanding. The third, John Vernon, died soon after his release, which was granted him six months before the expiration of his sentence, after he had been eighteen months in prison. . . . I have recorded but a portion — a small portion — of the sufferings inflicted. I have never paraded this, have never spoken about it, never written of it ; but I do think it is rather hard, after having undergone all these things, we should be held up as examples of ' lenient and considerate treatment '."

This was written in 1866, in answer to assertions that Ernest Jones had been treated with exceptional leniency during his two years in gaol. So far from this, it is plain that only his remarkable constitution kept him alive. Despite his privations, he managed during these two years of wretchedness to compose many poems, writing some of them in his own blood on scraps of paper gathered in defiance of the prison rules. His spirit remained alive, even when his body had almost given way. He came out of prison in July 1850, ready at once to take up again his work for the Charter with undiminished enthusiasm, and with as much energy as the state of his health would allow.

While he was in prison, his wife had been left penniless ; for her family had cast her off. She and the children were maintained by a regular allowance from the Halifax Chartists; and to Halifax Ernest Jones went on his release, to be welcomed back as candidate for the borough and to take stock of the state of Chartism two years after its great defeat. He found the movement in fragments. Feargus O'Connor was already well on the way to madness, and the failure of the Chartist Land Company, as well as the fiasco of 1848, had badly shaken his prestige. Bronterre O'Brien had broken away, and formed a National Reform League, on a broad programme which was meant to bring Owenites, Chartists, and Radicals of every type under a common banner. Lovett was pursuing his ideas of liberal education ; Thomas Cooper was leading his own group in strong hostility to O'Connor ; William Newton was pleading for a new movement which would conciliate, instead of antagonising, the Radical middle class. Amid this confusion Ernest Jones set to work to re-create the working-class movement for the Charter on a basis of unified national organisation. He toured the country — especially the North — seeking to revive the old Chartist spirit. He returned to the Chartist Executive, of which he became, before long, the only effective member. More and more, what was left of the Chartist movement fell into his hands ; and he made one attempt after another to persuade the working classes to accept the Charter as their primary object.

It would be fruitless here to trace these abortive activities year by year. In 1852 O'Connor was removed to an asylum, and the Chartist Convention, already a shadow of its old self, split on the issue of collaboration between the middle and working classes. Jones, standing with the opponents of collaboration, resigned from the Chartist Executive ; and at a Conference in Manchester later in the year he and his friends formed a new Executive, with him at its head, to work on the old, uncompromising lines. This became the leadership of the Chartist body, such as it was. It strove vainly — for example, in the abortive ' Mass Movement ' of 1854 — to enlist the support of the Trade Unions, then rapidly growing in power. But the Trade Unions would have none of it ; and year by year the Chartist Conventions had to record diminishing attendances, and a rapidly falling membership in the country.

Ernest Jones's efforts to keep Chartism alive were made partly through his speaking tours, in which he was untiring, and partly through his journals. In 1851 he started *Notes for the People* as a weekly journal. In the following year it became *The People's Paper*, which lasted until 1858. In these journals Jones published many of his poems and a number of stories ; but they are more notable for the articles in which he developed a definitely Socialist interpretation of the Chartist demands. He had come to hold that the Charter by itself supplied no answer to the social problem, that land schemes and home colonisation were utterly inadequate remedies for the evils of capitalist society, and that only Socialism could meet the real needs of the people. Strongly under the influence of Karl Marx, he stressed the irreconcilable antagonism between the interests of Capital and Labour, the increasing tendency for the control of wealth to become centralised in fewer hands, the necessity of political power as a means of destroying the class-monopoly of land and capital alike. Never an original social thinker, he was during these years an apt pupil — going often to Marx or Engels for advice, and attempting to create in Great Britain a class-war party on the basis of Marx's ideas. That he failed utterly was due not to defects of his own, but to the conditions of the time. The British workers in the 'fifties did not want a class-war gospel. They wanted — except a very few — to be let alone while they built up their defensive organisations inside the capitalist system. They had given up trying to overthrow the system itself, as soon as the chance had been offered them of doing something to improve their position within it.

Jones, however, could not for a long time realise how far the conditions had changed while he had been locked up in prison. Seeing the failure of the old Chartism, he attributed it to the vagueness of the Chartist social programme and to the inability of the leaders to understand the need for advancing towards a Socialist policy. Soon after his release he wrote, in criticism of the old leaders, as follows : " Another difficulty in the way of a popular movement is when it emancipates itself from one set of ideas to climb up to the next. This is hardly ever done without a certain amount of disruption, disorganisation, and strife. . . . As the intellect of the human race progresses, the scholar must necessarily outstrip his master. But it is a hard thing for the master to go to school again — he won't do it, he can't do it. He has created, or come into the movement with, a fixed set of ideas — he raises the movement up to the standard of his own intellect — he runs out the length of his mental tether, and there he stands : not so the movement. . . . When the master leaves off teaching, the scholar will teach himself and go on from where the instructor stopped. The latter cannot believe the fact — his old limbs cannot keep pace with the young traveller — his dim sight cannot distinguish the new goal to which he tends — and, fearful of the future, he drags his companion backward by the skirts — he becomes a *reactionary* Democrat. Then what bickering, what strife ensues ! A portion of the school have become personally attached to their old teachers, and stand still with them, despite their better judgement. . . . The public question becomes a private quarrel. . . . Thus, in every transition state, from one set of thoughts to another, a certain loss, a certain retardation is experienced. . . . It is one of these stages of transition through which we have now passed."

Here, plainly, is the account of the breach between Ernest Jones and the O'Connorites, who still clung to their remedy of land settlement and were strongly hostile to the new Socialist ideas. He was right in thinking O'Connorism obsolete; but he had still no conception of the difficulty of persuading the British workers to listen to the new Socialist gospel.

Notes for the People, and *The People's Paper* after it, had a hard struggle. Jones had no capital, and the distributors did their best to boycott his journals. His placards were torn down, not only by private opponents, but by the police. He had no money to pay contributors, and wrote almost the whole of his papers himself, often in the course of his speaking tours as leader of the Chartist Executive. Again and again he refused to accept the salary voted to him by the Chartist Convention, or to take any money for his work as a speaker; and he got nothing from his journals. He lived, poorly and precariously, on what he could make by his poems and his non-political writings, contributing any surplus that came his way over his modest needs to the support of the cause. He was quixotic about this : it is related of him that in one of his parliamentary contests he appeared in so deplorable a suit that his committee said he must have a new one. He replied that he could not afford it, and refused to accept it as a gift until they removed his old suit from his bedroom while he slept, and put a new one in its place. He ate very sparingly, trudged about from meeting to meeting on foot, whenever he could, and shortened both his own and his wife's existence by the immense burdens which he persisted in shouldering on behalf of the movement.

Meanwhile, his public reputation as a poet remained. His poems and novels were well reviewed, and sold enough to keep him and his and to save *The People's Paper* from death. In 1852 he stood again for Halifax, with two Whigs and a Conservative against him for the two seats. His poll measured the decline of Chartism. In 1847 he had secured 280 votes, against 511 and 507 for the successful Whig and Tory candidates. Now the two Whigs got 596 and 573, the Tory 521, and Jones only 37. Not even the Chartists voted solidly for him. The faction-fight within Chartism had destroyed

its influence, and bred deep personal animosities. In 1857
— the year of his wife's death — he tried again, this time at
Nottingham, Feargus O'Connor's old constituency, now held
by a Liberal and a Tory without any opposition except his.
He polled 614, against 2393 for the Liberal and 1836 for the
Tory — John Walter, of *The Times*. In 1859 he renewed
his attempt, only to be routed, this time by two Whigs, who
polled 2456 and 2151 against 1836 for a Tory and a mere
151 for Jones.

On this occasion again, the root of the trouble was dis-
unity. After the failure of the attempt to rebuild militant
Chartism on exclusively working-class foundations had
become manifest, Jones at last changed his policy, and began
to appeal for united action between the workers and the
Radical section of the middle class. In 1858 he convened at
the London Guildhall a national conference which launched
the Manhood Suffrage movement, with " registered, resi-
dential manhood suffrage " as its sole object. He became
president of the movement and was voted a salary of £8 a
week, which he refused to take. This Conference was to a
great extent the beginning of the new national Reform movement which led up to the Reform Act of 1867.

In 1858 *The People's Paper* died, and Jones's literary
journal, *The London News*, had to be sold in order to pay its
debts. His change of front had embroiled him with many
of his Chartist supporters ; specially vociferous against him
was G. W. M. Reynolds, the editor of *Reynolds' Newspaper*,
who accused him of pilfering funds subscribed for *The
People's Paper*. The entire baselessness of this charge was
exposed in the course of the libel action which Jones brought
against Reynolds ; but in the meantime the affair had split
his supporters at Nottingham, and caused him to cut a sorry
figure at the election. It came out during the action that
Jones had spent much of his own money on the paper, and
also that he had forfeited an income of £2000 a year from an
uncle, who had promised to leave it to him on condition
that he gave up his Chartist activities, but, on Jones's refusal,
left his fortune to his gardener instead.

In 1861 Ernest Jones, now seeking to build up the new
Reform movement which he had initiated in 1858, decided

to move with his family to Manchester, and there to resume the practice at the Bar which he had thrown over fifteen years earlier in order to devote himself to the Chartist movement. At Manchester he felt he could combine the earning of a tolerable living at the Bar with good work among the Northern Radicals. He was able to do this. He became, in fact, during the next few years the most influential political leader of the Lancashire working-class movement. On the outbreak of the American Civil War, he took an active part in supporting the cause of the North against the slave-owners, combating especially the view that the South should be favoured as the Free Trade party. " Why did the South secede ? " he said in one of his speeches ; and an auditor interjected, " For Free Trade ". Jones retorted, " Free Trade in what ? Free Trade in the lash, Free Trade in the branding-iron, Free Trade in chains ! " He also took a strong line against British intervention in the Danish-German War over Schleswig-Holstein.

Jones's most famous action during these years at Manchester was, however, his defence of the Irish Fenian prisoners who were charged with murder on account of their part in the successful rescue of two Fenians from a prison van — an affray in which a police sergeant was killed. In this and in subsequent Fenian trials he was complimented by the judge on his conduct of the case, though he did not succeed in saving the lives of his clients. In 1867, the year of the great Fenian trial, he also lectured extensively up and down the country for the National Reform League ; and one of these lectures, published under the title *Capital and Labour*, is important as showing that, despite his conversion to collaboration with the middle classes in order to get political reform, he had in no wise modified his essential Socialist views.

At the General Election of 1868, which followed hard upon the Reform Act of 1867, Ernest Jones was adopted as the working men's candidate for Manchester. At this election, the workers in the towns — those of them who were householders — had for the first time the right to vote. In this contest he came, for the first time in his career, within measurable distance of success. Manchester had gained a

353

third seat as a result of the new Act ; and there were three Liberals and two Conservatives in the field against him. He polled 10,662, against 15,486 for the leading candidate, a Tory, and 14,192 and 13,514 for the two successful Liberals, one of whom was the half-Radical Jacob Bright. A petition was mooted after the election against the return of the Tory, and early in 1869 a test ballot was taken among the Liberal and Radical electors with a view to choosing a candidate if the seat were declared vacant. Ernest Jones was chosen in this ballot ; but he was by then lying ill in bed, and near death — the consequence of a severe chill caught while he was returning home wet after a meeting. He died in Manchester in January 1869 — the day following his fiftieth birthday.

Unsuccessful careers are the hardest to assess ; and Ernest Jones was, by all ordinary standards, an unsuccessful man. He entered the Chartist movement at a time when it was already, little though many people realised the truth, in decay, because the conditions which had given it mass support were already ceasing to exist. Chartism had become a mass movement first as an expression of working-class protest against the cruel new Poor Law of 1834 ; it had received a renewed impetus during the deep distress of the early 'forties ; it had been based on the belief that nothing would be done to ease the workers' sufferings until they took matters into their own hands and brought Parliament itself under their control. But in 1846 Sir Robert Peel, by repealing the Corn Laws, gave the lie to the view that nothing could be done without the Charter. True, O'Connor and many other Chartist leaders had proclaimed that repeal was nothing but a manufacturers' dodge for reducing wages. But the fall in wages did not come — they rose instead ; and employment became more plentiful. There was never again in the nineteenth century a depression so deep and prolonged as that of the late 'thirties and early 'forties. Chartism had been above all else a hunger movement ; and as the pangs of hunger became less, not only did the hungry cease to parade the streets, but also the edge of sympathy was blunted among the more philanthropic section of the better-off.

That was why the European Revolutions of 1848 failed

to rouse the mass of the workers in Great Britain — that, much more than the deficiencies, notable as they were, in the Chartist leadership. Ernest Jones came into the movement at a time when loud and angry argument was proceeding between the rival factions standing for ' Physical Force ' and ' Moral Force ' as the means of getting the Charter. The very acrimony of the disputants was not unconnected with the fact that neither method really stood any chance of success. Jones at once rallied to the ' physical force ' party, and thereafter, right up to 1858, he stood always on the left of the movement — though never quite on its extreme left, which belonged to such men as William Cuffay, who was for ever plotting deeds of insurrectionary violence.

Jones rallied to the left of the movement because he was outraged by the callousness of the rich, among whom he had been nurtured, to the sufferings of the poor, and wanted instant and courageous action. There is no sign that he had at this stage any clear Socialist philosophy or programme, beyond a burning belief in the people's rights. He came into the Chartist movement as Feargus O'Connor's man ; and he was at first an enthusiastic believer in O'Connor's Land Scheme, which was based on peasant proprietorship, and was certainly not Socialist. He came to Socialism, and to a rupture with O'Connor, first through realising that Land Nationalisation was indispensable as a foundation for the re-settlement of surplus labourers upon the land, and then through seeing that the land monopoly was only part of a wider monopoly, based on the appropriation of the means of production by a limited class.

At this point he came into close contact with Karl Marx, at about the time when the *Communist Manifesto* was published. Versed in German ideas, he readily appropriated the Marxian gospel, put the class struggle into the centre of his thinking, and preached, albeit in embryonic form, the Marxian doctrine of surplus value. Capital, he proclaimed again and again, is only land *plus* stored labour ; it creates nothing. All creation is the work of labour ; but the capitalist, by virtue of his ownership, is able to take the lion's share. Moreover, the power of capital becomes, by a law of technical development, ever more centralised, and the isolated worker more helpless against it and more exploited. Trade Unionism, by combining the workers, can help them to bargain more effectively; but it is no more than a palliative. Consumers' Cooperation is another palliative. Nothing will avail, short of the destruction of the monopoly power that keeps the worker a slave. But this power can be destroyed only by socialisation, by common ownership of the land and the other essential instruments of production. In his propaganda Jones usually put the land monopoly in the forefront of his argument; but he applied the same reasoning to capital in all its forms : " Instead of capital having labour at its pleasure, and discarding it at will — and labour being dependent on such hire for its very existence — it is, on the contrary, labour that should dictate to capital the time and terms of its employment. . . . The system of wages is therefore vicious. . . . Working men, raise the cry — let us work for ourselves ! Labour should be lord of the earth, and we should be lords of our labour ! "

And again : " Cooperation is the soul of labour. . . . It is, however, evident that if this cooperative system is left to individual efforts, though these individuals act harmoniously together, it will advance far more slowly and meet with counteracting influences which it may be difficult if not impossible to overcome. Cooperation should be a State concern, realised by the power of the State."

Yet again : " I deny that Capital has any right over labour that creates it. I deny that it is warranted to dictate any terms, or offer any compromise. The block of marble might as well dictate to the sculptor who gives it value, beauty, and importance. . . . The complete sovereignty of labour over capital is the only Free Trade that can give freedom, is the only protection that can protect."

Ernest Jones was no theorist ; and he never presented more than a rudimentary version of Socialist doctrine. But the root of the matter was in what he said ; and in saying even so much he went far beyond the capacity of most of his hearers. His eloquence and energy achieved for Chartism no more than a ten years' prolongation of life beyond its natural span. Only when he returned to talking about what most men did understand, and were ready to hear — Franchise Reform — did he become again a national figure, leading more than a forlorn hope. Yet he never gave the impression of being a disappointed man. His sufferings in prison confirmed his faith, without making him bitter. He refused, as we have seen, to make capital out of them, in the same spirit as he refused to take even necessary rewards for his services to the working-class movement. He was very sensitive, and very proud ; and the calumny to which he was often exposed hurt him sorely. But he allowed nothing to deflect him from his self-chosen task. Even when no one listened or helped, he went on with his ceaseless propaganda, solacing himself with his poetry and, in his later years, when his means were rather less straitened, with his garden — his sole extravagance, as he said himself. He was a man whose sincerity and utter honesty came to be well recognised by his political enemies, and questioned, in his later years, only by those Chartists who regarded his later actions as apostasy. As a poet he had moments of lyrical quality, and as an orator he stood undoubtedly very high. But he subordinated both gifts to the demands of the cause. He was very single-minded, as well as very proud.

BIBLIOGRAPHY

A. *General*

THERE is no satisfactory general history of Chartism ; and before a comprehensive history can be written much more work needs doing on the story of the movement in the various parts of Great Britain in which the Chartists were active. The book upon which I, in common with all modern writers on the subject, have drawn most extensively is R. G. Gammage's *History of the Chartist Movement*, published originally in 1854, and reissued in a greatly improved edition in 1894. Dr. Gammage was himself a Chartist ; and his book contains a great many biographical particulars about the leaders of the movement. He is by no means an impartial writer, and is very hostile to Feargus O'Connor ; but his book is based directly on contemporary records, and is invaluable for its quotations from speeches and for its detailed account of the earlier phases of Chartism.

Among later general books, the best is still Mark Hovell's *The Chartist Movement*, published in 1918 (revised edition, 1925). The author was killed in the Great War before he had been able to finish his book, and it was finished from his notes by Professor T. F. Tout. The part which Hovell had practically finished (up to 1842) is very much better than Tout's continuation, which is slight and unsatisfactory. Hovell himself was so much on the side of Lovett and the ' moral force ' school of Chartism as to give a somewhat one-sided picture ; but his work is scholarly, and was based on wide reading of contemporary documents, including the files of *The Northern Star*.

A similar history, slighter but carrying on the record to the end of the movement, is Julius West's *History of the Chartist Movement*, published in 1920. This contains information concerning the international affiliations of Chartism — especially the Fraternal Democrats ; but it is greatly inferior to Hovell's book for the years up to 1842.

More recent is *But We Shall Rise Again : a Narrative History of Chartism*, by Reg Groves, published in 1938. Unlike the books so far mentioned, this is sympathetic to the ' physical force ' Chartists, and pays attention to the activities of the Chartist ' left wing ', *e.g.* Julian Harney. It also deals much better than the other books with the later phases of the movement, under the leadership of Ernest Johes. But it is brief, and has not room for much detail.

Le Chartisme, by Édouard Dolléans (2 vols., published in 1912), is a competent study, in French, by the author of the most convenient general history of modern working-class movements. But it contains little that is not in the books already mentioned.

H. T. N. Gaitskell's *Chartism : an Introductory Essay* is an excellent brief sketch, written primarily for students in Workers' Educational Association classes. It was published in 1929.

From Chartism to Labourism, by Theodore Rothstein (1929), is only in part concerned with Chartism. It is written from a Marxist point of view, and is valuable chiefly for its accounts of the international activities of Chartism during its later phases — especially the International Association and the work of Ernest Jones. It is, however, marred by inaccuracies.

Three specialised studies of Chartism have been published by Columbia University in its series of monographs in History, Economics, and Public Law (Vol. 73, 1916). These are *The Chartist Movement in its Social and Economic Aspects*, by F. F. Rosenblatt ; *The Decline of the Chartist Movement*, by P. W. Slosson ; and *Chartism and the Churches*, by H. U. Faulkner. They are all good ; and the first two are of real importance.

There is a good general account of Chartism in Max Beer's standard *History of British Socialism* (1920). This is better on the theoretical aspects than as a narrative of events. Chartism is also treated fairly fully in *The Common People* (1938), written by myself in collaboration with R. W. Postgate, and in less detail in my *Short History of the British Working-class Movement* (revised 1937).

These are all general accounts of Chartism. *The Age of the Chartists*, by J. L. and Barbara Hammond (1930), deals rather with the social background than with the movement itself. It is valuable from this standpoint, and should be read in conjunction with the famous *Condition of the Working Classes in England in 1844*, by Friedrich Engels (various editions). This in its turn is based largely on the Reports of the Factory Inspectors, on Edwin Chadwick's famous reports on *The Sanitary Condition of the Labouring Population* (*1842*) and on *The Health of Towns* (1845), and on the reports and evidence of the Royal Commission on *The State of Large Towns and Populous Districts* (1844) and on *The Employment of Children in Mines and Factories* (1842). These, as well as the early reports of the Poor Law Commissioners, can all be studied with advantage.

S. Maccoby's two volumes on *English Radicalism* (Vol. I, 1832–1852, published 1935 ; Vol. II, 1853–86, published 1938) are invaluable for the history of middle-class Radicalism during the Chartist period. They also cover Chartism itself, but rather incidentally. They have largely, but not wholly, superseded W. Harris's *The Radical Party in Parliament* (1885).

B. *Special Studies*

Fritz Bachmann's *Die Agrarreform in der Chartistenbewegung* (Bern, 1928) is valuable for O'Connor's Land Scheme and Chartist agrarianism in general. *One Hundred Years Ago : the Story of the Montgomeryshire Chartists* (1939) is a useful little book dealing with the uprisings in Newtown and Llanidloes in 1839. Frank Peel's *The Risings of the Luddites, Chartists*, etc. (1880) throws some light on the history of Yorkshire Chartism.

A. Müller Lehning's article on " The International Association " in *The International Review of Social History*, Vol. III, 1938, also published separately in book form (Leiden, 1938), is an excellent account of that body and of certain of the international activities of Chartism in its later phases. The letters of Marx and Engels also throw a good deal of light on Chartist personalities, especially Harney and Ernest Jones. Only a selection is available in English — *Marx–Engels Select Correspondence* (1934); but the full text is available, for the Chartist period, in French as well as in German.

C. *The Twelve Portraits*

(1) WILLIAM LOVETT.—The major source is Lovett's autobiography, *The Life and Struggles of William Lovett* (1876). There is a brief life of Lovett in the Fabian Biographical Series — *William Lovett*, by Barbara Hammond (1922), and an article in the *D.N.B.* by T. A. Hamilton. Lovett's other writings include *Chartism : a New Organisation of the People* (1841), written jointly with John Collins ; and *Social and Political Morality* (1853). The publications of the London Working Men's Association should also be consulted. These include *The People's Charter, being the Outline of an Act to provide for the Just Representation of the People of Great Britain and Ireland* (1838), *The Rotten House of Commons* (1836), and a number of addresses to the working classes on various subjects (mostly 1838). See also Lovett's trial (together with Benbow and Watson) in connection with the Fast-Day Procession of 1832, and his trial in connection with the Birmingham Riots of 1839 (various reports). *The English Chartist Circular* (edited by William Carpenter) should also be consulted, and the reports of the Complete Suffrage Union Conferences of 1842. See further the papers of the People's Convention of 1839, now in the British Museum.

(2) JOSEPH RAYNER STEPHENS.—There is an exceedingly bad *Life of Stephens* (1881), by G. J. Holyoake. Reference should be made to Stephens's own newspapers, *The Ashton Chronicle* (1848–9) and *The Champion* (1850–51), and to his contributions to *The Christian Advocate* and *The Political Pulpit*. A number of his sermons and lectures were published as pamphlets (see text). The report of his trial in 1839 should also be consulted, and the accounts of him given in Gammage's *History* and in *The History of the Factory Movement* by Alfred (Samuel Kydd) (1857). There is a notice in *The Dictionary of National Biography*, by Alexander Gordon.

(3) RICHARD OASTLER.—It is curious that there is no Life of Oastler. There is a useful pamphlet, *Richard Oastler, the Factory King*, by Arthur Greenwood (1913). A good deal of biographical information can be gleaned from Oastler's own publications, *The Fleet Papers* (1841–4) and *The Home* (1851–5). A collection of his *Speeches* was published in 1850. Oastler's history is treated fully in *A History of the Factory Movement*, by Alfred (Samuel Kydd). There is a notice in the *D.N.B.* by W. A. S. Hewins. See also *Sketch of the Life and Opinions of Richard Oastler* (Leeds, 1838).

(4) THOMAS ATTWOOD.—The principal authority is *The Life of Thomas Attwood*, by C. M. Wakefield (1885)—a poor book. For his currency views, see his numerous pamphlets — especially *The Remedy : or, Thoughts on the Present Distress* (1816), *Prosperity Restored* (1817), *Letters to Nicholas Vansittart on the Creation of Money* (1817), *Observations on the Currency, in Two Letters to Arthur Young* (1818), *Letters to Lord Liverpool* (1819), and the report of his public debate with William Cobbett in 1832. See also *The Gemini Letters* (1844), published by two of his disciples, and the reports of the Birmingham Political Union. J. Buckley's *Life of Joseph Parkes* (1926) and J. A. Langford's *Century of Birmingham Life* (1868) should also be consulted. There is a notice in the *D.N.B.* by W. B. Squire.

(5) JOHN FROST.—David Williams's *Life of John Frost* (1939) collects all the available information. *John Frost and the Chartist Movement in Wales*, by Ness Edwards (N.D.), is slight, but interesting. There is an article in the *D.N.B.* by G. F. R. Barker. There are several reports of Frost's trial after the ' Newport Rising ' of 1839. See also *The Rise and Fall of Chartism in Monmouthshire* (1840) — a contemporary account — and *The Chartist Riots at Newport* (Newport, 1889). Reference should also be made to the Memoirs of Dr. William Price of Llantrisant and to the booklet, *Dr. William Price of Llantrisant* (1939), by T. I. Nicholas. See also the full bibliography, *John Frost and the Chartist Movement in Monmouthshire*, by John Warner and W. A. Gunn (1939).

(6) JOSEPH STURGE.—There are two Lives of Sturge. The earlier, *Memoirs of Joseph Sturge*, by Henry Richard (1864), is much fuller on his pacifist and anti-slavery activities than on his connection with Chartism. This also applies in some degree to Stephen Hobhouse's *Joseph Sturge : his Life and Work* (1919), which is a competent little biography in most respects. See also article in *D.N.B.* by C. Fell Smith. Reference should also be made to *The Life of Edward Miall* (1884), by Arthur Miall, and to Miall's paper, *The Nonconformist* (from 1841), in which the pamphlet, *Reconciliation between the Middle and Labouring Classes* (1841), first appeared. See also the papers of the Complete Suffrage Union. Sturge's book on *The West Indies in 1837*, written jointly with T. Harvey, appeared in that year.

(7) THOMAS COOPER.—The principal authority is Cooper's autobiography, *The Life of Thomas Cooper* (1872). This can be supplemented for his later years from his *Thoughts at Fourscore* (1885). Cooper edited *The Kentish Mercury* (1840), *The Midland Counties Illuminator* (1841), *The Chartist Rushlight* (1841), *The Extinguisher* (1841), *The Plain Speaker* (with T. J. Wooler, 1849), and *Cooper's Journal* (1850), in addition to writing for many other papers. His best poem, *The Purgatory of Suicides*, written in prison, was published in 1845, and its sequel, *The Paradise of Martyrs*, in 1873. His *Poetical Works* appeared in 1877. His writings also include novels and stories — *Wise Saws and Modern Instances* (1845), *Captain Cobbler* (1848), *Alderman Ralph* (1853), *The Family Feud* (1855), and a story in verse, *The Baron's Yule Feast* (1846). Other works are *Two Orations against the Taking Away of Human Life* (1847), *The Land for the Labourers* (1848), *Letters to Young Men of the Working Classes* (1849), *The Bridge of History over the Gulf of Time* (1871), *Plain Pulpit Talk* (1872), *God, the Soul, and a Future State* (1873), *Evolution* (1878), and *Atonement* (1880). His *Wise Saws* was re-issued as *Old-Fashioned Stories* in 1874. There is also an article in the *D.N.B.* by J. Ramsay MacDonald.

(8) JOHN FIELDEN.—There appears to be no study at all of Fielden, except the brief notice in the Supplement to *The Dictionary of National Biography*, by Francis Espinasse. He himself published only a few pamphlets — *The Mischiefs and Iniquities of Paper Money* (1832), with a preface by William Cobbett, *National Regeneration* (1834), *The Curse of the Factory System* (1836), *Speech on the Sugar Duties* (1841), *A Selection of Facts and Arguments in Favour of the Ten Hours Bill* (1845). Reference to his struggle against the New Poor Law will be found in the early annual reports of the Poor Law Commissioners, and to his part in the Ten Hours Movement in *A History of the Factory Movement*, by Alfred (Samuel Kydd). See also *A Short History of Todmorden*, by J. Holden (1912), and my *Life of William Cobbett* (1924). Extracts from his speeches will be found in Baxter's *Book of the Bastilles* (1841).

(9) JAMES BRONTERRE O'BRIEN.—The principal source is an unpublished *Life of Bronterre O'Brien*, by Alfred Plummer, which the author has kindly allowed me to use. There is an article in the *D.N.B.* by Graham Wallas. O'Brien's principal writings are his translation of Buonarotti's *History of Babeuf's Conspiracy for Equality* (1836), his *Life of Robespierre* (1838 — only the First Volume was ever published), and his curious verse odes and elegies — *Ode to Palmerston* (1856), *Ode to Bonaparte* (1856), *Elegy on the Death of Robespierre, with an Historical Sketch* (1857), and *A Vision of Hell* (1859). His periodical writings are much more important. He contributed to Carpenter's *Political Letters* (1831) and *The True Sun* (1832), edited *The Midland Representative* (1831-2),

The Poor Man's Guardian (1832–5), *The Destructive, and Poor Man's Conservative* (1833–4), *The London Dispatch*, later *Hetherington's Twopenny Dispatch* (1836–9), *Bronterre's National Reformer* (1836–7), Bell's *London Mercury* (1837), *The Operative* (1838–9), and, with Carpenter, the *Southern Star* (1840). In 1838 he began to write regularly for O'Connor's *Northern Star*, and continued to do so until 1842, except while he was in prison. In 1842 he acquired and ran for a few months *The British Statesman*, and in 1844 he started *The National Reformer, and Manx Weekly Review* (1844–7), published in the Isle of Man. In 1849 he wrote for *Reynolds' Political Instructor* the articles published with additions after his death as *The Rise, Progress, and Phases of Human Slavery* (1885). In 1842 he published a pamphlet in vindication of his conduct in supporting Sturge's Complete Suffrage movement.

(10) GEORGE JULIAN HARNEY.—No published work on Harney appears to exist. He is not even in the *D.N.B.* Particulars have to be gleaned from Gammage's *History* and from scattered sources, especially an article, based on an interview by Edward Aveling, in *The Social Democrat* of January 1897. There is much information in his own papers, *The London Democrat* (1839), *The Democratic Review* (1849–50), *The Red Republican* (1850), *The Friend of the People* (1850–51, and again 1852), and *The Vanguard* (1852–3). In the late 'fifties and early 'sixties he edited *The Jersey Independent* ; and in the 'eighties and 'nineties he worked on *The Newcastle Weekly Chronicle*. He began to write for *The Northern Star* in 1841, and became sub-editor, under O'Connor, in 1843, and in 1847 editor, the connection lasting until 1850. In 1852 he bought *The Northern Star* and carried it on for a brief period, but had to give it up. There are numerous references to him in the letters of Marx and Engels and in Holyoake's writings (see later).

(11) FEARGUS O'CONNOR.—It is quite extraordinary that there is no Life of O'Connor. The *D.N.B.* has a fairly long article, by Graham Wallas ; and the other main source is the pamphlet containing the Funeral Oration, by William Jones, with a brief biography (1855). There is a chapter on him in Thomas Frost's *Forty Years' Recollections* (1880), and Gammage's *History* deals with him fairly fully. There is also some information in *The Labourer* (1847–8), which he edited jointly with Ernest Jones ; and of course *The Northern Star* (1837–52) is full of references to and contributions by him. See also *The Trial of Feargus O'Connor and Fifty-eight Others at Lancaster* (1843), edited by him and containing his accounts of the strikes, and the pamphlet *England's May-Day*, giving his speech at the opening of O'Connorville in 1847. O'Connor's book, *A Practical Work on the Management of Small Farms* (1843), contains some references to his own farming experiences in Ireland. Other writings of his include *The State of Ireland* (1822) and numerous pamphlets reprinted from *The*

Northern Star. Lovett and Cooper criticise him violently in their autobiographies.

(12) ERNEST JONES.—There is no published Life of Jones, beyond two pamphlets — *Ernest Jones : Who is he? What has he done?* (Manchester, N.D.), and *A Short Sketch of the Life and Labours of Ernest Jones*, by P. Davies (Liverpool, 1897) — and a notice in the *D.N.B.* by J. A. Hamilton. His own journals, *Notes for the People* (1851–2), *Evenings with the People* (1856), and *The People's Paper* (1852–8), as well as *The Labourer* (1847–8), which he edited with O'Connor, are valuable sources of information. He also edited *The London News* (1858), as a literary journal. See also Jones's *Open Letter to Chief Justice Wilde* (1848) and the report of his trial in that year. His pamphlets include *Capital and Labour* (1867), *Democracy Vindicated* (1867), and numerous off-prints from his journals. His *Chartist Songs and Fugitive Pieces* appeared in a number of forms, mostly undated ; and some of these were published with music, *e.g. The Song of the Lower Classes*, with music by John Lowry. Jones also wrote romances in prose and verse, novels, and much poetry. His juvenilia in verse were published by his parents in 1830, when he was only eleven. His first serious work was a romance, *The Wood Spirit* (1841), followed by a long poem, *My Life, or, Our Social State* (1845), and by numerous other works in both verse and prose.

D. *Reminiscences and Biographies*

In addition to books mentioned already, the following volumes of reminiscences by Chartists, or near-Chartists, are of value : George Jacob Holyoake's *Sixty Years of an Agitator's Life* (2 vols., 1892), and *Byegones Worth Remembering* (2 vols., 1905) [consult also Joseph McCabe's *Life and Letters of George Jacob Holyoake* (2 vols., 1908)] ; W. J. Linton, *Memories* (1895) ; Thomas Frost, *Reminiscences of a Country Journalist* (1886) ; Thomas Ainge Devyr, *The Odd Book of the Nineteenth Century* (Greenpoint, New York, 1882) ; E. Edwards, *Personal Recollections of Birmingham and Birmingham Men* (1877) ; Howard Evans, *Radical Fights of Forty Years* (N.D.).

Also the following biographies : *The Life of Francis Place* (1898), by Graham Wallas ; *The Life and Letters of J. A. Roebuck* (1897), by R. E. Leader ; *The Life and Times of Thomas Wakley* (1897), by S. Squire Sprigge ; *W. H. Chadwick, The Last of the Manchester Chartists* (1910), by T. P. Newbould ; *The Life of Robert Owen* (1907), by Frank Podmore ; *The Life of Robert Owen* (revised 1930), by G. D. H. Cole.

E. *Periodicals*

Most of the more important Chartist journals have been mentioned already, but the following are also worthy of attention :

The Northern Liberator, edited by A. H. Beaumont (1837–40);
The Western Vindicator, edited by Henry Vincent (1839); *The
Scottish Chartist Circular* (1839–41); *The People*, edited by Joseph
Barker (1849–50); *The Leader*, edited by Thornton Hunt (1850–
1859); *McDouall's Chartist Journal* (1841); *The Moral Reformer*,
edited by Joseph Livesey (1831–9); W. J. Linton's *English
Republic* (1851–5).

F. *Miscellaneous*

Thomas Carlyle's *Chartism* was published in 1840, and his
Latter-Day Pamphlets in 1850. Among novels, the most significant
are Benjamin Disraeli's *Sybil* (1845); Charles Kingsley's *Yeast*
(1851), *Alton Locke* (1854), and *Two Years Ago* (1851); Frances
Trollope's *Michael Armstrong, the Factory Boy* (1840); Mrs.
Gaskell's *Mary Barton* (1848), and *North and South* (1855).

INDEX OF PERSONS

GENERAL INDEX

373

THE END

PRINTED IN GREAT BRITAIN BY
LOWE AND BRYDONE (PRINTERS) LIMITED, LONDON